Cover picture:
Sheffield Park and Garden, East Sussex.

Produced by the Publishing Division of the Automobile Association
Editor Allen Stidwill
Designer Neil Roebuck
Picture Researcher Wyn Voysey
Index by D Hancock

Tours compiled and driven by the Publications Research Unit of the Automobile Association.

Photographs by British Tourist Authority, J Allen Cash Photolibrary, Jarrolds Colour Library, Woodmansterne Picture Library, S & O Mathews, Barnaby's Picture Library, Association Press, Topham Picture Library, Aerofilms Ltd, AA Photolibrary.

All maps by the Cartographic Department, Publishing Division of the Automobile Association. Based on the Ordnance Survey Maps, with the permission of the Controller of HM Stationery Office.

Town plans produced by the AA's Cartographic Department.

Filmset by Senator Graphics, Great Suffolk St, London SE1
Printed and bound by New Interlitho SPA, Milan, Italy

Published by the Automobile Association, Fanum House, Basing View, Basingstoke, Hampshire RG21 2EA

ISBN 0 86145 500 2
AA Reference 51936

Touring South & South East England

CONTENTS

The tiny church of St Thomas-a-Becket is set in isolated fields near the hamlet of Fairfield, Kent. Its interior is almost entirely of timber with box pews and a three-deck pulpit.

INTRODUCTION

At the heart of the region lies the great capital city of London, surrounded by beautiful and interesting places to see.

In Kent lie the orchards of the 'Garden of England', while Sussex is buttressed against the sea by the line of the majestic South Downs. There are the New Forest, Britain's best-loved woodland and the Chilterns to discover. Along the coast lie historic towns, massive ports and a whole variety of popular resorts. Inland are magnificent cathedral cities such as Canterbury, Chichester and Winchester, the delightful university town of Oxford, and mighty castles too, as at Arundel and Windsor. There are great houses like Chartwell, Hampton Court, Hatfield and Blenheim, and in London itself the pageantry and splendour of our capital city to experience.

This book reveals these treasures and more through its carefully planned motoring tours which provide the ideal way to explore this fascinating region. Each self-contained circular tour can be completed within a day and includes magnificent colour pictures to give a foretaste of what is to come.

As well as the tours this book includes a special 14 page feature on London together with 31 pages of invaluable town plans to guide you around the regions popular towns. There is also a large scale, 3 miles to the inch atlas of the region.

Touring South and South East England is just one in a series of six colourful *Regional Guides* which embrace the rich history and varied countryside of Britain. The other five guides in the series are: *Touring the West Country, Touring Wales, Touring Central England and East Anglia, Touring the North Country* and *Touring Scotland.* The six regions covered by the series are shown on the adjacent map.

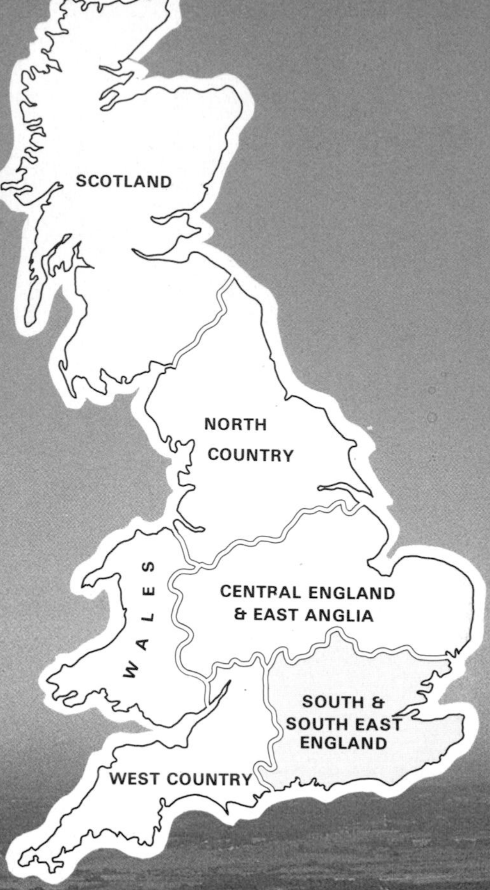

SCOTLAND
NORTH COUNTRY
WALES
CENTRAL ENGLAND & EAST ANGLIA
SOUTH & SOUTH EAST ENGLAND
WEST COUNTRY

ABOUT THE TOURS

The tours in this guide have been designed for clarity. Each tour occupies two pages and has a clear map accompanying the text. All the places described in the text are shown in **black** on the tour maps and are described as they occur on the road, linked in sequence by route directions. This precise wayfinding information is set in *italic*.

Castles, stately homes and other places of interest described in the tours are not necessarily open to the public or may be open only at certain times. It is therefore advisable to check the opening times of any place before planning a stop there. Properties administered by the National Trust, National Trust for Scotland and the Ancient Monument Scheme (NT, NTS and AM) are generally open most of the year, but this should be checked with the relevant organisation, as should precise opening times.

The Automobile Association's guide *Stately Homes, Museums, Castles and Gardens in Britain* is the most comprehensive annual publication of its kind and describes over 2,000 places of interest, giving details of opening times and admission prices, including many listed in this book.

The little village of Fulking lies serenely below the north slopes of the South Downs near Devil's Dyke, a spectacular cleft in the Down's 711-foot crest.

HOW TO FIND THE TOURS

All the motor tours in the book are shown on the key map below and identified by the towns where they start. The tours are arranged in the book in alphabetical order by start town name. Page numbers are also given on page vii. Each tour begins at a well-known place, but it is possible to join or leave at any point if more convenient.

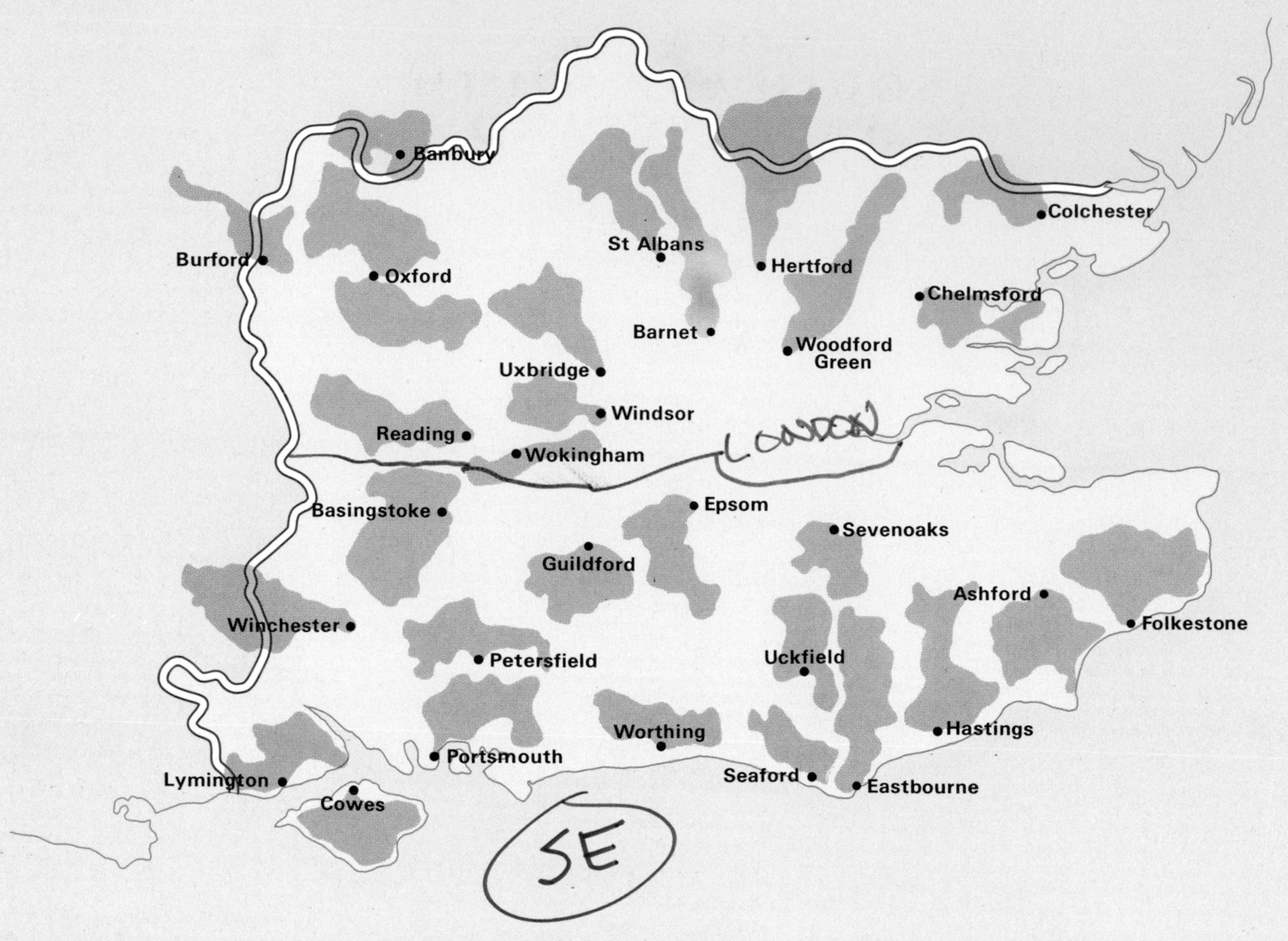

MAPS

Main Tour Route	
Detour/Diversion from Main Tour Route	
Motorway	
Motorway Access	
Motorway Service Area	
Motorway and Junction Under Construction	
A-class Road	A68
B-class Road	B700
Unclassified Road	unclass
Dual Carriageway	A70
Road Under Construction	
Airport	
Battlefield	
Bridge	
Castle	
Church as Route Landmark	
Ferry	
Folly/Tower	
Forestry Commission Land	
Gazetteer Placename	Zoo /Lydstep
Industrial Site (Old & New)	
Level Crossing	LC
Lighthouse	
Marshland	
Memorial/Monument	
Miscellaneous Places of Interest & Route Landmarks	
National Boundary	
National Trust Property	NT
National Trust for Scotland Property	NTS
Non-gazetteer Placenames	Thames /Astwood
Notable Religious Site	
Picnic Site	
Prehistoric Site	
Racecourse	
Radio/TV Mast	
Railway (BR) with Station	
Railway (Special) with Station	
River & Lake	
Woodland Area	
Scenic Area	
Seaside Resort	
Stately Home	
Summit/Spot Height	KNOWE HILL 209 KNOWE HILL 209
Viewpoint	

TEXT

AM	Ancient Monument
c	*circa*
NT	National Trust
NTS	National Trust for Scotland
OACT	Open at Certain Times
PH	Public House
RSPB	Royal Society for the Protection of Birds
SP	Signpost (s) (ed)

TOURING SOUTH AND SOUTH EAST ENGLAND

Motor Tours
Pages 2-75

AMONG THE COASTAL MARSHES

Towards the sea the Wealden hills flatten to Romney Marsh, a place of frogs and sheep where church towers can be seen for miles and the threat of flood is constant. At the sea's edge England's Napoleonic defences crumble peacefully, while massive walls repulse the ocean's eternal barrage.

ASHFORD, Kent
For hundreds of years Ashford has been a market town for Romney Marsh and the Weald of Kent. Its prime situation at the meeting of the two rivers Stour (East and Great) has made it a natural focus in the past, and its proximity to London has meant new growth as a population 'overspill' town. Today it is an important shopping and touring centre a mere 14 miles from the ancient city of Canterbury and within easy reach of the south Kent beaches. The town's industrial development began in the 19th century with the establishment of large railway works, which have closed. Future development with the channel tunnel project could increase Ashford's importance as a railway interchange. Medieval, Tudor and Georgian houses have survived despite development, and the 15th-century parish church retains much of its original character The Intelligence Corps Museum at Templar Barracks displays a fascinating array of mementos.

Leave Ashford on the A28 'Tenterden road, after 1 mile at roundabout take 3rd exit on to an unclassified road to reach Great Chart.

GREAT CHART, Kent
A 14th-century church with a 16th-century pest house in the south corner of its churchyard can be seen here. This long, narrow structure is a timber framed building once used to isolate victims of plagues. Court Lodge, a complete 13th-century stone house, stands near the church.

Continue through the village to rejoin the A28 to Bethersden.

BETHERSDEN, Kent
Marble from this village was used for the altar stairs at Canterbury Cathedral, but many humbler buildings also display its splendour. The quarries are now worked out. Brass memorials to forbears of the 17th-century poet William Lovelace can be seen in the local 14th-century church.

Continue through High Halden to Tenterden.

TENTERDEN, Kent
Typical Wealden houses, *ie* buildings faced with tiles and weather boards, line the broad, grass-verged High Street of this delightful town. Its high situation makes its 15th-century church tower (made of the famous Bethersden marble) visible across the Weald and from many miles out to sea. At one time the tower was used as a beacon to guide shipping. In the 15th century Henry VI admitted Tenterden to the Confederation of Cinque Ports, but the course of the River Rother later changed and the town port was replaced by nearby Smallhythe. Shipbuilding became a major local concern in the 16th century. The museum has various exhibits on the history of local trades and industries. Tenterden is the terminus for the preserved Kent and East railway.

Attractive gardens stretch along the banks of the River Rother at Rye.

Continue on the A28, drive over a level crossing, and pass the Rolvenden station of the Kent and East Sussex Railway on the left. Drive into Rolvenden.

ROLVENDEN, Kent
Surrounded by well-wooded country, this pleasant combination of weather-boarded (Kentish clad) houses and grass verges is typical of the county. The large 14th-century church preserves two squire's pews, and the restored postmill is a perfect example. Great Maytham Hall, now converted into flats, was designed by Sir Edwin Lutyens in 1910 and stands in gardens that were laid out by landscaper Gertrude Jekyll.

Drive to the church and turn left on to the unclassified 'Wittersham' road. Pass through Rolvenden Layne and cross the Rother Levels. Climb on to the Isle of Oxney, an isolated area of high ground. A detour can be made from the main tour route by turning left on to the B2082 to reach Smallhythe Place. Otherwise turn right on to the B2082 and drive to Wittersham.

SMALLHYTHE PLACE, Kent
Half-timbered Smallhythe Place dates from 1480 and was once the home of actress Dame Ellen Terry. It is now a museum displaying her personal relics (NT). The adjacent 15th-century Priest's House shares its grounds with the Barn Theatre.

The weather-boarded buildings in Tenterden's superb High Street are typical of the Kentish Weald.

WITTERSHAM, Kent
Wittersham is a quiet, charming village on the central ridge of the Isle of Oxney, between the River Rother and the Royal Military Canal. During the middle ages the tower of its 14th-century church was used as a shipping beacon. Inside the church is a finely carved lectern of late medieval origin. Wealden buildings comprising a windmill, oast houses, and a timbered cottage make an attractive group 1 mile east.

Proceed on the B2082 to cross the River Rother and continue over the Rother Levels. Pass through Iden, meet the A268, and pass through Playden to reach Rye (near the Royal Military Canal).

ROYAL MILITARY CANAL
Originally a defence against an expected Napoleonic invasion, this canal between Rye and Hythe now offers peaceful towpath walks and boat-hire facilities.

RYE, E Sussex
On a small hill rising out of fenland by the River Rother, this collection of attractive old buildings and cobbled streets was one of two Ancient Towns attached to the Cinque Ports. As such it was heavily fortified against the medieval French. This maritime importance seems odd today, but at that time Rye was almost encircled by sea. Its influence declined when the harbour silted up in the 16th century, and today the sea has receded. Many historic buildings have survived here, the oldest being probably the Norman and later church, which features a 16th-century clock with an 18ft free-swinging pendulum. Near by is the 13th-century Ypres Tower, which was built as a castle and used as a prison from the 16th to 19th centuries. Nowadays it holds nothing more sinister than a museum of local history. Weather-boarded and tile-hung houses, generally with timber frames, can be seen in Mermaid Street, Church Square, Watchbell Street, and High Street. The Mermaid Inn opened in 1420 and is possibly the oldest in the country. From the same century are The Flushing Inn, Stone House, Old Hospital, and Fletcher's House. Peacock's School was built in 1636, and 18th-century Lamb House (NT) was the home of novelist Henry James. Parts of the town walls remain, but 14th-century Landgate (AM) is the only original entry. The town stands on a small hill.

A detour can be made from the main tour route to Camber Castle by taking the A259 'Hastings' road.

CAMBER CASTLE, E Sussex
This ruined 16th-century coastal defence fort was one of several built in Kent by Henry VIII as a deterrent to the French navy.

3

Rolvenden's painstakingly restored windmill.

DUNGENESS, Kent
This desolate shingle promontory is the site of a nuclear power station that can be seen for miles over featureless Denge Marsh. A slender lighthouse was built here in 1961 because the old one would be obscured by the power station. The original still stands, slightly inland from its successor. Much of the promontory is taken by a 12,000-acre nature reserve frequented by seabirds and shoreline wildlife.

Innumerable drainage ditches prevent Romney Marsh reverting to its natural state.

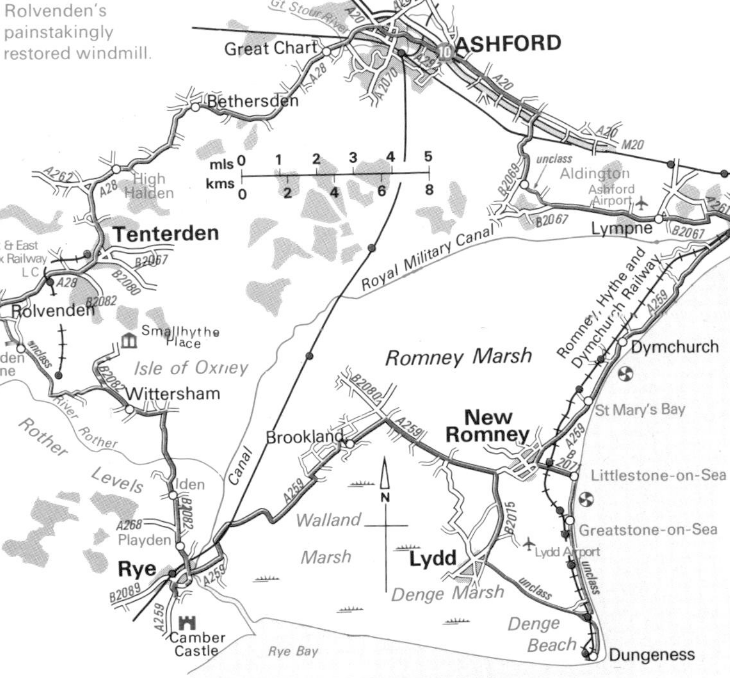

From Rye follow SP 'Folkestone A259' to reach Brookland, crossing the flat expanse of Walland Marsh on the way. Water is drained from the land by channels that crisscross the area on both sides of the route.

BROOKLAND, Kent
The 13th- to 15th-century church at Brookland displays an unusual wood and shingle belfry, and houses a Norman font thought to be unique in Britain. The latter is decorated with signs of the Zodiac and little vignettes depicting various seasonal activities.

Continue on the A259 for 1½ miles, meet crossroads, and turn right. In 4 miles turn right again on to the B2075 'Lydd' road to reach Lydd.

LYDD, Kent
Like Rye, Lydd was once a coastal town, but it now lies a good 3 miles inland. Its 14th-century church has a 130ft tower and has been described as the 'Cathedral of Romney Marsh'. A 140-acre water sports centre is on the outskirts of the town.

Proceed to the edge of Lydd, cross a railway bridge, then branch left on to the unclassified 'Dungeness' road. Shortly turn left again. To the right of the road are Denge Marsh and Denge Beach. After 3 miles (beyond Lydd) turn right to reach Dungeness.

ROMNEY, HYTHE, AND DYMCHURCH RAILWAY, Kent
Dungeness is the southern terminus of a 13½-mile narrow-gauge line which is claimed to be the world's smallest public railway. Steam trains run from Hythe, through New Romney, and along the seaward fringe of Romney Marsh to Dungeness.

Return along the unclassified road for 1 mile, then turn right and follow SP to reach Greatstone and Littlestone-on-Sea. At Littlestone-on-Sea turn left on to the B2071 to reach New Romney.

NEW ROMNEY, Kent
One of the ancient Cinque Ports but now 1 mile inland from the sea, New Romney's harbour was destroyed in 1287 by a violent storm which changed the course of the River Rother. Thanks to William Morris the town's Norman and later church was rescued from insensitive restoration in 1878.

Continue through New Romney and turn right on to the A259 'Folkestone' road to cross Romney Marsh.

ROMNEY MARSH, Kent
Most of this 204-square-mile tract has been reclaimed from the sea by drainage work started in Roman times. Flooding is an ever-present threat, as much of the area is still below sea level at high tide, but the land is too fertile to waste and the Marsh is famous for its wool. Tulip-growing is a newly developed local industry.

Continue through St Mary's Bay to reach Dymchurch.

DYMCHURCH, Kent
Situated on the edge of Romney Marsh, this old port is guarded by an ancient sea wall and was once a centre for smugglers. It is now a resort with vast stretches of sand and a variety of historic buildings. One of several Martello towers (AM) along the coast, built as defences against Napoleon, has been restored and houses a small exhibition site.

Continue beside the sea wall to Hythe.

Amongst the steam locomotives which operate on the Romney, Hythe, and Dymchurch Railway are two miniature versions of Canadian Pacific engines.

HYTHE, Kent
This Cinque Port is now a well-known resort. Just north is Saltwood Castle, a well-preserved medieval garrison fort complete with battlement walk, undercroft, armoury, and torture chamber

Leave Hythe by the A261 'Ashford' road and in 1 mile turn left on to the B2067 'Lympne' road. Proceed to Lympne.

LYMPNE, Kent
Views over Romney Marsh and the Channel extend from Lympne Castle, which was built and variously extended from Norman times to the 15th century. The Port Lympne Zoo Park, Mansion and Gardens affords an interesting visit.

Leave Lympne on the 'Tenterden' road B2067 and in 2½ miles bear right on to the unclassified 'Aldington' road. Continue to Aldington and turn right in the village on to the B2069 'Ashford' road passing pleasant woodland and cross a railway. After ¾ mile (from the railway) turn left on to the A20. Follow SP 'Ashford' to finish the tour.

'TO BANBURY CROSS'

Cut the corners of 3 shires, Oxfordshire, Northamptonshire and Warwickshire, gathering a taste of each while passing through truly English villages — satellites to Banbury, an old country town famous for its cakes and a children's nursery rhyme.

BANBURY, Oxon
'Ride a cock-horse to Banbury Cross' begins the nursery rhyme, which, with the fame of Banbury's cakes, has made the name of this town a household word. The deliciously spicy cakes first appear in town records from the 16th century, and can still be bought freshly baked here. However, the original Banbury Cross was destroyed in a Puritanical frenzy of 1602; the cross now standing in the town centre was erected in 1859. A beautiful old church went the same way — rather than restore it, the inhabitants blew it up in 1792 and replaced it with the present rather stark neo-Classical building. Similarly the old castle disappeared stone by stone, dismantled by the townsfolk to repair damage suffered by the town in 2 Civil War seiges. Despite these depredations, Banbury is a town of great charm, and although a thriving industrial, marketing and shopping centre, the character of its ancestry can be found in the twisting little medieval streets, old houses and inns — especially the gabled, half-timbered Reindeer Inn with mullion windows, in Parsons Street.

Leave Banbury on the A361 and continue to Bloxham.

BLOXHAM, Oxon
From the bridge over the stream, on whose banks grow alder and willow, ironstone houses spread up the valley walls, on one side to the 14th-century church and on the other to a hill crowned by the Victorian buildings of a public school. The old streets and houses in the centre are so closely pressed together they discourage modern additions, and so Bloxham has remained unspoilt and interesting.

At the end of the village turn left on to the Adderbury road, then left again into Milton Road. Pass the edge of Milton, then in 1 mile turn left for Adderbury. Turn left again on to the A423, then right on to the A41, SP 'Aylesbury,' and continue to Aynho.

AYNHO, Northants
On either side of the street apricot trees shade the weathered walls of stone cottages set back in unfenced gardens. The golden fruit of these trees was required by the Lord of the Manor as a toll. The recipients of the apricots were, for nearly 350 years, the Cartwright family, who lived in Aynho Park (OACT), a 17th-century mansion. Monuments to the Cartwrights feature in the church, below whose splendid tower are the village square, shops and a row of thatched cottages, built, like most of Aynho, of local limestone.

¾ mile beyond Aynho, branch left on to the B4031, SP 'Buckingham', for Croughton.

Banbury Cross is adorned by statues of Queen Victoria, Edward VII and George V

CROUGHTON, Northants
Croughton stands on the Oxfordshire border with an American Air Force base for company. Within the peaceful church are late 13th-century wall paintings, which were not discovered until 1930. Although unfortunately damaged by an unsuccessful attempt at protecting them with a layer of wax, these famous paintings are still reasonably clear, and include illustrations of the Flight into Egypt and the Epiphany.

Continue on the B4031 for 2 miles, then turn left on to the A43 for Brackley.

BRACKLEY, Northants
Although a busy place these days, Brackley, with a long tradition of fox-hunting, has retained its pleasant country town atmosphere. In the past, a number of important visitors have stayed here; in 1215 the Barons gathered in Brackley Castle (since demolished) to discuss the Magna Carta before meeting with King John, and Simon de Montfort tried to negotiate with Henry III's messengers here. The Earl of Leicester founded the Hospital of St John and St James in the 12th century, and his heart was buried in the chapel — only to be carelessly thrown away by a 19th-century workman who discovered a lead casket and threw away the 'bit of old leather' he found inside it. The Hospital, bought by Magdalen College, Oxford, in the 15th century, is now a well-known school and the chapel is one of the oldest school chapels in Britain.

Continue through Brackley and ¾ mile beyond the town turn left, SP 'Helmdon and 'Sulgrave', and continue to Helmdon. Here cross the bridge and turn left to Sulgrave. A detour (½ mile) can be made by turning right in Sulgrave for Sulgrave Manor.

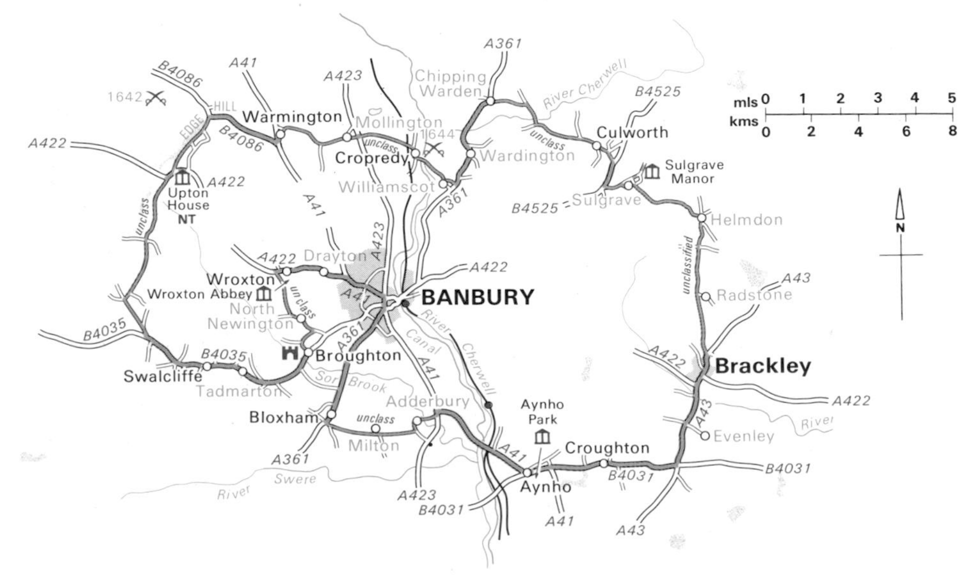

SULGRAVE MANOR, Northants
The forbears of American President George Washington lived in the Queen Anne north wing of Sulgrave Manor (OACT) between 1539 and 1610. The south wing was added in 1921, the same year the house opened its doors to the public. Carved above the porch entrance is the original American flag, 3 stars and 2 stripes, and in the hall hangs perhaps the most treasured possession of the house, an original oil painting of George Washington. Other relics include Washington's black velvet coat and a fragment of his wife's wedding dress. In the house there are great fireplaces, complete with their ancient implements; the original four-poster bed in the main bedroom; and a fascinating kitchen. The 14th-century church is closely linked to the manor and the Washington family, and includes the tomb of Laurence Washington, who built the house.

Continue on the Culworth road through Sulgrave, and in 1 mile turn right on to the B4525. In ½ mile turn left, SP 'Culworth', and at the T-junction turn left into Culworth.

CULWORTH, Northants
Culworth once had its own market and fair, but only a grocer's sign of a sugar-loaf and birch broom on a house by the green recalls these past days of importance. Charles I stayed in the village before the battle of Cropredy Bridge, and in the 18th-century the less respectable Culworth Gang, an infamous bunch of thieves, used it as their headquarters. The church has a tombstone of a negro slave who died in 1762 at the age of 16.

Continue for 1¾ miles, then turn right and later turn left for Chipping Warden. Join the A361 for Wardington, then in 1 mile turn right, SP 'Cropredy', and skirt the hamlet of Williamscot before reaching Cropredy.

CROPREDY, Oxon
Charles I won an early victory in Cropredy during his fight to keep the monarchy; a battle remembered by the 2 suits of armour hanging on the wall of an aisle in the spacious church. Chief among the church's treasures is the brass lectern, adorned by a glittering eagle. When the king came to fight his battle, the villagers hid the lectern in the River Cherwell for safety. Years later it was recovered, but one of the 3 brass lions which stand at the foot of the pedestal was missing. Another was made of bronze, which is why 2 lions shine brightly and the other is dull.

At the Brasenoes Arms PH in Cropredy, turn right, and in ¼ mile turn left, SP 'Mollington'. Later go over staggered crossroads into Mollington and continue to Warmington.

WARMINGTON, Warwicks
Warmington lies in rich farmland at the foot of Edgehill. Its cottages are gathered about a green, complete with a pond and sheep-dip, and nearby stands the Elizabethan gabled manor house of the village. Above the green the small brown-stone church is set on a steeply-sloping churchyard sheltered by shady pines. This was where soldiers killed in the Battle of Edgehill in 1642 were buried. The battle was the first in the Civil War between the Royalists and the Parliamentarians.

On entering Warmington bear left and cross the green and turn left on to the A41, then turn sharp right again on to the B4086, SP 'Kineton'. Continue for 2 miles with fine views from the Edge Hill plateau then turn left at a T-junction, SP 'Edge Hill'. Follow the hill for a further 1¾ miles before reaching the A422. From here a short detour can be made by turning left to Upton House.

A typical cottage in Culworth village

The great hall at Sulgrave Manor was part of the original house

UPTON HOUSE, Warwicks
A wealthy London merchant of James I's reign built Upton House (NT), but it was not until Lord Bearsted bought the house in 1927 and filled it with an art collection of impeccable taste that Upton became exceptional. For here are kept outstanding paintings of the Flemish and early Netherlands school, the Florentine school, and a particularly fine collection of the English 18th-century school, including works by Stubbs and Hogarth. The exquisite collections of 18th-century porcelain include Sèvres and Chelsea pieces. Upton's delightful gardens include terraces, wooded combes, a lake and a water garden.

The main tour turns right on to the A422, SP 'Stratford', then take the next turning left, SP 'Compton Wynyates'. Continue for 3½ miles to a crossroads and turn left, SP 'Banbury'. In 1 mile turn left on to the B4035 for Swalcliffe.

SWALCLIFFE, Oxon
William of Wykeham, founder of New College, Oxford (1324-1404) and a builder of cathedrals, built the lofty and buttressed tithe barn in Swalcliffe. An impressive arch of cathedral proportions opens into the massive interior, where great roof beams can be seen in the half-light. A fine church and manor house overlook the tumble of thatched cottages clustered about a hollow.

Continue on the B4035 through Tadmarton to Broughton. Here turn left, SP 'North Newington', then bear right past the entrance to Broughton Castle.

BROUGHTON CASTLE, Oxon
Broughton Castle (OACT) was last 'modernised' in about 1600, when the medieval fortified manor house of Sir John de Broughton was transformed into an Elizabethan manor by the Fiennes family. The improvements beloved by Victorians never took place because the 15th Baron was a notorious reveller and spendthrift, so no money was left for building. Indeed, the contents of the castle were auctioned to raise money in 1837, including the swans on the wide moat which surrounds the house. Across the bridge, through the battlemented gateway, great fireplaces, airy rooms, elaborate plaster ceilings and vaulted passages echo the past.

Shortly bear right again, then in ½ mile turn left for North Newington. Here turn right, SP 'Wroxton', then in 1¼ miles turn right on to the A422 and skirt the village of Wroxton.

WROXTON, Oxon
Mellowed, brown-stone cottages, many thatched, are overshadowed by Wroxton Abbey (OACT), a beautiful 17th-century house built on the foundations of a 13th-century Augustinian priory. The house possesses 3 paintings by Holbein and one by Zucchero, and of a more domestic nature, a quilt sewn by Mary, Queen of Scots.

Continue on the A422 through Drayton, then join the A41 for the return to Banbury.

AN UNSUSPECTED COUNTRYSIDE

Major highways following ancient Roman routes carry new towns and overspill developments deep into the countryside north of London. Between them, unsuspected by their traffic, are quiet rural areas where wood and parkland insulate splendid mansions from the modern rush.

BARNET, Gt London
Several charmingly-rural areas have survived here in spite of the capital's appetite for building land. Mill Hill has picturesque weather-boarded houses set neatly on the green ridge from which it takes its name. A 2-mile expanse of unspoilt countryside extends from Cockfosters to Monken Hadley, and Hadley Woods are delightful.

Leave Barnet Church with SP 'Hatfield, A1000'. After $\frac{1}{2}$ mile pass through Hadley Green.

HADLEY GREEN, Gt London
Hadley Common and Hadley Green meet at St Mary's Church, a 15th-century building of flint and ironstone, topped by an 18th-century copper beacon. Various Georgian houses and cottages cluster round the fringes of the green in a very village-like way.

Continue to Potters Bar, passing the Battle of Barnet (1471) Obelisk to the right. Meet crossroads and drive forward to pass the BBC radio station at Brookman's Park. In 2 miles bear left for Hatfield. Then forward at roundabout, in ½ mile bear left for Hatfield, at next roundabout forward passing the entrance to Hatfield House (right).

HATFIELD, Herts
Ancient Hatfield preserves many interesting buildings from its long history as a market town, not the least of which is the Tudor palace of Cardinal Moreton. Even this, however, with its Elizabeth I and Mary associations, is overshadowed by the famous and spectacular pile of Hatfield House (open). A chapel of the owners of the house, can be seen in the local church.

Proceed through Old Hatfield and meet traffic lights. Turn right here SP 'Hertford', then within $\frac{1}{2}$ mile cross a flyover and turn left to join the A414. A detour can be made from the main tour route by keeping forward on the A1000 and crossing the River Lee to Welwyn Garden City.

WELWYN GARDEN CITY, Herts
Although not the earliest of its kind in England (that honour belongs to Letchworth), Welwyn Garden City was begun in 1919 and represents an attempt to influence the living conditions of ordinary people.

Continue with the A414. In 2 miles enter a roundabout and leave by the 1st exit. After about 1 mile reach Cole Green and take the 2nd turning left on to an unclassified road SP 'Welwyn, B1000'. Continue for $1\frac{1}{4}$ miles and turn left to join the B1000. In another $\frac{1}{4}$ mile turn right on to an unclassified road across the River Mimram SP 'Archers Green'. At the end of this turn right for Tewin.

TEWIN, Herts
Tewin lies in wooded countryside above the charming River Mimram, east of the impressive 19th-century Digswell railway viaduct. Close by is beautifully-preserved Elizabethan Queen Hoo Hall.

Proceed to the green in Tewin and keep left for Burnham Green. Drive over crossroads for Woolmer Green.

WOOLMER GREEN, Herts
Local St Michael's Church, built in the late 19th century, was meant to incorporate a tower that was never erected.

Turn right on to the B197 and follow part of the old Great North Road to Knebworth.

KNEBWORTH, Herts
Several examples of the accomplished early 20th-century architect Lutyens' work can be seen in New Knebworth, including the Church of St Martin, Golf Club House, and 'Homewod'.

Meet crossroads and turn left on to an unclassified road SP 'Old Knebworth'. Pass under a railway bridge and turn right. After 1 mile Knebworth House lies to the right.

KNEBWORTH HOUSE, Herts
Among many fine paintings and relics displayed in this large house (open) are manuscripts belonging to historian Edward Bulwer Lytton, who lived here. The origins of the house itself are in the 15th century, but the building shows later influence. The grounds now form a Country Park.

Keep left with the 'Codicote' road and in $\frac{1}{2}$ mile turn right SP 'Kimpton and Whitwell'. Continue, then turn right on to the B656 SP 'Hitchin' and shortly pass the Vanstone Garden Centre on the left. Continue for $4\frac{1}{2}$ miles, passing a road on the right leading to St Ippollitts.

ST IPPOLLITTS, Herts
By all accounts St Ippollitts was a man skilled in the treatment of horses. The local church was rebuilt in 1879 from old materials.

Continue into Hitchin.

HITCHIN, Herts
Tilehouse Street and Bridge Street preserve the best of Hitchin's older houses, but many other features survive in this medieval wool town. The ancient market square and moated Hitchin Priory, the latter dating from the 1770s, are reminders of a prosperous past. Features of the town church include a fine old porch and good screenwork.

Leave the town by the A600 Bedford road. Continue to Henlow Camp.

HENLOW CAMP, Beds
Long-renowned as a flying centre, Henlow Camp is an RAF establishment situated some 2 miles south of the village from which it derives its name.

Drive to a roundabout and go forward. In $1\frac{1}{4}$ miles meet crossroads and turn right on to an unclassified road for Clifton.

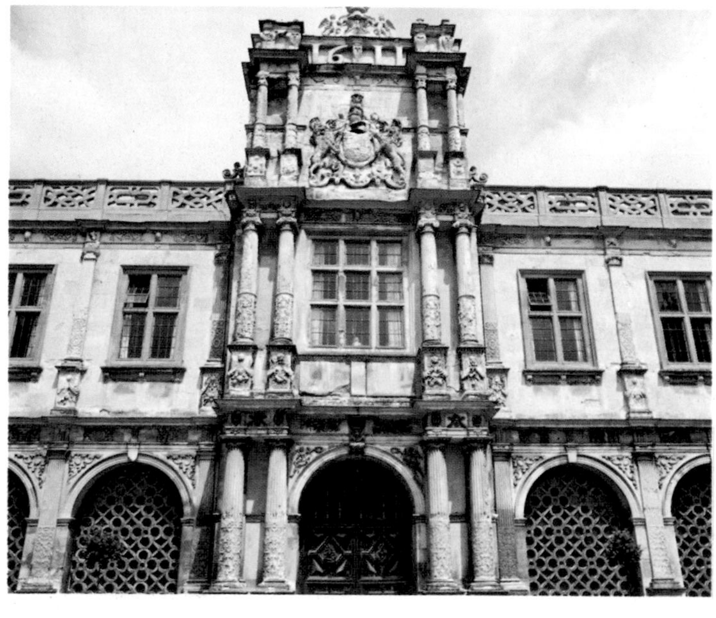

Hatfield House, which was built between 1608 and 1612, is one of the most outstanding examples of Jacobean architecture in England.

CLIFTON, Beds
A large 16th-century alabaster monument to Sir Michael Fisher and his wife is in Clifton Church.

Turn left, then immediately right, SP 'Stanford'. In $\frac{1}{4}$ mile pass the church and turn left. Cross the River Ivel Navigation, proceed for $\frac{1}{2}$ mile, and keep right for Stanford. Turn right on to the B658 SP 'Sandy' and keep straight on for Caldecote. Meet crossroads and turn left on to an unclassified road for Ickwell Green.

ICKWELL GREEN, Beds
Perhaps best known for the May Day revels still held round the enormous maypole that rises from its large green, this pretty village boasts several thatched cottages and a smithy where Georgian clockmaker Thomas Tompion once worked.

Turn left SP 'Old Warden' and in $\frac{1}{2}$ mile meet a T-junction. Turn right and pass Old Warden Airfield.

OLD WARDEN AIRFIELD, Beds
Historical aircraft and veteran cars can be seen in the Shuttleworth Collection at this small airfield, and flying displays are given occasionally.
Take the 'Shefford' road through Old Warden.

OLD WARDEN, Beds
The first Warden pear was grown in this pretty village. Old Warden Park house was built for Sir Joseph Shuttleworth in 1872, and is now used as an agricultural college. Nearby is the attractive Swiss Garden.
After $\frac{1}{2}$ mile meet a T-junction and turn left. Continue for 1 mile, pass under a railway bridge, and turn left. Follow SP 'Shefford' and eventually rejoin the A600. Cross a river and enter Shefford village.

SHEFFORD, Beds
Southill Park, a notable Regency house to the north of Shefford, was rebuilt by Henry Holland in 1800. It was once the home of Admiral Byng, who was unjustly shot for neglect of duty after losing a battle in 1757.

Proceed to traffic signals and turn right on to the A507 SP 'Ampthill'. In $3\frac{1}{4}$ miles turn left on to an unclassified road SP 'Silsoe'. In 1 mile turn left on to the A6 for Silsoe.

SILSOE, Beds
Silsoe's church is of early 19th-century date, but is a successful attempt at a traditional English church style. Nearby is Wrest Park House and Gardens (open).

Continue to Barton-in-the-Clay.

BARTON-IN-THE-CLAY, Beds
A 16th-century painting of St Nicholas is preserved in the village church. A viewpoint known as the Clappers, including 136 acres of lovely National Trust property crowned by Clappers Wood, rises to the west.
Turn left on to the B655, SP 'Hexton'. Climb on to the Barton Hills and drive to Hexton.

A winter scene at Hadley Green.

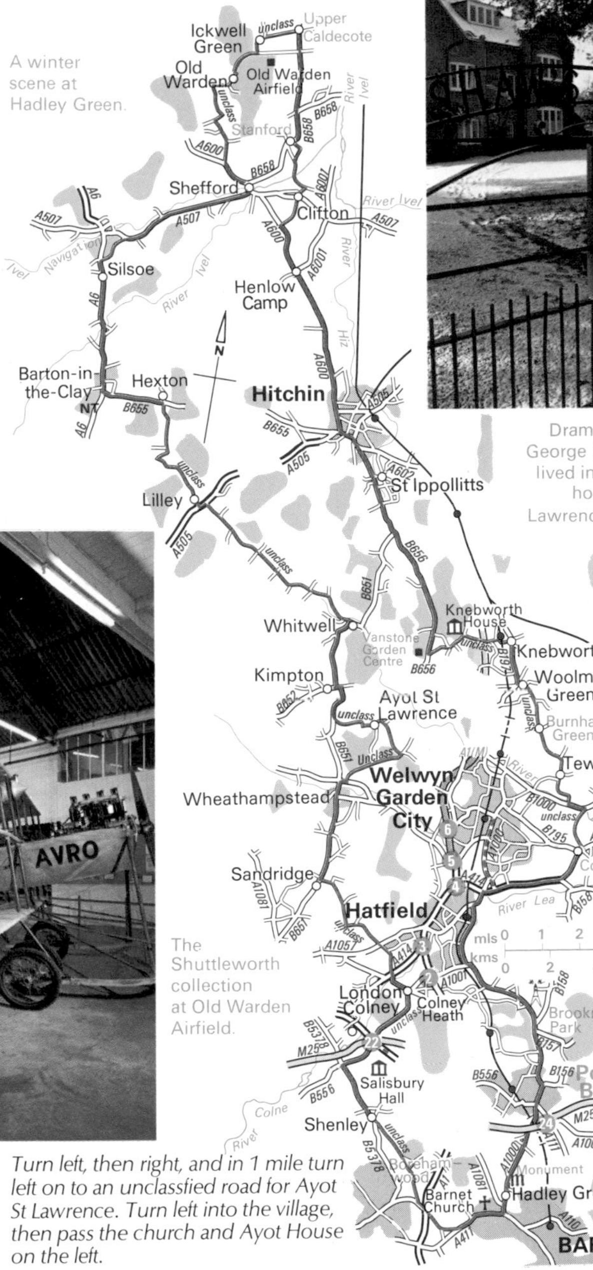

The Shuttleworth collection at Old Warden Airfield.

Dramatist and critic George Bernard Shaw lived in this Victorian house at Ayot St Lawrence for 44 years.

HEXTON, Herts
Nature lends a dramatic hand to the appearance of Hexton. All around are the undulating Barton Hills, and in the village itself the main street is lined with laburnums. The 19th-century St Faith's Church is guarded by giant yews.

Meet crossroads and turn right on to an unclassified road leading to Lilley.

LILLEY, Herts
Thomas Jekyll successfully copied a traditional style when he designed the attractive local church in 1870.

Keep forward over all crossroads and enter Whitwell.

WHITWELL, Herts
Brick-and-timber cottages and a charming old inn called The Bull make up this pretty village, set in unspoiled countryside.

Turn right on to the B651 SP 'St Albans', and ascend to the edge of Kimpton.

KIMPTON, Herts
The large flint Church of SS Peter and Paul stands at the north-eastern end of this village and is thought to date from the early 14th century.

Turn left, then right, and in 1 mile turn left on to an unclassified road for Ayot St Lawrence. Turn left into the village, then pass the church and Ayot House on the left.

AYOT ST LAWRENCE, Herts
Author George Bernard Shaw lived at Ayot St Lawrence from 1906 to his death in 1950 and his house – Shaw's Corner (NT) – is preserved as it was in his lifetime. His ashes were scattered in the garden.

Keep right and after 1 mile meet a T-junction. Turn right, then in a further $1\frac{1}{2}$ miles meet another T-junction and turn right on to the B653. Meet a roundabout and leave by the 1st exit on the B651 into Wheathampstead.

WHEATHAMPSTEAD, Herts
Modern industry has come to Wheathampstead, and many of its old cottages are now shops. Sarah Jennings, later the Duchess of Marlborough, is said to have been born at nearby Water End Farm. Features of the village itself include a 13th-century church and the 15th-century Bull Inn.

Continue along the B651 to Sandridge.

SANDRIDGE, Herts
Roman bricks and masonry were used to build a chancel arch in the local Church of St Leonard. Also in the building is a good 14th-century stone rood screen.

Turn left on to an unclassified road SP 'Colney Heath'. In 1 mile turn left at T-junction, and in ½ mile left again. In 1 mile at roundabout forward. Then in a further mile turn right across the dual carriageway and left on an unclassified road for Colney Heath. At roundabout take the 3rd exit SP 'London Colney' and continue.

LONDON COLNEY, Herts
Situated in Salisbury Hall is the interesting Mosquito Aircraft Museum. This contains 3 Mosquitos plus 18 de Havilland aircraft plus many interesting exhibits.

At roundabout take the 2nd exit SP 'Radlett'. A detour may be made from the main tour route by leaving the last-mentioned roundabout by the 1st exit on to the B556 then driving for ½ mile to Salisbury Hall.

SALISBURY HALL, Herts
Red-brick Salisbury Hall was built by Sir John Cuttes, treasurer to Henry VIII, and is encircled by a moat.

Continue and at 2nd roundabout turn left on to the B5378 for Shenley.

SHENLEY, Herts
Nicholas Hawksmoor, the great architect, lived at Porter's Park until his death in 1736. His house now serves as a hospital. Preserved on the village green is the old parish lock-up, once used for petty criminals.

Drive to the end of the village and go forward on to an unclassified road. In $2\frac{1}{4}$ miles join one-way traffic and follow SP 'Barnet'. Cross a flyover, then turn right and in 1 mile turn left on to the A411. Return to Barnet.

The pavilion in the grounds of Wrest Park at Silsoe dates from 1709.

THE DOWNS AND TROUT STREAMS OF NORTH HAMPSHIRE

Peaceful lanes wind their way across the rolling North Hampshire Downs, then descend through strings of enchanting Saxon villages, where trout streams meander through the chalklands past green watercress beds and banks of wild flowers.

BASINGSTOKE, Hants
A town that is still expanding, Basingstoke was once a pleasant country town, but now it is surrounded by huge housing estates and the centre has been rendered unrecognisable by modern shopping precincts. The older buildings have to be sought out, but among them is the Willis Museum which is a gold mine for all those interested in Hampshire's history and archaeology. A local man, Mr Willis, founded the museum with his collection of clocks: they were his profession and his hobby.

From Basingstoke town centre, or the Ring Road, follow SP 'Aldermaston' to the Aldermaston Road Roundabout. Leave on the A340 and in 2½ miles turn right, SP 'The Vyne (NT)'. In 1½ miles, at the T-junction, turn left (no SP), or, alternatively turn right for a short detour to The Vyne.

THE VYNE, Hants
A lovely Hampshire lane leads down to The Vyne (NT) and a more charming or unpretentious country house would be hard to find. William Sandys, councillor to Henry VI, built it, and his family lived in it for the next century. Chaloner Chute was the subsequent owner and his descendants lived there until 1956. Among the best features of the house are the Gothic ante-chapel, the chapel itself with fine Flemish stained-glass and Italian glazed floor tiles, the sunny oak gallery and the neo-Classical hall and staircase decorated in pale blue and white. All the furniture and furnishings have been collected by the Chute family over several centuries. This redbrick house is set in simple but pleasant grounds; a grassy sward rolls down to the edge of a long narrow lake at the back and fields stretch away beyond. Looking somewhat out of place is the Classical portico overlooking the lake. Dating from 1650, it is the earliest example of a portico found on an English house.

The main tour continues to the edge of Bramley. Here, turn left, SP 'Silchester', and in ¾ mile turn right. In 1¼ miles, at the crossroads, turn left and in ¾ mile branch right, SP 'Silchester Ruins'. Shortly, to the right, is Silchester Calleva Museum.

SILCHESTER CALLEVA MUSEUM, Hants
This museum, housed in the grounds of Silchester rectory, was instituted in 1951 as a contribution to the Festival of Britain. It contains finds from excavations at nearby Silchester — the old Roman town called *Calleva Atrebatum*. Displays of drawings and models represent Silchester as it was in Roman times, namely a market town and a provincial administrative centre with a population of some 4,000.

Continue to the next road junction and keep left, SP 'Aldermaston'. At the end turn right, then immediately right again. In 1 mile cross the main road, then turn left and continue to Aldermaston.

ALDERMASTON, Berks
Despite the huge Atomic Research Station and accompanying housing estates on Aldermaston's doorstep, the village itself has not been marred by modern development. Its main street of colour-washed brick and timbered buildings runs uphill to Aldermaston Court which is barricaded by huge wrought iron gates known as the Eagle Gates. At the bottom of the street is the Hind's Head, an old coaching inn with a distinctive ornate black and gold clock and a gilt weather vane in the shape of a fox.

Cloth used to be cleaned and thickened in the fulling mill at Alresford

Turn right on to the A340, and at the Hind's Head PH turn left, SP 'Brimpton'. In 1¼ miles turn right, cross the River Enborne, then turn left. At Brimpton follow the Newbury road, then in 2¼ miles turn left. In 1½ miles turn right on to the A339, then in another mile turn left, SP 'Burghclere'.

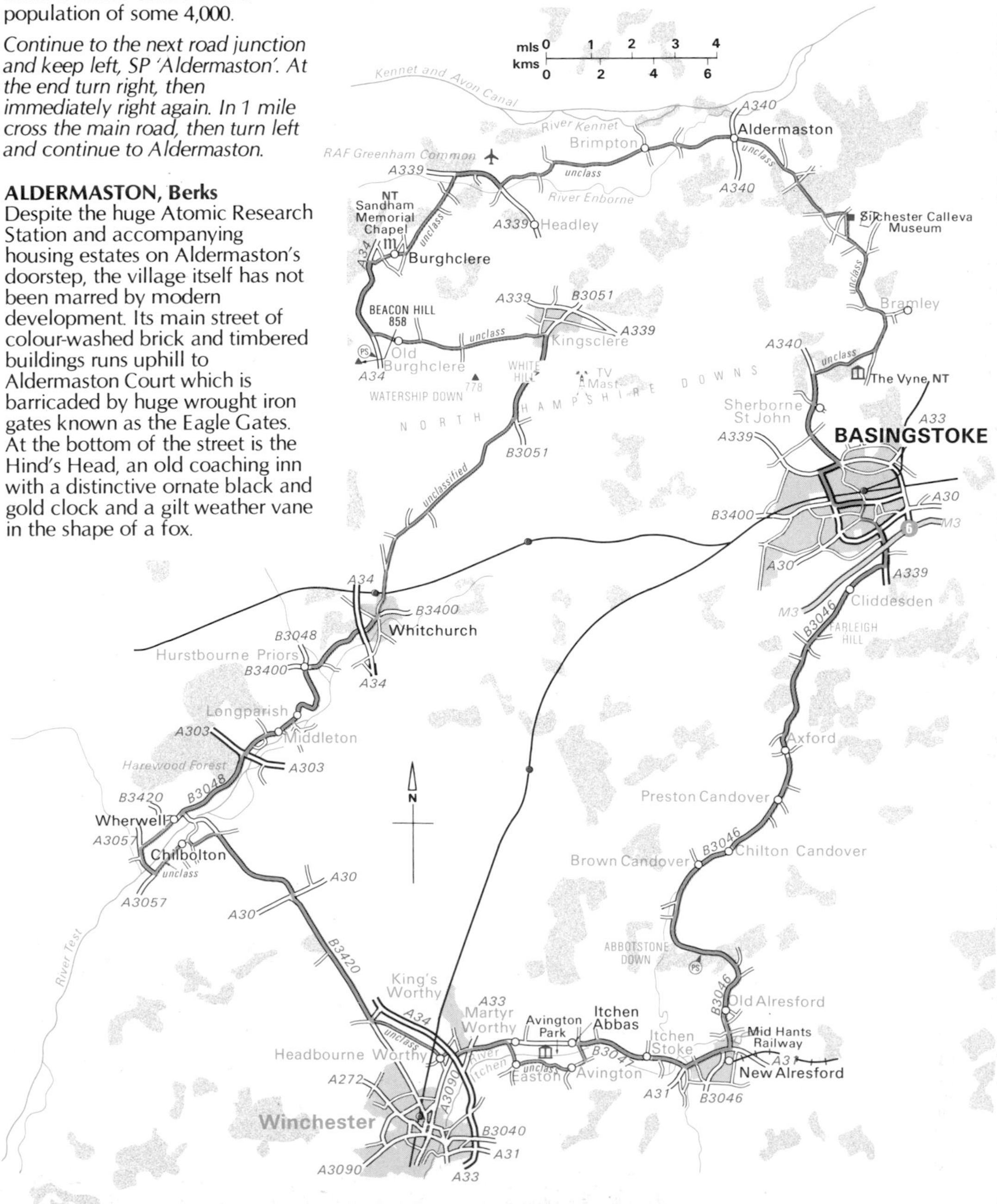

BURGHCLERE, Hants

In 1926 a chapel and 2 almshouses were built in the village of Burghclere to commemorate Henry Willoughby Sandham — a local World War I hero. The tiny Sandham Chapel (NT) is filled with visionary paintings by the English artist Stanley Spencer. Spencer served with the Royal Berkshire Regiment and the paintings here are his reflections of the war.

At the war memorial turn left and after ½ mile pass (right) the Sandham Memorial Chapel. At the A34, turn left, SP 'Winchester'. In 1¾ miles turn left, SP 'Kingsclere'. Ahead, on the A34, is Beacon Hill.

BEACON HILL, Hants

Beacon Hill rises to 858ft and is part of the chalk ridge running from Wiltshire through to Surrey and Kent. This windy, treeless viewpoint is a fine spot for picnicing and flying kites or model aeroplanes.

The main tour continues through the hamlet of Old Burghclere. In ½ mile bear right and follow a pleasant byroad along the foot of the North Hampshire Downs, with Watership Down prominent to the right, to Kingsclere. Here turn right, SP 'Whitchurch', then right again on to the B3051. Climb White Hill (to the left is a picnic area and Hannington TV mast) and continue for 5 miles, then turn left at the main road for Whitchurch.

WHITCHURCH, Hants

Anglers are familiar with the lovely trout-filled River Test and Whitchurch is one of the many villages lying along its valley. Of most interest here is the silk mill. The 18th-century brick building stands, crowned by a small bell tower, on an island in the river. Until the 1930s, when electricity deemed it redundant, water was the sole source of power. A shop (OACT) on the premises sells silk scarves, ties, shirts and so on, as well as an assortment of locally-made products.

At the mini-roundabout in Whitchurch turn right on to the B3400, SP 'Andover', and continue to Hurstbourne Priors. Here, turn left on to the B3048, SP 'Longparish', and follow a winding road along the Test valley to pass through Longparish (see tour 25). Beyond the village, at the A303, turn right then immediately left, SP 'Wherwell'. Remain on the B3420 into Wherwell.

WHERWELL, Hants

Elfrida, Saxon queen and mother of King Ethelred, founded a priory in this exceptionally picturesque thatched village. Unfortunately fires destroyed it and the few remains of the replacement nunnery are now part of priory house. The old pronunciation of the village name is 'Orrell'.

Continue through the village on to an unclassified road ahead, SP 'Fullerton'. In 1 mile turn left on to the A3057, then ½ mile further cross the River Test and turn left on to an unclassified road for Chilbolton.

CHILBOLTON, Hants

A huge, shiny, concave disc stands on the downs above Chilbolton on the site of an old airfield. This radio-wave reflector belongs to the Chilbolton Observatory, whose purpose is to discover more about the earth's atmosphere and interplanetary space.

At the end of Chilbolton turn right, SP 'Barton Stacey', then bear left. In ½ mile turn right on to the B3420, SP 'Winchester'. At the A30 turn right, then immediately left, to follow the line of an old Roman road. After 3½ miles, at the roundabout, follow SP 'The Worthy's', for Headbourne Worthy. Here, at the green, keep left then take the next turning right. In ¼ mile turn left on to the A3090 for King's Worthy. At the far end turn left and immediately right on to the B3047, SP 'Alresford'. After a mile, turn right and cross the River Itchen to Easton. At the Cricketers PH turn left and continue to Avington Park.

AVINGTON PARK, Hants

The River Itchen flows along the parkland boundary and its water meadows provide a tranquil setting for the 17th-century mansion (OACT), enhanced by cedar trees, tulip trees and a long avenue of limes. The front of the redbrick house is broken by a large, white, Doric portico on top of which sit 3 goddesses. For several years the house was lived in by the Shelley family. John, brother of the poet Percy, was the first. A previous owner, the Marquess of Caernarvon, built an attractive Georgian church in the park and all the woodwork — gallery, reredos, pulpit and box-pews — is carved from rich dark mahogany.

The silk mill at Whitchurch has always been a family business employing local women to work the looms

After leaving the park turn left into Avington village. In ¼ mile keep left and recross the River Itchen to reach the edge of Itchen Abbas.

ITCHEN ABBAS, Hants

Itchen Abbas is another of the lovely villages along this valley. With the old mill and the lazy brown trout in the river, it is easy to see why Charles Kingsley was inspired to write *The Water Babies* here. He used to stay at the pub, now rebuilt and called The Plough.

Leave Itchen Abbas on the B3047, SP 'Alresford', and continue to Itchen Stoke, then in 1 mile turn left on to the A31 for New Alresford.

NEW ALRESFORD, Hants

This is one of Hampshire's loveliest small towns. Its main street, appropriately called Broad Street, is flanked with lime trees and colour-washed Georgian houses. The writer Mary Mitford was born in one of them in 1787. A tributary of the Itchen flows around the town and there is a pleasant walk along its banks past an old fulling mill — a reminder of Alresford's medieval days as a wool town. Another reminder of the past is a lake at the edge of the town. In the 12th century the Bishop of Winchester dammed the village pond to form a natural harbour and make the river navigable to the sea.

MID HANTS RAILWAY, Hants

The chalk streams of Hampshire feed beds of bright green cress and provide them with ideal growing conditions. Over half the country's supply of watercress comes from Hampshire and for a long time Alresford Station was an important despatch point. The railway transported the cress all over England and came to be known as the Watercress Line. Neglected and unused for several years, enthusiasts have now restored part of the line and in summer steam trains run between Alresford and Alton.

At Alresford turn left, SP 'Basingstoke B3046', into Broad Street. At the end bear right and cross a causeway over the River Alre to Old Alresford. Cross wooded Abbotstone Down and continue through the Candover valley and down Farleigh Hill, into Cliddesden. In 1¼ miles turn left on to the A339 for the return to Basingstoke.

The lake at The Vyne was landscaped in the 18th century to enhance the view

AMONG THE COTSWOLDS

Wool and stone shaped this landscape. Mellow rock torn from hillsides cropped smooth by generations of sheep was built into great churches, houses, towns and villages by local skill applied with the profits from wool, medieval England's greatest resource.

BURFORD, Oxon
Like so many other wool towns in this part of the country, Burford is centred on a charming main street lined with honey-coloured buildings of local stone. The excellence of this building material is apparent in the fact that Sir Christopher Wren would specify no other for St Paul's Cathedral. The town's main street descends a steep hillside and crosses the River Windrush via a fine old bridge. Buildings of particular interest include 15th-century almshouses, the Great House of 1690, and basically Norman church which claims to be the second largest in Oxfordshire. Features of this splendid building include an imposing tower and spire, and somewhat macabre Civil War associations. In 1649 several Cromwellian mutineers were trapped in the building by their own forces, and on capture 3 of the imprisoned men were shot near the churchyard. The history of Burford is shown in the Torsey Museum and set in 200 acres of woodlands is the Cotswold Wildlife Park.

From the Bull Hotel in Burford follow the unclassified road to Asthall.

ASTHALL, Oxon
The banks of the Windrush afford a delightful view of Asthall Manor, a striking Elizabethan house with mullioned windows and an overall atmosphere of permanence. Alongside is the parish church, which is of Norman origin and features two interesting arches in the north chapel.

Meet a T-junction and turn right SP 'Witney'. Ascend, then turn left on to the B4047 and proceed to Minster Lovell.

MINSTER LOVELL, Oxon
Clustered stone-built cottages and the fine, partly-timbered Swan Inn nestle together to form this quaint little Windrush village. Of special note are the ruins of a 15th-century hall (AM), which boasts two gruesome legends. The first is of Lord Francis Lovell, who is supposed to have hidden in a secret room after the Lambert Simnel Rising of 1487. His whereabouts was known to only one servant, who died suddenly leaving the unfortunate Lord Francis incarcerated until his skeleton was reputedly discovered in 1718. A similar tale recounts the story of an unfortunate young Lovell bride who decided to hide in a large chest on her Christmas wedding night and became trapped.

At the White Hart Hotel turn left on to the unclassified 'Leafield' road. Descend and cross the River Windrush and continue to Leafield. Drive to the war memorial, turn left, then continue to the Fox Inn and bear right. Shortly pass the Leafield Radio Station. Continue to Shipton-under-Wychwood and turn right on to the A361 to enter the village.

The peaceful ruins of Minster Lovell Hall are haunted by macabre legends involving death by starvation and suffocation.

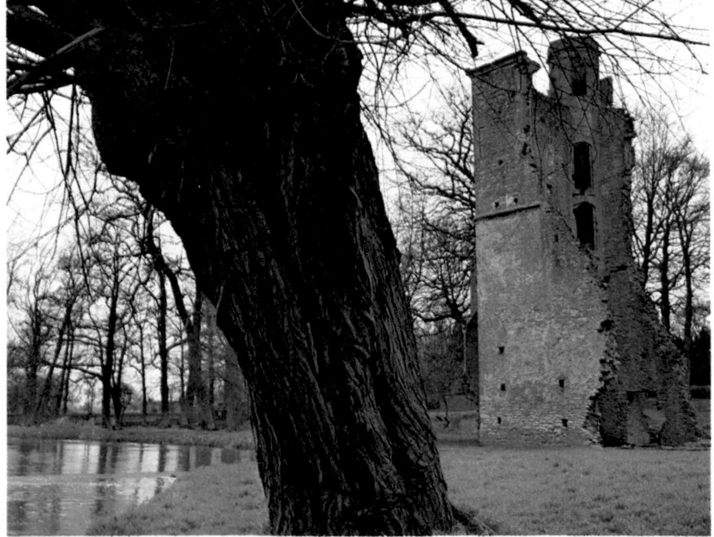

SHIPTON-UNDER-WYCHWOOD, Oxon
Restored Shipton Court is of Elizabethan origin and one of the finest buildings in the village; unfortunately it is closed to the public. More easily accessible is a fountain which was raised to the memory of 19 Shipton men who died in the wreck of the ship *Cosipatrick* in 1874. The Shaven Crown Inn has a Tudor gateway.

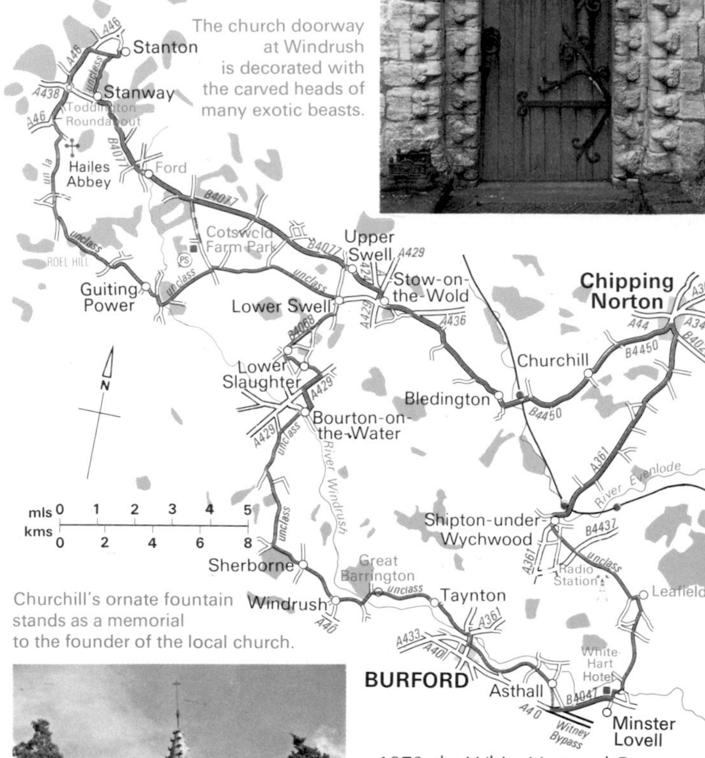

The church doorway at Windrush is decorated with the carved heads of many exotic beasts.

Churchill's ornate fountain stands as a memorial to the founder of the local church.

Cross the River Evenlode and continue to Chipping Norton.

CHIPPING NORTON, Oxon
The 'Chipping' element of this name means 'market', and for a considerable period the 'market at Norton' was the commercial centre for the Evenlode Valley. When the Cotswolds became one giant sheepwalk the town assumed new importance as a gathering place for wool merchants and other traders. Much of the town's attraction today is due to its many survivals from a prosperous past. Among these are numerous 18th-century houses and a 'wool' church that is among the finest in the county; 17th-century Almhouses, The Bliss Tweedmill of 1872, the White Hart and Crown and Cushion were once coaching inns. Four miles north-east is Chas Heton House, which contains tapestries and period furniture.

Follow the B4450 'Stow' road and drive to Churchill.

CHURCHILL, Oxon
Two famous men were born here in the 18th century – William Hastings, 1st Governor-General of India, and 'The Father of Geology' William Smith, who was the first man to map the rock strata of England and identify fossils peculiar to each layer. A restored church of 1826 crowns a nearby hilltop and displays a fine tower which can be seen for miles around. An unusual square-shaped fountain with open arches and pinnacles rising from a basin of flowing water stands as a memorial to Squire Langston, the original builder of the church.

Continue to Bledington.

BLEDINGTON, Glos
Situated near the River Evenlode, Bledington boasts its own Victorian maypole and a fine Norman church containing good examples of old glass. Nearby Maugersbury Hill forms an excellent viewpoint.

Later join the A436 for Stow-on-the-Wold.

STOW-ON-THE-WOLD, Glos
'Stow-on-the-Wold where the wind blows cold' is a local saying that aptly describes this, the highest hilltop town in the Cotswolds. It is set on a ridge between the upper valleys of the rivers Windrush and Evenlode and has an enormous market square with stocks and a 14th-century cross. This is the focal point of the town. Inside the local church is a splendid 17th-century painting of the Crucifixion by Belgian artist, de Craeyer. Hundreds of Royalists were imprisoned here after a Civil War battle fought in 1646.

Follow SP 'Tewkesbury' to join the B4077 and proceed to Upper Swell.

UPPER SWELL, Glos
This charming and unspoilt village comprises a cluster of houses and a tiny church. Its main feature is a fine manor house.

About 4½ miles farther a road on the left leads to Cotswold Farm Park.

COTSWOLD FARM PARK, Glos
Rare breeds of British farm animals are kept here in an authentic farmyard setting in beautiful countryside on the Cotswold Hills. Major attractions include a pet's corner, young stock, and rides round the park in a pony-drawn trap.

Continue on the B4077 through Ford. Descend to Stanway.

STANWAY, Glos
Magnificent wooded hills surround this attractive small village, which has a tithe barn mentioned in the Domesday Book. Stanway House, a focal point for the community, is approached through an imposing gateway in the style of Inigo Jones.

Meet crossroads and turn right on to an unclassified road, passing the grounds of Stanway House. In 1¼ miles turn right and drive to Stanton.

STANTON, Glos
Larch woods on Shenbarrow Hill shelter this unspoilt village, which is often described as the most attractive in the Cotswolds. Elizabethan Stanton Court and 16th-century Warren House are old manor houses of particular note, and thatched barns add the softness of straw or reed to the picture. Watching over all is the homely sentinel of the restored church.

Return and in ¼ mile bear right SP 'Cheltenham'. In ¾ mile turn left on to the A46 and continue to the Toddington roundabout. Keep forward at the roundabout, then in 1 mile take the 2nd turning on the left on to an unclassified road for Hailes Abbey.

HAILES ABBEY, Glos
For many years the 13th-century Cistercian foundation was a thriving centre of learning and religion, attracting pilgrims from all over the country. Nowadays it is a collection of ruins (AM, NT) with a small site museum in which tiles, bosses, and various early relics are preserved.

Return for 200 yds and turn left on to Roel Hill, which affords fine views of the surrounding countryside. Meet a T-junction and turn left, then turn right and continue to Guiting Power.

GUITING POWER, Glos
This picturesque village is attractively situated on the upper reaches of the River Windrush.

In ½ mile meet a T-junction and turn right SP 'Andoversford', then take the next turning left SP 'Stow'. Continue along a quiet country road to Lower Swell.

LOWER SWELL, Glos
Huge copper beeches and stone walls line the route into Lower Swell. In the village the small River Dikler flows past attractive bankside cottages and a working smithy. An elegant Georgian pillar topped by an urn stands on the village green and inside the local church are fine examples of Norman carving.

Turn right on to the B4068 SP 'The Slaughters', then turn left on to an unclassified road for Upper Slaughter.

UPPER SLAUGHTER, Glos
An outstanding 3-gabled Elizabethan manor house (open), with 15 tall chimneys and an avenue of mature trees, dominates this beautiful Cotswold village. Also here are a fine 17th- century parsonage and an attractive, partly Norman church.

Lower Slaughter's 19th-century brick mill contrasts sharply with the stone houses elsewhere in the village.

Pollarded willows and the enchantment of running water combine with the mellowness of old Cotswold stone in Burford's ancient river bridge, which spans the Windrush.

Drive to the end of the village and turn left, then continue to the neighbouring village of Lower Slaughter.

LOWER SLAUGHTER, Glos
As the River Eye winds its peaceful course between the rows of charming cottages which flank both its banks in this village it is spanned by many bridges, stone and wooden, and shaded by the dark-green umbrellas of stately yew trees. This scene of rural tranquillity is completed by a church with a 12th-century arcade.

Cross a bridge and turn right, then at the end of the village turn right again on to the A429. In ½ mile turn left on to an unclassified road for Bourton-on-the-Water.

BOURTON-ON-THE-WATER, Glos
This Cotswold-stone village – with its churches, shops, houses, sloping lawns alongside the River Windrush, and watermill – is reproduced at one-ninth actual size in the garden of the Old New Inn. Elsewhere in the village are the Birdland Zoo Gardens, a Village Life Exhibition and the Cotswolds Motor Museum.

Meet crossroads in the village and follow the unclassified 'Sherborne' road. Cross the river and bear right. Ascend, and in 3½ miles turn left for Sherborne.

SHERBORNE, Glos
Number 88, a cottage on the Windrush road, was once an old chapel and retains a fine Norman doorway. Sherborne House shares extensive grounds with Lodge Park, a charming 19th-century building that was erected as a grandstand for the audiences of deer coursing.

Leave Sherborne and continue to Windrush.

WINDRUSH, Glos
This village is named after the River Windrush. The local church faces a triangular patch of green surrounded by tall trees and has a Norman doorway considered to be one of the best of its type.

Keep left and continue for ¾ mile, then meet a T-junction and turn left for Great Barrington. Drive to the war memorial and bear right for Taynton.

TAYNTON, Oxon
Taynton's thatched grey-stone houses nestle together with a 700-year-old church on timbered slopes above the River Windrush. Stone for the building of Blenheim Palace was supplied by the famous quarries in this area.

After the village keep forward for the A424, then the A361. Cross a river and re-enter Burford.

THE CREEKS AND ESTUARIES OF THE ESSEX COAST

Beautiful, unspoilt scenery surrounds the Crouch and Blackwater estuaries — sheltered waterways haunted by wildfowl and seabirds and beloved by yachtsmen. The old riverports of Burnham-on-Crouch and Maldon are redolent of the salty character of the wild and lovely Essex coast, with its deserted creeks and lonely mudflats.

Low tide at the quay in Burnham-on-Crouch, well-known for its local oyster beds

CHELMSFORD, Essex
Roman workmen cut their great road linking London with Colchester straight through Chelmsford and built a fort here, *Caesaromagus,* at the junction of the Rivers Chelmer and Cann. The town has always been an important market centre and is now the bustling modern county town of Essex. The Marconi Company, pioneers in the manufacture of wireless equipment, set up the first radio company in the world here in 1899. Exhibits of the early days of wireless can be seen in the Chelmsford and Essex Museum in Oaklands Park, as can interesting displays of Roman remains and local history.

Leave Chelmsford town centre on the A130 Southend road. At the bypass roundabout, take the 3rd exit onto the B1009. After ½ mile, turn right at the Beehive PH in Great Baddow, and at Galleywood turn left onto the B1007 before crossing Galleywood Common to reach Stock.

STOCK, Essex
A fine old tower windmill and a delightful church with a traditional Essex-style wooden belfry and spire lend character to this pleasant village of well-kept houses. Some of the timbers in the church belfry are said to have come from Spanish galleons, wrecked in the aftermath of Sir Francis Drake's defeat of the Armada.

On entering Stock turn left onto the Wickford road. (Stock Church lies ahead on the B1007). Pass the windmill on the left before reaching a T-junction. Turn right here, then after ½ mile turn left before reaching the shores of Hanningfield Reservoir. In 1 mile turn left on to the Hanningfields road and continue to South Hanningfield.

SOUTH HANNINGFIELD, Essex
The placid waters of the reservoir that has been created by damming Sandford Brook transform the scattered rural settlement of South Hanningfield into a lakeside village. Standing by the shores of the lake is the 12th-century village church whose graceful belfry is a local landmark in the flat Essex countryside.

In 1½ miles turn right on to the A130, SP 'Southend', and 2 miles farther, at the Rettendon Turnpike roundabout, take the 1st exit on to the B1012. Later skirt South Woodham Ferrers.

SOUTH WOODHAM FERRERS, Essex
The desolate marshland overlooking the sheltered creeks of the Crouch estuary, a yachtsman's paradise, was chosen by Essex County Council as the site for one of its most attractive new town schemes. At the centre is a traditional market square surrounded by pleasant arcades and terraces built in the old Essex style with brick, tile and weatherboard.

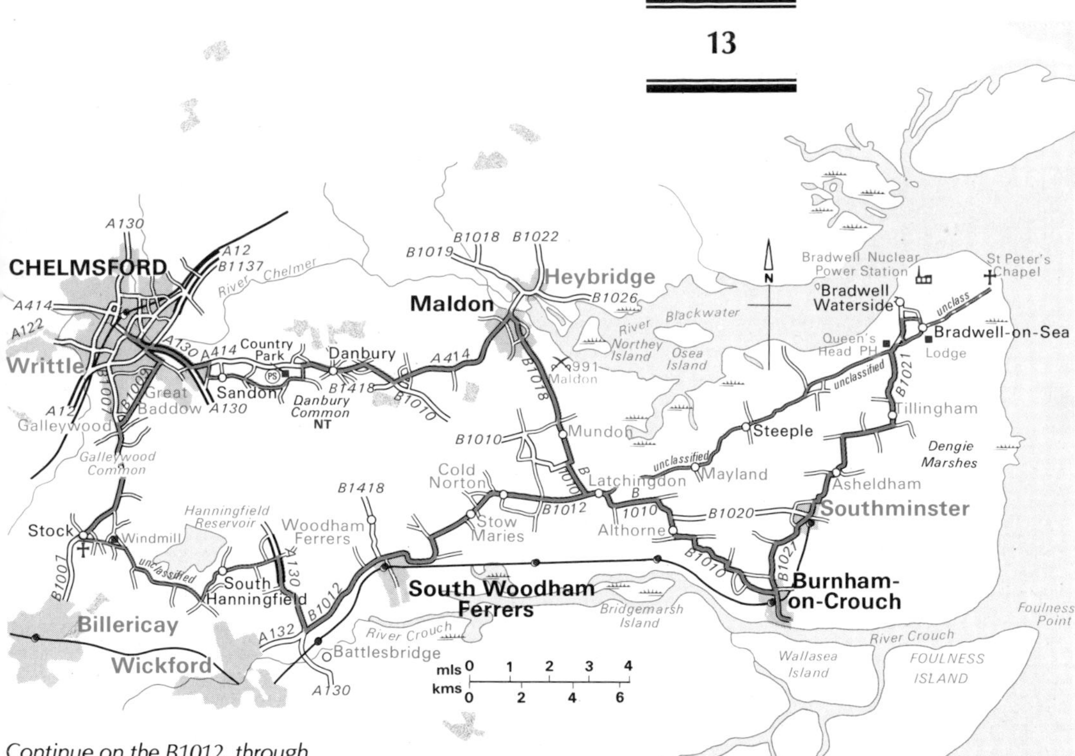

Continue on the B1012, through Stow Maries and Cold Norton to Latchingdon. Here keep forward on to the B1010, then at the church turn right. After 1½ miles turn right again and continue through Althorne. At the T-junction turn left and follow a winding road to the edge of Burham-on-Crouch. Turn right on to the B1021 for the town centre.

BURNHAM-ON-CROUCH, Essex
From the gaily-coloured cottages along the quay, the town climbs up the slopes above the seashore, its streets lined with an assortment of old cottages, Georgian and Victorian houses and shops. This is the yachting centre of Essex. In Tudor times sailing barges thronged the estuary where now yachts tack jauntily to and fro. Yachtsmen and holiday-makers come ashore to buy provisions, following a tradition that dates back to the medieval era when Burnham was the market centre for the isolated farmsteads of Wallasea and Foulness Islands and the inhibitants travelled in by ferry. The whole area was, and is to this day, famous for its oyster beds.

Return along the B1021 and at the end of the town keep forward on to the Southminster road. Continue northwards across the Dengie Peninsula.

DENGIE PENINSULA, Essex
The salty tang of sea air, brought inland by the east-coast winds, gives an exhilarating flavour to the marshlands of the Dengie Peninsula. Like the Cambridgeshire and Lincolnshire fens, the once waterlogged coastal region of this remote corner of Essex was reclaimed from the sea by 17th-century Dutch engineers. The views across the marshes encompass great sweeps of countryside, inhabited by wildfowl, seabirds and cattle grazing on the saltings. The old market town of Southminster and the marshland villages of Asheldham and Tillingham rise prominently from the flat expanse of the landscape.

In Southminster turn right at the church, then turn left on to the Bradwell road and at the next T-junction turn right. A winding road then passes through Asheldham to Tillingham. After another 1½ miles, at the Queens Head PH, turn right to reach Bradwell Waterside.

BRADWELL WATERSIDE AND BRADWELL-ON-SEA, Essex
Overshadowing the small coastal resort of Bradwell Waterside on the estuary of the Blackwater River, the massive bulk of Bradwell Nuclear Power Station stands as an incongruous 20th-century intrusion on this remote coastline. Bradwell-on-Sea, a village now a mile or so inland from the coast, is a cluster of attractive cottages set about a green leading to the church. Bradwell Lodge (open by appointment) a beautiful part-Tudor, part-Georgian manor house, has an unusually charming summer house. During the 18th century the portrait painter Thomas Gainsborough was a frequent visitor. Not far away, on the coast, stands the tiny 7th-century Saxon church of St Peter-at-the-Wall. It is one of the most ancient churches in England and is built across the line of the west wall of *Othona*, a great 3rd-century Roman fort.

From Bradwell Waterside return along the B1021 and in ¾ mile turn left for Bradwell-on-Sea village, then in 1 mile rejoin the B1021. At the Queens Head PH continue on to the unclassified Latchingdon road with occasional views of the Blackwater estuary, before reaching Steeple.

STEEPLE, Essex
This small village of thatched and weather-board cottages stands on the south bank of the Blackwater estuary, where brightly coloured yachts and the occasional stately sailing barge can be seen. Around the village stretches a rich green countryside of fertile meadows, patterned by lanes bordered with banks of trees.

Many of Tillingham's old cottages were built by the Church

Continue through Mayland back to Latchingdon. At the end of the village turn right on to the B1010, SP 'Maldon'. In 1 mile turn right again on to the B1018 and continue to Maldon.

MALDON, Essex
Just outside the fascinating old town of Maldon lies the site of one of the great decisive battles of England's early history. The Battle of Maldon was fought and lost in 991 when the English leader, Byrthnoth, was killed by the invading Danes after a fierce 3-day battle. As a result of this defeat, the English king, Ethelred the Unready, was obliged to pay an annual tribute of Danegeld to the conquerors; eventually the Danes overthrew him and Cnut became king. Maldon itself is a charming town, famous for its sea salt, produced for generations as a result of evaporating sea water. One of its churches, All Saints, has a unique triangular tower, and there are many intriguing shops and welcoming inns in its steep winding streets.

Leave Maldon on the A414 Chelmsford road and in 3¼ miles, at the roundabout, take the 3rd exit and continue to Danbury.

DANBURY, Essex
It is said that this village, crowning a high, wooded hill, takes its name from the Danes who invaded this part of the country in the Dark Ages. Remains of an ancient earthwork defence, thought to be Danish, can still be seen around the site of the church, which contains 3 beautifully carved wooden figures of knights dating from around 1300. To the south is Danbury Common (NT) where acres of gorse flower in a blaze of golden colour for much of the year; to the west, Danbury Country Park offers another pleasant stretch of open country.

At the end of the village turn left into Wells Lane. At the next T-junction turn right, SP 'Country Park'. Continue past Danbury Country Park to Sandon.

SANDON, Essex
The village green of Sandon has produced a notable oak tree, remarkable not so much for its height as for the tremendous horizontal spread of its branches. Around the green have been built the fine church and a number of attractive old houses, some dating back to the 16th century when Henry VIII's Lord Chancellor, Cardinal Wolsey, was Lord of the Manor of Sandon.

At Sandon bear left then immediately right, and at the end turn right. At the next T-junction turn left on to the A414, then at the roundabout go forward across the road bridge and turn right to join the A130 for the return to Chelmsford.

THE STOUR VALLEY AND THE RIVER COLNE

From the ancient Roman capital of Colchester, the tour circles round the most beautiful tracts of the Essex countryside; along the Stour valley celebrated in the paintings of Constable, to the old market town of Sudbury, birthplace of Gainsborough, and across the peaceful scenery of the Colne valley.

COLCHESTER, Essex
During the 1st century, Colchester was the capital of the south-east and an obvious target for Roman invasion. The walls of their city can still be traced around the old part of the town and the huge Balkerne Gate is magnificent to this day. By the time the Normans arrived, Colchester (the name coined by the Saxons) was an important borough and they built their tremendous castle on the foundations of the Roman temple of Claudius. All that remains is part of the lofty keep — the largest ever built in Europe — and the museum it now houses provides a fine record of Roman Colchester. Profits from cloth-making, which began in the 13th century, left a substantial legacy of churches and monastic buildings to Colchester and by the 15th century there were 15 parish churches in all. Most have long since been altered and restored and some, like All Saints' housing a natural history museum and St Martin's used as a public hall, have abandoned their rightful purpose altogether. Of St John's Abbey only its 15th-century gatehouse is left, but the stone from the older abbey went into the building of Bourne Mill (NT), a Dutch-gabled fishing lodge on the banks of Bourne Pond. There are several attractive and interesting corners of Colchester with buildings spanning 6 centuries. The Minories, a Georgian house, has an art gallery, period furniture, pictures, china and silver. Another Georgian house, Hollytrees, has 18th- and 19th-century costumes and domestic craft exhibits. Aptly named Siege House bears evidence of Civil War conflict as its timbers are riddled with bullet holes. Much of Colchester's notoriety comes from its oysters and roses. Reminders of a less industrialised past are the annual oyster feast — a civic banquet worthy of royal patronage — and the annual Colchester Rose Show. Both commodities flourish today as they have done since the 18th century.

Leave Colchester on the A134, SP 'Sudbury', and at the roundabout beyond the station take the 2nd exit. Pass through Great Horkesley and gradually descend into the Stour valley.

STOUR VALLEY, Essex/Suffolk
The River Stour forms a natural boundary between Essex and Suffolk, and picturesque bridges along its route join the 2 counties. Landscape artist John Constable immortalised the valley in his famous paintings, capturing to perfection the flat water meadows, willow-lined ditches, locks and watermills.

After crossing the river into Suffolk turn left on to the unclassified Bures road. A mile later pass the turning, on the left, to Wissington.

Market day at Sudbury

WISSINGTON, Suffolk
A Norman church with a later white weather-boarded bellcote, a few thatched farm buildings and a handsome redbrick house form an attractive group in this tiny hamlet. Inside the church are fragments of some interesting 13th-century wall-paintings which depicted stories from Christ's childhood and the lives of St Margaret and St Nicholas. Wiston Hall (not open) was built in 1791 for Samuel Beechcroft — a director of the Bank of England — by architect Sir John Soane.

Continue on the unclassified road following the Stour valley to Bures.

BURES, Suffolk
In AD 855 St Edmund, East Anglian king and martyr, was crowned in a chapel above this tiny town. Below, the town full of fine half-timbered buildings, steps across both sides of the river and the boundary. An ancient thatched building called Chapel Barn once belonged to Earls Colne Priory (no longer in existence).

At the main road in Bures, turn right on to the B1508, SP 'Sudbury'. Continue along the valley and later pass through Great Cornard to reach Sudbury.

SUDBURY, Suffolk
Thomas Gainsborough, portrait painter and landscape artist, was born in Sudbury during 1727. The house, 46 Gainsborough Street (then Sepulchre Street) is now a pleasant museum and art gallery devoted to him. A bronze statue of Gainsborough, complete with brush and palette, stands in the market place. This teems with life on market days, but otherwise is only gladdened by the splendid 19th-century Corn Exchange and St Peter's Church surveying the square. The church has a piece of embroidery 5 centuries old which is still used at aldermen's funerals. Sudbury was the largest of Suffolk's wool towns and has more the stamp of a manufacturing town than most of the others. Due to the Act of Parliament passed for improving the Stour's navigation, Sudbury became an important river port. However, the railway ended the era of the flat-bottomed Stour Barge, and the last one was sold by the Canal Company in 1913.

Leave Sudbury on the A131, SP 'Chelmsford'. At Bulmer Tye turn right on to the B1058 and continue to Castle Hedingham.

CASTLE HEDINGHAM, Essex
The castle (OACT), from which the village takes its name, was one of England's strongest fortresses in the 11th century. It belonged to the powerful de Veres, the Earls of Oxford, one of whom was among the barons who forced King John to accept the Magna Carta. Some idea of the castle's great size can be gained from the impressive stone keep which remains. Although not complete, 2 of its 4 round towers are left and its walls, 12ft thick, rise up to over 100ft. A brick Tudor bridge leads to it over the moat which has long since

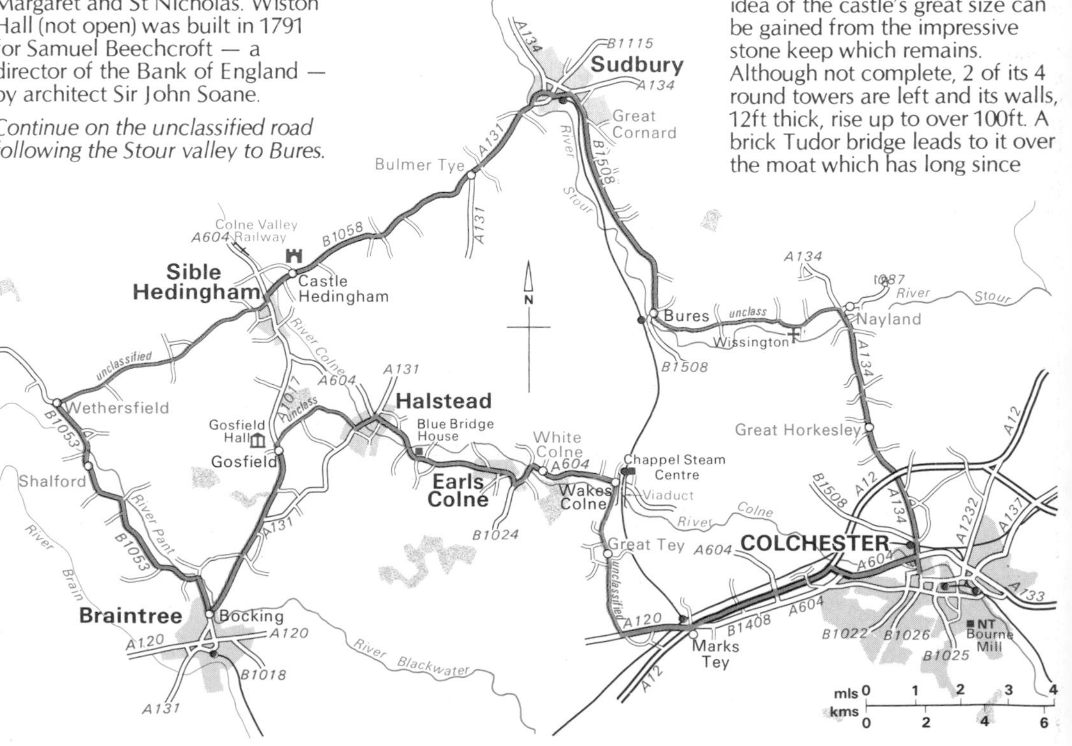

dried up. The village lying in the castle's shadow is a maze of narrow streets radiating from Falcon Square, which takes its name from the half-timbered Falcon Inn. Georgian and 15th-century houses mingle compatibly and the church, St Nicholas's, was built by the de Veres and is virtually completely Norman.

Continue on the B1058 then in ¾ mile turn left on to the A604 and enter Sible Hedingham.

SIBLE HEDINGHAM, Essex
Sir John Hawkwood was born here during the 14th century. He was one of the most famous soldiers of fortune during his time, and led mercenaries to Italy where he was eventually paid to defend Florence, where he died. There is a monument to him in the village church, decorated with hawks and various other beasts.

In Sible Hedingham turn right on to the unclassified Wethersfield road. Shortly turn right again, pass the church then turn left and continue to Wethersfield. In the village turn left on to the B1053 and follow the shallow valley of the River Pant. Pass through Shalford and after 5½ miles bear right to enter Bocking, which is combined with Braintree.

BRAINTREE AND BOCKING, Essex
Braintree was one of those ancient settlements that sprang up at the crossing point of 2 cross-country routes. Subsequent Roman occupation and development is evident from the many coins which have been found in the area. Braintree and Bocking have merged into a single town and they share the textile industry which has prospered here since the 14th century. Wool gave way to more exotic materials in the early 19th century, when the Courtauld family began the production of silk and this has been the main manufacture ever since. The other important industry here, dating from 1884, is the production of metal windows.

Courtauld's weather-boarded mill, which straddles the River Colne at Halstead

Leave on the A131 Halstead road. In 2¼ miles branch left on to the A1017, SP 'Cambridge', and continue to Gosfield.

GOSFIELD, Essex
A large lake built on the edge of Gosfield in the 18th century has been turned into a recreation centre. A paddling area has been roped off from the water-skiing area and rowing boats are available for hire. The lake and the village are all part of the Gosfield Hall (OACT) estate. It is not known for sure exactly when the Hall was built, or by whom, but it was Samuel Courtauld's (the silk manufacturing magnate) home for a time. A long Tudor gallery and some secret rooms are among the house's best features.

Tombs of 3 of the Earls of Oxford in Chapel Barn, Bures

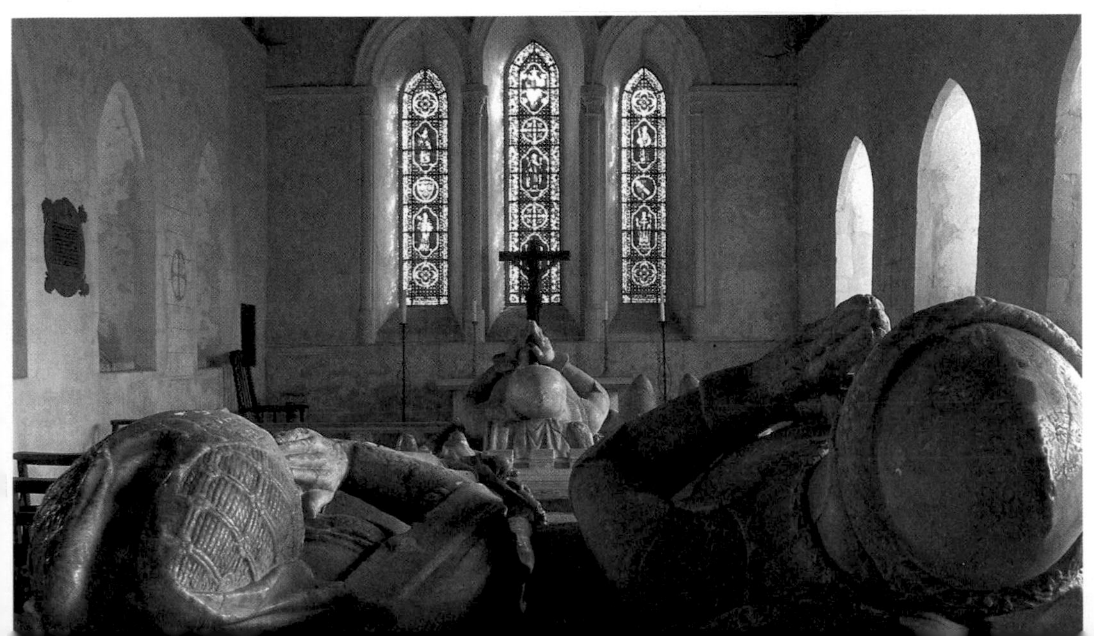

At the far end of the village pass Hall Drive on the left (which leads to Gosfield Hall), then turn right on to the unclassified Halstead road. In 2 miles turn left on to the A131 and enter Halstead.

HALSTEAD, Essex
Through-traffic pounds along Halstead's High Street which drops down from the top of the hill to the River Colne. Here the Courtauld family established a silk factory in 1826 and it is one of the best sights in the town. The river flows beneath the mill, a low, white, weather-boarded building with rows of windows along its sides. Outside the town lies Blue Bridge House with lovely 18th-century ironwork and red and blue brickwork.

Leave Halstead on the A604 Colchester road. After 1 mile, on the left, is the Blue Bridge House. Follow the valley of the River Colne to reach Earls Colne.

EARLS COLNE, Essex
The de Veres, Earls of Oxford, and the River Colne gave the village its name. Aubrey de Vere founded a Benedictine priory here in the 12th century and both he and his wife — William the Conqueror's sister — were buried there. A redbrick Gothic mansion marks the site now. A nucleus of timbered cottages preserves the village atmosphere, although modern housing is spreading fast. Nearby Chalkney Wood, running down to the Colne, is an outstanding beauty spot.

Continue on the A604 to Wakes Colne.

WAKES COLNE, Essex
A working steam centre has been opened at Chappel and Wakes Colne station and every aspect of steam locomotion can be studied here. Locos and items of rolling stock are on display and steam hauled rides are available on some weekends.

At the crossroads on the nearside of the railway viaduct turn right on to the unclassified Great Tay road. Climb out of the valley to reach Great Tey. Continue to the A120 and turn left for Marks Tey.

MARKS TEY, Essex
Norman inhabitants gave the village its name when they came over from Marck, near Calais. The church is distinctive with its oakboarded tower, but its chief treasure is its 15th-century font. This too is made of oak and has 8 intricately carved panelled sides.

At the roundabout take the 2nd exit, SP 'Colchester', and join the A12. Later join the A604 for the return to Colchester.

A MINIATURE LANDSCAPE

The Isle of Wight has everything offered by the mainland, but smaller. Here are high downs and soaring cliffs; long beaches fringed by farm and forestland; fishing villages and resorts popularized by royalty in the past and popular with sun seekers today.

COWES, Isle of Wight
This busy island port has a good harbour on the River Medina and is connected to East Cowes by floating bridge and ferry. The headquarters of the Royal Yacht Squadron is based at Cowes Castle, and the town is well known as England's premier yachting centre.

Leave Cowes following SP 'Gurnard' on the B3325. In ¾ mile keep forward on to an unclassified road for Gurnard. Reach a church and keep forward, then meet a T-junction and turn right into Lower Church Road. Continue to the next T-junction, turn left SP 'Yarmouth', and in a further 1½ miles meet another T-junction. Turn right and in another 1½ miles turn right again for Porchfield. Continue through wooded countryside and after 1½ miles turn right for Newtown.

NEWTOWN, Isle of Wight
Sited midway between Newport and Yarmouth, Newtown was created in the 13th century by the bishops of Winchester and stands on the beautiful Newtown River estuary (NT). The 18th-century Old Town Hall (NT) is notable.

In ¼ mile meet a T-junction and turn right, then in another ¾ mile meet another T-junction and turn right again on to the A3054. Proceed to Shalfleet.

SHALFLEET, Isle of Wight
Shalfleet's church displays very strong Norman features, particularly in the squat west tower and the good south doorway with its contemporary tympanum.

Continue to Yarmouth.

YARMOUTH, Isle of Wight
This Yar-estuary town is better known as a sailing centre than as a resort. Henry VIII built one of his many coastal defence forts (AM) here, and the triangular Fort Victoria of 1853 stands in the grounds of the Fort Victoria country park.

Following SP 'Freshwater', cross the Yar bridge, and in 1 mile bear right. Pass through Colwell Bay and continue to the small resort of Totland. Join the B3322 'Alum Bay' road and in ¼ mile reach a war memorial. Bear right to Alum Bay.

ALUM BAY & THE NEEDLES, Isle of Wight
Sandstone cliffs famous for their multi-coloured strata fringe this lovely bay. The isolated rock stacks of The Needles stretch out into the sea to the south-west, with Scratchell's Bay and a 200ft chalk arch beyond.

Return, and in ½ mile branch right on to an unclassified road SP 'Freshwater Bay'. To the right is Tennyson Down (NT), one of the West Wight Downs.

WEST WIGHT DOWNS, Isle of Wight
The high, gentle folds of the West Wight Downs (NT) occupy most of the island's south-west corner.

The brass cannons overlooking the Solent at Cowes are fired to start yacht races.

Continue to Freshwater Bay and join the A3055 SP 'Chale'. Bear right and ascend; skirting Compton Bay, and drive along a beautiful clifftop road that affords some of the finest views in the island. Later pass the edge of Brook village.

BROOK, Isle of Wight
Brook House dates from the 18th century, and Brook Chine (NT) is a beautiful cleft with 40 acres of grazing and 300 yards of superb seashore.

Continue through pleasant open country with good views. In 2¼ miles pass thickly-wooded Grange Chine to the right, with Brighstone Forest to the left and Brighstone Bay to the right. St Catherine's Point and St Catherine's Hill are prominent ahead before the tour enters Chale.

CHALE, Isle of Wight
Chale Abbey preserves a 14th-century hall, and the local church commands fine views of The Needles.

Drive to Chale Church and keep forward SP 'Ventnor'. In ½ mile turn right on to the B3399 road for Blackgang. A footpath from this point leads to Blackgang Chine.

BLACKGANG CHINE & ST CATHERINE'S HILL, Isle of Wight
It is thought that this dramatic chine derived its name from a gang of smugglers, but nowadays it harbours nobody more sinister than tourists visiting the Theme Park. Inland is 773ft St Catherine's Hill (NT), which affords excellent views and features 14th-century St Catherine's Oratory.

From Blackgang Chine return to the main route and turn right on to the A3055 SP 'Ventnor'. Pass under St Catherine's Hill and continue along the undercliff to St Lawrence.

Turn right (in Niton) and continue along Undercliff to St Lawrence.

ST LAWRENCE, Isle of Wight
Old St Lawrence's was Britain's smallest church until it acquired a porch and bell tower in 1842. Tropical Bird Gardens and glass makers are situated in the 20 acres of Old Park.

Continue to Ventnor.

VENTNOR, Isle of Wight
A paper recommending the local climate for the cure of certain illnesses transformed Ventnor from a fishing village to a focus of 19th-century society. Within the Botanic Gardens is the History of Smuggling Museum.

Follow SP 'Shanklin' and ascend, with fine sea views to the right. In ¾ mile a detour can be made from the main route to the delightful village of Bonchurch by turning right on to an unclassified road.

BONCHURCH & ST BONIFACE DOWN, Isle of Wight
The writers Dickens, Thackeray, and Macaulay all stayed in this delightful village, and the poet Swinburne lived at East Dene House. The village itself stands just below the island's highest point, 785ft Boniface Down (NT), and has a Victorian church.

Continue on the main drive, pass the Landslip viewpoint to the right of the road and reach Shanklin.

SHANKLIN, Isle of Wight
A group of thatched buildings, the Crab Inn, and St Blasius's Church are all that remain of the fishing village that stood here before the seaside holiday fad took over. The town's excellent sea-bathing, superb sandy beach, and good sunshine records attract increasing numbers of visitors every year. Shanklin Chine has a spectacular 45ft waterfall.

Continue through Shanklin and Lake to Sandown.

SANDOWN, Isle of Wight
The assets that contributed to the development of Shanklin have also made Sandown a popular holiday resort. Additional attractions include the Museum of Isle of Wight Geology and a good zoo.

Turn right on to the B3395 SP 'Bembridge' and drive to Yaverland.

YAVERLAND, Isle of Wight
Yaverland Manor House (not open) is the finest 17th-century building of its kind in the island.

Meet a T-junction and turn right. In ¼ mile it is possible to make a detour from the main route by turning right to the downs of Culver and Bembridge.

Until its collapse in 1764 one of the Needles was 120ft high.

lum Bay is famous for its multi-
oloured cliffs.

Vhippingham's
ermanic-looking church.

ULVER & BEMBRIDGE DOWNS,
sle of Wight
overing some 104 acres of east
Vight, these fine downs (NT) rise to a
43ft summit and drop sharply
owards the coast. Culver Down
eatures a bronze-age round barrow.

ontinue with the main tour to skirt
embridge Airport and at the far side
neet crossroads. Turn left on to an
nclassified road and in ¼ mile pass a
ootpath on the left leading to
embridge Windmill.

EMBRIDGE WINDMILL,
sle of Wight
ituated near one end of Bembridge
ligh Street, this stone-built mill (NT)
as a wooden roof and was erected
1700. Today it is the only windmill
eft on the island, and is maintained
n working order, but last used in
913.

ontinue into Bembridge.

BEMBRIDGE, Isle of Wight
Yachtsmen favour the nearby natural harbour at the mouth of the Eastern Yar. Numerous displays of nautical heritage from the early days of sail to the present time, are to be found in the Maritime Museum.

Follow the B3395 'St Helens' road and in 1¼ miles meet a T-junction. Turn right on to the B3330 into St Helens, then turn left SP 'Ryde' for Nettlestone. At Nettlestone branch right on to the B3340 SP 'Seaview'. On the right is the entrance to Flamingo Park. In ½ mile keep left, then meet a T-junction and turn left, then immediately left again. Turn right into Seafield Road for Seaview.

Yarmouth Harbour, crowded with yachts and other sailing craft.

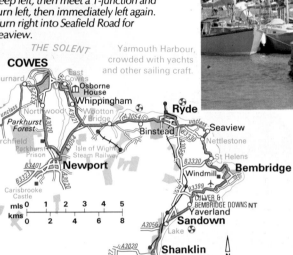

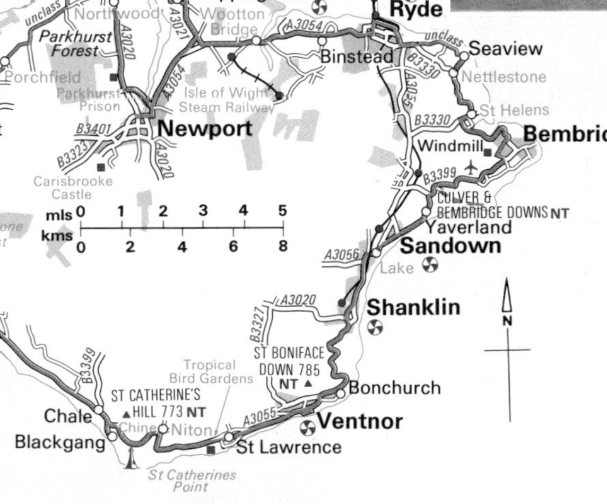

SEAVIEW, Isle of Wight
Much of the unspoiled fishing village is still evident in Seaview, a quiet resort offering good beaches and excellent shore angling.

Continue to a T-junction and turn right, then keep left on to an unclassified road and drive along the shoreline. In ½ mile pass through a toll gate, and 1 mile farther turn right on to the B3330. After a short distance turn right on to the A3055 for Ryde.

RYDE, Isle of Wight
Most visitors to the island enter at Ryde, a busy port that was a small fishing and smuggling village until the 18th century.

Follow SP 'Newport' to join the A3054 and pass through Binstead.

BINSTEAD, Isle of Wight
New Quarr Abbey stands near the 12th-century remains of its predecessor at Binstead, and the local church still shows some of its 13th-century origins in spite of Victorian restoration.

Keep forward through Wootton Bridge. In 1½ miles turn right SP 'East Cowes'. Meet a T-junction and turn right on to the A3021, then in 1¾ miles turn left on to an unclassified road SP 'Whippingham Church'. Continue to Whippingham.

The Indian-style Durbar Room at Osborne House was built in 1891 to accommodate state banquets.

WHIPPINGHAM, Isle of Wight
Prince Albert built the ornate church here in 1860, and Queen Victoria was a regular member of the congregation whenever the Royal Family was in residence on the island.

Pass Whippingham Church and continue to a T-junction. Turn left into Victoria Grove, then at the next T-junction turn left again to join the A3021 for East Cowes. Return along the A3021 'Ryde' road, passing the entrance to Osborne House to the left on the outskirts of the town.

OSBORNE HOUSE, Isle of Wight
Queen Victoria and the Prince Consort built Osborne House as a retreat from the pomp and ceremony of Windsor, and Her Majesty died here in 1901. The State apartments (open) remain as they were in her day.

Continue, and in 2 miles keep right SP 'Newport', and after another ½ mile turn right on to the A3054. Proceed to Newport.

NEWPORT, Isle of Wight
Situated at the head of the Medina estuary, this town is the capital of the island and stands on a site that has been occupied at least since Roman times. Mighty Carisbrooke Castle stands on the foundations of a Roman fort 1 mile south west. The 12th-century remains of the castle include a Norman keep and a 16th-century treadmill that used to be worked by prisoners to raise water. Today it is turned by a donkey for display purposes, and forms a fascinating exhibit in the Isle of Wight Museum.

Follow the A3020 'Cowes' road and pass Parkhurst Prison, backed by Parkhurst Forest.

PARKHURST FOREST, Isle of Wight
Parkhurst Forest is the largest stretch of woodland on the island, and one of the last British refuges of the native red squirrel.

Drive to Northwood and branch left on to the B3325. Continue to a T-junction and turn right to return to Cowes.

THE SUSSEX WEALD

Suspended between the North and South Downs is the high, broken patchwork of the Sussex Weald, a place of charming towns and villages on hillsides once cloaked by the vast, prehistoric Forest of Anderida.

EASTBOURNE, E Sussex
Consistently top of the seaside sunshine league tables, the thriving resort of Eastbourne has been popular since the beginning of the 19th century.

Leave Eastbourne seafront along the B2103 'Beachy Head' road, with fine views towards the cliffs of Beachy Head. Ascend, and turn left on to an unclassified road to reach the summit of this cliff range.

BEACHY HEAD, E Sussex
Beachy Head, the vast chalk promontory that marks where the South Downs are halted by the sea, is the starting point of the South Downs Way. This path runs west to beyond South Harting on the Hampshire border.

Continue past the Belle Tout lighthouse to Birling Gap.

BIRLING GAP, E Sussex
For centuries Birling Gap was a landing place favoured by smugglers but today the rocky shingle and sand beach is more popular with bathers. Between Birling Gap and Seaford are the great chalk cliffs known as the Seven Sisters.

Follow the tour inland to Eastdean.

EASTDEAN, E Sussex
Cottages and a small shop overlook Eastdean's sloping triangular green, and the local church houses a curious copy of a Norman font.

Turn left on to the A259 'Seaford' road, ascend steeply, then at the summit turn right on to the unclassified 'Jevington' road for Friston.

FRISTON, E Sussex
This downland village lies in a hilly area now popular with glider pilots. At one time its small Church of St Mary served as a landmark for mariners and smugglers alike.

Continue, with downland to the right and Friston Forest to the left. Also to the right is 659ft Willingdon Hill. Reach Jevington.

JEVINGTON, E Sussex
A sturdy Anglo-Saxon tower is carried by Jevington's flint-built church, and in the churchyard is the copper model of a square-rigged schooner once sailed by a Chinaman buried here.

Beyond Jevington descend through Wannock, with 702ft Windover Hill to the left.

WINDOVER HILL, E Sussex
A gentle climb to the summit of this hill is rewarded by excellent views, not the least of which takes in the prehistoric Long Man of Wilmington. Nobody knows who or what this giant turf-cut figure represents.

Continue to Polegate.

POLEGATE, E Sussex
Victorian St John's Church, like much of the rest of Polegate's architecture, is unremarkable but homely. The most notable building here is an early 19th-century windmill with all its sails intact.

At Polegate turn left on to the A22, SP 'London'. Pass through the flat countryside of Wilmington Wood. In $2\frac{1}{2}$ miles a detour from the main route is possible by turning right on to the A295 and driving to Hailsham.

HAILSHAM, E Sussex
The market at Hailsham is one of the largest in Sussex and continues a tradition that reaches back to Norman times.

In $\frac{1}{4}$ mile (beyond the Hailsham turning) turn left on to an unclassified road to Michelham Priory. Cross the River Cuckmere before reaching the priory.

MICHELHAM PRIORY, E Sussex
Remains of this small Augustinian priory (open), founded in 1229 for 12 canons and a prior, include a Tudor mansion, a 14th-century gatehouse, and an attractive bridge over the moat.

Continue and shortly turn right, and then turn immediately left, SP 'London'. Turn left on to the A22, then shortly right on to the unclassified 'Horam' road. Join the A267 and enter Horam. Continue on the 'Tunbridge Wells' road and pass through woodland scenery before reaching Cross-in-Hand, on The Weald.

Towering chalk cliffs dwarf the lighthouse at Beachy Head.

THE WEALD
The Weald is a high area of broken country suspended between the hills of the North and South Downs. Its towns and villages are rightly famous for their great character and beauty, and several wooded areas exist as reminders of the great Forest of Anderida that once cloaked these long, grassy slopes.

CROSS-IN-HAND, E Sussex
A working windmill stands in this charming village, which is sited at over 500ft on the Sussex Weald. Holy Cross Priory is partly in use as an old people's home, the house and grounds could be visited.

Cross high wooded country to Five Ashes. After $\frac{1}{2}$ mile (beyond Five Ashes), turn left on to an unclassified road. Later join the B2101 and enter Rotherfield, at the edge of Ashdown Forest.

ROTHERFIELD, E Sussex
Situated at the edge of Ashdown Forest, this village stands at 500ft near the source of the River Rother.

Keep forward, then branch right on to an unclassified road to leave by North Street. Drive to the A26. Turn right SP 'Tunbridge Wells', and pass through Eridge Green.

ERIDGE GREEN, E Sussex
Pretty estate cottages stand behind the local Victorian church, and near by is the sandstone outcrop of Bowles Rocks where trainee mountaineers practise.

Continue for 1 mile through Broadwater Forest, then turn left on to an unclassified road SP 'Groombridge'. After $\frac{1}{2}$ mile turn right SP 'High Rocks', then in a further $\frac{1}{2}$ mile bear right and pass High Rocks on the right.

HIGH ROCKS, E Sussex
Perhaps the largest sandstone outcrop in the area is High Rocks, which is used extensively by climbers.

Continue for $1\frac{1}{2}$ miles. Meet crossroads and turn right on to Major York's road. On the far side of Tunbridge Wells Common turn left on to the A26 and enter Royal Tunbridge Wells.

ROYAL TUNBRIDGE WELLS, Kent
In 1606 Lord North discovered chalybeate springs in the forest that stood here. Subsequently the town of Tunbridge Wells was founded, though building did not begin in earnest until the 1630s. By the end of that century it was a flourishing spa, and has remained so to the present day. Visitors to the picturesque raised parade known as the Pantiles may still 'take the waters'.

From the town follow SP 'Eastbourne A267' and re-enter E Sussex for Frant.

FRANT, E Sussex
Houses cluster round a large green here, and the 19th-century church contains fine stained glass of earlier date.

Turn left on to an unclassified road SP 'Bells Yew Green' and at the latter turn right on to the B2169 'Lamberhurst' road. Return to Kent. Drive through woodland, then pass a left turn leading to the ruins of Bayham Abbey.

BAYHAM ABBEY, E Sussex
Claimed to be the most impressive group of monastic remains in Sussex, this picturesque ruin (NT) dates from the 13th century and comprises a church, monastery buildings, and the former gatehouse – all easily identifiable (open).

After a further $\frac{1}{2}$ mile pass a left turn leading to The Owl House.

THE OWL HOUSE, Kent
Once the haunt of wool smugglers, this small half-timbered building (open) dates from the 16th century and stands in beautiful grounds. Features of the latter include woodland lakes and splendid collections of flowering shrubs.

In $1\frac{1}{4}$ miles turn left on to the B2100 and enter Lamberhurst.

LAMBERHURST, Kent
Although strung out along the busy Tunbridge Wells to Hastings road, this old village has managed to retain its own identity and features a fine 14th-century church.

About 1 mile south, off the A21, is Scotney Old Castle.

The weathered and fissured surfaces of such sandstone outcrops as Bowles Rocks, near Eridge Green, make ideal nursery faces for trainee mountaineers. All round the rocks are expanses of sand that have been worn from their surfaces.

SCOTNEY CASTLE, Kent
Ruins of this 14th-century tower and an attached 17th-century house (NT) stand in a landscaped and moated garden planted with trees and flowering shrubs (open). Apart from the interest of the buildings themselves, the gardens are among the finest in the country.

From Lamberhurst return along the 32100 'Wadhurst' road and re-enter E Sussex. In 3 miles turn left on to the 32099 to visit Wadhurst.

WADHURST, E Sussex
The churchyard of SS Peter and Paul features 30 iron grave slabs, a powerful indication of Wadhurst's one-time importance as an iron-smelting centre.

In 1¼ miles turn right on to an unclassified road SP 'Burwash Common'. Pass through woodland to Stonegate.

STONEGATE, E Sussex
This small village has a modern church and is attractively grouped round a junction of minor roads and lanes.

In Stonegate turn left on to the 'Burwash' road and after another ¾ mile turn right. Drive over a level crossing and cross the River Rother to enter Burwash.

BURWASH, E Sussex
In Burwash churchyard is a cast-iron grave slab that is claimed to be the oldest in the country. Pleasant old buildings in the High Street include timber-framed cottages.

Meet a junction with the A265 and turn right. Reach the war memorial and turn left on to an unclassified road SP 'Woods Corner'. In ½ mile pass a right turn leading to Bateman's.

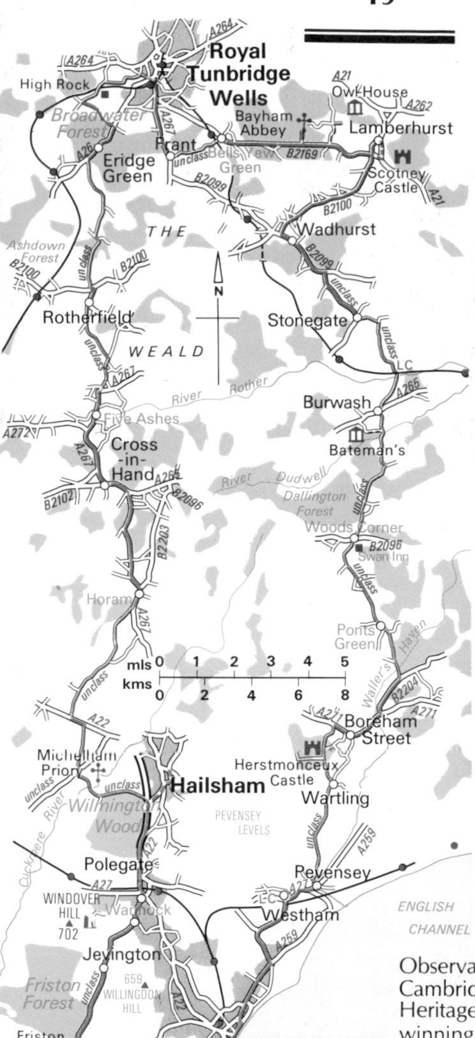

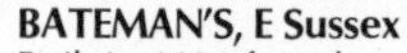

BATEMAN'S, E Sussex
Built in 1634 for a local ironmaster, this lovely house (NT) is best known as the one-time home of writer Rudyard Kipling. Much of the neighbourhood is featured in his *Puck of Pook's Hill.*

Climb to 646ft, cross the River Dudwell, and drive through Dallington Forest. Reach Woods Corner, and at the Swan Inn turn right then left on to the 'Pont's Green' road. Later follow SP 'Ninfield' and descend. Meet the B2204 and turn right SP 'Hailsham'. Later turn right on to the A271 for Boreham Street.

BOREHAM STREET, E Sussex
This village has an appealing character enhanced by attractive houses and the White Friars Hotel. Inside the latter is a 16th-century chimney breast.

Continue through Boreham Street and in ½ mile turn left on to an unclassified road passing Herstmonceux Castle.

HERSTMONCEUX CASTLE, E Sussex
Herstmonceux Castle, a fortified 15th-century moated manor house, was for a time a ruin, before being carefully restored in the 1930's. From 1948 to the mid eighties it was the home of the Royal Greenwich Observatory before its move to Cambridge. In the Sussex Farm Heritage Centre are some award-winning shire horses plus historic farm associated machinery.

Go forward to Wartling.

WARTLING, E Sussex
Wartling boasts a church with box pews, an 18th-century pulpit, and a wealth of fascinating Georgian monuments.

At Wartling bear right on to the 'Pevensey' road and cross the flat Pevensey Levels. Meet the A27 and turn right into Pevensey.

PEVENSEY, E Sussex
William the Conqueror disembarked here in 1066, and later built a stout castle within ancient Roman walls that had once been shaded by the vast Forest of Anderida. The village itself preserves Tudor buildings. The old Mint House contains a small museum.

Continue along the A27 to Westham.

WESTHAM, E Sussex
It is probable that the local church was once part of the ancient Hospital of St Cross, most of which stood outside the west gate of Pevensey Castle. Close by is a pair of 15th-century houses.

Turn left on to the B2191 SP 'Eastbourne'. Drive over a level crossing and later join the A259 to return to Eastbourne.

Rudyard Kipling lived at Bateman's from 1902 until his death in 1936. The interior of the house is preserved much as he left it.

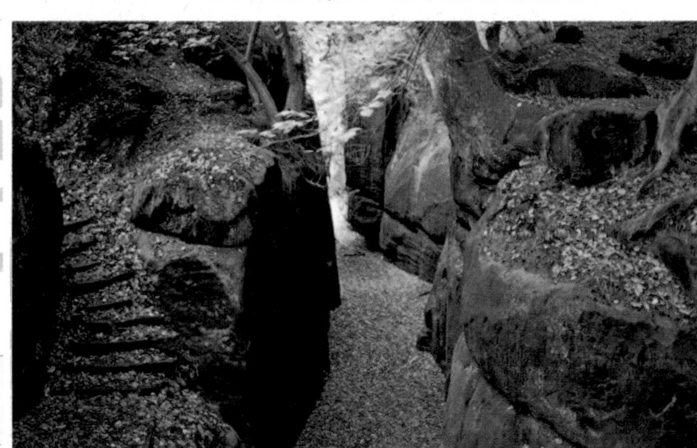

High Rocks is one of many sandstone outcrops situated near Tunbridge Wells.

Herstmonceux Castle was built when brick was newly fashionable in England.

THE EDGE OF THE NORTH DOWNS

Much of this is National Trust country, protected for its outstanding beauty. Valley woodlands and high, empty commons in Surrey rise to soaring outliers of the West Sussex downs, which roll summit after windy summit into the chalklands of south Kent.

EPSOM, Surrey
In the 18th century this pleasant market town was famous for the medicinal springs that gave their name to Epsom Salts; even before that it was known for horse racing. The popularity of the spa has waned, but that of the turf is still in good heart. Among the town's more notable buildings are 19th-century Durdans and 17th-century Waterloo House.

Leave Epsom from the southern end of the High Street, enter a roundabout, and take the 2nd exit to join the B280. Cross Epsom Common, with a picnic site to the right, and after 1½ miles approach traffic lights. A detour from the main tour route can be made by turning right at these lights for Chessington Zoo.

CHESSINGTON ZOO, Gt London
In 1931 Reginald Stuart Goddard founded this famous zoo in the grounds of Burnt Stub Manor, the successor to a house burned by Cromwellian troops. The grounds cover 65 acres and contain a large variety of birds, animals, and a children's zoo.

On the main route, continue forward from the traffic lights for 2 miles and turn left on to the A244 for Oxshott. Then turn right on to an unclassified road for Stoke D'Abernon.

STOKE D'ABERNON, Surrey
Preserved in the local church is Sir John d'Abernon's brass of 1277, thought to be the earliest memorial of its kind in the country. The old manor house is Tudor at heart, but received a brick face-lift sometime during the 18th century.

Turn right on to the A245 for Cobham.

A fine example of the screenwork at the church in Charlwood

COBHAM, Surrey
An inscription on the bridge here tells of an earlier structure raised by Queen Matilda, wife of Henry I, because one of her ladies drowned while crossing the pool.

At Cobham, turn left on to an unclassified road SP 'Downside and Ockham'. Cross the river bridge, then turn right and follow SP 'Ockham'.

OCKHAM, Surrey
Hidden among the trees of Ockham Park, close to the great house, is the village church. This is well known for its lovely 13th-century east window of 7 lancets, sometimes known as the Seven Sisters.

Drive to the war memorial and turn right on to the B2039. Take the next turning left on to an unclassified road. Meet crossroads and go forward for 3 miles to East Clandon.

Robert Adam was responsible for many of the fine rooms in Georgian Hatchlands, near East Clandon.

EAST CLANDON, Surrey
Timber cottages and large old barns give this place an enviable air of timelessness and peace, but the mainly 13th-century church has been poorly restored. Admiral Boscawen built 18th-century Hatchlands (NT) for his retirement, but died before he could enjoy it.

Turn left to join the A246 and continue to West Horsley.

WEST HORSLEY, Surrey
A church stood at West Horsley before the Normans came, but the massive tower dates from the 12th century. The body of the building shows traces of almost every subsequent century, including very good 15th-century screens. Sir Walter Raleigh's remains are said to lie under the south chapel.

Continue to East Horsley.

EAST HORSLEY, Surrey
The curious 19th-century mansion known as East Horsley Towers houses the Electricity Council's Staff College. Much older is the local parish church, which was altered considerably in the 13th century and restored almost out of recognition in the 19th. Beautiful recumbent figures of Thomas and Catherine Cornwallis and several old brasses can be seen inside.

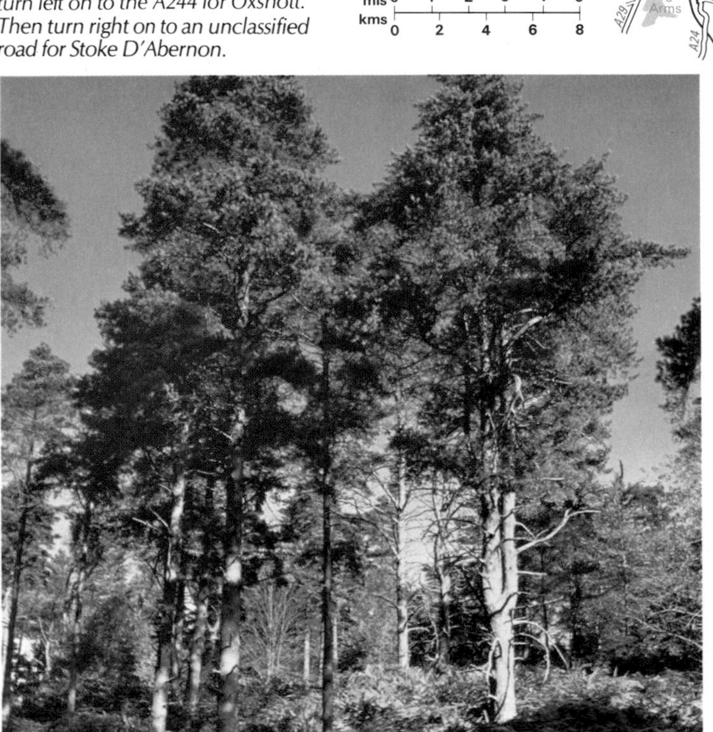

Left: Leith Hill Forest is a delightful mixture of woodland and heath. Below: 18th century Leith Hill Tower.

Continue for ½ mile, turn right on to an unclassified road SP 'Shere', and after another ½ mile bear left with SP 'Dorking'. Ascend through woodland to the summit of the North Downs, and after 1½ miles meet crossroads and turn right SP 'Abinger'. Descend (1 in 6) White Downs Hill and continue for 1 mile, then turn left on to the A25. After ½ mile turn right on to an unclassified road and ascend for 1¾ miles. A short detour can be made from the main tour route by turning sharp left to Friday Street.

NORTH DOWNS
This range of chalk hills starts near Farnham in Surrey and extends across Kent to the white cliffs of Dover, culminating in a 900ft summit near Woldingham.

FRIDAY STREET, Surrey
Old cottages and a single street leading to a lake fringed with pine and oak are the main features of this village. The Stephen Langton Inn recalls a prelate of that name who played a leading role in the signing of Magna Carta. Severell's Copse (NT) comprises 59 acres of woodland stretching from the lake to Leith Hill.

Return to the T-junction on the main route, turn left, then keep forward SP 'Leith Hill'. After 1½ miles pass a footpath leading left to Leith Hill.

LEITH HILL, Surrey
Much of the wooded countryside south of Friday Street is protected by the National Trust, including Leith Hill, Duke's Warren, and the estate of Leith Hill Place. The hill itself carries a picturesque tower whose top is 1,029ft above sea level – the highest point in Surrey.

Continue for 1¼ miles to join the B2126, then keep left for Ockley.

OCKLEY, Surrey
The local village green is sited on the course of the great Roman Stane Street. The local church enjoys a delightful setting and its tower dates from the 18th-century and a timbered porch is of 15th-century origin.

Turn left on to the A29. After the Kings Arms turn right on to the B2126. Continue for 1½ miles, then cross over the A24 to enter Capel. Turn right on to unclassified road SP 'Newdigate' in ½ mile turn left then turn right and enter Newdigate.

NEWDIGATE, Surrey
Typical of Wealden villages in general, Newdigate stands in an area that was once covered by dense forest. The forest has all but disappeared, but some of the great oaks that grew hereabouts can be traced to the massive pillars and arches of the local church tower.

Turn right and drive to Rusper.

RUSPER, W Sussex
Several half-timbered and tile-hung cottages survive in this pretty village, and St Mary Magdalene's Church boasts a sturdy 16th-century tower.

Bear left SP 'Crawley', continue for ½ mile, then turn right for Faygate. At Faygate turn left SP 'Crawley'. Meet a main road turn left on to the A264. To the right is St Leonard's Forest.

ST LEONARD'S FOREST, W Sussex
The forests of St Leonard's and Worth, along with various scattered woodlands, are among the only sizeable remnants left of the vast prehistoric Forest of Anderida.

After 2¾ miles turn left on to the A23 Crawley bypass. Follow SP 'London' through Crawley suburbs.

CRAWLEY, W Sussex
The planning of this new town is not without merit. Its industrial estates are well separated from the residential areas, and some of the worst effects of high-density building have been avoided by the imaginative use of open spaces. Some 2½ miles north of Crawley is the Greyhound Hotel, Tinsley Green, the venue for the international marbles championship, which began as a competition between two local men for the hand of a girl in marriage.

Continue with the A23 SP 'London' to pass Gatwick Airport.

GATWICK AIRPORT, W Sussex
London's second airport after Heathrow, provides many scheduled and charter flights. The spectators' viewing area is in the terminal.

Continue for 1 mile, enter a roundabout, and leave by the 1st exit on to an unclassified road leading to Charlwood and Leigh. A detour can be made from the main tour route by taking the 3rd exit from this roundabout into Horley.

HORLEY, Surrey
A knight's effigy of c1315 and a 15th-century brass can be seen in the local church, and the half-timbered Six Bells Inn dates from the 15th-century.
Continue to Charlwood.

CHARLWOOD, Surrey
The 11th- to 15-century church in Charlwood is noted for its screen work and wall paintings. The privately-run Gatwick Zoo & Aviaries covers 10 acres, with many of the animals and birds in natural settings.
Continue to Leigh.

LEIGH, Surrey
Charming old houses in this village are complemented by a green and a 15th-century church famous for its memorial brasses. Particularly good examples of the latter are those to the Ardernes, who lived in the area during the 15th century.

Pass through Leigh and after ¼ mile turn right at the Seven Stars (PH) for Betchworth, crossing the River Mole.

The lake at Friday Street is part of the National Trust property of Leith Hill.

BETCHWORTH, Surrey
High trees border the River Mole here, and the church preserves a great Norman chest of solid oak beneath its tower.

Meet a T-junction and turn left then right SP 'Walton-on-the-Hill'. Continue to a roundabout and take the 2nd exit on to the B2032. Climb (1 in 6) Pebble Hill to the downs. At the summit turn left on to the B2033 SP 'Box Hill'. Then bear left on to an unclassified road for Box Hill Country Park and picnic site.

BOX HILL, Surrey
Named after the box trees that grow on its flanks, 563ft Box Hill (NT) is a noted viewpoint and designated area of outstanding natural beauty, including both wood and downland scenery and a Country Park.

Descend to the bottom of the hill. Approach a T-junction and turn right SP 'Mickleham' B2209. Within ¼ mile turn right again on to an unclassified road SP 'Headley'. A detour can be made from the main tour by driving ahead for Mickleham.

MICKLEHAM, Surrey
Playwright George Meredith was born here in 1864. Yews from a Druid's Grove folly stand in the grounds of 18th-century Norbury Park.

Meet a T-junction and turn right on to the B2033. Headley Heath (NT) lies away to the right. Ascend and turn left on to an unclassified road for Headley SP 'Epsom'.

HEADLEY, Surrey
Yews mark the spot where Headley's 14th-century church was pulled down in the last century, and the spire of its 19th-century successor serves as a Surrey landmark. The church bell is a good 500 years old.

After 1¾ miles meet crossroads and turn right. Pass Epsom Downs racecourse.

EPSOM DOWNS RACECOURSE, Surrey
The course here has been the home of good racing since the reign of James I, and has been the venue for the Derby since 1780 perhaps one of Britain's most famous races.
Turn left on to the B290 and return to Epsom.

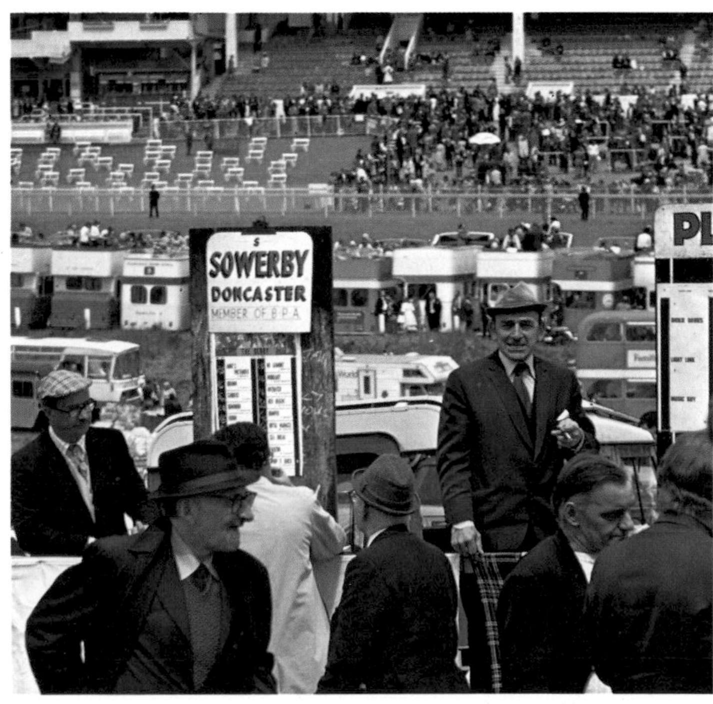

Derby Day at Epsom racecourse attracts racing enthusiasts from all walks of life.

FROM THE SEA TO THE NORTH DOWNS

At Dover soaring cliffs of dazzling white chalk mark the end of the North Downs' rolling march to the sea. Inland the massive towers of Canterbury Cathedral commemorate the halt of paganism, and the rebirth of Christianity in Kent.

FOLKESTONE, Kent
A popular holiday resort and a harbour for cross-Channel ferries, this ancient port still has a fishing fleet and fish market. A wide grassy promenade known as The Leas extends along the cliff top, and attractively wooded walks slope down to the beach. Spade House, the one-time home of writer H G Wells, now contains a museum.

Follow SP 'Hythe, A259' to Sandgate.

SANDGATE, Kent
The castle here belongs to a series built by Henry VIII after his religious break with Rome, when the threat of invasion seemed very real. Shorncliffe Camp, established on the plateau above Sandgate at the beginning of the 19th century, was founded to cope with the later threat of Napoleon's navy.

Continue to Hythe.

HYTHE, Kent
This ancient Cinque Port was very prosperous in the 12th and 13th centuries; its wealth today is assured by its popularity as a resort. Near by is the Royal Military Canal, which was built in 1804 as a defence against Napoleon but nowadays serves as a valuable leisure amenity. A terminus of the Romney, Hythe, and Dymchurch narrow-gauge railway is in the town.

Follow SP 'Ashford' and 'London' to Hythe Station, past the Royal Military Canal. Return along the 'Folkestone' road, before taking the B2065 'Elham' road and climbing to high ground. Fine views of the North Downs can be enjoyed from here. Continue, and cross the M20 and at roundabout take 2nd exit B2065 to Lyminge.

LYMINGE, Kent
There has been a Christian community at Lyminge since 633, when King Ethelbert's daughter and Bishop Paulinus founded their abbey here. Fragments of walling from the original buildings are incorporated in the Church of SS Mary and Ethelburga. Most of Lyminge is Victorian; the half-timbered Old Robus and 18th-century Old Rectory are notable exceptions.

Drive to the far end of the village take 2nd left on to an unclassified road SP 'Rhodes Minnis' passing through Sibton Park. In ½ mile (beyond Rhodes Minnis) branch left and climb through Lyminge Forest on to the North Downs. Cross the B2068 and turn right for Elmsted.

ELMSTED, Kent
Flint-built St James's Church in Elmsted is of Norman and later date and carries a medieval west tower. Inside is a late medieval half-timbered altar screen.

At Elmsted Church turn left, SP 'Wye', and continue to Hastingleigh.

HASTINGLEIGH, Kent
Norman and later St Mary's Church stands aloof from the village, half hidden from view by the fall of the downs.

Continue on the 'Wye' road to Wye Downs nature reserve.

WYE DOWNS AND NATURE RESERVE, Kent
Wye and Crundale Downs rise some 2 miles south-east of Wye and form part of the North Downs. The escarpment, covered with shrubs and woodland, is a nature reserve.

Continue to Wye.

THE NORTH DOWNS
This chalk range runs west from the White Cliffs of Dover to the Hog's Back near Guildford, and culminates in a 900ft hill at Woldingham.

WYE, Kent
Archbishop of Canterbury John Kempe founded a college of priests here in 1447, but King Henry VIII put paid to its religious teaching and it later served as a grammar school. Since 1900 it has been the agriculture school of London University. Other features of the town include a racecourse, a Georgian mill house, and 18th-century Olantigh—a venue for summer music festivals.

Follow SP 'Ashford' and cross the Great Stour River. Drive over a level crossing and turn right on to the 'Canterbury' road. After ¾ mile turn right on to the A28 and drive along the Great Stour Valley to Godmersham.

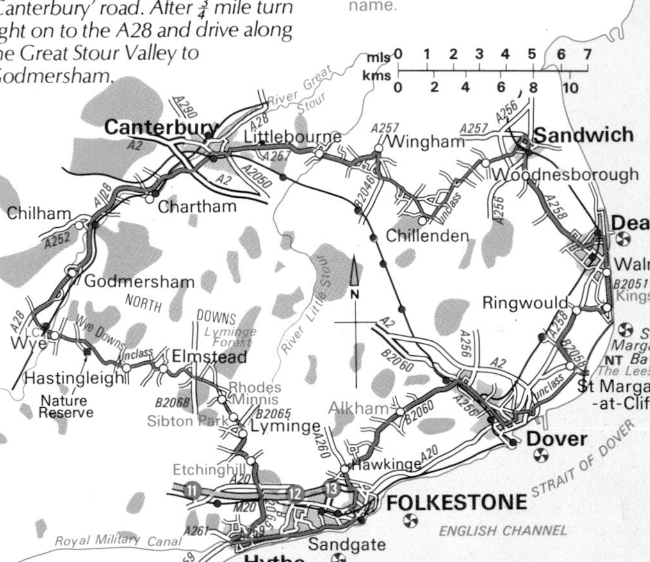

GODMERSHAM, Kent
A monument to Edward Knight, a close relative of novelist Jane Austen and owner of 18th-century Godmersham Park, can be seen in the local Norman and later church. Landscaped grounds surround the big house.

Continue to the outskirts of Chilham.

CHILHAM, Kent
Chilham village is gathered respectfully around a square at the gate of its castle, which was built for Henry II in 1174. The 300-acre grounds (open) feature wood and lakeside walks, gardens, plus medieval jousting displays.

Continue to the edge of Chartham.

CHARTHAM, Kent
This large Stour valley village is a well-known angling centre. St Mary's Church is of 13th-century date and boasts one of the oldest sets of bells in the country. East of the village is a ruined medieval chapel on a farm.

Continue to Canterbury.

Fishermen take aboard a net on the beach at Hythe.

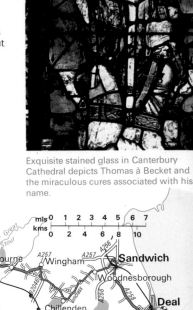

Exquisite stained glass in Canterbury Cathedral depicts Thomas à Becket and the miraculous cures associated with his name.

CANTERBURY, Kent
When the Romans came here they took over a Belgic Stourside community and developed it into the town of *Durovernum Cantiorum*, later to become a Christian community. When the Romans left the area was swept by waves of invaders who had little time for Christianity, but in the year 597 St Augustine's mission arrived to convert King Ethelbert of Kent and restore the town's dilapidated churches. Shortly afterwards Canterbury became the Metropolitan City of the Church of England. Long stretches of the city wall survive on Roman foundations, and the present cathedral dates from 1070. This fine structure is best known as the place where Archbishop Thomas à Becket was murdered for his denial of the king's authority over the church. Canterbury Castle has the 3rd largest Norman keep in Britain. King's School is thought to be the oldest extant.

Follow SP 'Dover' then 'Sandwich' to leave Canterbury on the A257. Continue to Littlebourne.

LITTLEBOURNE, Kent
Close to the local flint church is an ancient thatched barn. Neat single-

A number of Chilham's ancient houses were partly refaced in brick during the 18th century.

This portrait of the 1st Earl of Sandwich hangs in the Guildhall at Sandwich.

storey cottages dating from the 17th century stand at the end of the village green.

Continue to Wingham.

WINGHAM, Kent
Interesting buildings in this town include Debridge House and Wingham Court, both of which date from the 18th century. Many of the local buildings are picturesquely half timbered, and the Red Lion dates from the 15th century.

Turn right on to the B2046 'Folkestone' road, and in 1 mile turn left on to an unclassified road SP 'Chillenden'.

CHILLENDEN, Kent
The local church retains a good many Norman features. Chillenden Windmill, built in 1868 and restored in 1958, stands ½ mile north of the village.

Meet crossroads, turn left, and leave Chillenden by the 'Woodnesborough' road.

WOODNESBOROUGH, Kent
The church here suffered heavy restoration in the 19th century, but it retains a charming 18th-century cupola on the west tower. South-east of the church is a 17th-century brick cottage.

Continue to Sandwich.

SANDWICH, Kent
This, the oldest of the Cinque Ports, is now separated from the sea by 2 miles of sand-dunes. Among its many outstanding old buildings are the medieval Barbican, Fishgate, and a variety of houses and inns. St Bartholomew's Hospital guest house dates from the 15th century, and both the Guildhall and Manwood Court were built in the 16th. The Old House is a fine example of Tudor design. Much of the old beach between the town and Sandwich Bay is occupied by Sandwich Golf Course, which is famous the world over.

Leave Sandwich by the A258 'Dover' road and later turn left on to the A258 'Deal' road. Enter Deal.

Below: Dover's wonderfully preserved Roman lighthouse is thought to date from the 1st century. Right: the unmistakable White Cliffs of Dover would have been a familiar landmark to Roman sailors.

DEAL, Kent
Henry VIII built a castle (AM) in the shape of a six-petalled flower at Deal, though considerable protection was already offered by the notorious Goodwin Sands. These vast, shifting beds lie just 5 miles offshore and have caused hundreds of wrecks. In its early history the town was a limb of the Cinque Ports, but most of its development dates from the end of the 17th century. Local exhibits can be seen in the town museum, and collections from all over the world are shown in the Maritime Museum.

Proceed along the seafront on the 'Dover' road and branch left on to the B2057, SP 'Kingsdown'. Pass 16th-century Walmer Castle.

WALMER, Kent
The Henrian Castle (AM) here stands in attractive gardens and is the official residence of the Lord Warden of the Cinque Ports. The Duke of Wellington died here in 1852 and a number of his possessions are on display inside. Walmer Lifeboat is famous for the many rescues it has made from the Goodwin Sands.

Continue to the small resort of Kingsdown and turn inland SP 'Dover'. Drive to Ringwould, overlooking The Leas (NT).

RINGWOULD, Kent
Several bronze-age barrows can be seen near Ringwould on Free Down. The 12th- to 14th-century church has an attractive 17th-century tower.

Join the A258 'Dover' road for a short distance and turn left on to the B2058 for St Margaret's at Cliffe.

ST MARGARET'S AT CLIFFE, Kent
A variety of old buildings line the twisty main street. A haven of rural peace can be found in The Pines Garden (NT).

A short detour can be taken from the main route to St Margaret's Bay by keeping forward for 1 mile.

ST MARGARET'S BAY, Kent
This sheltered little bay, completely enclosed by towering chalk cliffs, is a popular starting point for cross-Channel swimmers. A narrow beach peters out to weed-bearded boulders and large pools in the chalk bedrock on each side.

Return to St Margaret's at Cliffe, turn left into unclassified Reach Road, and continue to a fine viewpoint overlooking Dover Harbour. Pass a footpath to the Blériot Memorial and turn left on to the A258. Enter Dover.

DOVER, Kent
Formerly the Roman walled city of *Dubris*, Dover was chief of the Cinque Ports and has a magnificent castle (AM) built on a site occupied since prehistoric times. Its strategic position gives it total command of the harbour, and successive English kings spent vast sums on its development. It was last used for military purposes during World War II. The Pharos, a surprisingly well-preserved Roman lighthouse, stands within the castle walls near the exceptionally fine Saxon Church of St Mary de Castro. Dover Town Hall incorporates the 13th-century Hall of Maison Dieu, and nearby Maison Dieu House dates from 1663. The oldest and best-preserved wall paintings north of the Alps can be seen in the Roman Painted House. A granite memorial in North Fall meadow marks the landing of Louis Blériot in 1909, after his historic cross-Channel flight.

Follow SP 'Canterbury' to leave Dover by London Road (A256). Pass a railway bridge and 1 mile farther on turn left on to the B2060 'Alkham' road, then passing Alkham, climbing through a North Downs valley to Hawkinge.

HAWKINGE, Kent
The Kent Battle of Britain Museum contains the largest and most comprehensive collection of remains of British and German aircraft from the Battle of Britain.

Return to Folkestone on the A260.

IN THE NORTH DOWNS

Some of the finest views in the south of England can be enjoyed from the great chalk ridge of the Hog's Back, which itself can be seen across miles of flat farm land scattered with small woods and copses. This is the country of the yellowhammer and skylark, of thorn-covered slopes and the gnarled creepers of old man's beard.

GUILDFORD, Surrey
Medieval kings built a great castle in this ancient town and merchants later developed it into an important centre of the wool industry. Nowadays the castle has vanished except for a 3-storey keep (open) in flower gardens, but the prosperity of wool is reflected in many fine old buildings. Charles Dickens thought the steep High Street 'the most beautiful in the kingdom'. At its summit is the 16th-century Grammar School, the contemporary Abbot's Hospital, and an 18th-century church. Farther down, the ornate clock of the 17th-century Guildhall hangs over the pavement near the Saxon tower of St Mary's Church, and the 19th-century Church of St Nicholas makes an interesting contrast at the bottom of the hill. The River Wey features an interesting 18th-century riverside crane powered by a 20ft treadmill. New buildings include Sir Edward Maufe's controversial cathedral on Stag Hill.

Leave Guildford town centre with SP 'Other Routes' and after 1 mile turn left on to the bypass SP 'Petersfield' then join the A3. After 2¼ miles drive under a road bridge, and in another mile pass the turning for Compton and Loseley House on the left. A short detour from the main route can be taken along the B3000 in the pleasant village of Compton and Loseley House.

The Hog's Back is criss-crossed by quiet country lanes.

COMPTON, Surrey
A gallery devoted entirely to Victorian painter and sculptor G F Watts displays some 200 of his works in this small village. He is commemorated by a mortuary chapel which features vivid interior decoration by his widow.

LOSELEY HOUSE, Surrey
Sir William More, a kinsman of the ill-fated Sir Thomas More, used stone from Waverley Abbey to build this magnificent Elizabethan mansion (open) near Compton. Fine ceilings are complemented by panelling from King Henry VIII's Nonsuch Palace, and every room is appointed with furniture and hangings from many periods.

Continue along the A3 for another ½ mile, then turn right on to the B3000 SP 'Farnham'. Proceed to Puttenham.

PUTTENHAM, Surrey
A handsomely aged church with a 15th-century tower enhances the quiet charm of this small village.

In the village turn left on to an unclassified road and continue along the southern slopes of the Hog's Back to Seale.

THE HOG'S BACK, Surrey
At its highest point this great whaleback ridge of chalk, an outlier of the North Downs, rises to 505ft above sea level. It stretches from Guildford to Farnham, with several parking areas along its length.

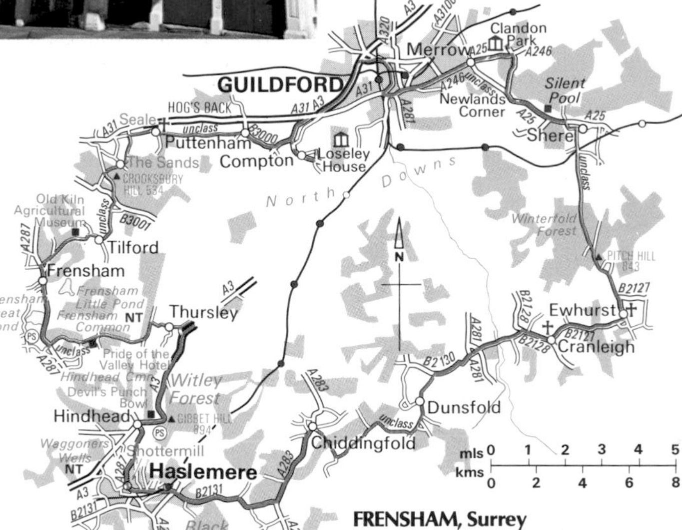

Drive past the church in Seale and turn left. Proceed for ½ mile and meet crossroads, then turn left for The Sands. Cross a main road SP 'Tilford' and pass 534ft Crooksbury Hill on the left. Continue to crossroads and turn left again SP 'Elstead'. After a short distance turn left on to the B3001 and take the next turning right on to an unclassified road for Tilford.

TILFORD, Surrey
Features of this pleasant village include two partly medieval bridges over the River Wey, and a huge old tree known as King John's Oak. The latter is said to be many centuries old. The village is noted for its Bach music festivals. One mile west is the Old Kiln Agricultural Museum.

Cross the River Wey twice with SP 'Frensham' and after ¼ mile turn left. Continue for another 1½ miles and turn left on to the A287 SP 'Hindhead'. Proceed through Frensham.

Guildford's fine 17th-century clock hangs high above the main street and can be seen for many yards in both directions.

FRENSHAM, Surrey
Frensham's lovely ponds are surrounded by woods and heathland on the Hampshire-Surrey border. The Great Pond covers 108 acres, and the Little Pond is resplendent with water lilies in late spring and summer. The 900-acre gorse and heather common (NT) features a line of large prehistoric bowl barrows, and much of the area is now protected as a country park. Frensham's restored church has a Norman font and, under the tower, a great copper cauldron reputed to be over 400 years old. Tradition holds that it belonged to a local witch called Mother Ludlam, and an 18th-century writer tells of it having been filled with ale to entertain the village 'at the wedding of poor maids'.

Cross Frensham Common to reach Frensham Great Pond and Country Park. Proceed for ¾ mile and turn left on to an unclassified road SP 'Thursley'. After 1½ miles reach the Pride of the Valley Hotel. Cross the main road and after 1¾ miles turn right for Thursley.

THURSLEY, Surrey
Old houses and charming cottages straggle along a winding lane to the village church which has a sundial on its shingled spire. A curious epitaph to an unknown sailor murdered by three ruffians at Hindhead in 1786 can be seen on a tombstone in the churchyard.

In ½ mile turn left and ½ mile further turn right on to the A3 'Hindhead' road. Drive over Hindhead Common, with the Devil's Punch Bowl on the right and Gibbet Hill, a picnic site, and Witley Forest on the left. Enter Hindhead.

Four great beams inside Thursley Church support its shingled steeple.

HINDHEAD, Surrey
Founded in the 19th century on the highest town site in Surrey, Hindhead offers some of the most beautiful surroundings in the county. The noted viewpoint of Gibbet Hill (NT) rises to 894ft in the north east, the deep combe of the Devil's Punch Bowl (NT) cuts through a sandstone ridge near by, and all around is Witley Forest. Off the B3002 1½ miles south west is the beauty spot of Waggoner's Wells (NT).

Follow SP 'Haslemere, A287' and descend to Shottermill, then keep forward on the B2131 for Haslemere.

HASLEMERE, Surrey
Haslemere stands in dense woods at the northern foot of 918ft-high Blackdown. For centuries the town has been a centre for craftsmen, and today the tradition is maintained at the Dolmetsch musical instrument workshops and museum (open). Aldworth, home of the great 19th-century poet Tennyson, stands on the slopes of Black Down. A number of 17th-century tiled houses survive behind a raised walk in the town, and the 19th-century Educational Museum of Sir John Hutchinson stands in the High Street (open). The town's annual music festival, usually held in July, is invariably devoted to the Baroque period.

Leave Haslemere on the B2131 SP 'Petworth', with Black Down (NT) on the right. After 2½ miles bear left SP 'Chiddingfold', and after a further ¾ mile meet a T-junction. Turn left on to the A283 for Chiddingfold.

CHIDDINGFOLD, Surrey
In medieval times this large village was very famous for its fine quality glass. Despite its large size it is one of the loveliest Wealden villages. At its heart is a pretty green with a thorn tree said to be 500 years old, a pond complete with ducks and water lilies, and the delightful 14th-century Crown Inn.

Drive to the Crown Inn and turn right on to an unclassified road SP 'Dunsfold'. Reach the far side of the green and bear right, then continue for 1 mile, turn left, and proceed to Dunsfold.

DUNSFOLD, Surrey
A modern lychgate and a tunnel of clipped yews lead to Dunsfold Church, which dates from the 13th century and has an attractive Tudor porch. Its pews may be the oldest still used in England.

One mile beyond Dunsfold turn right on to the B2130 SP 'Cranleigh'. Continue for 1 mile, then bear left and after ¼ mile turn right. Drive over staggered crossroads and continue for 1¼ miles. Turn right on to the B2128 and drive into Cranleigh.

CRANLEIGH, Surrey
Cranleigh is more than a village, and yet not quite large enough to call a town. Its pleasant green has a rural aspect, but the long main street lined with maples planted by Canadian soldiers in World War I might have been borrowed from a much larger place. In 1859 a surgeon called Napper and the local rector together founded the first cottage hospital.

Clandon Park was designed by a Venetian architect in the Palladian style.

Drive to the end of the village and turn left on to the B2127. After 2¼ miles turn left again into Ewhurst.

EWHURST, Surrey
Climbers come to Ewhurst to test their mettle on Pitch Hill, a sandstone outcrop that rises 1 mile to the north of the village. Ewhurst Mill has not worked for a century and was once a haunt of smugglers.

Keep forward in Ewhurst, on to the unclassified 'Shere' road. After ¾ mile bear left and cross Pitch Hill, with Winterfold Forest on the left, and drive into Shere.

SHERE, Surrey
Situated on the River Tillingbourne under the edge of the North Downs, this enchanting village has long proved an attraction to artists. The church, which figures in the *Domesday Book*, has a Norman tower with a medieval shingled spire. The White Horse Inn has a frame of ancient ship's timbers.

Drive to a T-junction and turn left SP 'Guildford'. Continue to the next T-junction and turn left again to join the A25. After ½ mile, off the main road to the right, is the Silent Pool.

SILENT POOL, Surrey
According to legend King John watched a local girl bathing here. She drowned herself in a fit of shame, and anybody visiting this quiet, tree-encircled water might easily imagine that her spirit lingers here still.

Ascend to Newlands Corner.

NEWLANDS CORNER, Surrey
This famous 567ft high North Downs beauty spot offers views across the Weald to the South Downs.

At Newlands Corner keep right on the A25. Descend for 1 mile and meet crossroads. Turn left on to the A25. By keeping straight ahead a short detour can be taken from the main route to Clandon Park.

CLANDON PARK, Surrey
Built in the early 1730s, this classical mansion (NT) features noteworthy plaster decoration, and stands in gardens refashioned by Capability Brown. A famous collection of china, furniture and needlework bequeathed to the nation by Mrs Hannah Gubbay in 1969 is displayed in these elegant surroundings.

Continue on the A25 to Merrow.

MERROW, Surrey
A footpath that starts between the church and inn at Merrow runs across gentle downland to a summit which affords views into 8 or 9 counties, depending on the weather.

Forward along the A246 returning to Guildford.

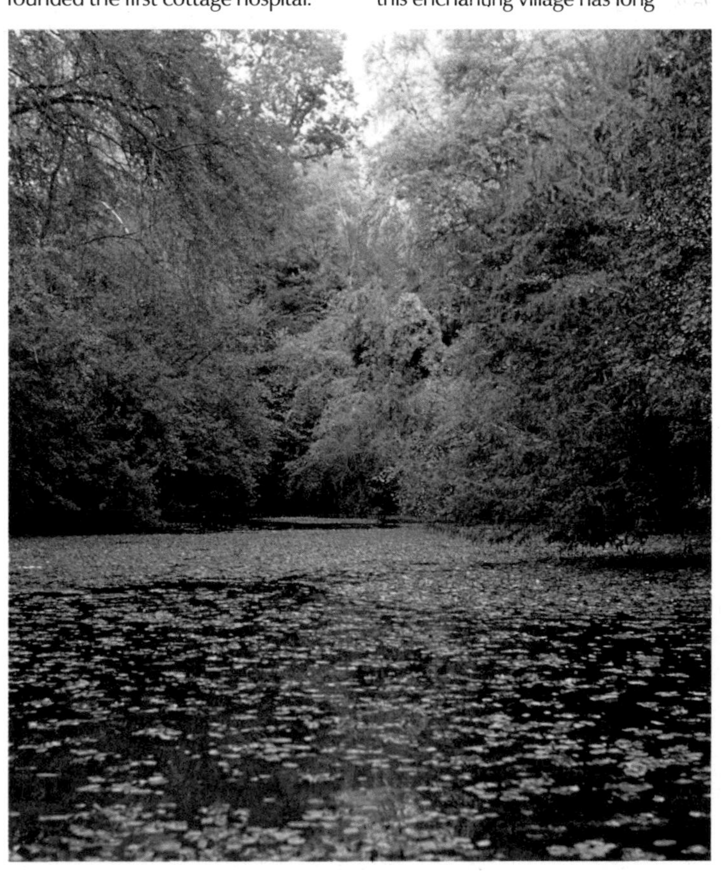

Tree-shrouded Silent Pool is connected in legend with King John.

THE KENTISH WEALD TO THE CINQUE PORTS

From Hastings, where English history was made in 1066 to Rye, a smugglers' paradise in the 18th century: both vital Cinque Ports. Inland, towards the Weald, the tour passes the windmills, weather-boarding and hop fields which characterise Kent.

HASTINGS, E Sussex
William the Conqueror ensured Hastings a firm place in English history when he assembled his army here in 1066, although the battle of Hastings actually took place at nearby Battle. His stone Norman castle now lies in ruins overlooking the town and can be reached via a cliff lift. During the Middle Ages Hastings was an important Cinque Port; until the end of the 15th century these south-east defence ports were duty-bound to supply ships and men in the event of invasion. However, when Hastings harbour silted up, the town turned to fishing for its livelihood. The Old Town to the east is the picturesque fishermen's quarter and the heart of the ancient town. Weather-boarded houses crowd down alleys to the shingle beach and the shops mostly sell sailors' bric-a-brac. Curious 3-storeyed square structures made of tarred wood stand on the beach; they are fishing net lofts and were originally built high to keep ground rent to a minimum. Fishermens' Museum which used to be the local chapel, is now packed with seafaring treasures.

Leave Hastings on the A259, SP 'Brighton', along the seafront. Pass through the neighbouring resort of St Leonards to Bexhill.

BEXHILL, E Sussex
In 1880, Lord de la Warr, member of an old Sussex family, developed this little town into a holiday resort. The rather ugly de la Warr Pavilion sitting on the sea front forms the focal point of the traditional range of seaside entertainments — concert halls, theatres, restaurants and sun lounges. Rather more attractive is the old village behind the coast line.

At Bexhill follow the A269, SP 'London', and pass through Sidley to Ninfield. Here turn right on to the Battle road and continue to Catsfield. At the end of the village turn right on to the B2095, SP 'Battle Station'. Later turn left on to the A2100 and enter Battle.

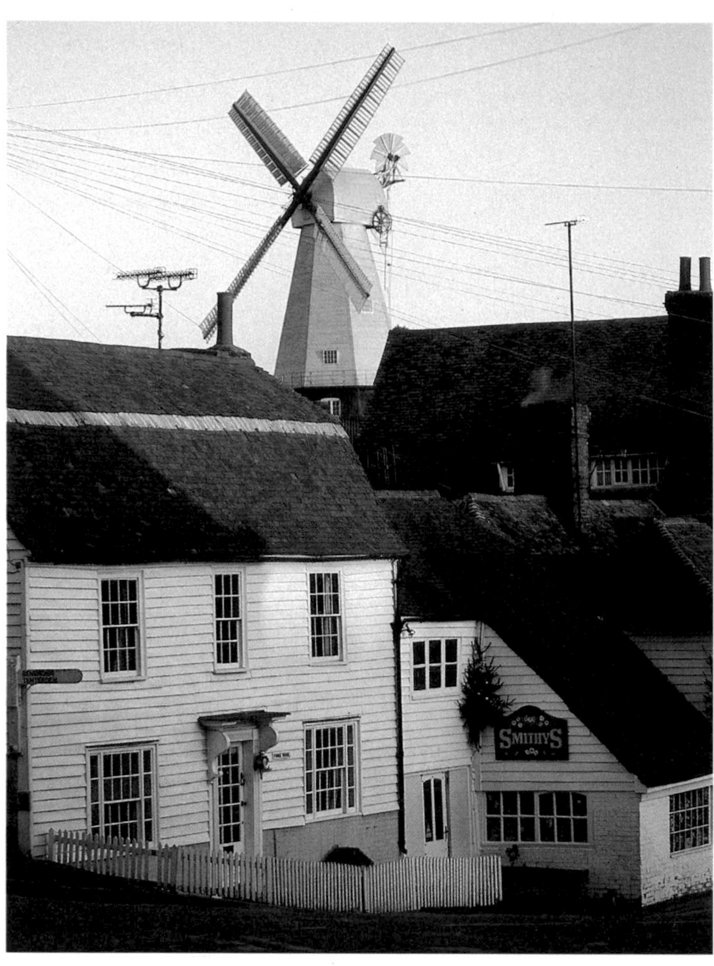

Above: Cranbrook's smock mill

Below: the cottage garden at Sissinghurst Castle

BATTLE, E Sussex
The Battle of Hastings took place just outside Battle, which is how the town got its name. King Harold II lost, and it was this defeat which gave the town an abbey, because William the Conqueror vowed beforehand that if he was the victor he would build one by way of thanks to God. When St Martin's Abbey was built, the high altar was placed on the spot where Harold fell. The abbey remains (OACT), actually of later buildings than William's, include a fine gateway, the monks' sleeping quarters and the cellars. In Langton House the history of Battle from Neolithic times to the present day is vividly illustrated and there are many pieces of Sussex iron from the industry which flourished over a 1,000 years ago. There is also a copy (1821) of the Bayeux Tapestry.

Remain on the A2100, SP 'London', then in 3 miles turn left on to the A21 and continue through Robertsbridge to Hurst Green. Beyond the village turn right on to the A265 and enter Kent before reaching Hawkhurst.

HAWKHURST, Kent
Hawkhurst was a onetime stronghold of the notorious Hawkhurst Gang — a group of smugglers who terrorised much of Kent and Sussex in the early 18th century. Now some way between village and town in size, the older part lies around a triangular green known as the Moor. Among the brick and weather-boarded houses around the green stands the church. Its 15th-century window tracery is particularly fine, as is the 14th-century east window.

Follow the A268, SP 'Flimwell/ Tonbridge'. A gradual climb passes through woodland into Sussex again at Flimwell. Here, at the crossroads, turn right to rejoin the A21. In 1 mile turn right on to the B2079 to reach Goudhurst.

GOUDHURST, Kent
Between the duck pond at the bottom of the hill and the church at the top, typical Kentish houses jostle each other up the main street. Goudhurst stands on a steep ridge of land and its church tower, 500ft above sea level, was used as a lookout post in both World War I and II. The church is 14th century, but the stocky tower dates from 1638, when a storm destroyed the original. Wooden painted figures inside represent Sir Alexander Colepeper and his wife and are the best of the church's many monuments.

At Goudhurst turn right on to the A262, SP 'Ashford', and in 1½ miles turn right again on to the B2085, SP 'Hawkhurst'. In 2 miles turn left, SP 'Cranbrook'. On reaching the A229 turn left, then take the next turning right on to the B2189 and enter Cranbrook.

CRANBROOK, Kent
Cranbrook was built from the profits of the cloth trade. With the streams to power fulling mills, oak trees to use as building material and fullers' earth to clean the cloth, it was an ideal centre for the industry. On the edge of the village stands one of the country's most splendid smock mills — their name supposedly coming from the resemblance to a man dressed in a smock. Built in the 18th century, its sails stretch up to nearly 100ft above the ground.

Remain on the B2189, SP 'Staplehurst', and later turn right on to the A229. In ¼ mile turn right again on to the A262, SP 'Ashford', and pass through Sissinghurst. ½ mile beyond the village a turning on the left leads to Sissinghurst Castle.

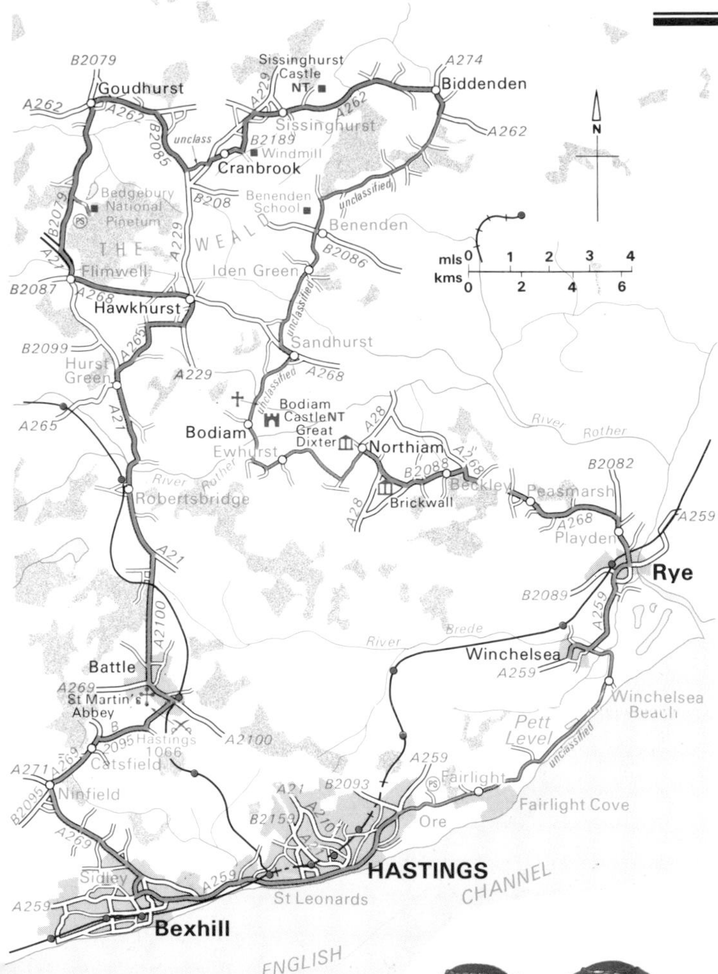

SISSINGHURST CASTLE, Kent
Vita Sackville-West and her husband Harold Nicolson transformed a few derelict buildings and a near wilderness into an imaginative and beautiful series of gardens, with the Tudor tower and 2 cottages as a centre-piece (NT). Each garden has an individuality of its own. There is the famous white garden (where only white or grey plants grow), the herb garden, the rose garden and many more. Redbrick walls and thick hedges divide the romantic gardens which lead naturally and enchantingly one to another. Vita Sackville-West's study — a glory-hole full of books, letters, diaries, photographs and personal mementoes — is in the tower.

The main tour continues on the A262 to Biddenden.

BIDDENDEN, Kent
Antique shops, tea shops, pubs and restaurants fill most of Biddenden's half-timbered buildings, for it is one of Kent's most popular villages. The quaint village sign depicts the 2 Maids of Biddenden — Eliza and Mary Chulkhurst. They were Siamese twins, said to be born in the 12th century although their dress on the sign is Elizabethan.

A carving of the Biddenden Maids who were joined at the hip and shoulder

At Biddenden turn right and continue on the Ashford Road, then in ¾ mile branch right, SP 'Benenden'. After 3¾ miles, at the T-junction, turn left passing Benenden School (right) and continue to Benenden. Cross the main road here and continue to Iden Green. In 2 miles turn left on to the A268 into Sandhurst, then turn right, SP 'Bodiam', to re-enter Sussex before reaching Bodiam.

BODIAM, E Sussex
Bodiam Castle (NT) outshines its village by far. The fortress was built in the 14th century to guard this vital crossing point on the River Rother, which was a potential route inland for French invaders. Although it was not attacked at that time, the castle met its fate during the Civil War when Cromwellian armies destroyed it. Now it stands serenely as an empty shell, clearly reflected in its wide lily-covered moat.

At Bodiam turn left on to the Ewhurst road and pass the castle (left). Cross the River Rother and in ½ mile turn left, SP 'Ewhurst Green'. Pass through Ewhurst Green and follow SP 'Northiam'.

NORTHIAM, E Sussex
The gnarled old oak tree on Northiam's village green is famous because Elizabeth I dined under it in 1573. During the occasion she took her shoes off, and let the villagers keep them when she left. They are now kept at Brickwall, so named because of its high surrounding walls. Brickwall was the home of the Frewen family for 400 years and is now a boys' school. At the opposite end of Northiam is Great Dixter (OACT). Nathaniel Lloyd, architectural historian, bought the house in 1911 and commissioned Sir Edwin Lutyens to enlarge and restore it, which he did to good effect. Curiously-clipped yews are the most striking feature of the gardens.

At Northiam turn right on to the A28 Hastings road and on leaving the village branch left on to the B2088, SP 'Rye'. Pass Brickwall House (right) and continue to Beckley. At the far end turn right on to the A268 and continue to Rye.

RYE, E Sussex
Ancient, timbered and Georgian buildings, the romance of a seafaring and smuggling past in every twisting cobbled street and its perch high up on a bluff within sight and smell of the sea, give Rye its considerable charm. When the sea lapped the town walls in the 14th century, Rye was one of the most prosperous ancient ports in Sussex. However, repeated, relentless attacks and burnings by the French, together with the silting up of the harbour, were the town's undoing. One of the buildings to survive the French deflagrations was Ypres Tower — the 13th-century town fort. It is put to good use now as the town museum, containing a fascinating variety of curios from bygone days. Rye so enchanted novelist Henry James that he made his home in the Lamb House (NT) until just before he died.

Leave Rye on the A259 Hastings road. Continue for 2 miles, then cross the river bridge and bear right, then turn sharp left for Winchelsea.

WINCHELSEA, E Sussex
Like Rye, Winchelsea was also a prosperous seaport and a member of the Cinque Ports, but nevertheless the sea has always been its enemy — firstly by completely submerging the old town in the late 13th century, and then by receding and taking with it the prosperity the port bestowed. Court Hall (OACT) is one of the oldest buildings and houses a museum of the town and surrounding area.

Return down the hill and turn right, then turn right again on to the unclassified road for Winchelsea Beach. Continue to Fairlight and later turn left on to the A259 for the return to Hastings.

These huts at Hastings, dating from the 16th century, are still used by fishermen to dry out their nets

FAMOUS COLLEGES AND HIDDEN VILLAGES

Unspoilt villages embodying the spirit of rural England speckle the open rolling fields that separate Hertford from Cambridge. Yet it is the city of colleges and courtyards, of beauty and learning, that reigns supreme.

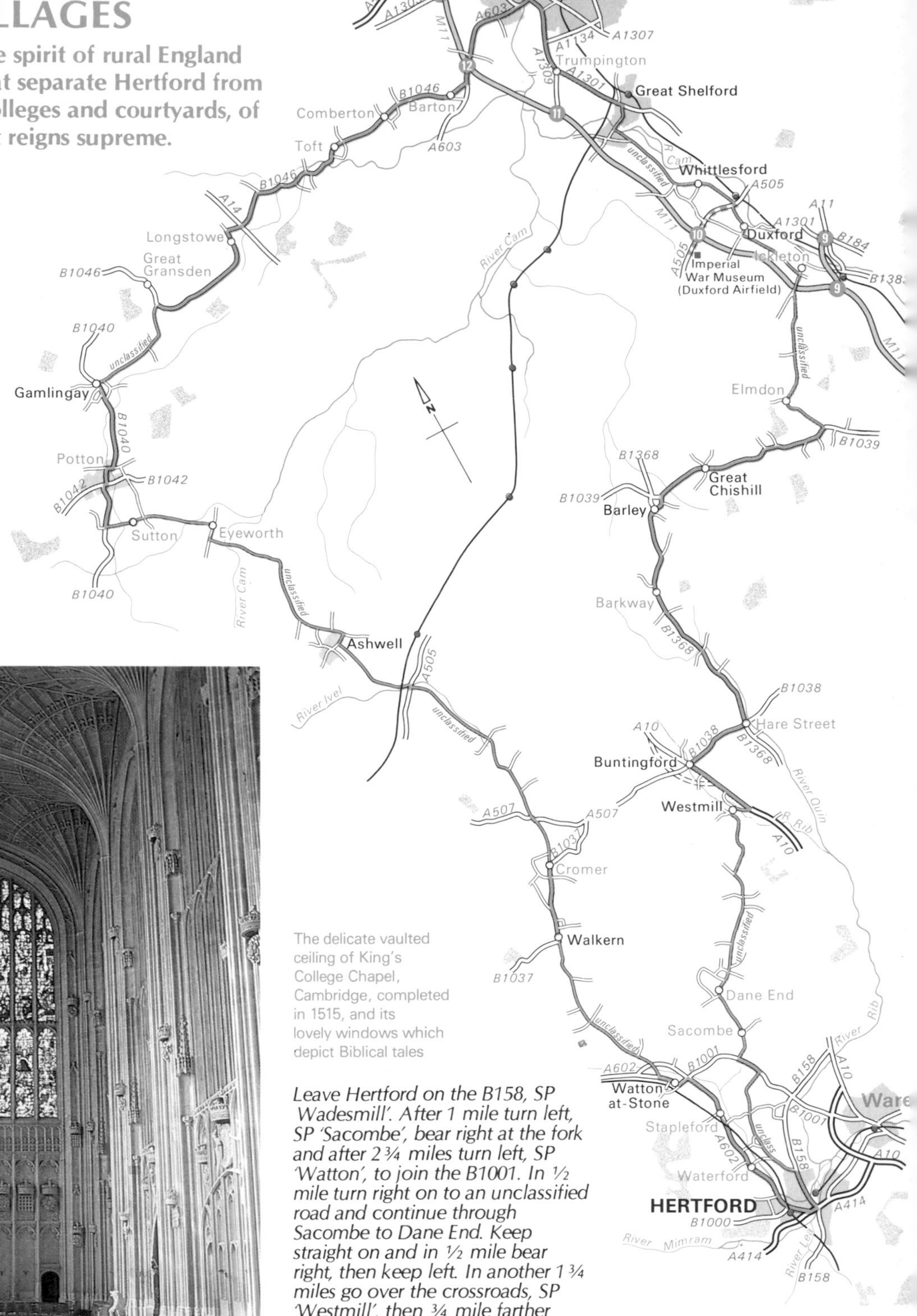

The delicate vaulted ceiling of King's College Chapel, Cambridge, completed in 1515, and its lovely windows which depict Biblical tales

HERTFORD, Herts
Old houses from Jacobean to the Georgian periods mingle well with new buildings in this old county town where 3 rivers, the Lea, the Beane and the Rib meet. Little remains of the old Norman castle except for the charming 15th-century gatehouse, one of the childhood homes of Elizabeth I, standing in pleasant parkland. At the heart of the town are the famous old buildings of Christ's Hospital School, founded by the governors of the Bluecoat School in London. Several appealing figures of Bluecoat children stand on the walls and above the entrance. Lombard House (not open), a lovely Jacobean building, was the home of the judge Sir Henry Chauncy who presided over the last trial for witchcraft ever held in England (see Walkern).

Leave Hertford on the B158, SP 'Wadesmill'. After 1 mile turn left, SP 'Sacombe', bear right at the fork and after 2 ¾ miles turn left, SP 'Watton', to join the B1001. In ½ mile turn right on to an unclassified road and continue through Sacombe to Dane End. Keep straight on and in ½ mile bear right, then keep left. In another 1 ¾ miles go over the crossroads, SP 'Westmill', then ¾ mile farther bear right to reach Westmill.

WESTMILL, Herts
Near to this exceptionally pretty village, complete with green and rows of tall-chimneyed cottages surrounding the church, stands one bought by the 19th-century essayist Charles Lamb. He is best know today for *Lamb's Tales from Shakespeare*, which he wrote with his sister, Mary. Button Snap is the evocative name of this thatched 17th-century cottage with tiny latticed windows, and it now belongs to the Lamb Society who have preserved and restored it (not open).

At the village green turn right, SP 'Puckeridge', and on reaching the A10 turn left for Buntingford.

BUNTINGFORD, Herts
The old Roman road of Ermine Street runs through this busy village. There is a fine range of almshouses, built in 1684 by Seth Ward who first became a distinguished scholar at Oxford, then Bishop of Exeter and finally of Salisbury.

By the nearside of the town centre turn right on to the B1038 for Hare Street. Here, turn left on to the B1368, and follow an undulating road through Barkway to Barley.

BARLEY, Herts
For more than 300 years the Fox and Hounds Inn has looked down from its hillside on the old cottages of Barley. The famous inn sign stretches right over the road; across the beam, huntsmen and hounds pursue a fox, which appears to be craftily disappearing into a hole in the roof of the inn.

Branch right, SP 'Great Chishill', to pass under the inn sign, and shortly to join the B1039. Cross into Cambridgeshire before reaching Great Chishill.

GREAT CHISHILL, Cambs
Great Chishill looks out peacefully over one of the quietest corners of Cambridgeshire. The showpiece of the village is the lofty 18th-century post mill, with white-painted timbers and a graceful fantail that turns the mill so that the sails always face into the wind.

Continue on the Saffron Walden road and after 3¼ miles turn left on to an unclassified road for Elmdon. In the village turn right on to the Ickleton road. In 3 miles, by the nearside of Ickleton village, turn left for Duxford.

DUXFORD, Cambs
Duxford's old watermill, listed in the Domesday Book, has attracted several famous visitors in the past, including Charles Kingsley, author of *The Water Babies.* Near the village, on the Battle of Britain airfield where World War II hero Douglas Bader served, is the Imperial War Museum's collection of military aircraft and armoured fighting vehicles; more than 60 historic aircraft are on view. The Duxford Aviation Society's collection of civil aircraft, including Concorde 01, is also open.

At Duxford turn right, then at the church turn left and after ¾ mile reach the junction with the A505. From here a detour can be made by turning left to visit Duxford Airfield. The main tour crosses the main road and continues to Whittlesford.

WHITTLESFORD, Cambs
The early 16th-century Guildhall, its overhanging upper storey supported on carved wooden posts, is only one of many attractive buildings around the village green. In the churchyard lies the graves of many brave young airmen who served at Duxford in World War II and fought and died in the Battle of Britain.

Continue on the unclassified road and in 2½ miles, at the T-junction, turn right for Great Shelford.

GREAT SHELFORD, Cambs
Great Shelford looks out towards the gently rolling Gog Magog Hills which lie just south of Cambridge. The hills take their name from a Romano-British giant who appears in legend, sometimes as 1 person, Gogmagog, sometimes as 2, Gog and Magog. By tradition dating back to at least the 11th century, the outline of 2 gigantic figures was carved on the hillside here at Wandlebury Camp, an Iron-Age fort.

On reaching the A1301 turn left towards Cambridge. At Trumpington turn right at the traffic signals on to the A1309 and continue into Cambridge.

CAMBRIDGE, Cambs
The distinguished and beautiful architecture of Cambridge's great colleges has stamped its personality on the heart of the city even more powerfully than at Oxford. The secluded college courtyards and gardens are usually open to the public, as are the many fine college chapels. The most lovely of these is without doubt King's College Chapel, with its graceful and intricate web of fan-vaulting. Visitors can stroll peacefully along the Backs, a green, sunlit sweep of lawns leading down from St John's, Trinity, Clare, King's and Queens' colleges to the river, where in spring and summer unhurried punts drift up and down. Peterhouse is the oldest college — founded in 1284 by the Bishop of Ely — but students had settled here from Oxford in individual groups attached to monastic schools as early as the previous century. The prettiest of the colleges is held to be Queens'. Its

Westmill village green, complete with water pump

Mathematical bridge leading from Cloister Court to the gardens is an interesting curiosity; it was designed in 1749 on mathematical principles and originally stood without nails or similar fixings. Even more famous is the Bridge of Sighs at St John's College, so-called from the one at Venice of which it is a copy. Cambridge, as might be expected, has several interesting museums. The Fitzwilliam contains an unrivalled collection of antiquities, paintings, manuscripts and rare objects. The University Botanic Gardens, rated second only to Kew, are best visited in the afternoons when the glasshouses are open.

From the south west side of the city centre follow the A603, SP 'Sandy'. After 2 miles cross the M11 then in ½ mile turn right on to the B1046, SP 'Comberton' and 'Toft', and enter Barton. Continue, SP 'St Neots', through Comberton to Toft. In 3½ miles, at the Fox Inn, turn right and immediately left across the main road for Longstowe. In another 3 miles turn left on to an unclassified road and continue to Gamlingay.

GAMLINGAY, Cambs
The cosy row of mellow redbrick almshouses that are the focus of this appealing village were built in 1665, the year of the Great Plague. Much of the village had been destroyed by fire in 1600, but fortunately the medieval church, a fine stone building, survived.

At the crossroads in Gamlingay turn left on to the B1040 and continue to Potton. Bear right then left through the square, and at the end turn left, SP 'Biggleswade'. In 1 mile, at the crossroads, turn left on to an unclassified road for Sutton — here cross a ford by the side of the old packhorse bridge. At the end of the village go over the crossroads, SP 'Ashwell'. In 1¾ miles, at the Ongley Arms PH, turn right and ½ mile later turn left, SP 'Ashwell'. After 4½ miles, at the war memorial, turn right into Ashwell.

ASHWELL, Herts
Ash trees around the River Rhee have given this lovely village its name. It stands amid open fields, its church tower rising 176ft above the surrounding countryside. Among the many timber-framed houses scattered about its streets, the pargeted and oak-beamed cottages attached to the 17th-century Guildhall form the most charming group. The old Tythe House (AM), which was once the office of the abbots of Westminster, has been restored and preserved as the village museum, where there is a fascinating collection of village history and rural life.

In Ashwell pass the Three Tuns PH and turn left, SP 'Bygrave' and 'Baldock', then go over the crossroads, SP 'Walkern'. In 2 miles cross the main road and 4½ miles farther join the A507, then keep forward on to an unclassified road to Cromer. Here, join the B1037 for Walkern.

WALKERN, Herts
In 1712, the last trial for witchcraft ever held in England took place in Walkern. A woman called Jane Wenham was accused by a local farmer of witchcraft and was tried and sentenced to death by Sir Henry Chauncy. Queen Anne granted her a pardon and as a result of her case the barbaric laws against witchcraft were repealed in 1736.

At the end of the village go forward on to an unclassified road, SP 'Watton'. After 4 miles turn left SP 'Hertford', and enter Watton-at-Stone

WATTON-AT-STONE, Herts
The elegant, canopied, cast-iron pump, dating from the early 19th century, and Watton Hall (not open), a house of overhanging gables, together form a traditional village group. The flint-built church, containing a wealth of medieval brasses, completes the picture.

At the roundabout take the 3rd exit on to the A602 for the return to Hertford.

LONDON

The Nation's Capital

One of London's best known landmarks — the Houses of Parliament, dominated by the familiar tower of Big Ben.

London History and London Landmarks

LONDON'S HISTORY begins in the middle of the 1st century AD when the invading troops of the Roman Emperor Claudius swept across south-east Britain to the Thames. The area was uninhabited marshland, and the Romans had to bridge the river to get to Colchester, then the most important town in the south-east. In time, they built roads converging on the bridge, river traffic increased, and a settlement grew up which they named Londinium. Its position ensured its prosperity and by the 3rd century it had become the centre of Roman administration and a prosperous walled city with a fort, a large temple, a basilica and a governor's palace. Recent excavations have shown that the present London Bridge is sited only a few hundred yards from the Roman one. Until the 17th century, London Bridge, lined on both sides with shops and houses, was the only access to the city from the south, and until the 16th century, London stayed more or less confined within the limits of the Roman walls. Southwark, on the south side of the bridge, was outside the jurisdiction of the city authorities, and by medieval times had become a refuge for criminals and the quarter where playhouses such as the Globe, forbidden within the City, could flourish.

Until after the reign of Edward the Confessor, English kings were not crowned at London. However, Edward had completed the rebuilding of Westminster Abbey just before his death, and Harold, his successor, was crowned there, as was William the Conqueror, who made Westminster his capital, at the same time conferring on London the status and privileges of a city, but also building the Tower as a symbol of his authority. London thus became truly the capital of England – but for centuries there were two centres of authority – Westminster where the monarch had his palace and where eventually parliament met, and the City where the powerful merchant guilds were supreme. Gradually wealthy landowners built themselves residences along the Strand, which linked the two centres, and the legal profession set themselves up on the site of the Temple of the Knights of St John.

From the 17th century onwards, London grew at an amazing rate, spreading far beyond the Roman and medieval walls. Even the Great Fire of 1666, to which we owe the creation of St Paul's Cathedral and many other churches designed by Wren, did not halt expansion, and surrounding villages like Chelsea, Marylebone, Islington, Kensington, Hampstead and Highgate were gradually swallowed up. The Victorian era, especially after the building of the railways, saw a phenomenal growth in size and population as trade with the Empire boomed and by 1901 the population of the capital stood at 4½ million, more than four times the number there had been in 1801.

The devastation of World War II has resulted in massive new office blocks, and whole areas of houses have been demolished to make way for high-rise or high-density flats, which have, say many, brought more problems than they have solved. Other post-war developments, such as the Barbican and the South Bank Arts Centre, have been widely acclaimed. Despite the drift of people from the centre, where housing is scarce and expensive, to the suburbs, London continues to grow and efforts are being made to attract industry back to the centre.

SURVIVOR OF THE BLITZ *St Paul's Cathedral, built after the Great Fire of 1666 as a symbol of the rebirth of the City, emerges defiantly from the smoke of a World War II bombing raid.*

WESTMINSTER'S LANDMARKS

WESTMINSTER ABBEY
Since the consecration of the abbey on 28 December 1065, the coronation of every English monarch has been held here, with the exception of the two uncrowned kings, Edward V and Edward VIII. It is also the burial place of all English monarchs from the time of Henry III, to whom we owe the rebuilding in Early English style of most of the abbey, to the reign of George III.

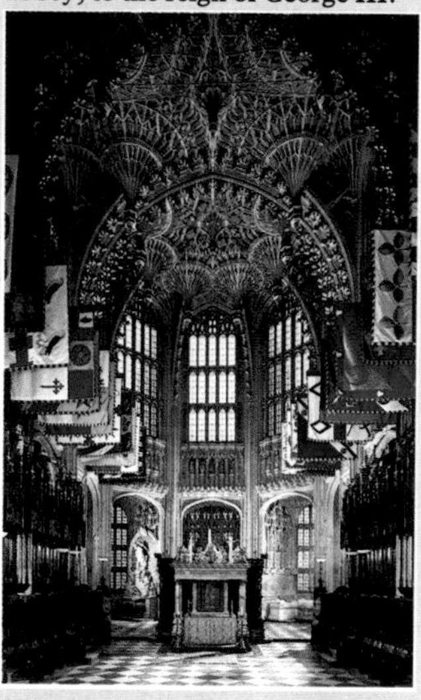

THE ABBEY *showing the delicacy of the fan-vaulting.*

Their tombs, particularly that of Edward the Confessor and that of Henry VII, housed in the beautiful, fan-vaulted chapel he had built in the early 16th century, are magnificent, but outnumbered by the thousand or so monuments to the great and famous. Poets' Corner is the best-known section, where many distinguished writers are remembered. Statesmen honoured include Disraeli and Gladstone, Churchill and Attlee.

WHITEHALL The old palace of Whitehall, burned down in 1698, was made the official residence of the sovereign by Henry VIII. The site is now occupied by government departments and by the Banqueting Hall, a Palladian masterpiece by Inigo Jones, which was planned as the start of a new royal palace. The ceiling of the main hall was painted for Charles I by Rubens. In the centre of the road is the Cenotaph, designed by Sir Edwin Lutyens and unveiled in 1920. Memorial services are held here every year in November. Leading off Whitehall is Downing Street, home of the Prime Minister and the Chancellor of the Exchequer.

WEST-END LANDMARKS

LEICESTER SQUARE
Devoted almost entirely to the cinema and other entertainments, the square was laid out in the 17th century on land belonging to the earls of Leicester. The streets between the square and Shaftesbury Avenue form the nucleus of London's Chinatown.

PICCADILLY CIRCUS AND SOHO The centre of London's West End and theatreland, Piccadilly Circus was once known as the hub of the Empire. At its centre is the famous statue of Eros, London's first aluminium monument, erected in 1893 to commemorate the social reformer, the 7th Earl of Shaftesbury. It represents, not Eros, but the Spirit of Christian Charity. Between Shaftesbury Avenue and its theatres and Oxford Street lies Soho, famous for its many restaurants and now notorious for sex shops and stripshows.

MARBLE ARCH Made redundant as a gateway almost as soon as it was built, Nash's imposing archway had to be moved from Buckingham Palace because it was too narrow to admit Victoria's State Coach, and was re-erected as the entrance to Hyde Park. By 1908, however, the traffic was too much for it, and it was removed to its present site, islanded by traffic on all sides, at the west end of Oxford Street, on the spot where the notorious Tyburn gallows used to stand.

POST OFFICE TOWER
Completed in 1964 and opened in 1966, the Post Office Tower, 580ft high and surmounted by a 40ft mast, is one of London's tallest buildings. At the top is a viewing platform and there used to be a revolving restaurant, but this has been closed for some years now.

ROYAL ALBERT HALL AND ALBERT MEMORIAL Much loved as the home of the Proms, the Royal Albert Hall, an immense, domed, circular structure opened in 1871, commemorates the Prince Consort, as does the elaborate Gothic memorial opposite, showing the Prince seated under a canopy and reading a catalogue of the Great Exhibition.

TRAFALGAR SQUARE
Famous for its flocks of pigeons and as a rallying point for demonstrations of all kinds, Trafalgar Square, on the site of the old Royal Mews, commemorates Lord Nelson's victory over the French in 1805. It was laid out between 1829 and 1841, but Landseer's lions, flanking Nelson's Column, were added in 1867 and the fountains, in which late-night revellers sometimes bathe, in 1948.

PICCADILLY CIRCUS *and the statue of Eros are the most famous and recognisable landmarks in London.*

CITY LANDMARKS

FLEET STREET AND THE STRAND Although many newspapers, including *The Times*, now have their offices elsewhere in London, Fleet Street is still synonymous with the power of the Press. Many of its pubs are the haunt of journalists and some, such as the Cheshire Cheese, have a long and distinguished history. The great Dr Johnson had his house in Gough Square, one of the many courts leading off the street. Fleet Street, which takes its name from the old Fleet River, runs from Ludgate to Temple Bar, the old boundary of the City with Westminster. The archway was removed in 1878, but a memorial plinth remains. St Bride's Church, designed by Wren, is known as the Parish Church of the Press, and its spire is said to have been the inspiration for the traditional three-tier wedding cake. The Strand is the continuation of Fleet Street towards Trafalgar Square. As the name suggests, this was the river bank until the building of the Embankment. Between the Strand and the river lie two of London's four Inns of Court, the Inner and Middle Temple, a peaceful enclave of mostly 17th-century courts, linked by steps and alleys. The Temple Round Church, one of only five in England, dates back to the time of the Knights Templar who originally occupied this site in the 12th century. Two other famous churches, both on islands in the Strand, are St Clement Danes of nursery-rhyme fame and, since its rebuilding after the war, the RAF church, and St Mary-le-Strand, designed by James Gibbs in 1714–19.

HOME OF THE PROMS *The Royal Albert Hall seats more than 5000 people in its huge, circular auditorium.*

THE BANK OF ENGLAND
This massive, windowless stone fortress stands rock-solid (whatever the state of the pound) in Threadneedle Street. Sir John Soane's original designs for the building can be seen in the Soane Museum but much of his structure was rebuilt by Sir Herbert Baker in the 1920s. Nearby are the Stock Exchange in Throgmorton Street, and Lloyds of London in Lime Street.

THE MONUMENT *offers a magnificent City panorama.*

THE MONUMENT Despite the towering office blocks, the Monument is still one of the City's most visible landmarks. Erected in 1677, it commemorates the Great Fire of 1666. From the top (202ft – the distance from its base to the place in Pudding Lane where the fire started) there are splendid views of the City.

OLD BAILEY Properly called the Central Criminal Court, the Old Bailey, crowned by the traditional figure of Justice, takes its popular name from the street where it is sited, near St Paul's. It was built where the old Newgate Prison, scene of public executions until 1868, used to stand.

THE BARBICAN London's most ambitious scheme for making the City a place to live as well as to work, the Barbican is a massive, self-contained complex west of Moorgate. Flats and tower-blocks look out on to a series of courtyards, gardens and a lake. At one end is the Museum of London at the other, an arts centre incorporating exhibition halls, a concert hall and a theatre, now the home of the Royal Shakespeare Company.

The River: Westminster to Greenwich

London owes its existence to the Thames and to the bridge the Romans built in the 1st century AD. Until less than a hundred years ago the river was busy with shipping of all kinds but nowadays even the distinctive flat-bottomed lighters have all but disappeared and the sailing barges are museum pieces.

To travel down the Thames from Westminster Pier to Greenwich in one of the many pleasure launches is to voyage past a fascinating panorama. After the splendours of Westminster, the City and the Tower of London, the scene changes to the warehouses and docks of the Pool of London and Limehouse, ending in the open spaces of Greenwich, and the Royal Naval College.

WESTMINSTER PIER AND BRIDGE Westminster Pier, just north of the bridge, is the embarkation point for many of the trips up and down the river. The bridge itself, built in the 19th century, seems to blend in with the Houses of Parliament.

THE HOUSES OF PARLIAMENT Kings from Edward the Confessor to Henry VIII lived here, but the Court had to move to St James in 1515, after a fire, and Henry VIII then built himself a new palace at Whitehall. Westminster Palace became the Houses of Parliament. In 1834 most of the old palace burnt down. Charles Barry designed the present Gothic building, and much of its intricate decoration was entrusted to Augustus Pugin. The buildings are 940ft long and include 1100 apartments and two miles of corridors. The clock tower at the north end, although smaller than the imposing Victoria Tower at the south end, is affectionately known the world over as Big Ben, although properly speaking this is the name of the 13½ ton bell that strikes the hours. Westminster Hall, 240ft long, may well be the largest Norman hall in Europe. Its magnificent hammer-beam roof dates from the reign of Richard II.

WESTMINSTER *The familiar shape of the Houses of Parliament and Westminster Bridge.*

COUNTY HALL A modern building with 750 ft of river frontage, it is the administrative headquarters of the Greater London Council.

CLEOPATRA'S NEEDLE This 69½ft-tall obelisk was given to this country in 1819 by the Viceroy of Egypt. It had been erected at Heliopolis in about 1500BC – but it has no real connection with Cleopatra.

THE SOUTH BANK COMPLEX This complex includes the Festival Hall, National Theatre and National Film Theatre, the Purcell Room, the Hayward Gallery and the Queen Elizabeth Hall.

WATERLOO BRIDGE By the 1920s John Rennie's 19th-century Waterloo Bridge was showing signs of structural weakness, and work began on this elegant replacement, designed by Sir Giles Gilbert Scott, in 1939.

SOMERSET HOUSE Elizabeth I lived in the palace that once stood on this site, and Oliver Cromwell lay in state here before his funeral. The present building dates from 1776 and a large part of it is occupied by the Registrar General's staff.

ST PAUL'S CATHEDRAL Sir Christopher Wren's magnificent Baroque cathedral replaced Old St Paul's, destroyed in the Great

THE TOWER OF LONDON *The massive keep or 'White Tower' built by William I dominates the riverside.*

Fire of 1666. Seen from the river, it retains its majesty despite surrounding office blocks. The height to the top of its cross is 365ft, and the dome is 112ft in diameter, with three galleries – the famous Whispering Gallery, the Stone Gallery and the Golden Gallery, the two latter giving fine views over London and the Thames. In the crypt are the tombs of Lord Nelson and the Duke of Wellington.

LONDON BRIDGE The medieval London Bridge was a remarkable structure, its 950ft length supported on 19 piers and bearing shops, houses and a chapel. The buildings were demolished in 1760 because of the danger of fire, and in 1831 the bridge itself was replaced by a five-arched granite bridge designed by John Rennie, and this was again replaced in 1968.

HMS BELFAST Almost opposite the Custom House is moored HMS *Belfast*, a World War II cruiser – the largest and most powerful ever built for the Royal Navy – now a museum.

THE TOWER OF LONDON In its time the Tower has been royal residence, prison, stronghold and place of execution – but it is now occupied by the Yeomen Warders, who wear picturesque Tudor costumes, the ravens, whose continued presence there is believed to guarantee its safety, and thousands of tourists who file through to see the Crown Jewels and a comprehensive collection of weapons and armour. William the Conqueror built the keep, known as the White Tower, between about 1078 and 1098, an outstanding example of Norman military architecture. Succeeding kings built and extended the defensive walls and added more towers. Many prisoners met their deaths here, including two of Henry VIII's wives, Anne Boleyn and Catherine Howard.

TOWER BRIDGE This, the most spectacular of London's bridges, was designed in the late 19th century by Sir John Wolfe-Barry. The roadway between the Gothic towers is carried on twin bascules which are raised to allow ships to enter the Pool of London; the original machinery is still in working order, though the steam engines have been replaced by electric motors for reasons of economy. A pedestrian high-level walkway has now been opened between the towers, and the original machinery can be inspected.

ST KATHARINE'S DOCK The buildings have now been adapted to a variety of uses and the docks themselves converted to marinas. The Maritime Trust's Historic Ship Collection illustrates the evolution from sail to steam and also includes the RRS *Discovery*, Captain Scott's vessel.

EXECUTION DOCK Pirates and sailors found guilty of serious crime on the high seas were hanged in chains here until three tides had washed over them. Nearby is the famous Prospect of Whitby public house.

THE GRAPES This picturesque old Limehouse pub stands near Regent's Canal Dock. Regent's Canal and the Grand Union Canal enabled goods to be shipped by barge from the Midlands to the Thames.

THE ISLE OF DOGS Charles II had his royal kennels here and this gave the island its name. Brunel's steamship *Great Eastern* was launched from a site near Millwall Docks.

GREENWICH The river gives the best view of Wren's superb Royal Naval College (originally a naval hospital). Behind them and behind the Queen's House (now part of the National Maritime Museum, rise the landscaped acres of Greenwich Park and at the top of the rise stands the Old Royal Observatory. Moored near the pier are two historic ships, *Cutty Sark*, and *Gypsy Moth IV*.

STEAM BARGES *(left) still common around Tower Bridge in the 1950s.*

THE PROSPECT OF WHITBY *is possibly the oldest of London's riverside pubs. In the foreground, the river police.*

CUTTY SARK *The only surviving example of the swift tea clippers lies in dry dock.*

Parks and Palaces

London is well-blessed with open spaces; they range from the compact green squares of residential districts to great open spaces like Hampstead Heath. Best-known, however, are the royal parks, tracts of land still owned by the Crown though the public is privileged to use them. London is also rich in royal palaces, as some past monarchs, such as Henry VIII, were keen builders. Today 'the Palace' denotes Buckingham Palace – but this has only been so for a comparatively short time, Queen Victoria being the first monarch to make her home there. The English Court remains 'the Court of St James', and it is to this that foreign ambassadors are still appointed.

GREEN PARK Charles II purchased this extension to St James's Park, from which it is divided only by The Mall, in 1667. He was fond of walking, and Constitution Hill, which runs alongside, is thought to have been the route of his favourite 'constitutional'. Green Park differs from the other Royal Parks in having no flowerbeds and no water.

GREENWICH PARK
Greenwich Park was enclosed in 1433 to form a setting for Bella Court Palace, built there a few years earlier by the Duke of Gloucester. In Tudor times it was popular as a hunting chase, and it was not until the reign of Charles II (who had a palace there) that the present, semi-formal layout was achieved. Wide expanses of lawn, broken by avenues of trees and an ornamental pond, sweep up towards Blackheath from the Maritime Museum and the Queen's House on the riverside. Fallow deer roam in a 13-acre tract of bracken and wild flowers known as The Wilderness, and there are three bird sanctuaries. The Old Royal Observatory (now a museum) stands in the park, as does a stone bearing a strip of brass marking the Meridian – zero degrees Longitude – to which measurements made all round the world are referred.

HYDE PARK Henry VIII designed Hyde Park specifically for the purpose of hunting when the land, previously the property of the Abbey of Westminster, came into his possession at the Dissolution. In Stuart times the park was used for horse-racing, and the one-and-a-half miles of Rotten Row (a corruption of 'Route du Roi') is still popular with riders. The Serpentine Lake was formed at the instigation of Queen Caroline by damming the underground River Westbourne; it provides facilities for rowing and sailing – or even year-round bathing for the intrepid few! At the north-east corner of the park, nearest to Marble Arch, is Speaker's Corner, where anyone prepared to face the heckling of bystanders can have his say.

KENSINGTON GARDENS
Kensington Gardens were once part of Hyde Park, but when William III came to the throne in 1689 he feared the effect of Whitehall Palace's damp atmosphere on his asthma and so acquired Nottingham House, at the west end of the park. This became Kensington Palace, its grounds Kensington Gardens – more formal than Hyde Park, though now divided from it only by a road and sharing the same stretch of water. Generations of children have flocked here to see the statue of Sir James Barrie's Peter Pan, the fantastically-carved Elphin Oak and the craft of model boat enthusiasts on the Round Pond.

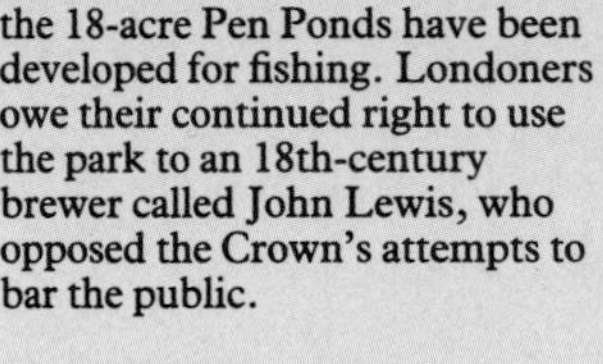

REGENT'S PARK Marylebone Park was renamed after the Prince Regent, later to become George IV, who was responsible for the elegant Nash residences built round its fringe; these were part of a huge neo-Classical development that would have covered the park itself had it been completed. Fortunately this was not feasible, and Nash laid out the area more or less as we know it today, with Inner and Outer Circles, artificial lake and Regent's Canal. Today there is boating on the lake, and pleasure cruises on the canal pass through London Zoo at the north end of the park. The Inner Circle encloses the rose-beds of Queen Mary's Garden, together with the Open-Air Theatre where performances of Shakespearian plays are given during the summer months.

RICHMOND PARK This, the largest of the royal parks, was originally an area of wild countryside enclosed by Charles I and used for hunting by his successors; King Henry VIII's Mound was constructed as a vantage point from which the monarch might survey the killing of his deer. The park is still fairly wild, the deer roaming freely through its coppices, but exotic shrubs have been introduced and the 18-acre Pen Ponds have been developed for fishing. Londoners owe their continued right to use the park to an 18th-century brewer called John Lewis, who opposed the Crown's attempts to bar the public.

ST JAMES'S PARK Until the reign of Henry VIII a 12th-century hospice for lepers, dedicated to St James the Less, stood here; Henry replaced it with St James's Palace, stocking the grounds with deer for the royal hunt. James I used the park to house a menagerie of animals from all over the world, many of them the gift of foreign royalty. The park remained swampy grassland, however, till the reign of Charles II, when it was redesigned in the formal French style. One of its attractions was an aviary (along the road still known as Birdcage Walk), and the islands of the ornamental lake were stocked with a collection of wildfowl.

LONDON'S ROYAL PARKS *are displayed clearly from the air as the 'lungs' of the capital.*

GREENWICH PARK *(right) and* ST JAMES'S PARK *(left) show the contrasting seasons: spring colours at Greenwich; mellow tones of autumn in St James's.*

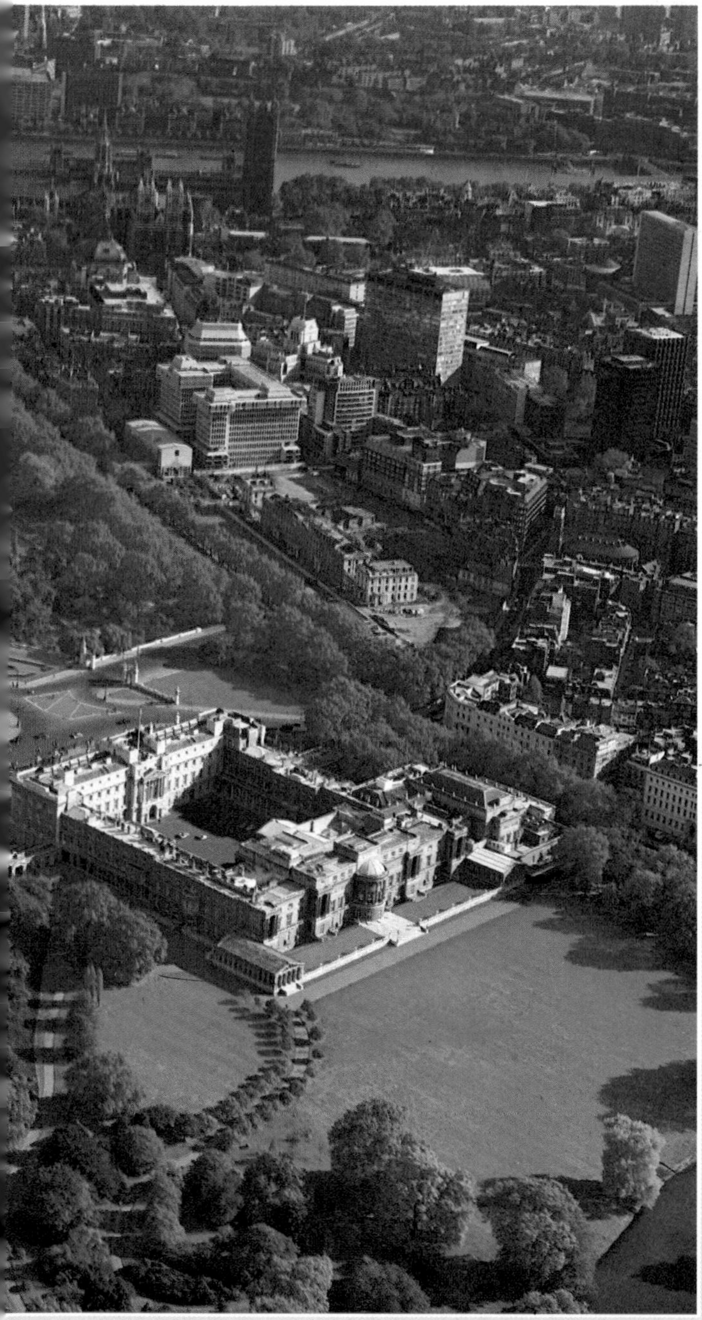

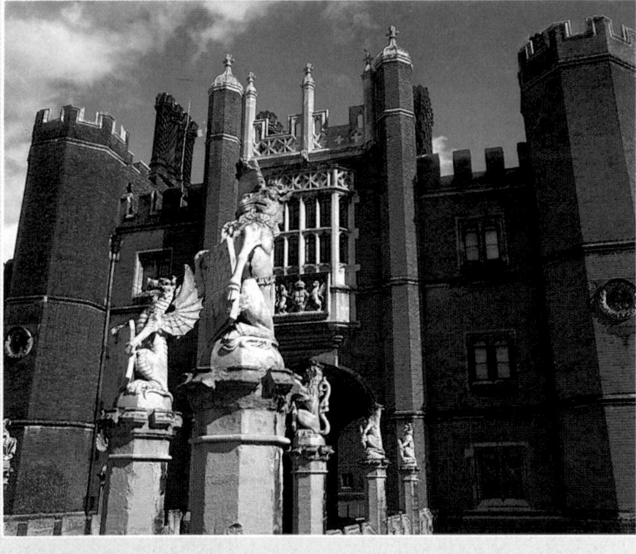

HAMPTON COURT *The great Tudor gatehouse dates from Henry VIII's time, but the heraldic 'king's beasts' are modern.*

THE VICTORIA MEMORIAL *was erected outside the Palace at the head of the Mall in 1911.*

BUCKINGHAM PALACE, *The Mall, SW1* Buckingham Palace – formerly Buckingham House, built in 1703 for the Duke of Buckingham and Chandos – has been the principal home of the sovereign since Queen Victoria came to the throne in 1837. The original brick building was bought by George III in 1761 as a dower house for Queen Charlotte, and in the reign of George IV it was remodelled and clad in Bath Stone by John Nash. Victoria put on a new frontage, however, having Marble Arch (Nash's grand entrance) moved to Hyde Park because it was too narrow for the state coach. In 1912 the east front of the building was refaced again, being given a classical façade of Portland stone to blend with the Victoria Memorial which stands opposite the top of the Mall. Buckingham Palace is open to the public only on such occasions as investitures, though it is possible to visit the Royal Mews and the Queen's Gallery.

HAMPTON COURT PALACE, *Hampton Court Road, Kingston-upon-Thames* When Cardinal Wolsey began work on Hampton Court in 1514 he intended to become the owner of one of the most magnificent palaces in Europe; later, however, he gave it to Henry VIII in a vain attempt to curry favour. Hampton Court, in its fine riverside park, was one of the king's favourite residences. He was often there, playing Royal Tennis (today's 'real' tennis) in the enclosed court and jousting in the area where the Tiltyard Gardens are now. Five of his wives lived there, and the ghosts of two (Jane Seymour and Catherine Howard) apparently haunt it. Anne Boleyn's Gateway, a fine example of Tudor brickwork, dates from this time, surmounted by Henry's fine astronomical clock. The intricate gardens, with their famous maze, were added by Charles II and are reminiscent of Versailles. The last monarch to live there was George II, and afterwards the palace, after extensive restoration, was opened to the public. There are priceless paintings to be seen, and fine tapestries and furniture – but perhaps most impressive of all is the magnificent hammerbeam roof in the Great Hall.

KENSINGTON PALACE, *Kensington Gardens, W8* Nottingham House, the London home of the Earl of Nottingham, was purchased by William III in 1683 and was remodelled as Kensington Palace by Sir Christopher Wren. It remained the home of the reigning monarch until George II died here in 1760; it was also the birthplace of Queen Victoria, who lived here until her accession to the throne. It is now the home of Princess Margaret, but the State Apartments, where there is fine work by Wren, Grinling Gibbons and William Kent, are open.

ST JAMES'S PALACE, *St James's St., SW1* This rambling, rectangular brick mansion was built for Henry VIII. It remained the official residence of the sovereign until the time of Victoria and was the birthplace of Charles II, James II, Mary II, Queen Anne and George IV. Charles I spent his last night in its guardroom before going to the scaffold in Whitehall. All that remains of the original structure is a fine Tudor gatehouse, in front of which the Brigade of Guards parade each day. The Chapel Royal has been much altered over the centuries, but it has the original Holbein ceiling; William III, Mary II, Queen Anne, George IV, Victoria and George V were married there, and it is the setting for the annual Royal Epiphany Gifts Service.
The Chapel is open to the public for services from October to Palm Sunday, though the Palace itself is not, being occupied by various Court officials.

London's Pageantry

Pageantry and ceremonial are colourful parts of London life, observed not only in the panoply of state and civic occasions but also in the meticulous observance of minor rituals so old that their origins have in some cases become obscured by time.

ROYAL CEREMONIES

THE STATE OPENING OF PARLIAMENT (*Late October or early November*) After the summer recess, the new session of Parliament is opened by a speech from the monarch. The Monarch, accompanied by other members of the royal family, rides from Buckingham Palace in the Irish State Coach, a gun salute heralding their arrival at Westminster. After changing into royal robes and crown in the Robing Room, the Monarch is escorted to the Upper Chamber, where the Lords in their ceremonial robes are already assembled. The official known as Black Rod summons the Speaker and Members of the House of Commons, having first knocked three times on the door with his staff, and the Monarch then outlines the proposed government legislation for the coming session.

TROOPING THE COLOUR (*Second Saturday in June*) This ceremony takes place on Horse Guards Parade on the occasion of the sovereign's official birthday. Wearing the uniform of one of the regiments of which he or she is Colonel-in-Chief, the sovereign rides out from Buckingham Palace and takes the salute of the Brigade of Guards and the Household Cavalry. This is followed by a display of marching and the 'trooping' (display) of the 'colour' (or flag) of one of the five regiments of foot guards.

THE DISTRIBUTION OF THE ROYAL MAUNDY MONEY (*March*) Each Maundy Thursday the sovereign personally distributes alms (now purses of money, representing the original gifts of food and clothing) and, since the reign of Charles II, a purse of specially minted Maundy money, to old folk chosen from various parts of London.

CHANGING THE GUARD *at Buckingham Palace. This daily ceremony is one of London's best-loved tourist attractions.*

DAILY CEREMONIES

THE CEREMONY OF THE KEYS (*10 pm*) Each evening the gates of the Tower of London are locked by the Chief Warder of the Yeoman Warders who is ceremonially challenged by a sentry as he nears the Bloody Tower. At 10 pm the Last Post is sounded and the Chief Warder hands over his keys to the Resident Governor and Major in the Queen's House. Applications to attend the ceremony can be made at the constable's office in the Tower.

THE CHANGING OF THE GUARD AT BUCKINGHAM PALACE (*11.30 am*) The guard, usually formed from one of the regiments of Foot Guards (the Scots, Irish, Welsh, Coldstream and Grenadier) is changed each morning. A band leads the new guard to the palace and the old one back to its barracks.

THE MOUNTING OF THE GUARD (*11 am weekdays, 10 am Sundays*) The Mounting of the Guard takes place at the Horse Guards, opposite Whitehall. The guard is formed from two units of the Household Cavalry – the Blues (identified by the red plumes on their helmets) and the Life Guards (white plumed).

CIVIC CEREMONIES

ELECTION OF THE LORD MAYOR AND LORD MAYOR'S SHOW A new Lord Mayor of London is elected every year on 29th September, Michaelmas Day. The retiring holder of the office and his aldermen attend a service at St Lawrence Jewry and then process to the Guildhall, where they make the final choice from the candidates put forward by the livery companies; the City bells ring as the old and new Lord Mayors ride to the Mansion House together in the state coach. On 8th November, after attending a luncheon at the Mansion House, together with liverymen of their companies, they go in procession to the Guildhall, where the insignia of office are finally transferred; bells ring in all the City churches as they return to the Mansion House. The new Lord Mayor publicly assumes office on the second Saturday in November, in the 600-year-old ritual of the Lord Mayor's Show. He is flanked by a bodyguard of pikemen and musketeers as he rides to the Royal Courts of Justice in the ceremonial coach, behind a procession of colourful floats depicting some aspect of London's history. The Lord Mayor's Banquet takes place at the Guildhall on the following Monday.

PROCESSIONS In early January the Lord Mayor and his officers lead processions to the opening session of the Central Criminal Court (Old Bailey); to the first sitting of the newly-elected Court of Common Council (January) and the Church of St Lawrence Jewry for the Spital Sermon, preached by a bishop on an Easter theme (second Wednesday after Easter).

OTHER CEREMONIES

JOHN STOW'S QUILL CEREMONY (*Around 5th April*) During the memorial service for John Stow, 16th-century author of *The Survey of London*, at the Church of St Andrew Undershaft, the Lord Mayor places a new quill in the hand of Stow's statue.

ROYAL EPIPHANY GIFTS SERVICE (*6th January*) Officers of the Household offer up gold, frankincense and myrrh – the currency equivalent of the gold then being distributed to old people – at a service in St James's Chapel.

THE LORD MAYOR'S SHOW *is a tradition dating back more than 600 years.*

TROOPING THE COLOUR.

CHARLES I COMMEMORATION CEREMONY (*30th January*) Each year, members of the Society of King Charles the Martyr and the Royal Stuart Society process from St Martin-in-the-Fields to the king's statue in Trafalgar Square to commemorate his execution on that day in 1649.

THE BLESSING OF THE THROATS (*3rd February, St Blaise's Day*) Throat sufferers commemorate St Blaise, who, on his way to a martyr's death, saved a child who was choking on a fishbone, in a service at St Ethelreda's Church in Holborn.

CAKES AND ALE SERMON (*Ash Wednesday*) Members of the Stationers' Company walk to St Paul's Cathedral to hear a sermon preached in accordance with the wishes of John Norton, a member of their Company who died during the reign of James I. Cakes and ale are distributed.

ORANGES AND LEMONS CHILDREN'S SERVICE (*End March*) The children from the local primary school attend a service to commemorate the restoration of the famous bells at St Clement Danes Church in the Strand, and each receives an orange and a lemon.

HOT-CROSS BUNS SERVICE (*Good Friday*) Morning service at St Bartholomew-the-Great, Smithfield ends with the distribution of hot-cross buns and money (provided by an ancient charity) to 21 local widows.

OAK APPLE DAY (*29th May*) Chelsea Pensioners celebrate the escape of the founder of the Royal Hospital, Charles II, after the Battle of Worcester, decorating his statue with oak leaves in memory of the oak tree in which he hid.

CEREMONY OF THE LILIES AND ROSES (*21st May*) Eton College and King's College, Cambridge, join in placing flowers on the spot where Henry VI, their founder, was killed in 1471.

THE KNOLLYS RED ROSE RENT (*24th June*) In the 14th century Sir Robert Knollys was fined for building a footbridge over Seething Lane to join two of his properties. The fine was a nominal one – a red rose to be delivered to the Lord Mayor on Midsummer Day – and payment is still made by the Churchwardens of All Hallows-by-the-Tower, who carry the flower to the Mansion House.

SWAN UPPING (*Around the last Monday in July*) The swans on the Thames between London Bridge and Henley belong to the Monarch and the Companies of Vintners and Dyers. The Monarch's Swan Keeper and the Swan Wardens and Swan Markers of the two Companies inspect the swans and mark the cygnets.

DOGGETT'S COAT AND BADGE RACE (*Late July/early August*) Six Thames watermen row against the tide from London Bridge to Chelsea Bridge, and the winner is presented with a scarlet coat with silver buttons and badge. This is the oldest rowing event in the world, instituted in 1715.

QUIT RENTS CEREMONY (*Late October*) In this, one of the oldest public ceremonies carried out in London, the City Solicitor makes token payment for two properties. The rents, accepted by the Queen's Remembrancer at the Royal Courts of Justice, comprise two faggots of wood, a billhook and a hatchet (for land in Shropshire) and six horseshoes and sixty-one nails (for a forge which once stood in the Strand).

PEARLY KING *at Battersea.*

WEMBLEY *Football fans.*

Calendar of Events

For Royal and Civic Occasions, see 'London's Pageantry'. Precise dates for most events may vary from year to year.

HAMPTON COURT *Henry VIII's astronomical clock.*

JANUARY
International Boat Show
(Earl's Court)

FEBRUARY
Cruft's Dog Show
(Earl's Court)

MARCH
Daily Mail Ideal Home Exhibition
(Earl's Court)
Druid Observance of Spring Equinox
(Tower Hill) around 21st
Harness Horse Parade
(Regent's Park) Easter Monday
Easter Parade
(Battersea) Easter Sunday
Oxford and Cambridge Boat Race
(Putney to Mortlake) end Mar/Apr

APRIL
London Marathon
Milk Cup Football Final
(Wembley Stadium)

MAY
May Day Procession
(Hyde Park) 1st May
Rugby League Cup Final*
(Wembley Stadium)
Summer Exhibition Opens
(Royal Academy)
London to Brighton Walk
(From Westminster Bridge)
FA Cup Final
(Wembley Stadium)
Chelsea Flower Show
(Royal Chelsea Hospital) end May/Jun

JUNE
Cricket Test Matches
(Lord's)
Lawn Tennis Championships
(Wimbledon) end Jun/Jul

JULY
Royal Tournament
(Earl's Court)
AAA Championships
(Crystal Palace)
Royal International Horse Show
(Wembley Arena)
Cricket – Benson & Hedges Cup Final
(Lord's)
First Night of the Proms
(Royal Albert Hall)
Open Air Theatre Season Starts
(Regent's Park)

AUGUST
Greater London Horse Show
(Clapham Common) Bank Holiday
Cricket – Test Matches**
(The Oval)
Outdoor Theatre Season Starts
(Holland Park)
Cricket – NatWest Bank Trophy Final
(Lord's)

SEPTEMBER
Battle of Britain Thanksgiving Service
(Westminster Abbey) around 15th
Druid Observance of Autumn Equinox
(Primrose Hill) around 23rd
Last Night of the Proms
(Royal Albert Hall)

OCTOBER
Costermongers' Harvest Festival
(St Martin's-in-the-Fields) 1st Sunday
Horse of the Year Show
(Wembley Arena)
Trafalgar Day Service and Parade
(Trafalgar Square)

NOVEMBER
RAC London to Brighton Veteran Car Run
(From Hyde Park)
Remembrance Day Service
(Whitehall – the Cenotaph) Sunday nearest 11th

DECEMBER
Smithfield Show
(Earl's Court)
International Show Jumping
(Olympia)
Carol Singing and Lighting of the Christmas Tree
(Trafalgar Square) from 16th
Switching on the Decorations
(Regent's Street)
New Year's Eve Celebrations
(Trafalgar Square)

* Rugby Union: Of matches involving England versus Scotland, Wales, Ireland and France, two take place at Twickenham between January and March in any given year. Matches against other foreign touring teams may also be held.
** Subject to fixtures.

Shops and Markets

Oxford Street, Bond Street, Regent Street and Knightsbridge are the traditional heart of London's shopping area, and many of the long-established department stores are found here. Charing Cross Road has its bookshops; Savile Row its high-class tailors; Soho its delicatessens; Tottenham Court Road its furniture. Street traders flourished before the days of shops, and their 'cries' are an evocative echo of Old London. Cheapside was once the centre of the City's trading ('ceap') being the Saxon word for barter or sale) but today there are markets all over the capital – large central wholesale markets and local 'village' and specialist markets.

BOND STREET Where Oxford Street is famous for department stores Bond Street is traditionally known for jewellers, art dealers and expensive boutiques. Many of the best of the latter have now colonised South Moulton Street, an attractive pedestrian way which leads off Brook Street.

KNIGHTSBRIDGE Harrods, the largest department store in Europe, lords it over the many expensive shops in Knightsbridge. Its magnificent foodhalls are a study in themselves, but every department is worth a visit, for the legend is that Harrods sells everything. For those who are daunted by the sheer size of the place, the streets round about, such as Beauchamp Place and Sloane Street, are full of interesting smaller shops and boutiques.

OUTLINED *in lights, Harrods is a world of luxury.*

OXFORD STREET Selfridges is the doyen of Oxford Street, with John Lewis, C & A, Marks and Spencer and a number of others also competing to attract the millions of shoppers who descend on the West End at weekends and, above all, at sales time.

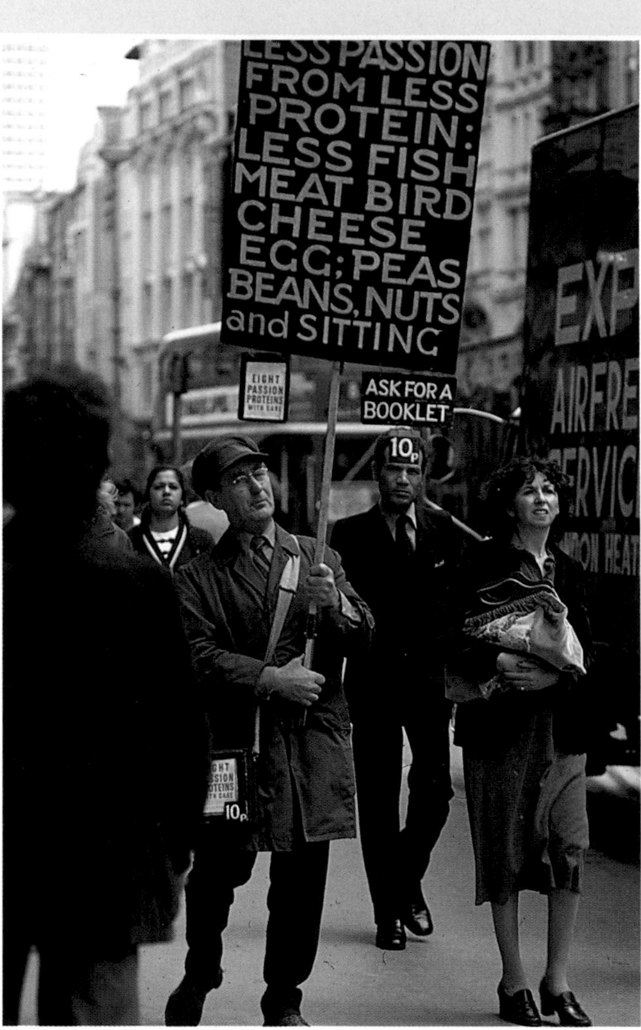

MISSIONARY ZEAL *urges this 'man with a message' to mingle with the Oxford-Street crowds in hopes of converts.*

PICCADILLY Not many shops have held their own against the tourist and airline offices that now dominate Piccadilly, but Fortnum and Mason stands firm, still supplying the finest in food and drink and a select range of fashion, from its original elegant premises. Swaine, Ardeney, Brigg & Sons specialise in riding equipment, leather goods and umbrellas. Richoux sells tempting pastries and confectionery and Hatchards, books. Facing these establishments, Burlington Arcade has many luxuries for sale, as has Jermyn Street, with its famous cheese shop, Paxton and Whitfield. Well-dressed gentlemen might order hand-made shirts in Jermyn Street, or perfume as a gift from J. Floris, established here in 1739, on their way to wile away a peaceful afternoon at one or other of the many exclusive gentlemen's clubs that dominate Pall Mall and St James's. At the west end of Jermyn Street, in St James's Street, it is still possible to have a bowler hat made to measure at James Lock, or to have fine leather shoes made at John Lobb, a few doors away.

REGENT STREET Most of the shops are to be found near Oxford Circus, where easily the most famous are Liberty and Jaeger. Liberty, housed in a distinctive, Tudor-style building, has always been a by-word for its beautiful fabrics. Nearby is Hamley's toyshop, a three-storey wonderland for children.

TOTTENHAM COURT AND CHARING CROSS ROADS High fashion in clothes is not to be found in either of these streets, but the best of modern furniture is displayed at Heal & Son and Habitat in Tottenham Court Road, and the whole range of bookshops, from paperback to antiquarian can be found in Charing Cross Road, where Foyles, occupying two buildings, sells not only these but very nearly all other categories of books. Music and musical instruments are also sold here.

TRADE MARKETS

NEW COVENT GARDEN This famous flower, fruit and vegetable market is now sited at Nine Elms, Battersea, but for hundreds of years it was held in the square in front of St Paul's Church, north of the Strand. It was originally the *Convent* Garden – a walled enclosure used by the monks of Westminster Abbey. After the Dissolution the land was eventually granted to the Earls of Bedford; the fourth Earl obtained permission from Charles I to build on the site, and an Italian-style piazza surrounded by gentlemen's residences was designed by Inigo Jones. Traders were soon attracted by the central square and its covered walks, and the market was well-known by the end of the 17th century. The 19th century saw the erection of special market buildings, and the second half of the 20th century the traffic problems that brought about its removal to the Nine Elms site. The old market has become the lively centre of a revitalised area; craft goods of high quality are sold at many of the stalls in the central market area, and a host of shops and restaurants have opened in the surrounding streets.

BILLINGSGATE Billingsgate Fish Market has also been moved from its original site because of traffic congestion in the City streets. It grew up round a medieval quay just below London Bridge, probably as early as the 9th century, although it did not receive its charter until 400 years later. In 1875 an arcaded building (which still stands) was erected to bring together the sale of all kinds of fish, 'wet, dry and shell', but in 1981 the market was transferred to a new site at the less-busy West India Docks. The name of Billingsgate has long been synonymous with bad language – its tradition of colourful expletive dating back to the original fishwives who squabbled round

SMITHFIELD *(left) is the last of the famous produce markets still operating in its original premises. Covent Garden (right) has turned to new crafts.*

the quay, but ably maintained by today's hard-pressed porter, carrying anything up to a hundredweight of fish balanced on his flat-topped 'bobbing' hat.

BOROUGH MARKET This Southwark market, a direct descendant of one held on old London Bridge, occupies buildings beneath the arches on a viaduct serving London Bridge station.

SMITHFIELD Smithfield, now one of the world's largest meat markets and famous for the quality of its beef, pork and lamb, dealt originally in hay, horses, cattle and sheep; its name recalls the 'smooth field' just outside the city walls to which the animals were driven through the streets of London until the practice was restricted by statute in the middle of the 19th century. At about the same time the market was modernised, when Sir Horace Jones built the Renaissance-style Central Meat Market Arcade, capable of holding up to 400 truckloads of meat at a time.

SPITALFIELDS The name of Spitalfields Market, in the East End, like that of Covent Garden recalls earlier Church ownership of the site: in the 12th century a priory dedicated to St Mary Spital was founded here. The surrounding land was fertile, and by the time of Charles II the volume of local produce for sale was such that he granted a market charter. During the 18th and 19th centuries the area was built up with close-packed houses that subsequently deteriorated into slums, but the market continued to deal in flowers, fruit and vegetables, though no longer locally produced.

OLD STREET CRIES

Street pedlars were, even until the beginning of this century, a familiar and colourful part of London life. The Rabbit Seller (top) and the Orange Girl (above), with her barrow of fine, ripe fruit, are woodcuts from a series by Bewick and his pupils.

STREET MARKETS

BERWICK STREET MARKET, *Berwick St, W1* One of the few survivors of the old Soho, Berwick Street Market (Monday to Saturday) offers excellent value in fruit and vegetables, and there are also shellfish, clothing and household goods stalls.

BRIXTON MARKET, *Electric Avenue, SW9* Brixton (Monday to Saturday) is a general market which reflects colourfully the local community it serves. Because of the largely West Indian population, many stalls are piled with exotic fruit and vegetables, and the compelling rhythms of Caribbean music throb in the background.

CAMDEN PASSAGE MARKET, *Camden Passage, N1* This market which has grown up near the Angel, Islington, is devoted to antiques, curios and bric-à-brac of all kinds. Some of its shops and stalls open all week, but Saturday is the liveliest day.

COLUMBIA ROAD MARKET, *Shoreditch, E2* Well-known to keen gardeners, Columbia Road Market (Sunday mornings) offers a wide variety of flowers, plants and shrubs.

CAMDEN LOCK MARKET, *Camden Lock Place, NW1* Antiques, bric-à-brac, period clothes, and crafts are on sale (weekends) in this lively market which has grown up around Camden Lock in Chalk Farm.

LEADENHALL MARKET, *Gracechurch St, EC3* Specialising in meat and poultry, this City market (Monday to Friday) also offers fish, fruit and vegetables and plants. Its origins go back to the 14th century.

NEW CALEDONIAN MARKET, *Bermondsey Sq, SE1* The New Caledonian is primarily a dealers' market in antiques, though members of the public are not excluded. Much of the serious trading, however, takes place before the official opening time of 7 am on a Friday.

PETTICOAT LANE, *Middlesex St, E1* This is probably the most famous of London's street markets, typically Cockney in character and very popular with tourists. It is actually sited in Middlesex Street but was dubbed Petticoat Lane in the 17th century, when it was the place where the local poor could buy cast-off clothing of their richer neighbours. Today's market (Sunday mornings) still sells clothing of all sorts, but it also deals in most household items.

PORTOBELLO ROAD, *Notting Hill, W11* A general market during the week, with a West Indian flavour, Portobello Road assumes its distinctive character on a Saturday, when a multitude of antique stalls, arcades and shops are opened up. The items offered for sale range from expensive antiques through Victoriana to pure junk. The scene is enlivened by buskers and street entertainers.

PORTOBELLO ROAD *Bric-à-brac stalls line the street.*

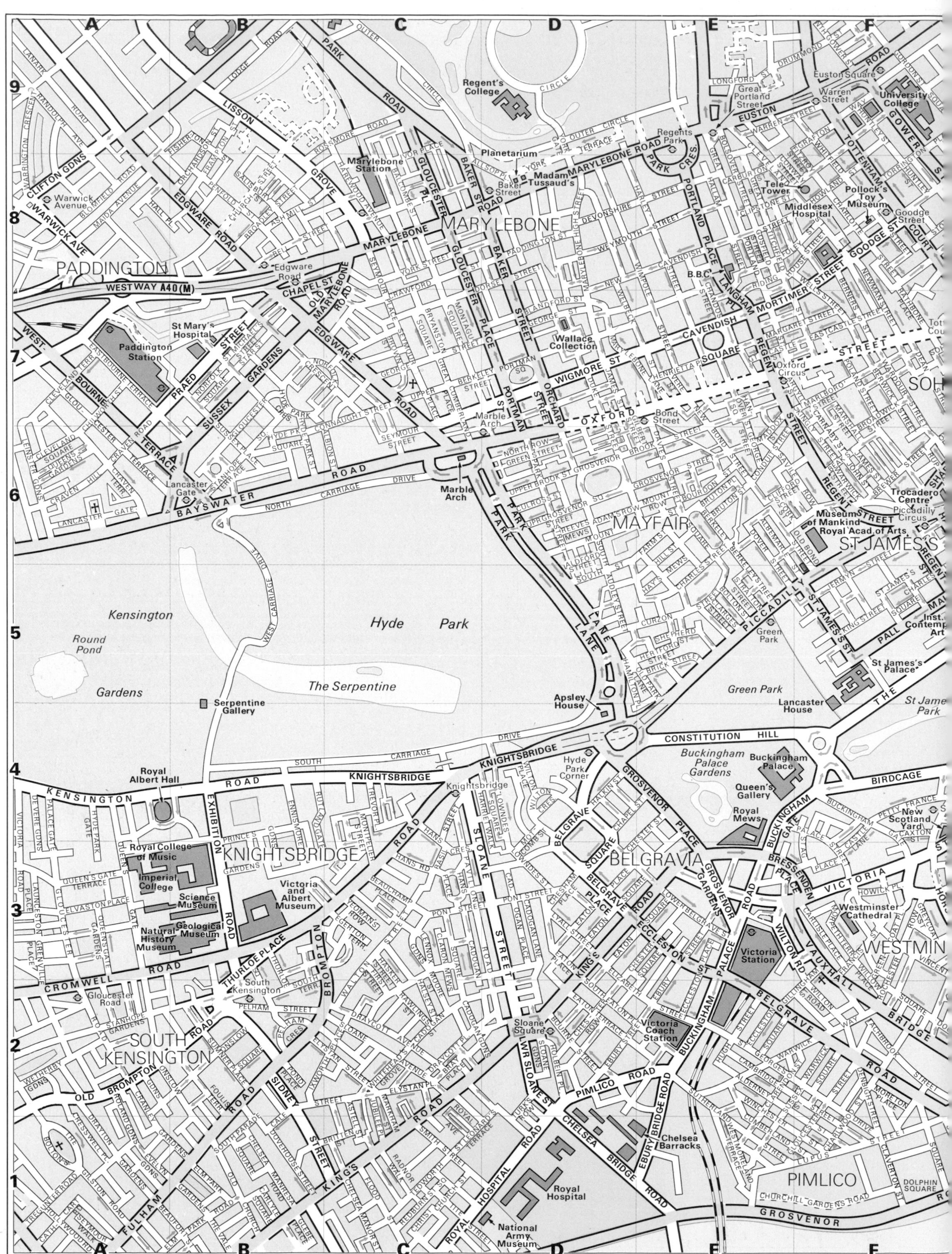

PADDINGTON
MARYLEBONE
MAYFAIR
ST JAMES'S
KNIGHTSBRIDGE
BELGRAVIA
SOUTH KENSINGTON
PIMLICO
Regent's College
Marylebone Station
Planetarium
Madam Tussaud's
Great Portland Street
Warren Street
Euston Square
University College
Regents Park
Telecom Tower
Middlesex Hospital
Pollock's Toy Museum
Goodge Street
Warwick Avenue
Edgware Road
B.B.C.
Paddington Station
St Mary's Hospital
Wallace Collection
Oxford Circus
Bond Street
Marble Arch
Lancaster Gate
Trocadero Centre
Piccadilly Circus
Museum of Mankind
Royal Acad. of Arts
Kensington Gardens
Round Pond
Hyde Park
The Serpentine
Serpentine Gallery
Apsley House
Green Park
St James's Palace
Lancaster House
Inst. Contemp. Arts
St James's Park
Royal Albert Hall
Hyde Park Corner
Buckingham Palace Gardens
Buckingham Palace
Queen's Gallery
Royal Mews
New Scotland Yard
Knightsbridge
Royal College of Music
Imperial College
Science Museum
Natural History Museum
Geological Museum
Victoria and Albert Museum
Victoria Station
Westminster Cathedral
South Kensington
Gloucester Road
Sloane Square
Victoria Coach Station
Chelsea Barracks
Royal Hospital
National Army Museum

THE FOREST AND THE SEA

Here the woods and heaths of the New Forest meet the lovely Solent shore. Ponies and semi-wild cattle graze through oak-fringed glades where kings once hunted, and wander at will wherever there are no grids to bar them entry.

LYMINGTON, Hants
Early wealth came to Lymington from its saltworks, but these were closed in the 19th century and the town now makes a comfortable living as a busy holiday resort, yachting centre, and Isle of Wight ferry terminal. Its wide High Street, lined with 18th- and 19th- century houses, climbs from the waterfront to a church with a huge tower crowned by an exotic cupola of 18th century date.

Follow SP 'Beaulieu B3054', cross the Lymington River, and climb into the New Forest. Cross Beaulieu Heath to the pleasant picnic spot of Hatchet Pond. Turn right, then 1 mile farther turn sharp right again on to the unclassified 'Buckler's Hard' road.

BUCKLER'S HARD, Hants
This small Beaulieu River village thrived for several centuries as a shipbuilding yard. A fascinating little maritime museum recalls those times, and the deep estuary is put to peaceful use by yacht owners. The short village street of 18th-century houses was the creation of the 2nd Duke of Montagu, who planned a town and docks here to receive produce from his own extensive foreign estates.

THE SOLENT, Hants
Much of this tour is in sight of The Solent, a narrow and very busy channel that separates the coast of Hampshire from that of the Isle of Wight. It was formed by the submersion of an ancient river valley whose headstream was the Frome and tributaries the Itchen and Test. Most of the coast on the Hampshire side is designated an area of outstanding natural beauty.

Return along the 'Beaulieu' road and after 2 miles turn right on to the B3054. Enter Beaulieu.

BEAULIEU, Hants
Beaulieu's idyllic position among the woods and hills of South Hampshire is enhanced by the superb ruins of its abbey (open). Largely destroyed at the Dissolution, this important foundation retains a beauty that 'mocks the spoilers still' and preserves its great gatehouse (open) as the home of Lord Montagu. Ruined walls pierced by graceful door and window apertures surround trim lawns that were once the floors of large monastic buildings. Elsewhere in the grounds is the well-known National Motor Museum (open), which features an excellent collection of veteran and vintage cars, cycles, and motorcycles.

Continue through woodlands along the B3054 'Hythe' road for 1 mile, then turn right and immediately right again on to the unclassified 'Lepe' road, passing through woodland, and after 2½ miles enter Exbury.

A beech glade near Knightswood Oak.

EXBURY, Hants
The gardens of Exbury estate are famous for their magnificent rhododendron and azalea displays in late spring (house not open). The village itself stands near the creeks and saltmarshes of the Beaulieu River estuary, in an area of the Solent shore designated as being of outstanding natural beauty.

Turn left into the village and after another 2 miles bear left, with views across The Solent to the Isle of Wight. Continue along the foreshore at Lepe, now part of a country park, then turn inland. After ¾ mile turn right on to the Calshot road. Drive for another 2½ miles, meet a T-junction, and turn right on to the B3053 to enter Calshot.

CALSHOT, Hants
Immediately obvious in this otherwise pleasant little place is the intrusive chimney of its power station. Rather more pleasing to the eye is the low, round tower of Calshot Castle, a coastal fort built by Henry VIII. It occupies a commanding position on a promontory at the end of a long shingle beach. Calshot foreshore is part of a country park.

Return along the B3053 SP 'Southampton' and drive to the edge of Fawley.

Huge timbers from New Forest trees were once left to weather in the wide street at Buckler's Hard before being used to build ships.

SOUTHAMPTON WATER, Hants
Between Calshot and Eling, the route of this tour is never far from the shores of Southampton Water, a maritime highway busy with the traffic of tankers, tugs, liners, ferries and pleasure craft. Southampton port, at its head, has long been one of the most commercially and strategically important harbours in the country. The Crusaders embarked here, the *Mayflower* set sail from the local docks, and Philip II of Spain landed here on his way to marry Mary Tudor in Winchester Cathedral. Today the Water guides great vessels from all over the world into the haven of England's premier cruise passengers port.

FAWLEY, Hants
Esso's petroleum refinery, which dominates Fawley, is an unlovely building but has some claim to fame through sheer size.

Drive to the next roundabout and follow SP 'Hythe' on to an unclassified road. After 1 mile turn right into Frost Lane and descend, over a level crossing, to the shores of Southampton Water. Continue to Hythe.

HYTHE, Hants
Excellent views of Southampton docks and the shore are afforded by the Hythe ferry. Ship-spotting enthusiasts will find the village pier a handy vantage point.

Leave Hythe Pier with SP 'Totton', then after ½ mile meet a T-junction and turn right. Continue for 2 miles, then on the nearside of the next roundabout turn sharp right on to the 'Marchwood' road. Continue through Marchwood and after 2 miles at staggered crossroads turn right on to the 'Eling' road and continue to Eling.

ELING, Hants
Situated on a creek off the head of Southampton Water, this ancient port has a toll-bridge reputed to be the smallest of its kind in Britain and a working tide mill (open).

Cross the toll-bridge and follow SP 'Lyndhurst' to join the A35, and follow to Ashurst.

ASHURST, Hants
The New Forest Butterfly Farm has an extensive display of tropical butterflies in large glasshouses.

THE NEW FOREST, Hants
This district between the River Avon and Southampton Water comprises some 92,000 acres of undulating forest and heathland threaded by small streams and scattered with ponds. Many species of trees thrive in the mixture of clays, peat, and gravels here, affording cover to various species of deer and the famous New Forest ponies. Parts of the forest are nature reserves.

Continue over heathland to Lyndhurst.

Exhibits on display at the Montagu Motor Museum include historic record-breakers.

The boats in Lymington Harbour sprout a forest of masts.

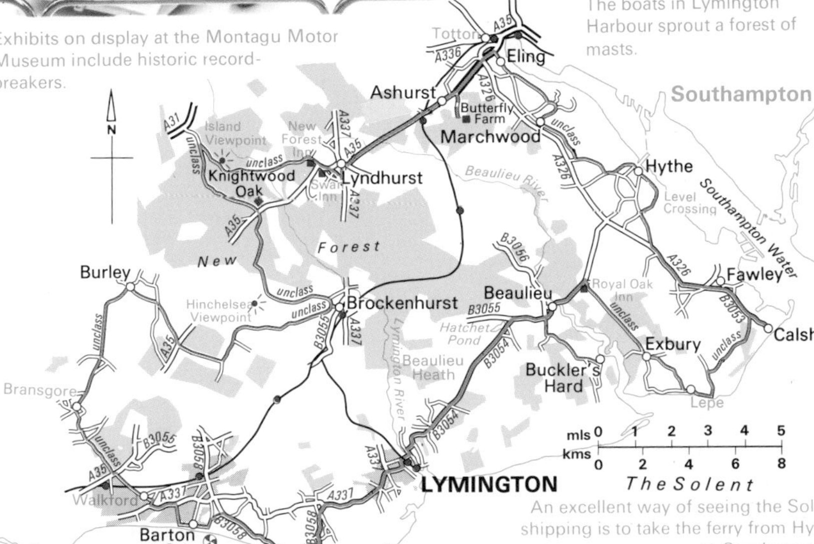

An excellent way of seeing the Solent shipping is to take the ferry from Hythe to Southampton.

The Knightswood Oak stands near Lyndhurst.

LYNDHURST, Hants
Lyndhurst is the capital of the New Forest and an extremely popular tourist centre. Woodlands lap the boundaries of the town, and it is not unusual to meet one of the area's semi-wild ponies or cows ambling through the streets. The Victorian parish church features stained glass by Burne-Jones, William Morris and others, and a large mural by Leighton. Alice Liddel, on whom the heroine of *Alice in Wonderland* was based, is buried here. West of the church is the Queen's House, where the Verderers' Court still sits to administer the forest.

Follow the 'Bournemouth' road to the Swan Inn and turn right on to the unclassified 'Emery Down' road. After $\frac{1}{2}$ mile reach the New Forest Inn and turn left SP 'Bolderwood'. Continue along one of the forest's most attractive byways. After 3 miles pass the Island Viewpoint and a common on the left, then turn sharp left (no SP) to re-enter fine woodlands along the Bolderwood Ornamental Drive. After a further 2 miles reach the Knightswood Oak on the left.

KNIGHTSWOOD OAK, Hants
The huge Knightswood Oak has a girth of more than 21ft and is thought to be 600 years old.

Keep forward from the Knightswood Oak and cross a main road to drive along the Rhinefield Ornamental Drive, bordered by fine conifers and rhododendrons. Cross heathland and pass through the outskirts of Brockenhurst. Turn left across a ford and drive to the town centre.

BROCKENHURST, Hants
Many people find this handsome, lively village an ideal base from which to explore the New Forest. The local church is of Norman origin and claims to be the oldest foundation in the forest. *Domesday* records a church on this site, and the enormous yew in the churchyard may well have been planted over 1,000 years ago. Brusher Mills, a famous New Forest snake-catcher responsible for the demise of over 3,000 adders, is buried here.

Recross the ford and follow SP 'Burley' across wide heathland with picnic areas and good views. Pass Hincheslea Viewpoint on the right and in $4\frac{3}{4}$ miles enter Burley.

BURLEY, Hants
Nearby Castle Hill rises to 300ft and affords good views over this pretty village. An intriguing collection of souvenirs, trophies, and weapons can be seen in the local Queen's Head Inn.

Take the 'Bransgore' road, cross more heathland, and reach the Crown Inn in Bransgore. Turn left here SP 'Lymington' and cross pleasant countryside. After 2 miles turn left and right across a main road, with the Cat and Fiddle Inn on the right. Drive beyond Walkford and turn left on to the A337. After $\frac{3}{4}$ mile turn right on to the unclassified 'Barton on Sea' road. Continue for $\frac{1}{2}$ mile and turn left, then meet a T-junction and turn right to enter Barton on Sea.

BARTON ON SEA, Hants
This resort's low clay cliffs form part of the Barton Beds, a geological series noted for its fossil shell, bone, and shark remains. Good views from the clifftop greensward extend to the chalk stacks of the Needles, and Isle of Wight.

Reach the end of the Promenade and turn left to follow SP 'Milford on Sea' across heaths and commons. Turn right on to the B3058 and drive to Milford on Sea.

MILFORD ON SEA, Hants
A popular resort since Victorian times, Milford on Sea offers good bathing from its sand and shingle beach and excellent views across the Solent to the Isle of Wight. All Saints' Church has a picture by Perugino at the west end of the south aisle. On a promontory about $2\frac{1}{2}$ miles south east is Hurst Castle.

HURST CASTLE, Hants
Built by Henry VIII in 1544, this fort (AM) was later occupied by Cromwell's forces and served as a prison for Charles I in 1648. Restoration work was carried out in 1873, and access today is by foot along a shingle promontory or by boat from Keyhaven.

From Milford on Sea, continue along the B3058 'Lymington' road and turn right on to the A337 before re-entering Lymington.

NORTH OF THE SPIRED CITY

Just a few miles from the city of learning and dreaming spires are the vast victory estate of Blenheim, an ancient Saxon demesne that was the playground of the high aristocracy, and the gentle contours of the Vale of Oxford.

OXFORD, Oxon
This ancient and world renowned university town stands on three main waterways – the River Cherwell, the River Thames (known locally as the Isis), and the Oxford Canal. It is first mentioned in the Saxon Chronicle of 912, but all the indications are that there was a thriving community on the site at least 200 years earlier. Organized teaching has existed at Oxford since the 12th century, and the collegiate system became established in the 13th century as the various religious orders consolidated. Town and gown were often at loggerheads in medieval times, particularly when university privileges conflicted with the interests of local merchants. Charles I established his parliament here, and Oxford served as the Royalist headquarters during that troubled time of civil war. The town's street plan forms an intriguing network centred on Carfax, a junction of four streets and the centre of the old community. Perhaps the most notable of the four is High Street, which is known locally as 'The High'. At the east end is Magdalen, one of the richest colleges in Oxford, and a little closer to Carfax is St Edmund Hall – a unique relic of a residential society founded for graduates in 1220. The High's centrepiece is the University Church of St Mary the Virgin, which is instantly recognizable by its beautiful 14th-century spire. Wren designed the Sheldonian Theatre, at the east end of Broad Street, and the 19th-century bulk of Ashmolean Museum displays a varied array of fascinating and often valuable collections.

From Oxford follow SP 'The East A420'. Pass through Headington.

HEADINGTON, Oxon
Stone for many of the Oxford colleges was worked in the once-famous Headington quarries. The village church dates from the 12th century and incorporates a fine Norman chancel arch. Morris dancing is a long-standing local tradition, and Headington's own troupe of dancers performs annually on Whit Monday.

Continue to a roundabout and take the 2nd exit into unclassified Bayswater Road. After $\frac{3}{4}$ mile turn right, SP 'Stanton St John'. Drive forward to a T-junction and turn right, then left, into Stanton St John.

STANTON ST JOHN, Oxon
John White, the chief founder of Massachusetts in New England, was born here in 1575. Milton's grandfather also lived here. The village has thatched farms, stone cottages, an ancient manor house, and a lovely old church.

Drive to the church, turn left, then follow SP 'Oakley'. Enter that village.

New College, Oxford, was founded by William of Wykeham in 1379. Architect James Wyatt restored the chapel buildings in the 18th century.

OAKLEY, Bucks
Oakley House stands at the south end of the village and is of 17th-century date. Early 13th-century St Mary's Church contains a number of old coffin-lid monuments.

From Oakley approach a main road and turn right on to the B4011. Take the next turning left on to an unclassified road for Brill.

BRILL, Bucks
Isolated Brill is a lovely village which stands at 700ft above the Vale of Aylesbury. Its two greens are fringed with charming cottages and almshouses, and its Tudor manor house radiates the warmth of mellow red brick. Brill windmill (open) dates from 1668 and may be one of the oldest postmills to have survived anywhere in Great Britain.

Proceed to the Sun Hotel, turn left into Windmill Street, and pass the old windmill. Later ascend, then descend to join the B4011 to Blackthorn. After 1 mile turn left on to the A41 for Bicester.

BICESTER, Oxon
The site of Roman Alchester lies a mile to the south of Bicester, and the modern A421 follows the line of an old Roman road close by. No Roman remains have been found at Bicester itself, but the *castra* element in its name suggests that there was once a garrison here. If that was the case then the military tradition continues, for nowadays it is the base for one of the largest army depots in the country. Local roadsides have wide grass verges for the convenience of the many horseriders hereabouts.

Follow SP 'Oxford, A421', then turn right on to the A4095 SP 'Chipping Norton'. Proceed for 1 mile, then go forward on to the B4030 to Middleton Stoney. Cross a main road and continue to the outskirts of Lower Heyford.

LOWER HEYFORD, Oxon
Set on a slope overlooking a wide valley and the River Cherwell, Lower Heyford has a 13th-century church which carries a 15th-century tower and is entered via a 15th-century porch complete with sundial. The font dates from the 17th century.

Cross the Oxford Canal and River Cherwell. (Rousham House is on the left).

ROUSHAM HOUSE, Oxon
Near the River Cherwell is Rousham House, a 17th- and 18th-century building which boasts the only garden layout by William Kent to have survived intact (open).

Continue to the Hopcrofts Holt Hotel, and turn right on to the A423 for Deddington.

DEDDINGTON, Oxon
One of many small towns near the lovely River Cherwell, Deddington is built of honey-coloured local stone and is rich in Civil War associations. Many of these may be 'local colour', but King Charles I is reputed to have slept at 16th-century Castle Farm while in the area. The local church is of 14th-century date and has a very fine north porch. Its tower was rebuilt in 1635 after the first attempt fell down.

Turn left on to the B4031 'Chipping Norton' road and pass through Hempton. After 3 miles keep left and join the A361. After $\frac{1}{2}$ mile turn left on to the B4022 SP 'Enstone'. Continue for 1 mile and turn left again on to an unclassified road for Great Tew.

GREAT TEW, Oxon
Delightful cottages of thatch and stone combine with the old village stocks here to present a truly traditional picture of rural England. A number of interesting monuments can be seen in the church, and the manor house has been rebuilt in its original gardens.

After $\frac{1}{2}$ mile turn right SP 'Little Tew'. Drive to crossroads and turn left to rejoin the B4022. After a further 3 miles drive over staggered crossroads and skirt Enstone. Proceed to Charlbury.

CHARLBURY, Oxon
Set in the Evenlode Valley, Charlbury is a compact little town with many narrow streets containing 18th-century buildings, including shops and inns. Within Wychwood Forest is Cornbury Park, although the Earl of Leicester once resided here when he was a favourite of Elizabeth I, the majority of the building dates from the 17th and 18th centuries. Ditchley Park is a fine 18th-century house by James Gibb, it lies 2½ miles to the north east and is occasionally open in the summer.

Continue along the B4022, crossing the River Evenlode, with Wychwood Forest to the right. Later turn right into Witney.

WITNEY, Oxon
The name 'Witney' is synonymous with blanket making, an industry that has grown from the town's close proximity to rich wool country and the availability of ready power from the River Windrush. *Domesday* records that two mills stood here, and doubtless there were others even before that. The main street extends for almost a mile to a green set with lime trees and graced with fine houses built with the profits of wool and weaving. Prosperity is similarly mirrored in the 17th-century Butter Cross, which stands on 13 stone pillars and displays both a clock tower and a sundial. The old Blanket Hall of 1720 displays a curious one-handed clock. Witney's

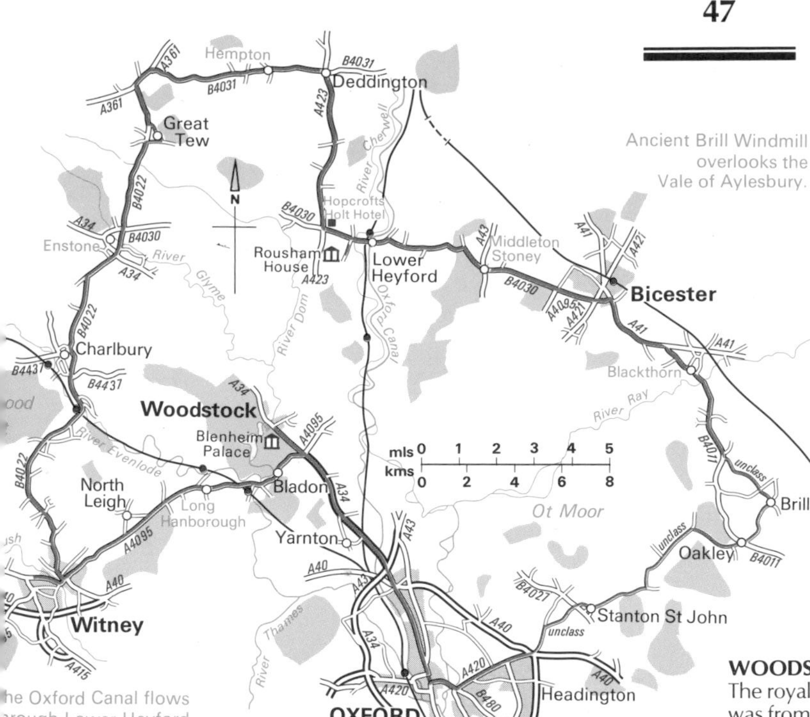

he Oxford Canal flows
ırough Lower Heyford.

hurch carries a 156ft-high spire that erves as a landmark for many miles.

eturn along the A4095 'Bicester' oad to the outskirts of North Leigh.

ORTH LEIGH, Oxon

eatures of North Leigh include a isused windmill and a church with a axon tower. Inside the church is a loom' painting and an unusual ollection of coffin plates. North-east f the village are superb Roman emains (AM) on one of the best villa tes in this country.

ontinue on the A4095 and pass ırough Long Hanborough to Bladon.

LADON, Oxon

ir Winston Churchill, his wife, and oth his parents are buried in Bladon hurchyard. The church itself is a 'ictorian reconstruction of a uilding that had previously ccupied the site for many centuries.

)rive 1 mile farther and approach a oundabout. Turn left on to the A34 or Blenheim Palace and Woodstock.

LENHEIM PALACE, Oxon

ohn Churchill, 1st Duke of Aarlborough, won more than a ictory when he crushed the French t Blenheim in 1704. Queen Anne warded him and his heirs forever e Royal Manor of Woodstock with e Hundred of Wootton, while a no less grateful parliament voted him half a million pounds to pay for the building of Blenheim Palace. The duchess rejected plans for the house drawn up by Wren and chose instead Sir John Vanbrugh's suitably grandiose scheme. The gardens were originally laid out by Henry Wise, and the grounds – later modified by Capability Brown – cover 2,500 acres and include a vast lake, Triumphal Way, and sunken Italian garden. The palace itself is an Eldorado of art treasures and fine furnishings. One-time prime minister and war leader Sir Winston Churchill was born here in 1874.

Ancient Brill Windmill overlooks the Vale of Aylesbury.

WOODSTOCK, Oxon

The royal demesne of Woodstock was from Saxon to Tudor times the site of a great country manor that served as the playground of royalty. Various members of the high aristocracy were born here, some installed their mistresses or hunted here, and several died here. Elizabeth I was imprisoned here by Mary for a while, but the tables were resoundingly turned when the Virgin Queen returned in triumph after her accession to the throne. Woodstock House was, unfortunately, a total casualty of the Civil War and has all but vanished. In the town itself is a grand town hall that was built in 1766 by Sir William Chambers with money donated by the Duke of Marlborough. Tradition has it that the very famous Bear Inn dates back to 1237. There are a great number of very old and attractive stone houses in the streets of Woodstock.

Return along the A34 towards Oxford. After $3\frac{1}{2}$ miles meet an unclassified right turn leading to Yarnton.

YARNTON, Oxon

Yarnton's manor house was built in 1612 and has since been well restored. Above its porch are the Spencer Arms. The local church, which dates from the 13th century, carries a 17th-century tower and contains a fine Jacobean screen.

Continue along the A34 for the return to Oxford.

Blenheim Palace, which covers 3 acres of ground, was built for the Duke of Marlborough between 1705 and 1722.

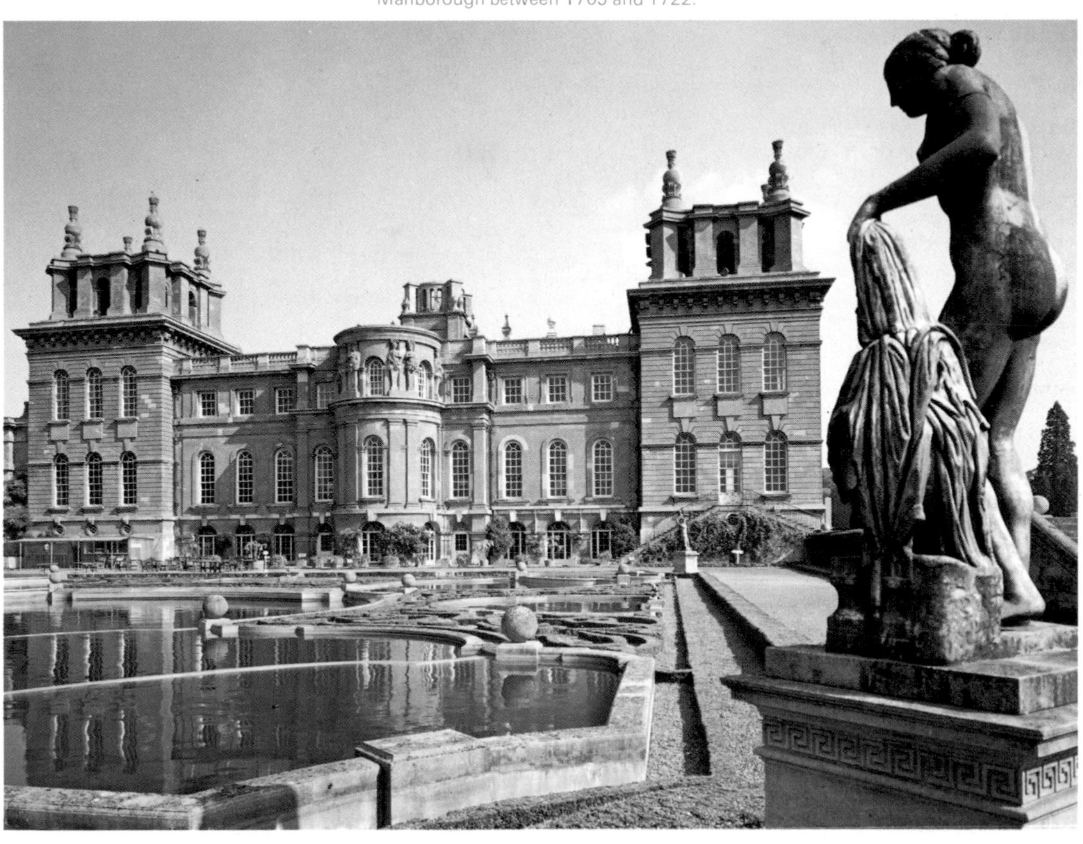

OXFORD AND THE ISIS

Matthew Arnold's city of dreaming spires still enchants the visitor to Oxford, home of the oldest university in Britain. From Oxford, where the Thames is still called the Isis, the river winds its slow way through the broad green water meadows surrounding Abingdon and Dorchester.

OXFORD, Oxon
The splendour of the college architecture lends an unequalled dignity to Oxford's busy streets. Their enclosed courts and well-kept gardens (OACT) are a timeless haven from the pace of daily life outside. University, Merton and Balliol Colleges were all founded in the 13th-century and the oldest is probably Merton (1264). Edmund Hall is the only survivor of the medieval halls that pre-dated the colleges themselves. Most of the significant buildings in the city are connected with the university; The Bodleian Library's collection of rare manuscripts makes it second only in importance to the Vatican Library in Rome; the Ashmolean Museum, the oldest in the country, founded in 1683, contains opulent treasures from the Orient as well as from all the countries of Europe; the circular Sheldonian Theatre, opposite Blackwells, great rambling bookshop in the Broad, was designed in 1664 by Christopher Wren and from its cupola there are panoramic views of the city. The Broad, the Cornmarket and the High are the streets where life goes on. Here, and in the maze of side streets and winding narrow lanes that lead off, are most of the old colleges, the students' pubs, little restaurants, antique and curio shops. Eights Week, when college teams of rowing eights compete against each other in late spring, attracts hundreds of visitors to the lovely Meadows.

Leave on the A420, SP 'The West ' and 'Swindon'. In 1¼ miles turn right, then at the roundabout take the 2nd exit. In ¾ mile branch left, SP 'Eynsham', then turn right on to the B4044. After crossing the picturesque Swinford Bridge (toll) go forward to the outskirts of Eynsham and turn left on to the B4449. In 2 miles turn left to Stanton Harcourt.

STANTON HARCOURT, Oxon
The majestic tombs marking generations of the Harcourt family fill the Norman church which looks down upon medieval fishponds and the lovely 17th-century parsonage. Several thatched cottages grace the village, and there is a 15th-century tower in the grounds of the old manor house (not open). The poet Alexander Pope lived here while completing his translation of Homer's *Iliad* in 1718. Also in the manor grounds is an outstanding example of a medieval kitchen, with an octagonal pyramidal roof.

Morris Dancers celebrating May morning outside the Sheldonian Theatre, Oxford

Continue to the edge of Standlake and turn left, SP 'Kingston Bagpuize'. In ½ mile turn left on to the A415, SP 'Abingdon'. Recross the Thames at Newbridge and continue to Kingston Bagpuize. Here turn left then right. In 2½ miles cross the A338, and in another 2½ miles go forward at the roundabout for the outskirts of Abingdon. Keep forward at the mini-roundabout for a diversion to Abingdon.

ABINGDON, Oxon
A mixture of Georgian houses and buildings dating back to the 13th century characterise this old Thameside town, once the county town of Berkshire, but now within Oxfordshire's boundaries. The 17th-century County Hall, standir on graceful columns, houses the Town Museum specialising in local history, and the Guildhall h a fine 18th-century Council Chamber. Several portraits line its walls, including one by Gainsborough of George III and Queen Charlotte. Down by the river stands the abbey gatehouse and a reconstructed Elizabethan theatre where plays and operas are performed in summer. Of Abingdon's 2 churches, St Helen's is the more beautiful, its elegant spire dominating the town and surrounding water meadows.

The main tour turns right on to the B4017, SP 'Drayton'. At Drayton turn left on to the B4016 for Sutto Courtenay.

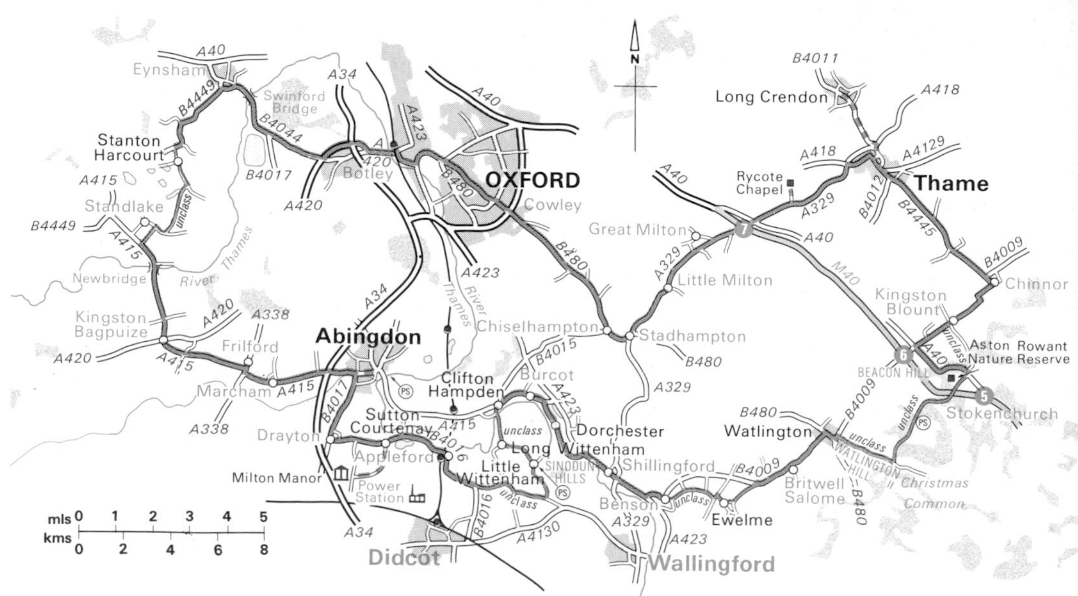

Rycote Chapel, with its fine wagon roof, has not altered since the 15th century

SUTTON COURTENAY, Oxon
One of the loveliest villages on the Thames, Sutton Courtenay's half-timbered houses and cottages are to be found along winding lanes and around a spacious green shaded by scented lime trees. In the churchyard rest the graves of Lord Asquith, who was Prime Minister at the outbreak of World War I, and Eric Blair, better known as George Orwell, author of *Animal Farm* and *1984*.

A diversion can be made to Milton Manor House by turning right in Sutton Courtenay on to an unclassified road.

MILTON MANOR, Berks
The 3-storey central portion of the Manor (OACT) was built during the 17th-century, but the 2 wings were added a century later by the Barret family. The house is remarkable for its elegant Gothic library, designed after the style of Horace Walpole's famous mansion at Strawberry Hill. The library contains a fine collection of English porcelain including Spode, Rockingham and Crown Derby.

Continue through Appleford, then go forward on to the Wallingford road. At the T-junction turn right and at the next T-junction, turn left. In ¾ mile turn left again, SP 'Little Wittenham'. Continue past the Sinodun Hills to Little Wittenham.

LITTLE WITTENHAM, Oxon
The hamlet lies in the shelter of the twin Sinodun Hills, which are crowned by a distinctive group of beech trees known as the Wittenham Clumps. A path through Wittenham Wood leads up to the ancient hill fort that commands the heights and provides superb views, westwards towards the Vale of the White Horse and eastwards to the Chiltern Hills.

In Little Wittenham turn left to reach the edge of Long Wittenham.

LONG WITTENHAM, Oxon
Half-timbered houses, an old inn and a medieval church form the long main street of this pleasant village. The Pendon Museum at the west end has fascinating detailed miniature scenes of rural life in the 1930s. Also part of the museum is the Madder Valley model railway. Built by one man, John Ahern, it pioneered the idea of setting model railways in a scenic landscape. Although Madder Valley is fictitious, many of the buildings along it are based on actual places around the country.

Continue on the Clifton Hampden road alongside the Thames. Cross the river and turn right into Clifton Hampden.

CLIFTON HAMPDEN, Oxon
By the old 6-acre bridge across the River Thames stands the Barley Mow Inn, immortalised by Jerome K. Jerome in *Three Men in a Boat*. On the other side of the river are the timbered, thatched cottages of Clifton Hampden.

In Clifton Hampden turn right on to the A415, SP 'Dorchester'. ½ mile beyond Burcot turn right on to an unclassified road for Dorchester.

DORCHESTER, Oxon
Dorchester's beautiful cobbled High Street contains a pleasing variety of interesting old buildings and the lanes leading off it are equally fascinating. In Samian Way, for example, is Molly Mop's thatched cottage; it was built in 1701 and the flint and brick walls are patterned in stripes and diamonds. The 200ft-long Abbey Church, standing on the site of a Saxon cathedral, is hidden among willow trees on a bend of the River Thame. It is famous for its magnificent sculpture and stained-glass window that traces the ancestry of the Virgin Mary.

In 1 mile turn right on to the A423 for Shillingford. In 1¼ mile turn left on to the B4009, SP 'Watlington', and enter Benson. Bear right through the village with the Ewelme road and in 1½ miles turn left, then right, into Ewelme.

EWELME, Oxon
Almost unchanged since the 15th-century when they were built, the almshouses, the old schoolhouse, and the church, form an exceptional medieval group among the brick and flint cottages of this charming village where watercress grows by the stream that runs parallel to the main street. Alice, Duchess of Suffolk, a granddaughter of the poet Geoffrey Chaucer, was responsible for them, and her imposing alabaster tomb is the most famous feature of the church. The grave of Jerome K. Jerome lies in the churchyard.

In Ewelme turn left on to the Watlington road and in 1 mile turn right on to the B4009. In 2½ miles join the B480 then turn left, SP 'Town Centre', into Watlington.

WATLINGTON, Oxon
Tucked away at the foot of the Chilterns, astride the prehistoric track known as the Icknield Way which stretches from Wiltshire up to The Wash, Watlington's Georgian architecture blends with the stone and half-timbered buildings of earlier centuries. At the centre stands the 17th-century brick market hall.

At the Market House in Watlington turn right (one-way) into Hill Road, and climb Watlington Hill, past the Watlington Mark — a chalk design cut into the hillside. At the top turn left, SP 'Kingston Blount'. After 1½ miles pass a picnic area on the right and in 1 mile cross the M40 and pass (left) the Aston Rowant Nature Reserve.

ASTON ROWANT NATURE RESERVE, Oxon
The whole of the Chiltern Hills, where the slopes and the high chalk ridges are clothed with beech woods, has been designated for preservation as an Area of Outstanding Natural Beauty. Wildlife and plants are specially protected by a number of National Nature Reserves such as Aston Rowant (OACT), which lies on one of the highest ridges of the Chilterns.

Pass the Stokenchurch Wireless Mast before turning left on to the A40 and descending wooded Beacon Hill. At the foot, turn right on to the B4009, SP 'Princes Risborough'. Continue through Kingston Blount and in 1¼ miles turn left to reach the edge of Chinnor and go forward on the B4445 to Thame.

THAME, Oxon
The architectural styles of 5 centuries are well represented at Thame, where the picturesque gabled 15th-century Birdcage Inn could have served as the model for many Christmas card and fairy story illustrations. It stands on the immensely wide High Street, the scene in autumn of the annual fair. The Spread Eagle Inn was mentioned in John Fothergill's book of country inns. *An Innkeeper's Diary*. At the north end of the street stands an old stone house (1570) which used to be Thame Grammar School, its most famous pupil was the Civil War leader John Hampden.

A detour can be made by turning right in the High Street on to the Aylesbury road. After ½ mile, at the roundabout, take the B4011 to Long Crendon.

LONG CRENDON, Bucks
In the thatched cottages of Long Crendon needle-making flourished as a cottage industry until factories took the trade away in the 1830s. A long half-timbered building (NT), the Courthouse, dating from the late 14th-century, stands near the church. Its upper storey contains one long room with an open-beamed roof, which was used as a court house in the reign of Henry V and perhaps also as a wool staple hall during the 14th and 15th centuries.

The main tour turns left in Thame on to the Oxford road. In ¾ mile, at the roundabout, take the A329. In 2 miles an unclassified road on the right leads to Rycote Chapel.

RYCOTE CHAPEL, Oxon
This outstanding example of a medieval chapel was built by the Quartermaine family from Thame and consecrated in 1449. The interior is furnished with beautiful Jacobean pews and medieval benches; the gilded stars on the ceiling were originally cut from rare European playing cards. Elizabeth I and later Charles I both visited the chapel.

Continue on the A329 through Little Milton to Stadhampton and turn right on to the B480, SP 'Oxford'. After 4 miles enter the suburbs of Oxford before crossing the Ring Road for the return to the city centre.

HAMPSHIRE DOWNS AND SUSSEX LANES

West of Petersfield are the rolling chalk downs of Hampshire, bare summits rising from wooded flanks watered by trout streams. East are the great wooded commons, winding lanes, and picturesque villages of Sussex.

PETERSFIELD, Hants
In its early years Petersfield's prosperity was based on the wool trade, but as this began to decline it became an important coaching centre on the busy London to Portsmouth road. Today it is a thriving country town full of fine old houses in evocatively-named streets. A once-gilded equestrian statue of William III guards the central square, where a market is held every Wednesday and Saturday. The extensive waters of Heath Pond lie south east of the town on the B2146.

Leave Petersfield on the A3 'Guildford' road and continue to Durford Heath.

DURFORD HEATH, W Sussex
The 62-acre expanse of Durford Heath (NT) includes 4 acres of Rogate Common with its abundance of wildlife.

Continue along the A3 for ¾ mile. Reach the Jolly Drover Inn and turn right on to an unclassified road SP 'Rogate' to enter Sussex. After ¼ mile turn left on to the Fernhurst road and drive through wooded country to Milland.

MILLAND, W Sussex
Although close to the Portsmouth road, this straggling village preserves an air of remoteness and seclusion. St Luke's Church of 1878 stands in front of the primitive Old Church which it replaced.

Continue beyond Milland for 1½ miles and turn right with SP 'The Old Cottage'. Ascend to Woolbeding and Pound Commons (NT).

WOOLBEDING COMMON, W Sussex
Woolbeding Common, part of a 1,084-acre estate (NT), includes some 400 acres of common heath and woodland open to public access.

Descend past Woolbeding's Saxon church.

Cowdray House was built *c*1500.

WOOLBEDING, W Sussex
Domesday describes Woolbeding as 'a perfect manor containing a church, mill, meadow, and wood.' The mill has gone, but the village is as delightful as that ancient description suggests. All Hallows' Church boasts a good Saxon nave.

Cross the River Rother, meet the A272, and turn left to enter Midhurst.

MIDHURST, W Sussex
This small market town stands on the south bank of the River Rother, at the centre of one of Sussex's most beautiful regions. South lie the downs, and north are the picturesque ruins of Cowdray House (see Easebourne).

Leave Midhurst by the A286 'Guildford' road, cross the river, and turn left through Easebourne.

EASEBOURNE, W Sussex
Formerly more important than Midhurst, immaculate Easebourne is very much an estate village. Among its many well-kept houses are Sycamore Cottage in Easebourne Lane, and The Priory, attached to the south side of St Mary's Church. Tudor Cowdray House (not open) was ruined by fire in 1793.

Leave Easebourne and climb through woodland to the 530ft Henley Common viewpoint. Continue to Fernhurst.

FERNHURST, W Sussex
Almost certainly the last stronghold of the Sussex iron-smelting industry, this large village has settled into attractive rural retirement amid the woods and valleys of the Weald.

Meet crossroads in Fernhurst and turn left on to an unclassified road. Drive through wooded country with SP 'Linchmere', and after 1 mile branch right SP 'Liphook'. Enter Linchmere.

LINCHMERE, W Sussex
Linchmere boasts a tiny green outside the enlarged hill chapel that serves as its church. Magnificent views from here extend over a deep valley flanked by steep slopes.

After Linchmere turn left on to the B2131 to re-enter Hampshire. Enter Liphook.

LIPHOOK, Hants
Most of Liphook straggles untidily along the main Portsmouth road, but here and there it preserves something of a village atmosphere. Bohunt Manor (open) stands in a lovely woodland and water garden.

A detour from the main route can be made here by turning left on to the unclassified 'Midhurst' road and driving for 1½ miles to Hollycombe.

HOLLYCOMBE, W Sussex
The Hollycombe Working Steam Museum and Woodland Garden (open) has a remarkable collection of equipment ranging from old fairground rides to a 2ft-gauge railway through woodland banks of rhododendrons and azaleas. Attractions include traction engine rides and demonstrations of steam ploughing, threshing, and rolling.

At the Royal Anchor Hotel in Liphook (on the main route) at mini roundabouts turn right then sharp left SP 'Greatham' passing Longmoor Camp and Woolmer Forest. Continue to Greatham. In Greatham turn left on to the A325 and follow SP 'Alton'. Reach a church and after another ¼ mile turn right on to the B3006 and drive on to the east Hampshire Downs for Empshott. Continue along the B3006 to Selborne.

SELBORNE & SELBORNE HILL, Hants
It is not just the beauty of its scenery or the architectural distinction of some of its houses that have made this lovely village famous. It is also featured in Gilbert White's classic field study entitled *The Natural History of Selborne*. White, who was born in the Vicarage in 1720, made one of the first and best studies of wildlife inter-action within a defined area. He died in The Wakes, a fine house that now contains a library and the Gilbert White Museum (open). Visitors today can still see the church meadows and high beech hangers where he made many of his observations, and climb the steep Zig-Zag Path to the excellent viewpoint of Selborne Hill (NT).

In 3½ miles turn left on to an unclassified road for Chawton. A short detour can be made from the main route here by keeping forward on the A32 to Alton.

Midhurst's mainly 19th-century church looks over a town that preserves beautiful buildings from many periods of architecture.

The Gilbert White Museum at Selborne.

ALTON, Hants
In years gone by this historic market town grew quietly prosperous on brewing and the manufacture of woollen cloth. Fine Georgian buildings grace the main street, and a Tudor cottage that was once the home of the poet Spenser is in Amery Street. Exhibits in the Curtis Museum include a collection of craft tools and other bygones.

Continue back to the main tour route and enter Chawton.

CHAWTON, Hants
In Chawton is the unassuming 18th-century house where novelist Jane Austen once lived. Now a Jane Austen Museum (open), this was her home from 1809 till her death, and all her later books were written here.

Reach a roundabout at the end of Chawton and take the 2nd exit on to the A31. Climb to 600ft at Four Marks continue on the A31 to roundabout, take 3rd exit and follow into Alresford.

NEW ALRESFORD, Hants
During the medieval period New Alresford grew to be one of the 10 greatest wool towns in the country. Aptly-named Broad Street, considered the finest village street in Hampshire, leads downhill to scattered Old Alresford. At the north-west end of the village is the large and picturesque lake.

A short detour can be made from the main route by turning left into Station Road to visit the Mid Hants Railway.

MID HANTS RAILWAY, Hants
The original Watercress Line, as this railway has come to be known, was threatened with closure in 1973 and initial efforts to keep the whole line open were not successful. In 1975 the Winchester & Alton Railway Company raised enough money to open 3 miles of track between Alresford and Ropley. All associated buildings in the 10 miles to Alton were also acquired.

New Alresford's Broad Street, said to be the finest village street in Hampshire, is lined with attractive Georgian houses and lime trees.

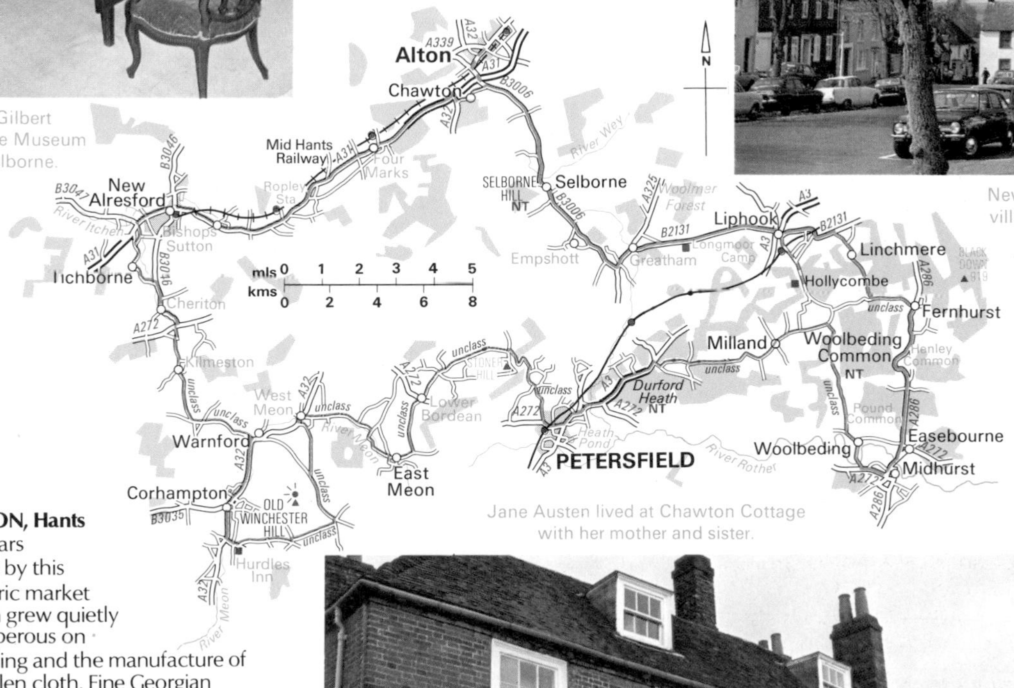

Jane Austen lived at Chawton Cottage with her mother and sister.

Leave Alresford on the Winchester road and after ½ mile meet crossroads. Turn left on to an unclassified road to Tichborne.

TICHBORNE, Hants
Tichborne is a delightful collection of thatched 16th- and 17th-century houses with an unspoilt little church and a 19th-century manor house. Some 800 years ago the ailing lady of the manor, distressed by the poverty of the villagers, begged her husband to help them. Mockingly he agreed to set aside part of his estate to provide corn for the poor in perpetuity, but that would be only so much land as she could crawl round while one torch burned. Tradition has it that she managed to encompass an amazing 23 acres of ground before the flame – and her life – expired. The land concerned still known as The Crawls, and every year the villages receive a dole of 30cwt of flour blessed by the local priest.

Continue for 1 mile past the village, meet a T-junction, and turn right on to the B3046 for Cheriton. Follow SP 'Petersfield' for ½ mile, then cross a main road on to the unclassified 'Droxford' road. Drive through Kilmeston, climb rolling hills, then later turn left on to the 'Warnford' road for a descent to the Meon Valley. Continue to Warnford.

WARNFORD, Hants
This beautiful Meon Valley village has a 12th- to 17th-century church with a massive Norman tower. Ruins of a 13th-century building, misleadingly known as King John's House, is located at Warnford Park.

Meet a T-junction and turn right on to the A32 'Fareham' road. Cross the River Meon and continue into Corhampton.

CORHAMPTON, Hants
This pleasant River Meon village boasts a rare Saxon church with a contemporary sundial. The walls of the ancient nave slant crazily to the south, but the building is quite safe.

After another mile turn left on to the B2150 'Waterlooville' road, then pass the Hurdles Inn and take the next turning left (no SP). Follow SP 'East Meon' over crossroads and after another ½ mile bear left. Cross downland to meet a T-junction and turn left again on to the 'West Meon' road. Continue to the slopes of Old Winchester Hill.

OLD WINCHESTER HILL, Hants
Why this noted beauty spot should be so named is a mystery, for the city of Winchester lies a good 12 miles to the west. The hill's windswept summit rises to nearly 700ft, affording excellent views over half the county, and a 1¾-mile nature trail has been laid out on its flanks.

Branch right on to a narrow road and later turn right on to the A32. Drive into West Meon and turn right on to the unclassified 'East Meon' road. Continue along the attractive Meon Valley to the edge of East Meon.

EAST MEON, Hants
'Father of angling' Izaak Walton once fished here, and the village is still a popular trout centre. The Norman church is arguably the finest of its kind in Hampshire.

Follow SP 'Petersfield' and in ½ mile turn left on to the narrow 'Lower Bordean' road. Later cross the A272 into the very narrow 'Colemore' road and follow SP 'Petersfield' to a T-junction. Turn right, descend the attractive Stoner Hill, and return to Petersfield.

ROYAL NAVAL BASE BENEATH THE SUSSEX DOWNS

Portsmouth, historic seat of the Royal Navy, opens the way to the hidden creeks and harbours of the Hampshire and West Sussex coasts sheltered beneath the magnificent beech hangers that cloak the South Downs.

PORTSMOUTH, Hants
Naval tradition is everywhere in Portsmouth. The docks, founded by Richard the Lionheart at the end of the 12th century, now cover more than 300 acres. Here the most famous ship in British history, HMS *Victory*, Nelson's flagship at the Battle of Trafalgar in 1805, lies peacefully at anchor. It has been restored and fitted out to show what conditions on board ship were like. Nearby, the Royal Navy Museum has a fascinating display of model ships and figureheads, and a huge and impressive panorama representing the Battle of Trafalgar. Also in the dockyard is the Mary Rose, Henry VIII's flagship, which was raised from the seabed after a famous rescue mission. A major exhibition accompanies the restored ship. In old Commercial Road is the birthplace of Charles Dickens, which is now a museum of his life and times (OACT).

From Portsmouth city centre follow SP 'Southsea' to the seafront, then turn left along the Esplanade to Southsea.

SOUTHSEA, Hants
Henry VIII built a castle (OACT) at Southsea in 1539 to defend Portsmouth harbour. Now it houses a naval museum and archaeological exhibits. Southsea is well off for museums: Cumberland House in Easter Parade, has local natural history displays and an aquarium; the Eastney Beam-Engine House is the hub of an industrial archaeology museum and the Royal Marines Museum is to be found in Eastney Barracks.

From Southsea follow South Parade and in ¾ mile turn left into St George's Road. Pass Eastney Barracks (right) and at the roundabout, take the 2nd exit. At the next roundabout, take the A2030, SP 'Out of City'. The tour then runs alongside Langstone Harbour and in 2 miles at the roundabout, take the A27, SP 'Chichester' and continue to Emsworth.

EMSWORTH, Hants
Emsworth, tucked away between 2 of the many small creeks of Chichester Harbour, is an ancient port, famed for its oyster fisheries. Yacht building is the traditional occupation here and yachts jostle in the small, picturesque harbour. On the jetty is a majestic old tide mill.

At Emsworth turn left on to the B2148 Horndean road, pass under a railway bridge then bear left. In 1 mile turn right into Emsworth Common Road and enter Southleigh Forest. Continue to Funtington and join the B2146. In 1 mile turn right, SP 'Bosham', and pass through West Ashling. At the roundabout junction with the A27 a diversion can be made by taking the 2nd exit for Bosham.

The cottages crowded along Bosham's quayside all have steps to their front doors to protect them from the frequent flooding of the harbour at high tide

North Street — typical of Chichester

BOSHAM, W Sussex
The village green leading from the waterfront up to the fine old church, the brick and tile-hung cottages along the strand and the sheltered harbour, all create a scene that appeals to painters and yachtsmen alike. Inhabitants of Bosham claim that it was here, and not at Southampton, that King Cnut unsuccessfully challenged the waves to withdraw. As evidence they point to the tomb that was discovered in the church about 100 years ago and said to belong to Cnut's daughter.

The main tour joins the A27 Chichester road and continues to Fishbourne.

FISHBOURNE, W Sussex
The little Sussex village of Fishbourne is outshone by the splendid Roman palace built here c AD 75. Archaeologists have unearthed a 6-acre site, the largest Roman building yet found in Britain. The north wing, with the famous 'boy on a dolphin' mosaic floor, is open, and parts of the original hypocaust (underground central heating system) and baths can also be seen. Outside, archaeologists have reconstructed the gardens as they might have been in Roman times.

Beyond Fishbourne turn left on to the A259 and follow SP 'City Centre' into Chichester.

CHICHESTER, W Sussex
The county town of West Sussex is a delightful criss-cross of old streets, lined with handsome Georgian houses and shops. The city was founded by the Romans in AD 43, and the old Roman street plan can still be traced in North, South, East and West Streets. These divide the town in 4, meeting at the splendid octagonal market cross built in the 15th century by Bishop Story. The prettiest of the old streets are The Pallants and Little London, where an 18th-century Corn Store has been converted to the City Museum and the museum of the Royal Sussex Regiment. Chichester's great Norman cathedral contains 2 outstanding works of modern art: a dazzling tapestry by John Piper and a painting by Graham Sutherland.

From the Ring Road in Chichester follow SP 'Worthing' to the Chichester Motel Roundabout. Here follow SP 'Goodwood' and in ½ mile, at the T-junction, turn left. Later, on the right, is the entrance to Goodwood Park and House.

GOODWOOD HOUSE, W Sussex
Seat of the Dukes of Richmond and Gordon, Goodwood House (OACT) was built during the late 18th century in Sussex flint. It is a treasuretrove of fine pictures, notably Vandyck's portraits and George Stubbs' paintings of racehorses; furniture; tapestries and Sèvres porcelain. Wooded parkland surrounds the house and high above on the downs is Goodwood Racecourse — once part of the estate. The glorious scenery of the downs provides a superb setting and the views are quite breathtaking.

Climb on to the South Downs to reach Goodwood Racecourse. Here turn left and later pass the entrance, on the left, to the Weald and Downland Open Air Museum just before Singleton village.

THE WEALD AND DOWNLAND OPEN AIR MUSEUM, W Sussex
All types of buildings from southern and south-eastern England have been accumulated at this open-air museum (OACT), the first of its kind to be established in this country. Here you can see, for example, a Wealden farmhouse, a charcoal burner's hut, a forge, a pottery and a smithy — just a few of the many old rural buildings from England's past.

Continue to the A286 and turn right, SP 'Midhurst', into Singleton. Continue through Cocking to Midhurst.

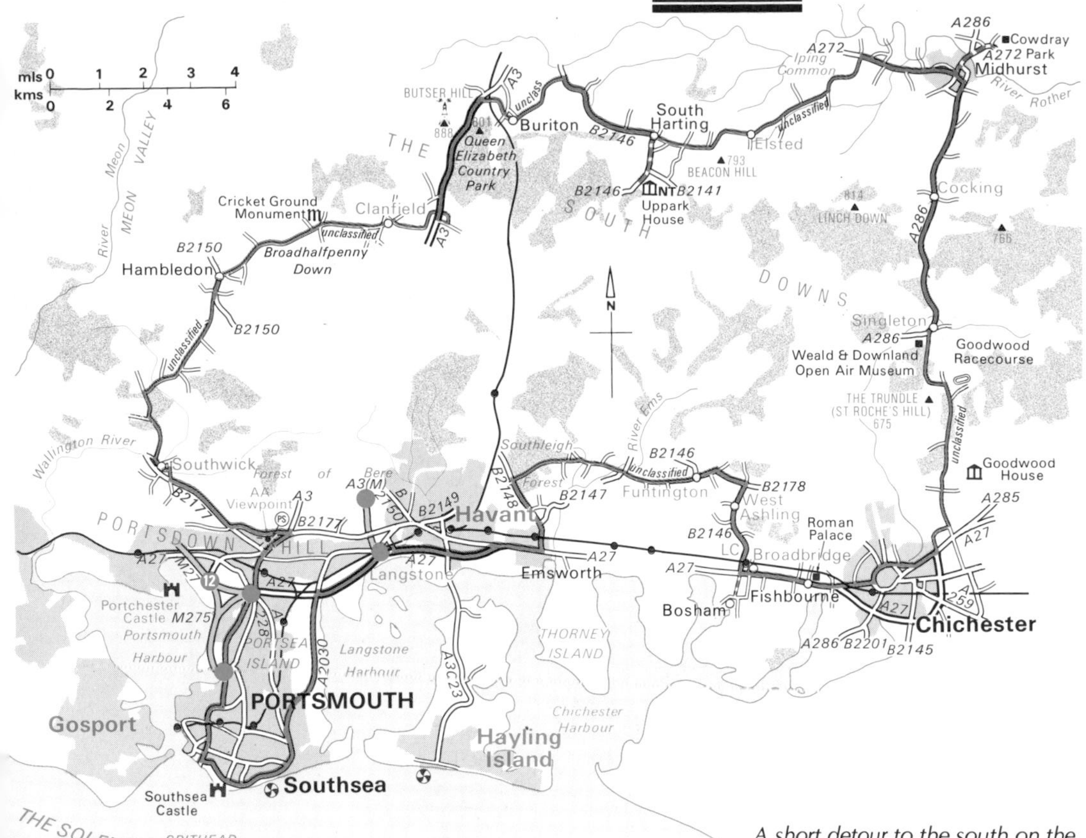

MIDHURST, W Sussex
The little town of Midhurst sits snugly in the Rother valley to the north of the downs. The quaintly named Knockhundred Row leads from North Street to Red Lion Street, where the old timbered market house stands. Of the many picturesque buildings, the half-timbered Spread Eagle Inn, dating back to medieval times, is perhaps the finest. A curfew is still rung in the church every evening at 8 p.m. in memory of a traveller who, lost in the forest long ago, followed the sound of the church bells and so was saved.

To the east of the town is Cowdray Park.

COWDRAY PARK, W Sussex
Viscount Cowdray of Midhurst bought the estate earlier this century and preserved the ruined house (OACT), once the seat of the Earls of Southampton which was destroyed by fire in 1793. The superb parkland forms an appropriate setting for the aristocratic sport of polo which was imported into England from India in the last century.

Leave Midhurst on the A272, SP 'Petersfield'. In 2½ miles turn left SP 'Elsted' and 'Harting'. Cross Iping Common, and continue through Elsted to South Harting.

SOUTH HARTING, W Sussex
The slender church spire rises out of the wooded farmland surrounding this attractive village, whose main street is lined with old houses, some of brick, some tile-hung and some of Sussex clunch — a local soft limestone. It was at Harting Grange (not open) that the 19th-century novelist Anthony Trollope spent the last 2 years of his life.

A short detour to the south on the B2146 Emsworth road leads to Uppark.

UPPARK HOUSE, W Sussex
A magnificent house in a magnificent setting on the downs, Uppark (NT) was the home of Lord Grey, 1st Earl of Tankerville, in about 1690. A later owner, Sir Matthew Fetherstonhaugh (pronounced Fanshawe) furnished it with exquisite furniture and rare carpets. His wife Sarah brought with her a wonderful Queen Anne dolls' house, complete with furniture, glass and silverware. Their extravagant and highly sociable son, Sir Harry, inherited Uppark and brought to the house a beautiful 15-year-old girl, Emma Hart, who later became Lord Nelson's Lady Hamilton. Sir Harry married his 20-year-old dairymaid when he was 70 and left her the entire estate. The young lady spent the rest of her life conserving Uppark and it remained largely unchanged throughout the 19th century. The novelist H. G. Wells spent much of his youth here, for his mother was housekeeper.

From the Ship Inn at South Harting, follow SP 'Petersfield' along the B2146. After 2 miles re-enter Hampshire, then in just over ½ mile turn left for Buriton.

BURITON, Hants
Glorious beech hangers drop down into Buriton, whose traditional green with its duck pond is surrounded by attractive cottages, an old church, a rectory and a stone manor house. The latter was the home of famous historian Edward Gibbon, best remembered for his mammoth work, *The Decline and Fall of the Roman Empire.*

Continue through the village and in about a mile turn left on to the A3, SP 'Portsmouth'. In 2 miles, on the left, is the entrance to the Queen Elizabeth Country Park.

QUEEN ELIZABETH COUNTRY PARK, Hants
The wooded downland south of Buriton was opened by the Forestry Commission in Jubilee Year (1977) as the Queen Elizabeth Country Park (OACT). Marked trails wind through the park and there is a reconstruction of an Iron-Age settlement to be seen, as well as a craft centre displaying items used to farm the hills for the past several hundred years.

In 1 mile turn left SP 'Clanfield' then left again. At the roundabout take the 1st exit. From Clanfield cross Broad Halfpenny Down to Hambledon.

HAMBLEDON, Hants
On Broadhalfpenny Down near Hambledon, opposite the Bat and Ball Inn, stands a monument commemorating the beginning of cricket. The Hambledon Cricket Club were the first, in 1760, to play the game in an organised manner. To the west of the attractive village, on a south-facing slope, lies one of England's few successful vineyards (open by appointment), producing a white wine similar to German hock.

In Hambledon turn left on to the B2150, then in ¾ mile branch right SP 'Fareham'. After 2½ miles, at the T-junction, turn left, SP 'Southwick', at the next T-junction turn left for Southwick. Here follow SP 'Portsmouth' to join the B2177. At the roundabout at the top of Ports Down Hill take the 1st exit, SP 'Havant'. Nearly 1 mile further is an AA Viewpoint. Continue on the B2177, then shortly, turn right, SP 'Portsmouth', to join the A3. Descend to Cosham and return to Portsmouth city centre via the A3, or the M275.

Bayleaf House, built in Kent between 1420 and 1480, was reconstructed at the Weald and Downland Museum in the 1970s

BERKSHIRE'S WOODED VALLEYS AND ROLLING DOWNS

The rhythmic thud of horses hooves breaks the early-morning silence as racehorses at exercise gallop over the springy turf of the Lambourn and Berkshire Downs, high above the sheltered villages of the Kennet and Thames.

READING, Berks
The old town has all but disappeared under the impact of the 20th century, but it is still pleasant to stroll along the pretty riverside walk where the Thames runs between Reading and its quiet suburb of Caversham. In Whiteknights Park, the Museum of English Rural Life contains an interesting collection of agricultural implements and reminders of village life as it used to be. The town museum has remains from the nearby Roman fort of Silchester and the old Norman abbey, founded by Henry I who is buried in the Church of St Laurence. The Abbey Gate still stands in Forbury Street and here, from 1785-7, Jane Austen and her sister Cassandra attended a school that occupied 2 rooms above the gateway. Oscar Wilde wrote the moving *Ballad of Reading Gaol* about his imprisonment here from 1895-7.

Leave Reading on the A4, SP 'Newbury'. In 4¼ miles, at the motorway roundabout, take the 2nd exit, SP 'Theale'. At the next roundabout take the A340, SP 'Pangbourne', then turn left on to an unclassified road for Bradfield.

BRADFIELD, Berks
Set in the wooded valley of the River Pang, Bradfield, largely 18th-century, is best known for its public school, Bradfield College. It was founded in 1850 by Thomas Stevens, the local vicar, whose main concern was to train the pupils as choirboys for his church. The school has an open-air theatre, renowned for its good productions of Greek and other classical plays.

At Bradfield turn left, SP 'Bucklebury'. In 1 mile turn right through Southend Bradfield, then Chapel Row. Cross Bucklebury Common and continue to Upper Bucklebury. At the far end branch right, SP 'Cold Ash', and continue through well-wooded countryside. After 1½ miles pass the outskirts of Cold Ash, then in ¾ mile go over the crossroads and descend to Ashmore Green. Here, branch right into Stoney Lane (no SP) and continue to the suburbs of Newbury. At the T-junction turn right, then turn left on to the B4009 and continue to the edge of Newbury. For the town centre take the 3rd exit at the roundabout.

NEWBURY, Berks
This old market town is nowadays best known for its racecourse where major steeplechase and hurdling events are held in the winter season. In the past, the town was noted for its weaving industry and its most famous resident was Jack of Newbury, John Smalwoode, who started life in the Tudor period as a penniless apprentice and became an immensely wealthy clothier. In 1513 he led 100 men to fight at the Battle of Flodden, and was important enough to act as host to Henry VIII. He paid for the building of the beautiful Tudor church of St Nicholas, where a brass (1519) commemorates him. The remains of his house can be seen in Northbrook Street, and the 17th-century timbered cloth hall now houses the town museum.

Count Gleichen's statue of King Alfred, a tribute to a great warrior who united Saxon England, stands in Wantage market

At Newbury the main tour joins the bypass, SP 'Hungerford A4'. At the next roundabout take the B4494, SP 'Wantage', and in nearly ¾ mile pass on the left the turning to Donnington Castle.

DONNINGTON CASTLE, Berks
The gatehouse and the massive round towers of the gateway of Donnington Castle (AM) stand as a reminder of the 2 Civil War battles of Newbury. The Royalist leader Sir John Boys beat off 2 attacks in 1643 after the first battle, even though his castle was pounded almost to rubble by cannon shot. Again in 1644, after the second battle, Donnington played its part by defending the king's retreat to Oxford, but the castle gradually fell into picturesque ruin.

Continue on the B4494 and in ¼ mile bear left (still SP 'Wantage'), then gradually climb over the well-wooded Snelsmore Common — now a country park. In 1 mile, before the motorway bridge, turn left on to an unclassified road for Winterbourne. At the far end of the village turn right, SP 'Boxford', and later descend into the Lambourn valley to Boxford.

BOXFORD, Berks
Old, weathered cottages and a lovely gabled watermill standing on a clear, bubbling stream make an idyllic rural picture in this charming Berkshire village set in the Lambourn valley.

Boxford watermill on the River Lambourne

Turn left and cross the river bridge, then keep left. At the main road turn right by the Bell Inn, SP 'Easton' and 'Welford', and continue to Great Shefford. Here, join the A338, then keep forward on to the unclassified Lambourn road and later skirt East Garston.

EAST GARSTON, Berks
Under the shelter of the Berkshire Downs nestle a medley of old brick and timber cottages, some thatched, some tiled. On the street that leads up to the church is an appealing group of black and white cottages, each with its own little bridge across the river.

Continue along the valley, through Eastbury for Lambourn.

LAMBOURN, Berks
Horses could be said to outnumber people in Lambourn, where almost every house has its own block of stables, and on the springy turf of Lambourn Down strings of highly bred racehorses can be seen at exercise against an exhilarating backdrop of open countryside. The village itself, in its downland setting, makes an attractive sight, especially around the medieval church where there are old almshouses and an ancient village cross.

At the crossroads turn right on to the B4001, SP 'Wantage', and cross the Lambourn Downs. After 6 miles, at the crossroads, turn right on to the B4507 for Wantage.

WANTAGE, Berks
The statue of King Alfred in the market place at Wantage commemorates the fact that this pleasant old town in the Vale of the White Horse was his birthplace in 849. No Saxon relics survive, but the town contains a number of attractive Georgian buildings.

Follow SP 'Newbury B4494' and climb on to the Berkshire Downs. After 4 miles turn left on to an unclassified road for Farnborough. Continue across the downs to West Ilsley and then East Ilsley.

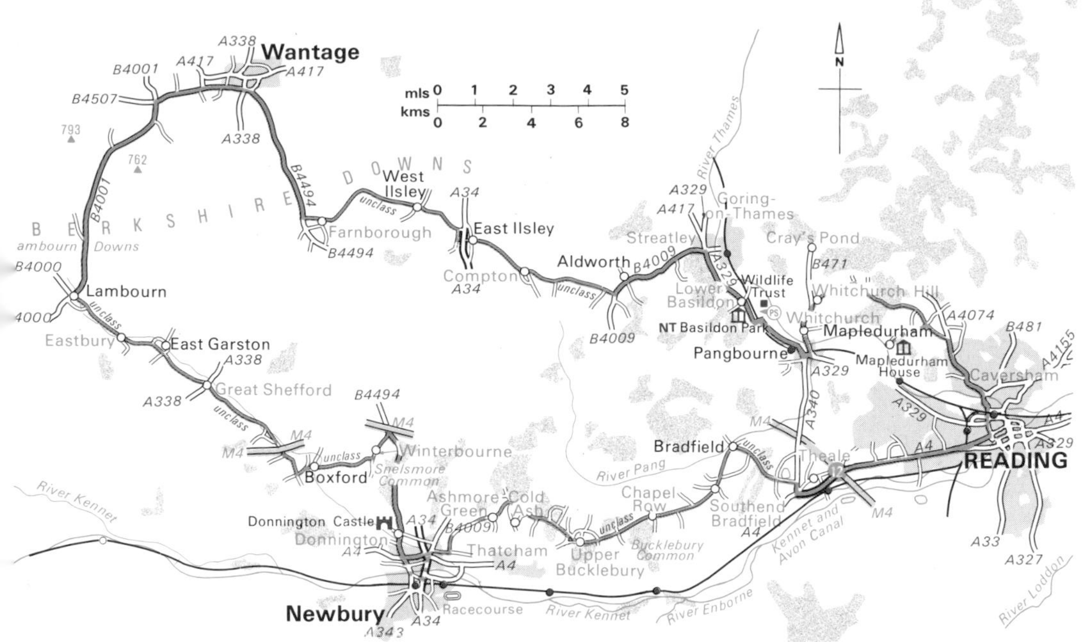

WEST AND EAST ILSLEY, Berks

At these twin villages the traveller stands in the heart of the Berkshire Downs, amid a seemingly endless panorama of superb country. East Ilsley seems to exist solely for the training of horses. There are stables everywhere and fenced-off rides cover the surrounding hills.

At East Ilsley bear left for Compton. Continue on the Pangbourne road then in 2¼ miles turn left on to the B4009, SP 'Streatley', and skirt the village of Aldworth.

ALDWORTH, Berks

The 9 'giants' of Aldworth were all members of the de la Beche family. Three of them are nicknamed John Long, John Strong and John Never-Afraid. A fourth one, John Ever-Afraid, has disappeared, but according to legend he was buried halfway up the church wall to fulfil an oath — he swore that the devil could have his soul if he was buried inside or outside the church. The village well, now disused, has the distinction of being one of the deepest (372ft) in the country.

The tour descends into the Thames valley to reach Streatley. At the traffic signals turn right on to A329, SP 'Reading'. Beyond Lower Basildon pass Basildon Park (right).

BASILDON PARK, Berks

This imposing 18th-century house, built by John Carr of York, was used by troops in both World War I and II but otherwise stood empty from 1910 until Lord and Lady Iliffe bought it. After lovingly restoring the house, they gave it to the National Trust in 1977. The splendid plasterwork inside is attributed to William Roberts of Oxford.

½ mile further, on the left, is the Child Beale Wildlife Trust.

CHILD BEALE WILDLIFE TRUST, Berks

Colourful exotic birds, including ornamental pheasants, peacocks and flamingoes, strut around this unusual garden. A lake, a river and garden statuary provide an attractive setting for walking, and there is a special area for children.

Continue alongside the River Thames to Pangbourne.

PANGBOURNE, Berks

Kenneth Graham, author of *The Wind in the Willows,* lived and died at Pangbourne, and it is easy to imagine his characters Mole and Rat rowing up and down the river here, where the Thames meets the Pang. Above Pangbourne's pleasant houses is the Nautical College, founded in 1917 by Sir Thomas Devitt.

At the mini-roundabout in Pangbourne turn left, then left again on to the B471, SP 'Whitchurch'. Cross the Thames by a toll bridge and enter Whitchurch. After ¾ mile, at Whitchurch Hill, turn right, SP 'Goring Heath'. Nearly 1½ miles farther turn right again, SP 'Reading', then in 2½ miles pass on the right the turning for Mapledurham.

MAPLEDURHAM, Oxon

Wooded hills surround this peaceful little village where pretty cottages, 17th-century almshouses and an old watermill, the last one on the Thames to preserve its wooden machinery, are attractively grouped by the river. Mapledurham House (OACT) is a lovely brick manor house built in the reign of Elizabeth I by Sir Michael Blount, who entertained her here. Two of his descendants, the sisters Mary and Martha Blount, were friends of the 18th-century poet and satirist Alexander Pope, who wrote in a poem addressed to one of them: 'She went from Op'ra, park, assembly, play/To morning walks and pray'rs three hours a day;' John Galsworthy chose the village for the site of Soames Forsyte's country house in the *Forsyte Saga.*

Continue on the Reading road then in ¾ mile turn right on to the A4074 and later descend into Caversham. At the traffic signals turn right and recross the Thames for the return to Reading.

Mapledurham, one of England's largest Elizabethan houses, was the home of the Blount family for 12 generations

EXOTIC ANIMALS IN THE CHILTERNS

Just a stone's throw from Hertfordshire's densely populated towns lie unsuspected areas of wooded countryside hiding Whipsnade's and Woburn's free-roaming wild animals — creatures as much at home here in the Chilterns as in their far-off native lands.

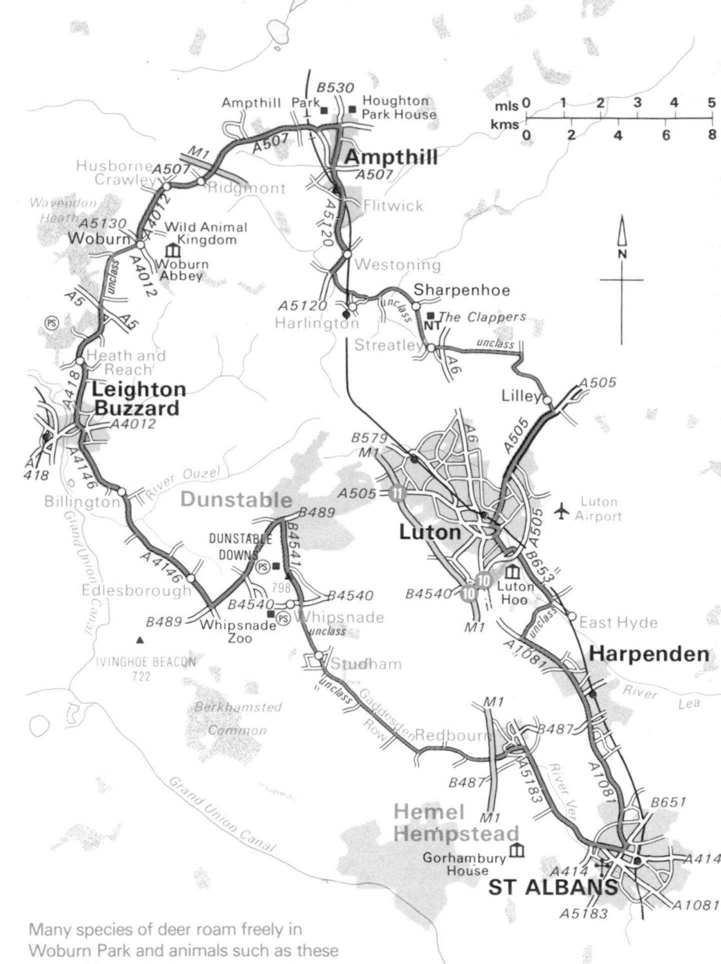

ST ALBANS, Herts

The remains of *Verulamium,* once the most important Roman town in Britain, lie across the River Ver to the west of the present city of St Albans. Here stand the ruins of the great amphitheatre and part of a hypocaust (underground heating system). The Verulamium Museum contains some spectacular mosaic pavements and many other fascinating relics. Modern St Albans takes its name from the first Christian martyr in Britain, Alban, a Roman convert who lived in *Verulamium*. The mighty abbey was founded in 793 on the hill where he is thought to have been killed, and contains his shrine. Made of Purbeck marble, the shrine was lost for years; it was discovered in the last century, shattered into fragments, and restored by Sir Giles Gilbert Scott. The only English Pope to date, Nicholas Breakspear, was a native of St Albans, son of an abbey tenant. He was elected in 1154 and took the name of Adrian IV. Several old streets meander around the town centre where the 15th-century curfew tower rises 77ft high, and there are a number of historic houses to be found. The Old Fighting Cocks Inn claims to be one of Britain's oldest pubs, and on the site of the Fleur de Lys Inn, in French Row, the King of France was held prisoner after the Battle of Poitiers in 1356. Other places of interest are the Kingsbury Watermill Museum, where the 'Handmeade' is preserved — a working watermill of the 16th century; the Organ Museum; the City Museum which houses part of the Salaman Collection of craft implements, and the beautiful gardens of the National Rose Society where more than 1,650 sorts of roses bloom.

Leave St Albans on the A1081, SP 'Harpenden'.

Many species of deer roam freely in Woburn Park and animals such as these pygmy hippos live in spacious enclosures

HARPENDEN, Herts
Harpenden means 'spring or valley of the harpers', and this pleasant small town set in lovely, wooded countryside, is much sought after by London commuters. Its High Street is full of interesting and attractive old houses and shops, and the common, bright with gorse, looks out over the peaceful slopes of the Harpenden valley.

Continue on the Luton road and in 1¾ miles pass the Fox PH, then ¼ mile farther turn right, SP 'New Mill End'. In another 1½ miles turn left on to the B653 SP 'Luton'. Later, to the left, pass Luton Hoo.

LUTON HOO, Beds
The colourful Edwardian diamond magnate Sir Julius Wernher, decided to have Robert Adam's Classical 18th-century stone-built mansion remodelled in 1903 to suit his own extravagant tastes. His fabulous collection of art treasures includes Faberge jewels and Imperial robes worn at the court of the Russian Tsars, paintings by Titian and Rembrandt, rare tapestries and old porcelain (OACT).

Continue into Luton.

LUTON, Beds
Luton is now Bedfordshire's largest town, a thriving centre of light industry and famous for its international airport. In the past, however, it was famed for the making of pillow-lace and the elegant straw-plaited hats worn by ladies to protect their complexions from the sun. Exhibits in the Wardown Museum illustrate the history of these crafts from a bygone era.

Leave on the A505, SP 'Hitchin', and after 3¾ miles pass the Silver Lion PH, then branch left, SP 'Lilley', and turn left into Lilley.

LILLEY, Beds
This quiet little village on the prehistoric track called the Icknield Way was the home of a 19th-century eccentric, John Kellerman. He claimed to be the last descendant of the medieval alchemists and to possess the secret of turning base metal into gold. The family crest of the Salusburys, local landowners, is carved on many of the cottages.

Continue on the unclassified road and in nearly 2 miles turn left, SP 'Streatley'. In another 2 miles cross the main road for Streatley. Here, turn right and continue to Sharpenhoe.

SHARPENHOE, Beds
A footpath winds from Sharpenhoe, a tiny village nestling at the foot of a steep hill, to a lovely area of high woodland known as the Clappers (NT). The views from the top explain why John Bunyan chose this for the 'Delectable Mountain' of *Pilgrim's Progress.*

Capability Brown landscaped the formal gardens of Luton Hoo which houses the splendid Wernher art collection

Turn left, SP 'Harlington', and in 1¾ miles turn on to the Westoning road and skirt the village of Harlington. After another 1¼ miles turn right on to the A5120, SP 'Ampthill', and continue through Westoning to Flitwick. Here, cross the railway bridge and turn left to reach Ampthill.

AMPTHILL, Beds
Sheltered by low hills, Ampthill presents a charming mixture of thatched cottages, Georgian houses, old coaching inns and a parish church set in a pretty square. Ampthill Park (house not open), is famous for the ancient oak trees in its grounds. Catherine of Aragon, first wife of Henry VIII, was dismissed to Ampthill when the king decided to divorce her.

A short detour can be made to visit the ruins of Houghton Park House, 1 mile north of the town.

HOUGHTON PARK HOUSE, Beds
The 17th-century mansion (AM) that was once the home of the Countess of Pembroke, sister of Sir Philip Sidney, fell into ruins nearly 200 years ago. This is thought to have been the 'House Beautiful' of *Pilgrim's Progress*, the book that John Bunyan wrote while a prisoner in Bedford gaol. The hill on which the gaol stands is thus his 'Hill of Difficulty'.

At Ampthill the main tour turns left on to the B530 SP 'Woburn'. In ¾ mile turn right on to the A507. Pass through Ridgmont and at Husborne Crawley join the A4012. In 1¾ miles turn left for Woburn

WOBURN, Beds
The village of Woburn has a number of attractive buildings dating from the post-coach era, and is filled with antique shops and boutiques catering for the thousands of visitors drawn to Woburn Abbey (OACT), seat of the Dukes of Bedford. This most flamboyant of all Britain's stately homes is famous for its Wild Animal Kingdom. Herds of rare species of deer and numerous other exotic animals are housed in the beautiful 3,000-acre park and there are many other attractions, to suit the whole family. The abbey itself is a spacious 18th-century mansion designed by Henry Holland and contains a notable collection of paintings by Canaletto, Velasquez, Gainsborough and Van Dyck.

At Woburn turn right, SP 'Leighton Buzzard'. In 2 miles turn left and then right on to the A418 and continue through Heath and Reach to reach Leighton Buzzard.

LEIGHTON BUZZARD, Beds
A graceful 5-sided market cross with 2 tiers of arches holding carved figures, erected in 1400, stands at the centre of the market town. One of the attractive old buildings nearby, the Wilkes Almhouses, is the scene of a curious ceremony which takes place annually in May: while portions of the founder's will are read aloud, a choirboy stands on his head. As Leighton Buzzard has now been joined to Linslade on the opposite bank of the Ouzel, the town is sometimes called Leighton-Linslade. From Pages Park station, the Leighton Buzzard Light Railway, converted from industrial track, runs through nearly 4 miles of lovely wooded countryside.

Leave on the A4146, SP 'Hemel Hempstead'. Pass through Billington into Buckinghamshire, then continue to Edlesborough. In 1 mile turn left on to the B489, SP 'Dunstable'. Occasional views of the Whipsnade White Lion cut into the hillside can be seen on the right before reaching the outskirts of Dunstable. Here, at the mini-roundabout, turn right on to the B4541, SP 'Whipsnade', and climb on to the Dunstable Downs.

DUNSTABLE DOWNS, Beds
Rising dramatically from the surrounding farmland, Dunstable Downs, a steep scarp of the Chiltern Hills, is an ideal centre for gliding. Part of the downs, an area of woods and common land where many species of wildflowers grow, belongs to the National Trust. Two ancient highways cross the hills: the great Roman road of Watling Street, and the Icknield Way, a much older prehistoric track that may have been named after the tribe of the Iceni, whose queen, Boudicca, was eventually defeated by the Romans. Five Knolls, just outside Dunstable, is a group of round barrows where several Bronze-Age skeletons, knives and weapons have been excavated.

Near the top of the climb pass a picnic area and bear right. In 1¼ miles, at the crossroads, go forward SP 'Studham'. Alternatively, turn right on to the B4540 to visit Whipsnade Zoo.

WHIPSNADE ZOO, Beds
Over 2,000 wild animals roam the large paddocks of the 500-acre park set in the beautiful Chiltern countryside. Lions, tigers, bears and rhinos can be seen in almost natural conditions and there are many rare birds too. A passenger railway drawn by steam locomotives takes visitors through several of the paddocks, including the White Rhino enclosure. Special features include the dolphinarium and the children's zoo and farm.

The main tour continues to Studham. At the clock tower keep forward, SP 'Gaddesden Row', and in ½ mile go over the crossroads then bear left. Pass through Gaddesden Row and at the Plough PH bear left. In 2 miles turn left, SP 'Redbourn'. Later pass under the motorway bridge and turn left for Redbourn. Here turn right and at the roundabout take the 2nd exit on to the A5183, SP 'St Albans'. After 3 miles, near the Pré Hotel, a drive on the right leads to Gorhambury House.

GORHAMBURY HOUSE, Herts
Sir Francis Bacon, the Elizabethan writer and scholar who some believe to have been the real author of Shakespeare's plays, was born here. He rose to be Lord Chancellor of England under James I but was finally disgraced and impeached for embezzlement. His memorial stands in St Michael's Church, St Albans, a life-size marble figure showing the great philosopher alseep in a chair. The Tudor manor where Bacon lived is now partly ruined, but the present 18th-century house (OACT) contains relics of the Bacon family as well as a fine collection of Chippendale furniture.

Continue on the A5183 for the return to St Albans.

By the 1800s Alfriston's Clergy House was being used as labourers' cottages

LEWES AND THE SOUTH DOWNS

Two lovely river valleys cut through the downs on their way to the sea with its high white cliffs. In between, low-lying water meadows and wooded lanes hide dignified manor houses and medieval hamlets with historic Lewes at their heart.

SEAFORD, E Sussex
A flat, exposed stretch of land — once wild and empty but now covered with buildings — separates Seaford from the sea. The port lost its importance as long ago as the 16th century when the River Ouse changed its course after a particularly violent storm and flowed into the sea at Newhaven instead. East of Seaford, high white cliffs of chalk stretch away from Seaford Head to Beachy Head. On the promontory of Seaford Head, beside the clifftop path to Cuckmere Haven, lie remains of an Iron-Age hill fort. During excavations broken flint axes, saws and arrowheads were found buried in 2 small pits; they were probably religious offerings.

From Seaford, follow the A259 Eastbourne road. Cross the Cuckmere River by the Exceat bridge, then in ¼ mile turn left on to the unclassified Litlington road. To the right of the A259 at this junction is the Seven Sisters Country Park.

SEVEN SISTERS COUNTRY PARK, E Sussex
Nearly 700 acres of downland and marshland have been turned into the Seven Sisters Country Park. Nature trails wind through the countryside and fishing is available along the Cuckmere valley. An old barn at Exceat houses the park information centre, and here there are interesting permanent displays of local history and temporary exhibitions.

Continue on the Litlington road and after nearly ½ mile pass the turning for Westdean (right).

WESTDEAN, E Sussex
Westdean village sits peacefully at the end of a No Through Road and seems remote from the hectic 20th century. Its cottages, mostly flint, cluster round a pond, a dovecot (AM) and the ruins of the medieval manor house (AM). Inside the Church of All Saints is a Jacob Epstein bronze bust of Lord Waverley, Home Secretary during World War II. It is possible that the site of this little village may be where Alfred the Great first met Asser, the monk who later became Bishop of Sherborne and wrote an account of the king's life.

Continue on the Litlington road and after another ½ mile, pass Charleston Manor on the right.

CHARLESTON MANOR, E Sussex
Only the grounds of this part-Norman, part-Tudor and part-Georgian manor house are open. However, the romantic gardens, full of bulbs and flowering shrubs contained by yew hedges and flint walls, are exceptionally pretty. Particularly interesting are the huge restored tithe barns, one thatched, the other tiled, and the medieval dovecot with its conical roof and revolving ladder.

Continue through Litlington and after ¾ mile turn left, SP 'Alfriston'. In another ¾ mile, turn left to recross the Cuckmere River. At the next T-junction, turn left for Alfriston.

ALFRISTON, E Sussex
The High Street of this tiny market town runs south from its square. Here stands the old market cross, shaded by the branches of a massive chestnut tree. On either side of the High Street are timbered buildings, some hung with tiles, some with weather-boarding, but virtually all are pre-18th century. Among the finest buildings are the 3 inns: The George, The Market Cross and The Star. The latter is most famous, both for its external carvings and the brightly coloured ship's figurehead which stands outside, and for its associations with smugglers. Alfriston was a well-known hideout for these outlaws in the early 19th century as it was on their route up the Cuckmere valley from the sea 3 miles away. Behind the High Street, overlooking the river and a large green known as the Tye, is Alfriston's church. Named Cathedral of the Downs because of its size, the cruciform church is particularly lovely and has some of the best flintwork in the country. On the edge of the green is the Clergy House (NT). This 14th-century building was, in 1896, the first to be bought by the newly formed National Trust.

Return along the unclassified Dicker road and after 1 mile pass Drusillas Zoo Park on the right.

DRUSILLAS ZOO PARK, E Sussex
Hiding in the heart of the Cuckmere's low-lying water meadows and sleepy villages is Drusillas Zoo Park. Apart from the zoo itself, there are a great variety of different attractions here. These include a butterfly house, a farm, an adventure playground, a bakery selling its own freshly baked bread and a railway to take passengers on a round trip through the park.

On reaching the main road turn left at the roundabout and take the A27, SP 'Lewes'. After 4½ miles a detour to the left may be taken to West Firle.

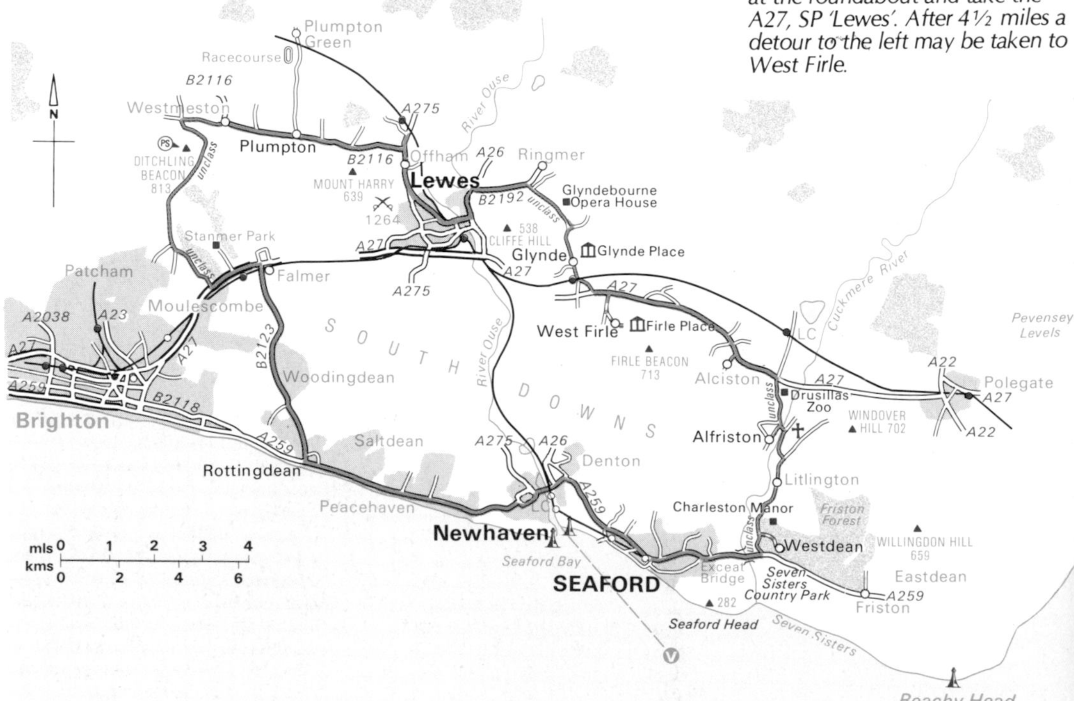

Anne of Cleves House, 16th-century, stands in Southover High Street, Lewes

WEST FIRLE, E Sussex
Such is the feudal atmosphere of West Firle (curiously there is no East Firle) that it still seems to be part of the estate attached to Firle Place (OACT). The village hides on the edge of the parkland and the Gage family crest over the inn confirms its connection with the great house. The Gages have owned Firle Place ever since the 15th century, and the main part of the house dates from that time. No alterations of any consequence were made to it until 1774, when the front was rebuilt to incorporate a gallery for the 1st Viscount's splendid art collection. Half an hour's walk away from the village is Firle Beacon, a magnificent viewpoint with distant views of the sea.

Continue on the A27 and in ½ mile turn right on to an unclassified road for Glynde.

GLYNDE, E Sussex
Like Firle, the small village of Glynde has a great house on its doorstep, Glynde Place (OACT). The present Elizabethan manor was built of flint and Caen stone in 1569, but the impressive stable block was added in the 18th century. The stable buildings surround a delightful courtyard of smooth lawn, roses and climbing plants. Bronzes, needlework and a pottery can be seen at Glynde Place, but one of its most prized possessions is a drawing by Rubens. This was a study for the painted ceiling of the Banqueting House at Whitehall.

At the far end of the village pass Glynde Place, and in ¾ mile bear left, SP 'Ringmer'. After 1 mile pass Glyndebourne Opera House.

Although sheep still graze the chalky slopes of the South Downs, many acres are now being used for arable farming instead

GLYNDEBOURNE, E Sussex
When John Christie, onetime science master at Eton, inherited his ancestral home at Glyndebourne, he decided to indulge his great love of opera and build an opera house in the grounds of his Tudor mansion. Since opening in 1934, Glyndebourne has become internationally famous for its opera festivals performed from May to August. The idyllic setting, the elaborate champagne picnics on the beautiful lawns and the elegance of evening dress, combine to produce a magical atmosphere at Glyndebourne that is unforgettable.

Continue, and on reaching the B2192 turn left, SP 'Lewes'. At the A26 turn left to reach Lewes.

LEWES, E Sussex
With the downs rising up around it and the River Ouse flowing through it, Lewes was an ideal site on which to build a defensive fort and the Normans made full use of it. William de Warenne, husband of William the Conqueror's daughter Gundrada, originally built his castle of wood on 2 artificial mounds. Later a stone keep was built but little except this and the gateway remain, however, because in 1620 the castle was demolished and the stone sold off as building material for 4d a load. The imposing outer gatehouse, called Barbican House, is 14th century and a museum of Sussex archaeology is kept here now. Wide views from the top of the keep encompass Offham Hill. It was there that Henry III unsuccessfully fought Simon de Montfort in 1264 at the Battle of Lewes. East Sussex's charming country town of steep streets, little alleyways and neat, red-roofed Georgian houses covers no more than a square mile. Nearly every building is of interest; Anne of Cleves House — so called because it was one of the properties Henry VIII gave Anne as payment for divorcing him — is open as a folk museum. There is another museum in Regency House and this is devoted to military heritage and includes a short history of the British army. Traditionally, every November 5 the streets throng with torch-lit processions and bonfires blaze in celebration of Guy Fawkes.

Leave the town centre on the A275, SP 'East Grinstead'. Pass through Offham then in almost ½ mile turn left on to the B2116, SP 'Hassocks'. Continue along the foot of the South Downs to Plumpton.

PLUMPTON, E Sussex
A church, a post office, an inn, an old rectory and Plumpton Place make up the old village of Plumpton; the modern village, 2 miles away, is called Plumpton Green and lies handy to Plumpton Racecourse. Plumpton Place (not open) a half-timbered, E-shaped house, was restored by Sir Edwin Lutyens after World War II. Above the village a V-shaped group of fir trees commemorate Queen Victoria's Golden Jubilee.

Continue to Westmeston. Here, turn left on to an unclassified road, SP 'Underhill Lane'. At the next crossroads turn left and climb to the summit of Ditchling Beacon (813 ft) — one of the highest points on the South Downs. 2½ miles later, turn left, SP 'Moulsecombe'. In another 1¼ miles turn left on to the A27 and pass Stanmer Park (the site of the University of Sussex). Branch left then turn right on to the B2123, SP 'Rottingdean', and pass through Woodingdean to reach Rottingdean.

ROTTINGDEAN, E Sussex
Flint and brick cottages brighten up the High Street of this onetime smuggling town which has the salty flavour of the sea. Rudyard Kipling, author of *Jungle Book*, stayed here as a boy with his uncle, the painter Sir Edward Burne-Jones. Some of Burne-Jones' glasswork can be seen in the church, which overlooks a green with a pond — a particularly attractive corner of the town. A Georgian house, remodelled by Sir Edwin Lutyens, contains the library, an art gallery and a museum with some Kipling exhibits and a good toy collection.

At Rottingdean turn left on to the A259, SP 'Newhaven', and continue along the coast road through Saltdean and Peacehaven to Newhaven.

NEWHAVEN, E Sussex
Well-known as a cross-channel departure point to France, Newhaven teems with passengers both coming and going to the Continent. The town was called Meeching until the 1560s, when the Ouse changed its course (see Seaford) and Newhaven seemed more appropriate.

From Newhaven follow SP 'Eastbourne' and remain on the A259 for the return stretch to Seaford.

THE WEALD OF WEST KENT

Since medieval times the wealthy have come to West Kent to build their great houses amongst the woods and weathered rocks of the High Weald. Below is a different world of rich valleys full of twisty lanes, fruit orchards, and the smell of growing hops.

SEVENOAKS, Kent
Tradition has it that this town was named from a clump of 7 oaks that once grew here. The original trees have long gone, but in 1955 new ones were taken from Knole Park and planted on the common. It was Knole Park that brought prosperity to Sevenoaks in the 15th century when Archbishop Bourchier acquired it and rebuilt the manor house (NT) as a palace for archbishops of Canterbury. Nowadays the town is largely residential, with an air of confident ease typical of long-established communities. Cricket has been played on The Vyne wicket since 1734.

Leave Sevenoaks with SP 'Westerham' (A25). After 1 mile turn left on to the A25. There are fine views towards the steep wooded escarpment of the North Downs to the right. Continue into the village of Sundridge.

SUNDRIDGE, Kent
Sundridge's pride is the 15th-century timbered hall-house in its main street. The great hall is several storeys high, and its original stone hearth is still to be seen. The house was restored in 1923. Nearby Ovenden House dates from 1745, and 13th-century Sundridge Church contains a number of good brasses.

Keep forward and enter Brasted.

BRASTED, Kent
In spite of traffic the main village street still retains much of its character. At one point it opens on to a small green fringed by half-timbered houses. Brasted Place, in a fine park adjoining the village, was built by Robert Adam in 1784 and subsequently became the home of Napoleon III. About $1\frac{1}{2}$ miles south of the village is 600-acre Brasted Chart (NT), which offers pleasant walks and drives.

Continue along the A25 to Westerham, passing Quebec House on entering the village.

QUEBEC HOUSE, Kent
On the eastern outskirts of Westerham village is early 17th-century Quebec House (NT), famous as the boyhood home of General Wolfe. Relics of this hero of the Battle of Quebec, who died winning the victory that made Canada British, are preserved inside the house. His statue stands in Westerham High Street.

Continue into Westerham village.

WESTERHAM, Kent
General Wolfe was born in the vicarage here in 1727. He stayed at the George and Dragon in 1758, during what was to prove his last visit to the town. Another famous person with Westerham connexions was Sir Winston Churchill, whose statue stands on the tiny green. Westerham Hill is an 800ft- high viewpoint crossed by the Pilgrims' Way.

Continue on the 'Redhill' road. At the end of the village turn left on to the unclassified road for Squerryes Court.

SQUERRYES COURT, Kent
The Warde family have lived in this 17th-century mansion from the time of General Wolfe to the present day, and it was here in 1741 that Wolfe received his commission. A room is set aside for Wolfe mementos, and other parts of the house feature fine paintings and tapestries.

This statue of General Wolfe stands on the green in Westerham.

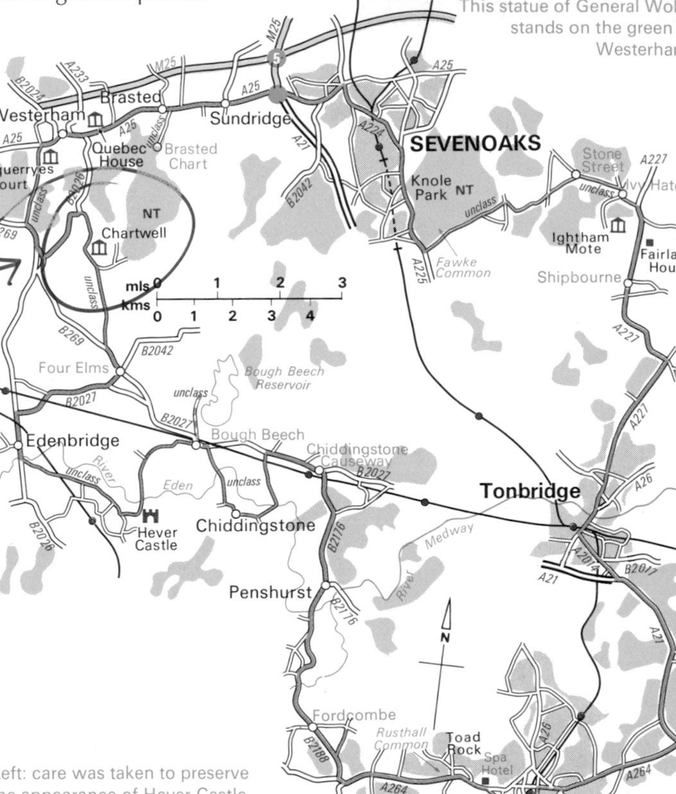

Left: care was taken to preserve the appearance of Hever Castle during restoration. Below: beautiful Italian statuary is a feature of the grounds at Hever Castle.

Ascend through thickly-wooded country and turn left on to the B269 'Edenbridge' road, with fine views across the Weald. In $\frac{3}{4}$ mile turn left on to the B2026 'Westerham' road. Climb on to wooded Crockhamhill Common. After the common turn right on to an unclassified road to Chartwell.

CHARTWELL, Kent
Chartwell will always be associated with Winston Churchill. It was his country home from 1922 until his death, and part of it now houses a Churchill museum. Other rooms are arranged much as they must have been in his lifetime. The Churchilliana on display include photographs illustrating every stage of his life, gifts given to him by other world leaders, and his Nobel Prize. A good many of his paintings are to be seen in the house, and in his studio at the end of the garden.

Beyond Chartwell descend to the Eden Valley and turn left on to the B2269 'Tonbridge' road. At Four Elms turn right on to the B2042 SP 'Edenbridge', and shortly join the B2027. After 1½ miles turn left on to the B2026 into Edenbridge, and drive along the main street.

EDENBRIDGE, Kent
Several old buildings survive in Edenbridge main street, particularly between the 16th-century Crown Hotel and the bridge over the River Eden. The mainly 13th-century church carries a massive tower crowned by a spire of later date.

Cross the River Eden, take the first turning on the left, and proceed along an unclassified road to Hever Castle.

HEVER CASTLE, Kent
In Tudor times 13th-century Hever Castle was the home of the Boleyns, whose daughter Anne married Henry VIII and bore him the future Queen Elizabeth I. The building began life as a fortified farmhouse, but was made into a crenellated mansion at the beginning of the 15th century. The fortunes of the house waned with the fall of the Boleyns, and by the beginning of this century it had once more reverted to use as a farmhouse. It took a wealthy American, William Waldorf Astor, to restore it to its present magnificence. The superb gardens feature Tudor-style flower beds and a 35-acre lake. Both house and gardens are open to the public.

Leave the castle and continue to Bough Beech. A detour can be made from here to Bough Beech Reservoir: turn left on to the B2027, cross a railway bridge, then turn right on to an unclassified road to the reservoir.

BOUGH BEECH RESERVOIR, Kent
This reservoir is the haunt of migrant waders, ducks, wintering divers, grebe and geese. Access is by written permission only.

Leave Bough Beech and join the B2027 for 200 yards, then turn right on to the unclassified 'Chiddingstone' road. Drive to crossroads and turn left for Chiddingstone. Ahead, at the crossroads, is the entrance to Chiddingstone Castle.

CHIDDINGSTONE, Kent
Chiddingstone, a National Trust village, has a beautifully preserved street lined with half-timbered 16th- and 17th-century houses that were probably built with iron-industry money. At the top of the street is 19th-century Chiddingstone Castle. The Chiding Stone, from which the village takes its name, is a large sandstone rock behind the street. Nagging wives were once brought here to be chided by the assembled village population.

After ½ mile (beyond the village) branch left. In 1¾ miles turn right on to the B2027 for Chiddingstone Causeway. Pass the local church and turn right to follow the B2176. Enter Penshurst.

PENSHURST, Kent
At the centre of Penshurst, behind a screen of tall trees, is 14th-century Penshurst Place. The Sidney family and their descendants have lived here for more than 400 years, and Sir Philip Sidney – diplomat, courtier, and poet – was born here in 1554. The family became Earls of Leicester, and the village contains the original Leicester Square.

Leave Penshurst and follow the B2188 'Tunbridge Wells' road through the Medway Valley to Fordcombe.

FORDCOMBE, Kent
This 19th-century picture village of half-timbered and tile-hung cottages is grouped round a pleasant green. It was built at the instigation of Lord Hardinge, whose seat was near by at South Park.

Beyond Fordcombe turn left on to the A264. Cross Rusthall Common and note a left turn leading to Toad Rock.

TOAD ROCK, Kent
Amongst the many eroded sandstone outcrops in the Tunbridge Wells area is Toad Rock, on Rusthall Common, which has been weathered to look like a toad. Other unusual rock formations are to be found at nearby Happy Valley.

In ¼ mile reach the Spa Hotel and turn right on to Major York's road. Proceed to the far side of the common (carpark for the Pantiles) and turn left on to the A26 into Royal Tunbridge Wells.

ROYAL TUNBRIDGE WELLS, Kent
Extensive parks and gardens impart a quiet charm to this elegant Regency town. The 17th-century Church of St Charles the Martyr is the oldest here and Holy Trinity dates from the 19th century. The latter was built by Decimus Burton, who also laid out lovely Calverley Park. Medicinal waters discovered by Lord North in 1606 – the main reason for the foundation of the town – may still be drunk at the Pantiles, an 18th-century raised promenade fringed with lime trees.

Leave the town with SP 'Hastings' to join the A264. Later turn left on to the A21 'Sevenoaks' road. Pass woodland and branch left on to the A2014. Later turn right and enter Tonbridge.

TONBRIDGE, Kent
A settlement has existed here at least since Anglo-Saxon times. The River Medway played an important part in the town's early prosperity, and the later introduction of the railway increased its importance as a centre of communication. Today Tonbridge is a mixture of market town and rail depot built round a ruined Norman to 14th-century castle on a mound.

Cross the River Medway and follow SP 'Gravesend, A227'. Ascend to Shipbourne.

The variety of architectural styles in the houses at Chiddingstone creates a beautiful village landscape.

SHIPBOURNE, Kent
Most of the Victorian village that makes up Shipbourne lies to the west of the green. St Giles' Church was reconstructed in the 1880s.

Beyond the village pass Fairlawne House.

FAIRLAWNE HOUSE, Kent
Situated just ¾ mile north of Shipbourne, this splendid house (unfortunately not open to the public) dates from the 18th century and features a Great Room designed by the architect Gibbs.

Pass Fairlawne House and ascend. At the top of the hill turn left on to an unclassified road SP 'Ivy Hatch'. Take the next turning left and descend a narrow lane to Ightham Mote.

IGHTHAM MOTE, Kent
Medieval Ightham Mote, a small manor house set in lovely meadowland, is considered to be the most complete of its kind in Britain (open at certain times). Its low bulk is encircled by a moat, and its fine wooded grounds feature a tree-fringed lake. Peacocks are kept in the gardens.

Return to Ivy Hatch and keep left on the 'Seal' road. After a short way turn left again and drive to the village of Stone Street. Bear left on the 'Fawke Common, Riverhill' road and continue through heaths and woodland. Later cross Fawke Common, meet a main road and turn right on to the A225. Descend, and reach the entrance to Knole Park on the right.

KNOLE PARK, Kent
In 1456 Thomas Bourchier, then Archbishop of Canterbury, bought an ordinary manor house called Knole Park. He and his successors developed this humble beginning into a great palace, but when Archbishop Warham died in 1532 Henry VIII seized the estate for himself. Elizabeth I granted it to Sir Thomas Sackville in 1566, who died while improvement work on the interior of the house was still in progress. Knole Park (NT) (open) looks much as it must have done then.

Return to Sevenoaks.

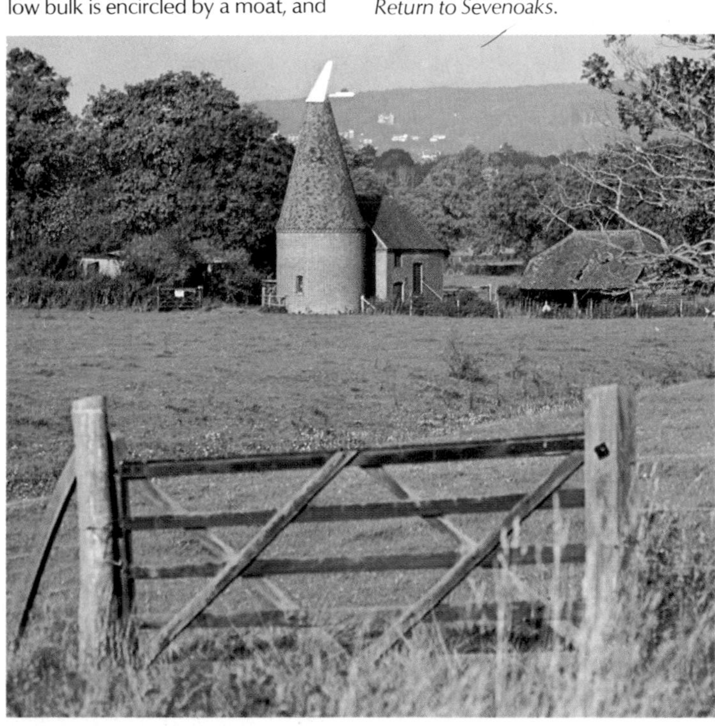

Kent is renowned for oast houses like this one near Bough Beech.

ASHDOWN FOREST AND THE FOREST WEALD

Never far from the quietly civilised villages of East Sussex and the Kent borders are the woods and heathlands of Ashdown Forest — a tame fragment of the vast primeval wilderness that covered much of south-east England in ancient times.

UCKFIELD, E Sussex
Standing on a hillside above the valley of the River Ouse, Uckfield looks towards the great sweep of the downs. Traditional Sussex houses, brick and tile-hung, or weather-boarded, line its attractive main street.

Leave Uckfield on the Eastbourne Road. In 2½ miles cross the A22, SP 'Isfield', and 1¼ miles farther keep left on the Ringmer road to shortly pass the entrance to Bentley Wildfowl Gardens.

BENTLEY WILDFOWL GARDENS, E Sussex
A succession of ponds, surrounded by luxurious belts of trees and bushes, create an ideal habitat for many varieties of interesting wildfowl; spectacular flocks of rose-coloured flamingoes, black swans and ornamental pheasants bring a blaze of exotic colour to the Sussex countryside.

At the T-junction 2 miles later, turn left on to the B2192, SP 'Halland', then in 1½ miles turn right on to an unclassified road for Laughton.

LAUGHTON, E Sussex
Between wooded countryside to the north and the flat marshlands of Glynde Level to the south, stands the little village of Laughton. A curious buckle emblem can be seen on the church tower, on the ruined tower of Laughton Place south of the village, and on several buildings round the area. This was the badge of the Pelhams and dates back to the Battle of Poitiers in 1356, when Sir John Pelham captured the French King and was awarded the Badge of the Buckle of the King's Swordbelt by a grateful Edward III.

Turn left on to the B2124, SP 'Hailsham'. On reaching the A22 turn right then take the next turning left, SP 'Chiddingly'. In ¾ mile turn left again for Chiddingly.

CHIDDINGLY, E Sussex
The tall church spire soars above the cottages of this small, quiet village. From the church, you can see for miles over the downs, and on a clear day it is possible to pick out the chalky outline of the Long Man of Wilmington — a giant figure cut out of the turf above Wilmington. Inside the church is an outsize monument to members of the Jefferay family, with 2 large standing figures in elaborate Elizabethan dress.

Turn left in the village, SP 'Whitesmith', and in 1 mile at the T-junction, turn right, SP 'Waldron'. Continue for 2 miles, then turn right and immediately left on to the Heathfield road. In 1½ miles, at the crossroads, turn left SP 'Blackboys'. On reaching the main road turn left then immediately right, SP 'Buxted'. After 1¾ miles turn left and continue to Buxted.

Weather-boarding, typical of Kentish cottages, like these in Groombridge, was added to give extra protection

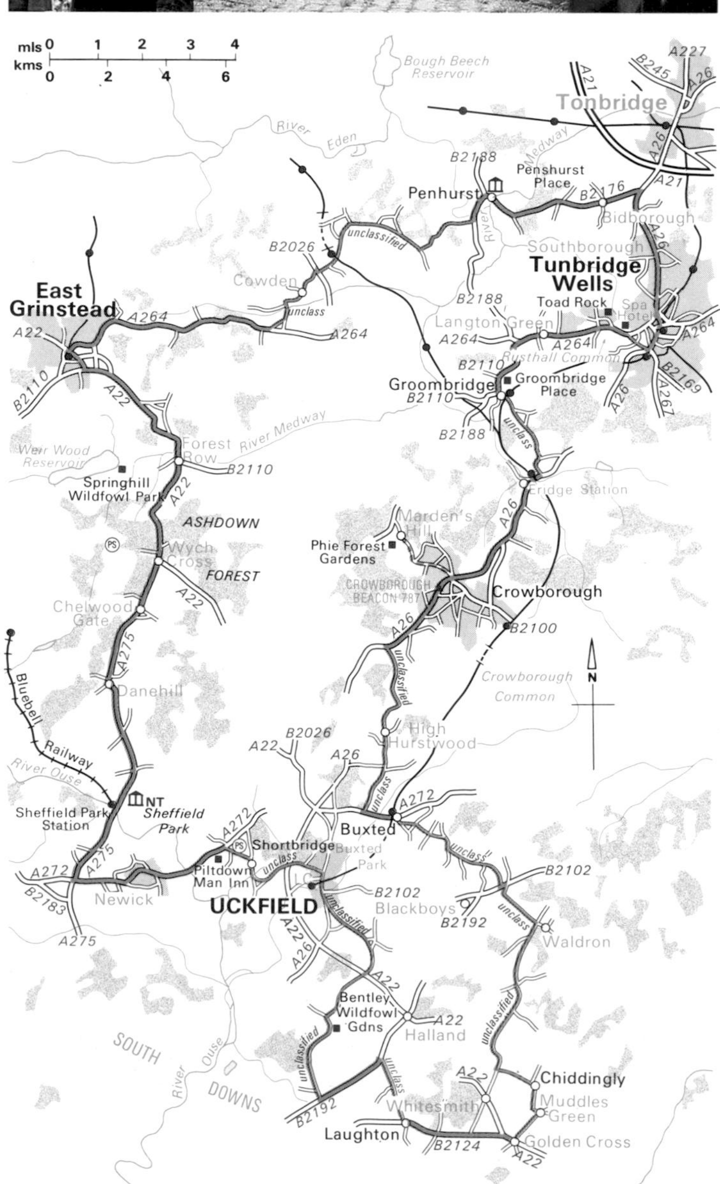

BUXTED, E Sussex
Hogge House, a 16th-century black and white timbered building at the gates of Buxted Park, was the home of Ralph Hogge, a local iron-master, the first man to cast an iron cannon in 1543. The old village that he knew was allowed to fall into ruins during the 19th century because Lord Liverpool, the owner of Buxted Park (not open) wanted to improve the view from his mansion. Consequently Liverpool moved the village to its present site near the station. The parish church still stands in the park. It is dedicated to St Margaret of Scotland and her emblem, the marguerite, is carved around the pulpit and embossed on the ceiling.

At Buxted turn left on to the A272 and skirt the grounds of Buxted Park. After ¾ mile turn right on to an unclassified road and continue to High Hurstwood. Bear left into the village, then ascend to skirt part of the Ashdown Forest. On reaching the A26 turn right, passing over Crowborough Beacon (792ft), and enter Crowborough.

CROWBOROUGH, E Sussex
Crowborough has grown up around a triangular green, and climbs up over the slopes of the 796ft Beacon Hill from where there are superb views. A relatively modern town — its oldest house dates from the 19th century — it owes its charm to its position on the eastern edge of Ashdown Forest. Nearby the Phie Forest Gardens are a favourite place for country walks and picnics.

Remain on the A26 and in 3 miles pass Eridge Station, then immediately turn left on to an unclassified road for Groombridge.

GROOMBRIDGE, E Sussex/Kent
Groombridge spans the county border between East Sussex and Kent. The old part of the village, in Kent, is exceptionally pretty, with 18th-century brick and tile-hung cottages grouped around a triangular green which leads to the gates of Groombridge Place, (not open) a delightful Jacobean moated manor house set in lovely gardens (open by appointment).

In Groombridge turn right on to the B2110, SP 'Tunbridge Wells'. Pass the grounds of Groombridge Park (right), then in 1¼ miles turn right, on to the A264. Continue through Langton Green and after crossing Rusthall Common, a side road on the left may be taken to visit the curious Toad Rock, so called because of its distinctive shape. Continue on the A246 and in ¼ mile at the Spa Hotel, turn right, SP 'Brighton'. On the far side of the common turn left on to the A26 to enter Tunbridge Wells.

'UNBRIDGE WELLS, Kent
his delightful town owes its xistence to Lord North who, in 606, discovered the medicinal prings in what was then a andstone outcrop in the Forest of shdown. Many of its houses date rom the late 17th and 18th enturies, by which time it had ecome a fashionable spa. The amous Pantiles, an elegant olonnaded walk lined with ashionable shops and shaded by rees, takes its name from the arge roofing tiles, 15 of which urvive, laid to appease Queen nne who had protested at the nuddy state of the ground. The own museum contains a ascinating collection of Tunbridge Vare — small boxes and trinkets lecorated with a mosaic of tiny ieces of wood — and Victorian aintings, toys and dolls.

.eave Tunbridge Wells on the A26, P 'Tonbridge' and 'London'. Pass hrough Southborough, then in mile turn left on to the B2176, P 'Penshurst'. Continue through 3idborough to Penshurst.

'ENSHURST, Kent
he pretty village of Penshurst lies etween the Rivers Medway and den. Around the approach to the hurchyard is a charming group of imbered cottages, the central one aised up on pillars to form an rchway. Penshurst Place (OACT) vas the home of the gallant lizabethan soldier-poet Sir Philip idney who, when dying after the 3attle of Zutphen, gave the water offered to him to an enemy oldier, saying: 'Thy necessity is greater than mine'. The manor ouse, set in lovely 17th-century gardens, was originally built in the 15th century by Sir John de Pulteney, 4 times Lord Mayor of ondon, and his magnificent medieval great hall survives. Descendants of Sidney, the de L'Isle family, still live at Penshurst.

Branch left on to the B2188, and in ¾ mile turn right, SP 'Chiddingstone'. After 1½ miles, at the T-junction, turn right, and ¾ mile farther keep left, SP 'Cowden'. In another mile turn left, then in 1½ miles cross the main road to reach Cowden. Go through the village and turn right on to the East Grinstead road. On reaching the A264 turn right for East Grinstead.

EAST GRINSTEAD, W Sussex
The old centre of East Grinstead, originally a small market town, remains unspoilt, and in the main street are many Tudor half-timbered buildings. The most attractive group is Sackville College (OACT): gabled, 17th-century almshouses built around a quiet courtyard with the dignified air of an Oxford college.

Leave on the A22 and continue to Forest Row. Springhill Wildfowl Park lies 1½ miles to the west.

SPRINGHILL WILDFOWL PARK, E Sussex
Rare varieties of ducks and wild geese, flamboyant peacocks, graceful swans, flamingoes and cranes inhabit this 10-acre forest garden that surrounds an attractive 15th-century farmhouse on the borders of Ashdown Forest.

Continue on the Eastbourne road into part of the Ashdown Forest.

ASHDOWN FOREST, E Sussex
Ashdown Forest, lying between the North and South Downs, covers more than 14,000 acres. Extensive though it is, Ashdown is merely a remnant of the vast primeval Forest of Anderida which cut Sussex off from the rest of the country. It remained a wild and dangerous area until Elizabethan times when the great trees were felled to provide fuel for the forges of the Wealden iron industry.

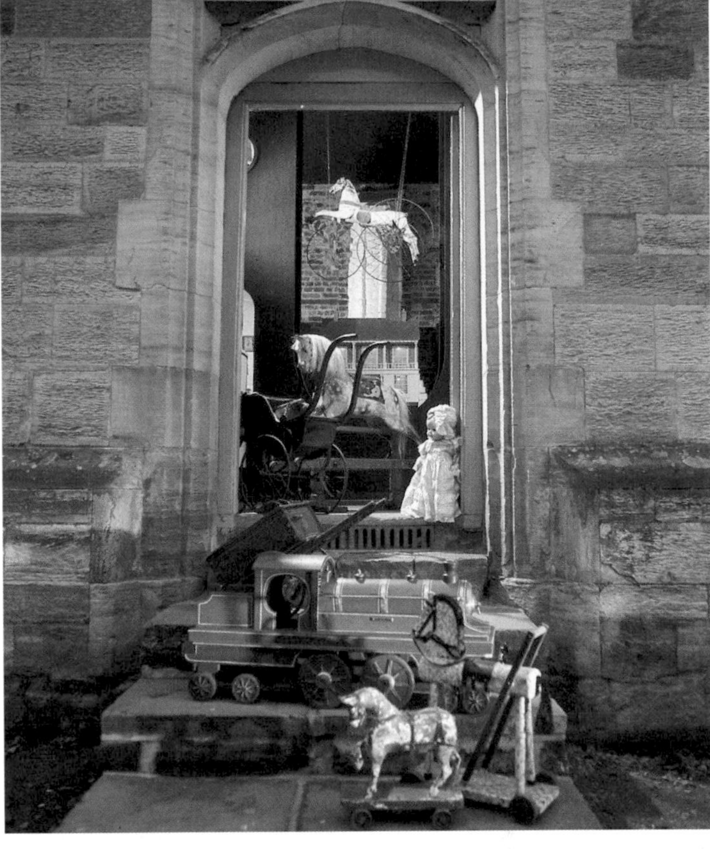

A collection of toys and games can be seen in the stable block of Penshurst Place

At Wych Cross turn right on to the A275, SP 'Lewes'. Continue through Chelwood Gate and Danehill to Sheffield Park.

SHEFFIELD PARK, E Sussex
The gardens (NT) of the elegant 18th-century house (OACT) built by Wyatt for the Earl of Sheffield, are one of the great showplaces of Sussex. The original landscape design, featuring broad, curving lakes was carried out by Capability Brown and his pupil Humphry Repton. Two more lakes were added later, and around the 4 stretches of water A. G. Soames, who bought the property in 1909, created gardens and walks of rhododendrons, azaleas, maples, birches and other trees.

Careful planting at Sheffield Park ensures a blaze of colour all year round

THE BLUEBELL RAILWAY, E Sussex
At Sheffield Park station you can take a step back into the past by travelling on the famous Bluebell line, where vintage steam trains trundle along the old East Grinstead to Lewes track, through 5 miles of glorious Sussex countryside to Horsted Keynes.

Continue on the A275 and 2 miles later turn left on to the A272. Pass through Newick to reach Piltdown.

PILTDOWN, E Sussex
Between Newick and Uckfield stands an inn called the Piltdown Man. Its name and the inn sign which depicts on one side an apelike skull and on the other a club-wielding caveman, commemorate one of the greatest archaeological hoaxes of all time. In 1912 a respectable young lawyer called Charles Dawson caused a sensation by announcing his discovery of the skull of a creature that was joyfully hailed as evidence of the 'missing link' between *homo sapiens* and the great apes. Piltdown Man remained a 'fact' for more than 40 years, until scientific dating techniques established in 1953 that the skull had been cobbled together from the jaw of an orangutan and the deformed cranium of a medieval skeleton.

After passing the Piltdown Man Inn turn right, SP 'Shortbridge'. At Shortbridge, cross the river and turn left for the return to Uckfield.

THE BUCKINGHAM CHILTERNS

Great rounded hills crowned with beeches enfold valleys where pure chalk streams are home to the speckled trout. Here and there steeples rise dark against the green flanks, proclaiming downland villages famous for their beauty.

UXBRIDGE, Gt London
Uxbridge stands on the banks of the River Colne and the Grand Union Canal. Its Old Crown and Treaty House featured in an historic meeting between Charles I and Parliament in 1645. St Margaret's Church dates from the 14th and 15th centuries, but its tower was rebuilt in 1820. The Market House dates from 1789.

Follow SP 'Denham' then 'Beaconsfield' to leave Uxbridge on the A4020, crossing the Grand Union Canal and the River Colne. Proceed to the Denham roundabout and take the 3rd exit on to the A40. Denham village lies off the road to the right.

DENHAM, Bucks
Denham is a most attractive village of fine houses, old inns, and ancient brick and timber cottages. St Mary's Church, which dates from the 15th century, contains wall paintings of the Day of Judgement and a 13th-century font. The local Wesleyan Chapel was built in 1820. At the end of the main street is 17th-century Denham Place, which stands in grounds landscaped by Capability Brown. Savay Farm is a 14th-century hall house.

Continue for 2 miles, with the River Misbourne to the right of the road, and meet traffic signals. Turn right on to the A413, SP 'Amersham' and proceed for 2¼ miles. Go forward to skirt Chalfont St Peter.

CHALFONT ST PETER, Bucks
A complete contrast in building styles is offered by two local churches. One is a Victorianized 18th-century structure and the other a 20th-century creation. The once-fashionable gothic-revival style is evident in Chalfont House, which was built for General Churchill.

Go forward to skirt Chalfont St Giles. A detour from the main route to Milton's Cottage can be made by driving to the Pheasant Inn and turning left on to an unclassified road.

MILTON'S COTTAGE, Bucks
Milton lived in this timber-framed and brick cottage (open) during the plague year of 1665. He completed *Paradise Lost* here and began *Paradise Regained*.

CHALFONT ST GILES, Bucks
St Giles' Church has a 13th-century heart in Victorian dress. The village has a small green bordered by ancient brick and timber cottages. Artefacts relating to life in the Chilterns are on show at the Chiltern Open Air Museum.
Continue to Amersham.

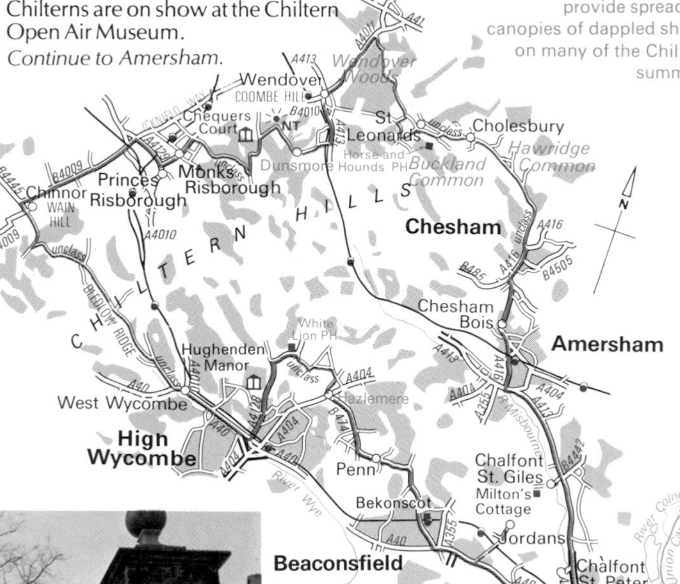

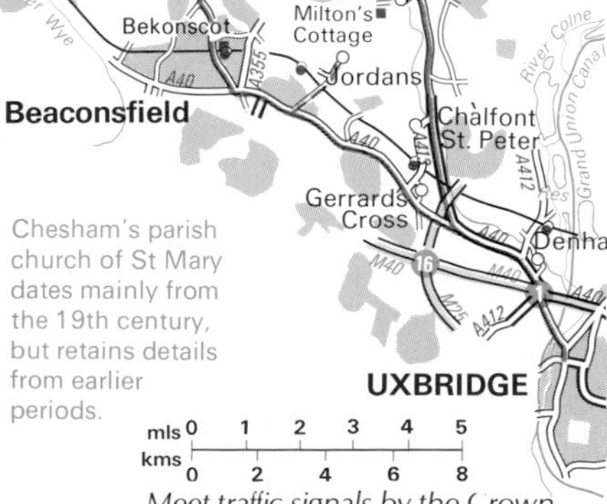

Chesham's parish church of St Mary dates mainly from the 19th century, but retains details from earlier periods.

Ancient beech trees provide spreading canopies of dappled shade on many of the Chiltern summits.

AMERSHAM, Bucks
Amersham is a lovely collection of old houses, quaint cottages, and ancient inns in the Misbourne Valley. Sir William Drake built the Town Hall in 1682, some 15 years after the almshouses bearing his name. Beech woods grace the Chiltern countryside around the town.

Meet traffic signals by the Crown Hotel and turn right into Church Street. Within 1 mile approach more traffic signals and turn left on to the A416 for Chesham Bois.

CHESHAM BOIS, Bucks
St Leonard's at Chesham Bois is a 19th-century restoration, but the arch of its south entrance may have been part of a medieval church. Memorial brasses can be seen inside.

Continue on the A416 to Chesham.

CHESHAM, Bucks
Chesham stands in the Chess Valley, with attractive Chiltern countryside to the north-west. Georgian houses and cottages exist here. The George Inn in the High Street dates from 1715. A charter granted by King Henry III in 1257 gave Chesham its market, held every Wednesday.

In Chesham bear left then right with one-way traffic SP 'Berkhamsted'. Meet a roundabout, drive forward for about a ¼ mile, and turn right. Continue to a T-junction and turn left. Within ½ mile keep forward to an unclassified road SP 'Tring'. In 1¾ miles bear left to climb on to the Chilterns.

THE CHILTERN HILLS
Wooded in the west but mostly windswept and bare near Ivinghoe in the east, the Chiltern Hills extend in a majestic line from Goring in the Thames Valley to a point near Hitchin, and culminate in 835ft Coombe Hill above Wendover. Many of the chalk 'downs' are crowned with ancient beech groves. The North Bucks Way, a 30-mile walk from Wolverton to Chequers, is open for public use.

Keep forward to Hawridge Common and continue to Cholesbury.

CHOLESBURY, Bucks
Cholesbury Common boasts a fine tower windmill which started life as a smock mill in 1863. Its form was revised after it had been declared unsafe in 1884, and it has now been converted into a private house. Iron-age Cholesbury Camp covers 15 acres near by.

Continue to Buckland Common, then drive to the Horse and Hound (PH) and keep left. Take the next turning right to St Leonards.

ST LEONARDS, Bucks
The Church of St Leonard, rebuilt after the Civil War and restored in 1845, has plastered walls and carries a squat bell turret surmounted by a spire.

Follow the 'Aston Clinton' road. Descend Aston Hill through Wendover Woods T-junction A4011. Turn left and continue along the A4011 to Wendover.

WENDOVER, Bucks
Many delightful brick and timber cottages survive here, plus a collection of quaint inns which includes the Red Lion Hotel, where Oliver Cromwell slept in 1642. Bosworth House, in the main street, is of 17th-century origin. Both the local windmill and a watermill have been converted into houses. The ancient Icknield Way crosses the Chilterns near by on its way from east to south-west England.

Turn left on to the A413 SP 'Amersham'. Within $\frac{1}{4}$ mile turn left again, then continue for $1\frac{1}{2}$ miles and turn right on to an unclassified road. Ascend to Dunsmore, go forward with SP 'Kimble', and follow the narrow road over a shoulder of Coombe Hill.

COOMBE HILL, Bucks
About $1\frac{1}{2}$ miles west of Wendover is Coombe Hill (NT) – 106 acres of downland in the highest part of the Chilterns. Excellent views include Aylesbury and the Chequers Woods.

Descend to Chequers Court.

CHEQUERS COURT, Bucks
Chequers is a notable 16th-century house that was given to the nation by Lord Lee of Fareham, as a thank-offering for the ending of World War I. About 3 miles from Princes Risborough in hundreds of acres of parkland, it is the Prime Minister's official country residence and contains valuable Cromwellian relics.

Turn left SP 'Great Missenden'. In $1\frac{1}{4}$ miles turn sharp right SP 'Princes Risborough', and in 1 mile descend Longdown Hill. Turn left on to the A4010 for Monks Risborough.

MONKS RISBOROUGH, Bucks
A well-known local landmark is the 80ft chalk cross cut on a slope overlooking the Icknield Way. Its upkeep was traditionally the duty of the earls of Buckingham.

Continue to Princes Risborough.

PRINCES RISBOROUGH, Bucks
Among several picturesque old houses surviving here is a 17th- and 18th-century manor house (NT).

At roundabout take 3rd exit A4129 SP 'Thame'. In 1 mile at roundabout turn left on to the B4009. Proceed to Chinnor along the line of the Icknield Way.

Above: this pastel of John Milton at the age of 62 hangs in Milton's Cottage. Right: this picturesque, creeper hung cottage is where the poet ended his days in blindness and loneliness, a disillusioned old man.

CHINNOR, Oxon
A Chiltern village with a cement works sounds incongruous, even to 20th-century ears, but Chinnor has just such an industry. Its moated manor house and attractive church are more typical of the area.

Meet crossroads and turn left, then within $\frac{1}{4}$ mile go forward along an unclassified road with SP 'Bledlow Ridge'. Wain Hill viewpoint lies to the left.

WAIN HILL, Bucks
Cut into the solid chalk slope of Wain Hill is the 75ft-long Bledlow Cross, one of two turf-cut crosses in the county.

In $\frac{1}{2}$ mile ascend Chinnor Hill and turn sharp left for the climb to Bledlow Ridge.

BLEDLOW RIDGE, Bucks
The climb to Bledlow Ridge is steep, but well worth the effort for it commands breathtaking views.

Descend to West Wycombe.

WEST WYCOMBE, Bucks
This town has a beautifully-preserved main street (NT) which enshrines architecture dating from the 15th to 19th centuries. The town's Church of St Laurence stands isolated on a 600ft-high hill at the site of a village which has long gone. Artificial chalk caves in the area once housed the notorious Hell Fire Club founded by Sir Francis Dashwood who owned the mansion in West Wycombe Park (NT). Nearby is a small motor museum.

Join the A40 and drive through the village to High Wycombe.

HIGH WYCOMBE, Bucks
High Wycombe has been important since Roman times, and once earned a very good living from wool and lace. It is now well known for the manufacture of furniture, particularly chairs, and has a museum dealing solely with the craft in Castle Hill House. The Guildhall and octagonal Little Market House are scheduled as Ancient Monuments.

Leave High Wycombe following SP 'Great Missenden, A4128' and cross the River Wye. Within $1\frac{1}{2}$ miles reach Hughenden Manor on the left.

HUGHENDEN MANOR, Bucks
Hughenden Manor was the home of Disraeli, Prime Minister of Great Britain under Queen Victoria. It was remodelled in 1862 but his study still remains as he left it.

After about $\frac{1}{2}$ mile turn right. Ascend for $\frac{3}{4}$ mile and approach the White Lion (PH). Turn right again into unclassified Cryers Hill Lane and proceed to a T-junction. Turn left SP 'Penn' and in 1 mile turn right. In $\frac{1}{2}$ mile approach traffic signals at Hazlemere and drive straight over crossroads on to the B474 SP 'Beaconsfield'. Go forward to Penn.

PENN, Bucks
Penn is in one of the loveliest parts of the Chilterns. Village inn and church stand side by side overlooking the green in the company of fine Georgian houses, and the view from the churchyard is exceptional.

Continue through Penn to the outskirts of Beaconsfield and Bekonscot Model Village.

BEKONSCOT MODEL VILLAGE, Bucks
Situated in Warwick Road, Beaconsfield New Town, this model has cottages, churches, waterways, a railway, an airport, farms, and fields, at the scale of one inch to one foot.

Continue into Beaconsfield.

BEACONSFIELD, Bucks
Beaconsfield has a green bordered by roads of Queen Anne and Georgian houses, and ancient inns with notable histories. The half-timbered Royal Saracen's Head was once a coaching stop. Although St Mary's Church is medieval in origin it wears a Victorian face; the poet Edmund Waller lies buried here.

At roundabout turn left A40 SP 'London'. Continue for ½ mile, enter a roundabout, and leave by the 1st exit. After another ½ mile at roundabout the unclassified left turn leads to Jordans.

JORDANS, Bucks
The most famous of all Quaker Meeting Houses stands here. It was built in 1688 and is only a few years younger than Old Jordans Farm, where Quaker meetings were held prior to its completion.

Continue along the A40 to the outskirts of Gerrards Cross.

GERRARDS CROSS, Bucks
This largely residential district has a Byzantine-style church of 1859 and a few Georgian houses.

Continue along the A40 and enter Denham roundabout. Leave by the A4020 exit and return to Uxbridge.

A painted ceiling dominates the Blue Drawing Room in 18th-century West Wycombe Park.

SANCTITY IN STONE

Centuries before Christianity the primitive peoples of England raised the huge megaliths of Stonehenge. Much later came the cathedrals, the Norman permanence of Winchester and soaring early-English completeness of Salisbury.

WINCHESTER, Hants
Venta Belgarum to the Romans, this one-time capital of Wessex boasts an 11th-century and later cathedral that is the second longest in Europe. Inside are richly-carved chantry chapels, the oldest iron grille in England, and coffins holding the bones of Saxon kings. Survivals from the distant 13th century include excellent stretches of the city walls, the hall of Pilgrims' School, and the 13th-century and later Deanery. Winchester College, founded by William of Wykeham in 1382, retains much of its original structure and stands near the ruined Bishop's Palace of Wolvesey Castle. Castle Hall dates from the 13th century, and 16th-century Godbegot House stands on the site of a palace built by King Canute. Close to the centre of town the River Itchen rushes through a lovely old mill (NT) of 1744 before winding through attractive gardens alongside the medieval walls.

Follow SP 'Stockbridge' to leave Winchester on the A272, and in $4\frac{3}{4}$ miles reach the Rack and Manger Inn. Turn right on to an unclassified road SP 'Crawley'. After another 1 mile reach a pond and turn left into Crawley village.

CRAWLEY, Hants
Almost too perfect to be true, this picture-book village has timber-framed cottages, an old pub, and a duckpond. Its homely church has Norman features, and its Court dates from the late 19th century.

Drive to the far end of the village and keep left, then in $1\frac{1}{4}$ miles turn right to rejoin the A272. Proceed to Stockbridge Down.

STOCKBRIDGE DOWN, Hants
Situated on the north side of the A272, this lovely area of open downland (NT) features a group of bronze-age round barrows and the south-west ditch and rampart of iron-age Woolbury Camp hillfort.

Later descend and enter the Test Valley, then continue to the edge of Stockbridge.

STOCKBRIDGE, Hants
People from all over the world come here to fish the Test, one of the most sought-after game rivers in the country. Stockbridge itself is a one-street town of mainly Victorian buildings. The Town Hall, the Grosvenor Hotel, and the White Hart Inn are all early 19th-century, and only the 13th-century chancel of the old church remains.

Meet a roundabout and take the 2nd exit on to the A30, then drive to the next roundabout and branch left on to the A3057 SP 'Andover'. In 1 mile turn left on to an unclassified road SP 'Longstock', then cross a bridge and cross the River Test to Longstock.

LONGSTOCK, Hants
Thatched cottages strung out along a narrow, winding lane form the spine of this pretty village. Medieval tiles can be seen behind the altar of the 19th-century church, which is also notable for its beautiful chancel arch.

Turn left, then at the end of the village turn right (no SP) on to a narrow by-road. In $\frac{3}{4}$ mile meet a T-junction and turn right. Continue across open downland, then in another $\frac{3}{4}$ mile keep forward SP 'Grateley'. Pass Danebury Ring on the left.

DANEBURY RING, Hants
At the top of a 469ft hill is Danebury Ring, an iron-age camp that has been thoroughly excavated in recent years. It has been acquired by the County Council as a Heritage Site and public amenity area.

In 2 miles meet a main road and turn left on to the A343. Pass the Army Aviation Museum, then after 1½ miles reach Middle Wallop. Meet crossroads and turn right on to the B3084 for Over Wallop.

OVER WALLOP, Hants
Although St Peter's Church in Over Wallop displays 12th- and 13th-century traces, much of its old structure has been hidden by Victorian restoration. Inside is a 15th-century font.

In 2¼ miles enter Grateley, keep forward on the B3084 passing Quarley Hill on the right, in 1¾ miles at a T-junction turn left on to the A303 SP 'Amesbury'. After ¾ mile at a roundabout take 2nd exit A303 SP 'Amesbury and Exeter', join the dual carriageway and after 5 miles bypass Amesbury before reaching a roundabout.

Danebury Ring consists of three lines of ramparts and ditches and encloses 13 acres.

In Saxon times Winchester was the capital of England.

The church at King's Somborne.

AMESBURY, Wilts
At Amesbury the Avon is crossed by a five-arched Palladian bridge which complements the stately flow of the river. Amesbury Abbey is of the 19th century and stands in a park in which beech clumps have been planted to represent the positions of English and French ships at Trafalgar. The Church of SS Mary and Melor is a flint-built Norman structure containing a contemporary font fashioned from Purbeck marble.

At the roundabout keep forward then in 1¾ miles turn right on to the A344 SP 'Devizes'. Continue to Stonehenge.

Stonehenge is probably the most famous prehistoric monument in the world.

STONEHENGE, Wilts
Almost nothing is known about this most famous of all prehistoric megalithic monuments. From time to time the public imagination is caught by theories of sun-worship rites and primitive astronomical computers, but it is likely that these have as little factual base as the neo druidical ceremonies enacted here every Midsummer's Night Eve. Originally Stonehenge (AM) comprised an encircling ditch and bank dating from the stone age, but this simple base was later developed into circles of sarsen stones around a horseshoe of trilithons enclosing the enigmatic Welsh bluestones. Several stones still stand where they were first erected thousands of years ago, and the largest measures almost 30ft high from its deeply buried base to its top. Much of the surrounding land belongs to the National Trust.

Continue on the A344 and in 1½ miles turn left on to the A360 SP 'Salisbury'. In 1 mile meet a roundabout and keep forward, passing Normanton Down.

NORMANTON DOWN, Wilts
In the Normanton Down area there are no fewer than 26 round barrows of various types, and a single long barrow dating from an earlier period. Excavations of this remarkable group have shown them to be Wessex Graves dating from the early bronze age. Hundreds of other examples survive near Stonehenge.

Follow an undulating road across part of Salisbury Plain, and after 3 miles meet crossroads. Turn left on to an unclassified road SP 'The Woodfords'. Continue to Middle Woodford.

MIDDLE WOODFORD, Wilts
Most of Middle Woodford Church was rebuilt in Victorian times, though the great flint and rubble tower is a survival from earlier days. Heale House, where Charles II once hid and from which he rode forth to view Stonehenge, only the eight acre gardens are open.

At Middle Woodford meet a T-junction and turn right to follow the River Avon to Lower Woodford.

LOWER WOODFORD, Wilts
High downs rise on either side of this tiny village, which is the lowest of three Woodfords strung along the Avon Valley. The only building of any real note here is the manor house (not open), but the local countryside is enchanting.

In 2 miles cross a river bridge and turn left, then immediately right and shortly pass the earthworks of Old Sarum.

OLD SARUM, Wilts
In Roman times this important centre was linked by the Port Way to *Calleva Atrebatum*, a significant garrison town near Silchester in Hampshire. After a while Old Sarum became the site of a great cathedral, but a combination of water shortage, military troubles, and exposure to inclement weather prompted a move to Salisbury in 1220. The cathedral was demolished in 1331 and the materials transported to the new site for the superb building that stands today.

Reach the main road and turn right on to the A345. Continue to Salisbury.

SALISBURY, Wilts
Salisbury's 404ft cathedral spire, the tallest in England, dominates most approaches to this lovely city. The cathedral itself is a perfect example of early-English architecture, set amid an enchanting medley of houses in the ancient cathedral close. Many other old buildings survive in the city.

From Salisbury follow SP 'Southampton' to leave on the A36. In 2¼ miles at the start of the dual carriageway, turn right on to an unclassified road SP 'Alderbury', continue into Alderbury.

ALDERBURY, Wilts
Alderbury House is said to be built of stone from the old belfry of Salisbury Cathedral. The small farm at nearby Ivychurch is on the site of a Norman priory, and local St Mary's Church is of Victorian date.

At Alderbury continue to the end of the village, cross bridge and follow SP 'West Grimstead'. Drive to that village and keep forward SP 'West Dean', and in 3 miles meet a junction and turn right for West Dean.

WEST DEAN, Wilts
Half hidden among trees at the top of a hill are remains of the old St Mary's Church of West Dean. New St Mary's was built of flint and brick in 1866. Close to the ruins is a good 16th-century barn.

Turn right SP 'Lockerley', then beyond East Dean go over a level crossing and continue to Lockerley. In ½ mile bear right, and ¼ mile farther pass under a railway bridge. Drive to the nearside of a green and turn left SP 'Dunbridge'. At Dunbridge turn left on to the B3084 and drive over a level crossing and river bridge. In ½ mile turn right on to an unclassified road SP 'Mottisfont Village'. Meet a T-junction and turn right. Pass the entrance to 18th-century Mottisfont Abbey.

MOTTISFONT, Hants
Remains of a 12th-century priory are incorporated in 18th-century Mottisfont Abbey (NT), which houses an excellent collection of paintings by Rex Whistler.

Cross the River Test then later meet the main road and turn left on to the A3057. Follow the Test Valley to King's Somborne.

KING'S SOMBORNE, Hants
A ring of bells in the Church of SS Peter and Paul is inscribed 'completed in the Jubilee Year of Queen Victoria, 1887'. The building itself is of ancient foundation but was much restored in 1885. The architect Sir Edwin Lutyens designed modern Marsh Court.

In King's Somborne turn right on to an unclassified road SP 'Winchester', then take the next turning left. After another ¾ mile turn right SP 'Farley Mount' then climb through well-wooded country to Farley Mount. This country park has an excellent picnic site. Meet a fork junction and bear left to follow a pleasant by-road. Go forward over all crossroads for 3 miles, then turn left on to the A3090 to re-enter Winchester.

The River Test is renowned for its trout fishing.

REACHES OF THE THAMES AND ROYAL WINDSOR

The stern towers of Windsor's mighty castle look down in royal splendour on the ever-changing life of the Thames, where boats ply busily to and fro between leafy banks and beneath elegant bridges.

WINDSOR, Berks
The largest inhabited castle in the world rambles over 13 acres on a chalk bluff above the River Thames. Windsor Castle has been a royal residence since Henry 1's reign and every subsequent ruling English monarch has made additions to it. However, George IV contributed most and he was responsible for the distinctive multi-towered skyline of today. The parts of the castle open to the public are St George's Chapel, burial place of kings and queens; Queen Mary's Dolls' house, designed by Sir Edwin Lutyens and exquisitely perfect to the tiniest detail; the state apartments, full of outstanding paintings, carvings, furniture and porcelain; and the enormous Round Tower which surveys 12 counties. Most of the town's architecture is a mixture of Victorian and Georgian with the notable exception of the Guildhall (OACT). Sir Christopher Wren, whose father was Dean of Windsor, completed it in 1689 and it now displays various exhibits of local history, with portraits of kings and queens lining the walls.

WINDSOR GREAT PARK, Berks
Stretching south of the castle from the river to Virginia Water are some 4,800 acres of glorious open parkland, dense beech woods and beautiful formal gardens. Both Home Park, the private land around the castle, and the Great Park, are dissected by the Long Walk. This magnificent avenue of chestnut and plane trees leads from the castle to Snow Hill. Here, at the park's highest point, stands a towering equestrian statue of George III. Savill Gardens and the Valley Gardens within the park are both woodland areas of great beauty. Rhododendrons, azaleas, roses, camelias and magnolias are just some of the lovely flowers and shrubs that provide colour in them all year round.

Leave Windsor on the A308, SP 'Maidenhead'. In 4 miles pass under the motorway bridge and turn right on to the B3028 for Bray.

BRAY, Berks
The song called *The Vicar of Bray* has made the village name familiar. Just which vicar it refers to is uncertain, but Simon Aleyn of Tudor times seems to be the most popular candidate. The almshouses are a particularly attractive feature of this Thameside village. They were founded by William Goddard in 1627 and a figure of him stands over the gateway. A pretty lane leads from the main street to the churchyard, which is entered through a timber-framed gatehouse. This may have been the chantry house, for the chantry Chapel of St Mary stands inside the churchyard. It was used as a small school in the early 17th century.

In the 1820s Windsor Castle was transformed from a hotch-potch of apartments to a magnificent palace at a cost of about £1,000,000

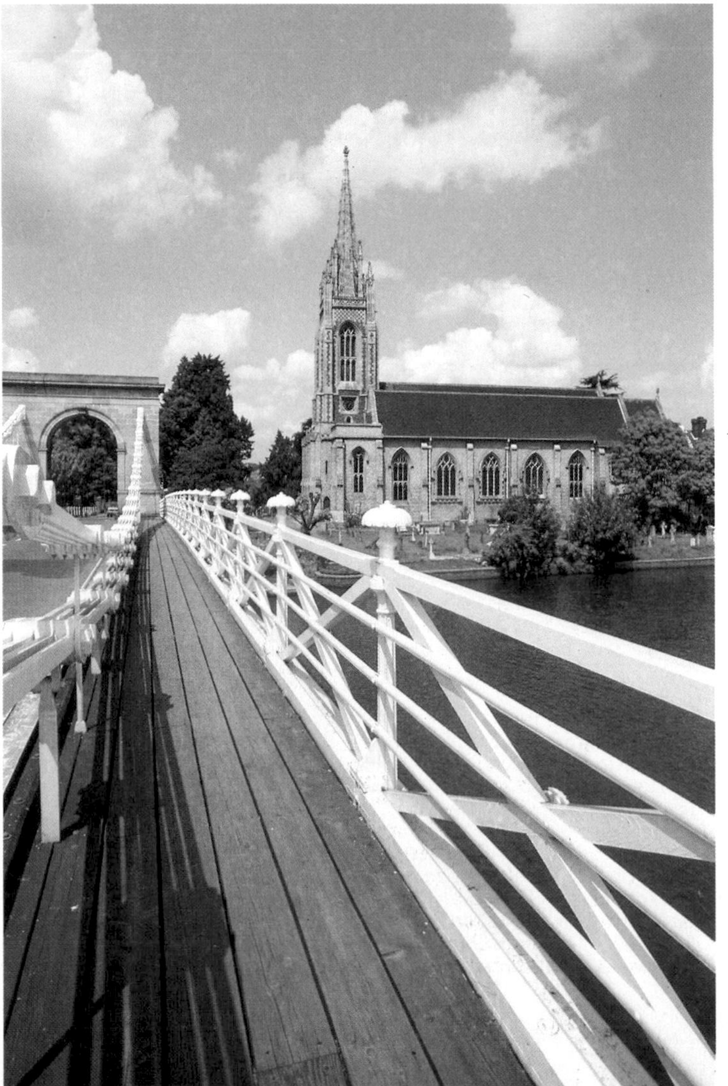

Marlow's suspension bridge, built in 1831, and the 19th-century Church of All Saints — one of the town's 3 churches

At the end of the village bear right, continue for 1 mile to the edge of Maidenhead then turn right on to the A4 (no SP) and shortly cross Maidenhead Bridge.

MAIDENHEAD, Berks
Maidenhead, so near to London and on one of the loveliest stretches of the Thames, has become a popular residential commuter town. The town first began to grow in the 13th century around the bridge which was replaced in 1772 by a fine stone one. During the Civil Wars and the 17th century Revolution Maidenhead was a strategic point. The Henry Reitlinger Bequest Museum in Oldfied House (OACT) by the bridge is filled with glass, pictures, ceramics and sculptures, as well as numerous other treasures. Just upstream is Boulters Lock Inn — a popular stopping place for river navigators since the 18th century.

After crossing the Thames continue for nearly ½ mile, then turn left on to an unclassified road, SP 'Wycombe'. After 2 miles, on the left, is the entrance to Cliveden.

CLIVEDEN, Berks
A house has stood at Cliveden (NT) since 1666, but it has not been the present one. Two fires burnt down the original and its successor, and this third house, built in the 19th century, is largely the work of Sir Charles Barry. Between the wars it was owned by the Astors and was a popular meeting place for influential politicians and social celebrities. The grounds are exceptionally beautiful, due to natural terrain as much as design. The site slopes down to a part of the Thames called Cliveden Reach and the views from the back of the house are superlative. Here, the huge terrace drops down to a great carpet of lawn patterned with low box hedges, and beyond lies the Italian Garden. Other features of the grounds include woodland walks, a monumental Victorian fountain, an elaborate water garden with a Japanese pagoda and glades of dark green ilex trees that provide an ideal setting for the stone statues scattered within them.

Continue on the unclassified road and in just over ¼ mile turn left, SP 'Bourne End'. In ¾ mile turn left still SP 'Bourne End'. Nearly ½ mile farther turn left on to the A4094, SP 'Cookham', and later cross the River Thames for Cookham.

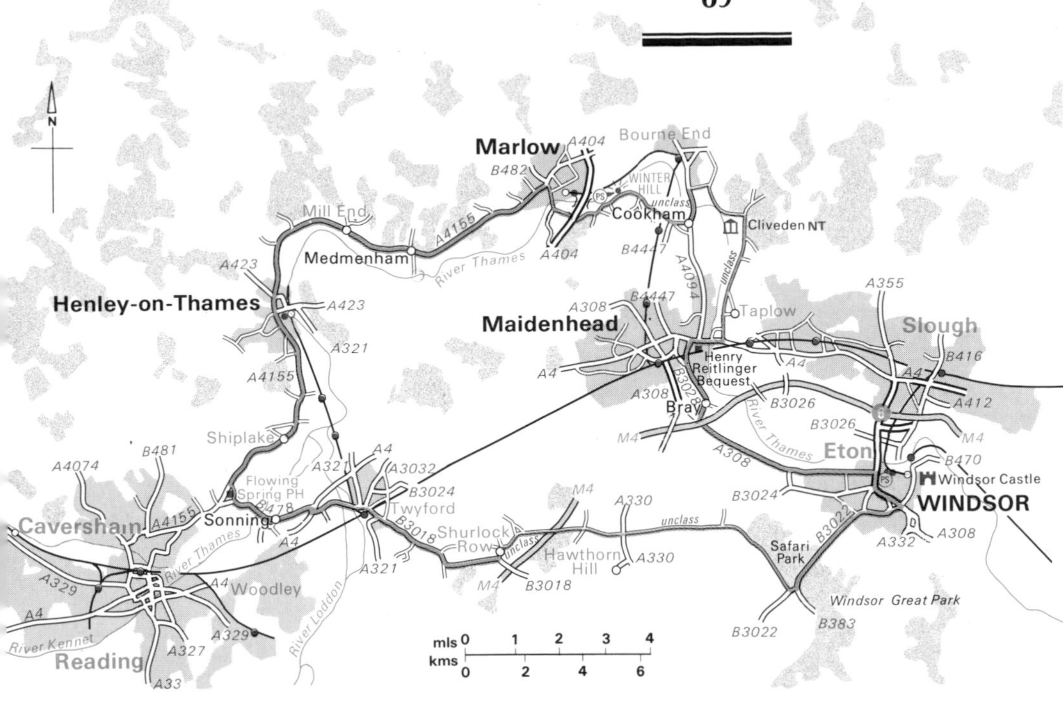

Looking upstream at Henley towards the 16th-century tower of St Mary's Church, distinguished by its flint and stone chequerwork and 4 octagonal turrets

COOKHAM, Berks
The modern painter, Stanley Spencer, was a native of Cookham. More people throng the streets and river since his days, but the redbrick cottages facing the green and the river scenes are easily identified in many of his paintings. Several of Spencer's works can be seen in the King's Hall Gallery in the unspoilt High Street. One of the boathouses along the river acts as the office of the Keeper of the Royal Swans. He is in charge of the annual ceremony of Swan Upping — the counting and marking of all cygnets on the Thames.

Turn right into the main street (B4447), SP 'Cookham Dean'. In almost ½ mile, before the White Hart Inn, turn right, SP 'Winter Hill Golf Club'. ¼ mile beyond the viewpoint of Winter Hill turn right, then right again, and descend through thick beech woods. At the next T-junction, turn right and cross the Thames for Marlow.

MARLOW, Bucks
The jewel of this busy town is its fine suspension bridge which was renovated to mint condition in 1966. It spans the river near a cascading weir and the beautiful beech trees of Quarry Wood form a backdrop for this, the lock and the lock house. By the bridge is the Compleat Angler Hotel, named after Izaak Walton's book about the delights of fishing as a pastime. Marlow's broad main street and West Street are full of unspoilt buildings from the 16th to 18th centuries, among which was the home of Shelley and his wife.

At the end of Marlow High Street turn left on to the A4155, SP 'Henley' and continue to Medmenham.

MEDMENHAM, Bucks
A clique of roisterers in the 18th century came to be known as the Hellfire Club and their headquarters were at Medmenham. The leader, Sir Francis Dashwood, was a Chancellor of the Exchequer, and he rebuilt the Norman abbey here in which to hold his scandalous parties. Finally, public exposure and disgrace ended the club's activities for good. There is little sign of those revelries in the village today, with its groups of cottages, 15th-century manor house and 16th-century inn with dormer windows.

Continue on the A4155 to Henley.

HENLEY-ON-THAMES, Oxon
Henley is the most famous of the Thames resorts due to the prestigious annual regatta held here in July. The first inter-varsity race took place here in 1829 and within 10 years it was a recognised national event enjoying royal patronage. The graceful bridge in Henley is 18th century, appropriately decorated with the faces of Father Thames and the goddess Isis. Apart from the boating available throughout the summer and the pleasant walks along the towpaths, there are lots of interesting shops, inns and teashops in Henley. Most of the inns are old coaching houses with squares that were once the scene of bull and bear fights. Kenton theatre, completed in 1804, is the 4th oldest theatre in England.

Leave Henley on the A4155, SP 'Reading'. In 2 miles pass the Shiplake war memorial, and after another 2½ miles, at the Flowing Spring PH, turn left (one-way), SP 'Sonning'. At the end turn left again on to the B478 (no SP) for Sonning.

SONNING, Berks
Eleven arches form the 18th-century bridge across the Thames at Sonning. The village is pretty and unspoilt, with little streets of cottages, grander Georgian houses and a lock gaily bedecked with flowers. The Bishops of Salisbury lived here centuries ago, but the only sign of their palace is a mound in the grounds of Holme Park.

Bear left through the village and at the roundabout take the 2nd exit on to the A3032, SP 'Twyford'. In Twyford turn right on to the A321, SP 'Bracknell'. After crossing the railway bridge keep forward on to the B3018 and remain on it to Shurlock Row. Turn left on to an unclassified road, SP 'Maidenhead', into the village, and at the far end turn right on to the Hawthorn Hill road. Later pass over the M4 and in 1¼ miles cross the A330, SP 'New Lodge'. In 4 miles turn left on to the B3022, SP 'Windsor', then turn left again and shortly pass Windsor Safari Park and Seaworld (left).

WINDSOR SAFARI PARK AND SEAWORLD, Berks
This was one of the first Safari parks to spring up in Britain. Apart from the fascinating drive-through reserves, aviaries and caged animals, there is a modern dolphinarium too. Here, bottle-nosed dolphins perform their incredible tricks, vying for popularity with the killer whale.

Continue on the B3022 for the return to Windsor.

WOKINGHAM, Berks
Wokingham boasted a bell foundry in the 14th century, and the silk industry flourished here in Elizabethan days. Rose Street preserves timbered houses and the Rose Inn, where poets Dean Swift, Pope, and Gay spent a wet afternoon together. Gay utilized the time in composing verses to the landlord's daughter, Molly Mog. Several almshouses exist in and around the town, and Lucas Hospital of 1665 – at Luckely – is considered particularly fine.

Follow SP 'Reading, A329' to leave Wokingham via Broad Street. In ¼ mile approach the clock tower, then turn left on to the B3349 SP 'Arborfield' and go over a level crossing. After 2¼ miles turn right for Arborfield Cross.

ARBORFIELD CROSS, Berks
To the left of Arborfield Cross, off the A327, is Arborfield Garrison. Within the complex is the Royal Electrical and Mechanical Engineers Museum, which is open to the public most weekdays.

Turn right and immediately left on to an unclassified road SP 'Swallowfield'. Continue for 2 miles and turn right. Swallowfield Park is on the right.

SWALLOWFIELD PARK, Berks
Swallowfield Park lies almost on the Hampshire border, at the meeting of the rivers Loddon and Blackwater. Swallowfield Park house was rebuilt in the late 17th century and remodelled by William Atkinson in 1820.

At the park gates turn left across the Blackwater River to reach Swallowfield. Turn left SP 'Basingstoke', at T-junction turn left on to the main road B3349 for Risely. Bear right and in ½ mile at T-junction turn right and at roundabout take 1st exit SP 'Basingstoke' A33. A detour from the main route can be made by taking 2nd exit unclassifield road for 2 miles at T-junction turn left and left again for entrance, for Stratfield Saye Park. Then return to the main route.

STRATFIELD SAYE PARK, Hants
This rather unstately stately home (open) was built in the reign of Charles I and purchased by the 1st Duke of Wellington in 1817. The duke intended to use the £600,000 voted to him by a grateful nation to build a new house in the superb park, but funds did not permit this and so the great soldier set about making the existing building as comfortable and convenient as he could. Central heating was installed in the passageways, and there were 'new-fangled' water closets of blue-patterned china in every room. It has been the home of the dukes of Wellington ever since.

On the main route, drive to the Wellington Monument and turn left on to an unclassified road, SP 'Hook & Eversley', cross Heckfield Heath, and continue for ½ mile. At roundabout take 2nd exit B3011, then after ½ mile branch left on to an unclassified road. Continue, cross the River Whitewater, then after 2½ miles meet crossroads and drive forward. A short detour can be made to the village of Eversley by turning left here and continuing for ½ mile.

ROYAL PARKS AND HAMPSHIRE WOODS

Close to Windsor is the semi-cultivated countryside of royal parkland; farther away, near the Duke of Wellington's country estate, are dark ranks of conifer plantations and the lighter greens of oak and birch tangled with honeysuckle.

Eversley's ancient origins are suggested by the picturesque nameplate on its village green.

EVERSLEY, Hants
St Mary's Church at Eversley was built in the 18th century, and is distinguished in having had naturalist Charles Kingsley as rector. The north aisle was built in his memory. Bramshill House, a Jacobean mansion regarded as one of the finest in the country, is now the Police Staff College.

Join the A327 for Eversley Cross and drive to The Chequers (PH). Turn left on to the B3016 SP 'Wokingham' and continue to Finchampstead.

FINCHAMPSTEAD, Berks
Finchampstead's pride is the splendid avenue of Wellingtonia pines which runs 1 mile east to Crowthorne. Its church has a white-painted body of Norman date and carries an 18th-century tower built in red brick. The whole building stands on a prehistoric earthwork, as if aloof from the village.

Turn right, then after ¼ mile meet a war memorial and turn right on to the B3348 SP 'Crowthorne'. Pass Finchampstead Ridges on the right.

FINCHAMPSTEAD RIDGES, Berks
This 60-acre heather and woodland National Trust property offers excellent views over Berkshire, Hampshire, and Surrey countryside.

Continue, enter a roundabout, and take the first exit on to the A321. After 1 mile at roundabout take 3rd exit B3430 on to Nine Mile Ride.

NINE MILE RIDE, Berks
Nine Mile Ride follows the line of a Roman road through delightfully wooded country. At the Bracknell end, to the south, is the 20-acre iron-age hillfort of Caesar's Camp, part of which is now a public recreation ground with a picnic site.

After 2¾ miles at roundabout take 2nd exit SP 'Bagshot'. Continue passing Caesar's Camp (see Nine Mile Ride) and at roundabout take 2nd exit on to the A322. Proceed for 1½ miles on to the A332 'Ascot' road. Continue for 1¾ miles and bear right. Approach a roundabout and leave by the 3rd exit on to the A329, with Ascot racecourse on the left, and enter Ascot.

ASCOT, Berks
Ascot has strong Queen Anne connections. It was she who instituted the Royal Ascot race meeting in 1711, a fashionable event still held in June and patronized by members of the Royal Family. The Ascot Gold Cup was presented for the first time in 1807.

Continue to Virginia Water, which can be seen on the left.

VIRGINIA WATER, Surrey
This 1½-mile-long artificial lake, laid out by Thomas Sandby for George III, is situated at the south-east corner of Windsor Great Park and is well known for its beauty. Colonnades brought from the Roman port of Leptis Magna stand on its bank in contrast to a 100ft totem pole set up in 1958 to mark the centenary of British Columbia. The nearby Valley Gardens are most inviting.

Continue at T-junction and turn left on to the A30. Pass the Wheatsheaf Hotel and proceed for 1¼ miles, then turn left on to an unclassified road for Savill Gardens (left).

THE SAVILL GARDENS, Berks
Windsor Great Park is noted for its magnificent horticultural areas, but none is more popular than the wooded 20-acre Savill Gardens. Its variety of flowers provide a wealth of colour throughout the seasons.

Continue to The Sun (PH) and go forward for ¼ mile before turning right for Englefield Green.

ENGLEFIELD GREEN, Surrey
This large residential district lies within easy reach of delightful Windsor Great Park. Its 250-year-old Barley Mow Inn was once a popular coaching stop. Late 19th-century Royal Holloway College stands among gardens and playing fields between Englefield Green and the railway. It was one of the first women's colleges ever built and became a constituent college of London University in 1900.

Cross a main road and pass a left turn to Cooper's Hill RAF Memorial.

Windsor Castle has dominated its surroundings ever since William the Conqueror started it in the 11th century.

An equestrian statue of George III by sculptor Richard Westmacott stands on a granite base at the end of the Long Walk in Windsor Great Park.

COOPER'S HILL RAF MEMORIAL, Surrey
The Commonwealth Air Forces Memorial on Cooper's Hill commemorates 20,000 allied airmen who died, with no known grave, in World War II. The site, which gives views of Windsor Castle and seven counties, overlooks Runnymede.

Return to main route then after 300 yards bear left and descend Tite Hill to the edge of Egham. Enter a roundabout and leave by the 1st exit to rejoin the A30. After another ¾ mile enter another roundabout and leave by the 3rd exit on to the A308. Continue to Staines.

STAINES, Surrey
The old market town of Staines, at the junction of the rivers Colne and Thames, is entered via a superb road bridge built by Rennie and opened by William IV. The by-pass & M25 crosses by a modern bridge. West of the local church the London Stone marks the limit of the City of London's former jurisdiction. Sir Walter Raleigh was brought here to be tried because at that time London was in the grip of the plague.

Return along the A308 SP 'Windsor'. In 1 mile meet a roundabout and take the 3rd exit to pass Runnymede.

RUNNYMEDE, Surrey
About $\frac{1}{2}$ mile north-west of Egham are the 60-acre riverside meadows of Runnymede. It was here in 1215 that King John was prevailed upon by his barons to seal the draft of Magna Carta, from which seed – almost by accident – grew the English ideal of personal liberty. Overlooking the meadows is Cooper's Hill, which is crowned by the RAF Memorial and has the American Bar Association's Magna Carta Memorial at its foot. Halfway up its slopes is a memorial to the assassinated US President, John F Kennedy.

Continue through Old Windsor.

OLD WINDSOR, Berks
Old Windsor parish stretches from the River Thames to Virginia Water, including the semi-wild countryside of the Great Park and parts of Windsor Forest. Edward the Confessor had his palace here before the new Windsor of today existed, and William the Conqueror held a Great Council (Witan) here in 1070 – just 4 years after the Norman invasion of Britain.

At roundabout take 1st exit A308; to the left lies Windsor Great Park. Later enter a roundabout and leave by the 3rd exit, into King's Road, to enter Windsor.

WINDSOR, Berks
Windsor is a largely Georgian and Victorian town that owes its existence to its magnificent castle. William the Conqueror first appreciated the site's strategic importance over Old Windsor and built a palisaded fort within a moat. Practically every English monarch who has taken the throne in the 900 years since then has contributed to its development, and today it is the largest inhabited castle in the world.

Leave the town with SP 'Bagshot A332', to return along King's Road. In $\frac{3}{4}$ mile enter a roundabout and leave by the 2nd exit to enter Windsor Great Park.

An immense variety of trees and shrubs is displayed in the magnificent formal landscapes which surround Virginia Water.

Sumptuously decorated rooms full of splendid furniture are features of the seat of the dukes of Wellington, at Stratfield Saye Park.

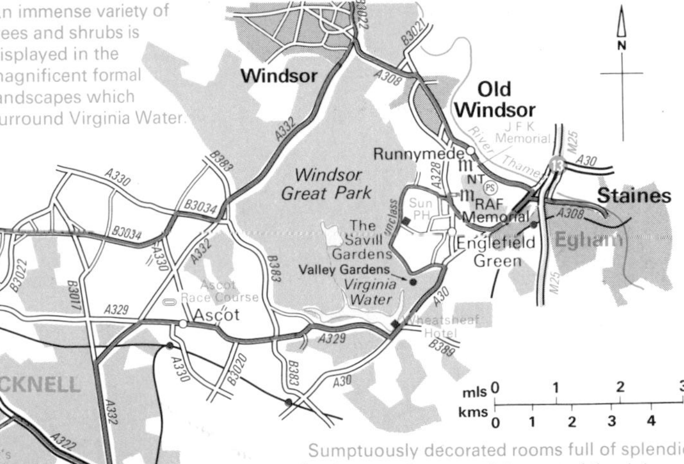

WINDSOR GREAT PARK, Berks
Within the boundaries formed by Home Park and the castle to the north, and by all that remains of Windsor Forest's royal chase to the south and west, Windsor Great Park encompasses an area of almost 5,000 acres. Ancient King's Oak, near Forest Gate, is claimed to be the largest in the park. Legend has it that antlered Herne the Hunter meets here with his ghastly pack before chasing across the night skies. Most of the park is accessible by well-kept footpaths.

Continue for 4 miles before bearing right, then turn left SP 'Ascot'. After another $\frac{1}{4}$ mile meet crossroads and turn right on to the B3034 SP 'Winkfield'. After $\frac{3}{4}$ mile turn left on to the A330 SP 'Ascot'. After $\frac{1}{2}$ mile turn right on to the B3034, then go forward over all crossroads to join the A3095. Continue for $\frac{1}{4}$ mile then turn left to rejoin the B3034 and continue for 1 mile. Cross a humpback bridge, keep left, and enter Binfield.

BINFIELD, Berks
Alexander Pope sang in the choir of the local church as a boy. Among the church's treasures is a fine old hour glass.

Approach crossroads and turn left on to an unclassified road. After ½ mile bear right. Continue, at T-junction turn right on to the B3408, in 1 mile at roundabout take 2nd exit A329 to return to Wokingham.

EPPING AND THE VILLAGES OF ESSEX

Most of the great forest that covered West Essex in Norman times has been cut down, though Epping and Hatfield remain. The magic of Essex today is its village life, which has a timeless quality that echoes the tranquillity of forest communities in ancient days.

WOODFORD GREEN, Gt London
Sir Winston Churchill was MP for Wanstead and Woodford from 1924 to 1964. His statue on Woodford Green is by David McFall.

From Woodford Green follow the A104 'Epping' road and in ¾ mile turn left on to the A110 SP 'North Chingford'. In another $\frac{3}{4}$ mile turn right on to an unclassified road into Forest Side. Continue to a T-junction and turn right into Ranger's Road (A1069) to pass the Royal Forest Hotel and Queen Elizabeth's Hunting Lodge.

QUEEN ELIZABETH'S HUNTING LODGE, Gt London
Queen Elizabeth's Hunting Lodge is a wood-and-plaster building thought to have been erected towards the end of the 15th century so that the sovereign of the day could enjoy a grandstand view of the chase. After having served as a keeper's lodge for a number of years it now houses the Epping Forest Museum.

EPPING FOREST, Essex
Epping Forest owes its creation to the Norman Conquest. It was maintained as a royal hunting area through the reigns of various monarchs, and in the reign of King Charles I its bounds were fixed to embrace some 60,000 acres. In 1882 what was left of it was formally opened as a publicly-owned area by Queen Victoria.

Enter Epping Forest and in 1 mile meet a T-junction. Turn left on to the A104 and in 1¼ miles meet a roundabout. Leave by the 1st exit on to an unclassified road SP 'High Beach', then bear right SP 'King's Oak' for High Beach.

HIGH BEACH, Essex
It is arguable whether this village is named 'Beech' after the area's principal tree or 'Beach' denoting a gravel bank. Either would seem to be appropriate. The poet Tennyson spent his early manhood here.

Beyond the King's Oak (PH) the Epping Forest Conservation Centre lies to the right. Continue to the next road junction and turn left, then descend and in ¾ mile cross the main road. Continue for 1 mile and turn right SP 'Epping' to pass through Upshire. Ascend to re-enter the forest, then meet a T-junction and turn left to join the B1393. Continue to Epping.

EPPING, Essex
Epping lies outside the forest and has managed to retain its own identity as a small market town of some charm, despite the proximity of London. Winchelsea House and Epping Place, in the High Road, are both of 18th-century date.
Drive to the green at the end of the town and branch left on to the B181, SP 'Roydon'. In $1\frac{1}{4}$ miles bear right. After $\frac{3}{4}$ mile, having passed over Cobbin's Brook, reach a T-junction and turn left. Continue through Epping Green to Roydon.

ROYDON, Essex
About $1\frac{1}{2}$ miles south-west of Roydon are the ruins of Tudor Nether Hall, a Manor house that belonged to the Coltes family. It was here that Thomas More came to woo and win the elder daughter of John Coltes. Preserved in the village itself are the old parish cage, stocks, and a whipping post.
Turn left with SP 'Hertford' and shortly cross the River Stort and a level crossing to enter Hertfordshire. In $\frac{3}{4}$ mile turn right with SP 'Chelmsford' to join the A414. After 3 miles go forward on unclassified road through High Wych, and at T-junction turn left on to the A1184 to Sawbridgeworth.

This superb brass is one of 15 preserved in Sawbridgeworth's 14th-century church.

SAWBRIDGEWORTH, Herts
A number of fine Georgian and older buildings survive in this small town, and to the south is Pishiobury – a fine house built by James Wyatt in 1782 and now a school. Ancient brasses are preserved in St. Mary's Church.
Meet crossroads and turn right on to unclassified road SP 'Chelmsford'. Turn right onto the A1060 then turn left on to the B183 SP 'Takeley' for Hatfield Broad Oak.

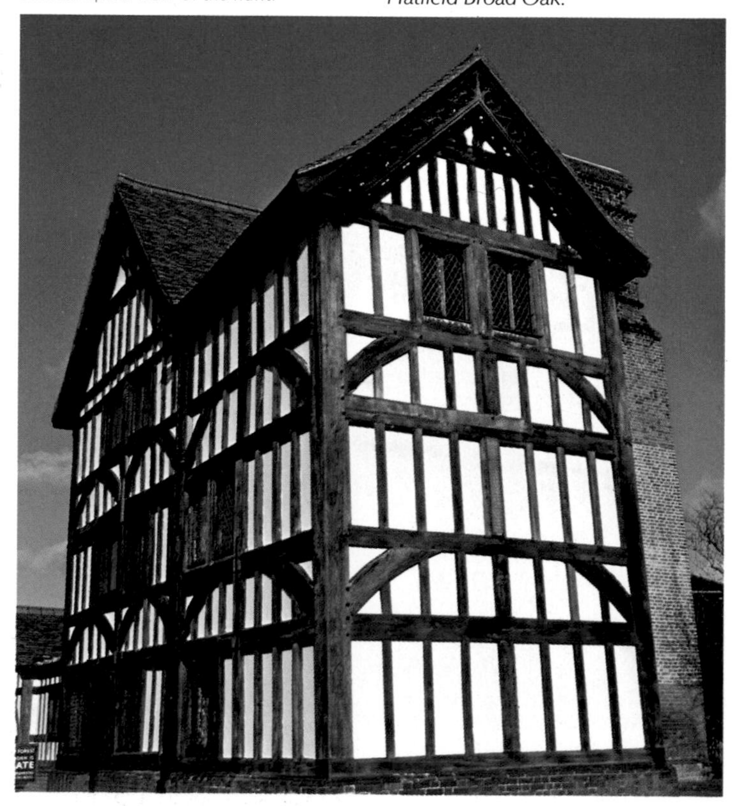

The two upper floors of Queen Elizabeth's Hunting Lodge were originally designed without infilling between the beams, thus enabling an uninterrupted view of the hunt.

HATFIELD BROAD OAK, Essex
Notable features in this markedly-pretty village include a Norman and later church, 18th-century almshouses, and several distinctive Georgian houses.

Keep left and in $1\frac{1}{4}$ miles turn left on to an unclassified road SP 'Hatfield Forest'. In $\frac{3}{4}$ mile keep forward and skirt the Hatfield Forest Country Park.

HATFIELD FOREST, Essex
Once a part of the ancient Royal Forests of Essex, 1,049-acre Hatfield Forest is now protected by the National Trust and offers splendid woodland walks along its chases and rides. Additional amenities include boating and fishing.

Continue, and later turn right on to the A120 for Takeley.

TAKELEY, Essex
Takeley, on the line of the old Roman Stane Street, has an interesting Norman and later church with Roman masonry in the fabric of its walls. Inside is a modern font surmounted by a 6ft-high medieval cover. Good timbered houses and 17th-century barns can be seen in the village.

Drive to traffic signals and turn left off the A120 on to an unclassified road SP 'Broxted'. In $1\frac{1}{2}$ miles note Stansted Airport to the left. In another $1\frac{1}{4}$ miles turn right into Molehill Green. Continue with SP 'Thaxted' and pass through Broxted.

BROXTED, Essex
Broxted's church shows a happy blend of 13th- and 15th-century styles, with the nave and chancel from the earlier period and a belfry and north aisle from the later. Church Hall is of late 16th- to mid 17th-century date.

Beyond the village join the B1051 for Thaxted.

THAXTED, Essex
Many old houses survive to remind the visitor that this was once a very prosperous town. The 15th-century church was clearly built by a community with a great deal of money to spend. The timbered Guildhall dates from the 16th century and incorporates an earlier ancient lock-up. Several old almshouses and a tower windmill can be seen in the area.

Turn left on to the B184 and continue through the village. At the end meet the Fox and Hounds (PH) and turn right on to the B1051 for Great Sampford.

GREAT SAMPFORD, Essex
This pretty village has attractive gabled houses, and opposite the Bull Inn is an Elizabethan manor house. A large pond and three-cornered green complete the picture.

Turn right again on to the B1053 and continue to Finchingfield.

An essential part of Finchingfield's charm is its typically English village green.

FINCHINGFIELD, Essex
Possibly the most photographed village in Essex, Finchingfield is a picture-book community complete with a church on a hill, a picturesque windmill, quaint old cottages, and a charming green enlivened by the noisy population of its duckpond. St John's Church has a sturdy Norman tower that indicates its origins, but the main body is an attractive mixture of styles. One mile north west is Spains Hall and Gardens.

Drive to the war memorial and turn right on to the B1057 for Great Bardfield.

GREAT BARDFIELD, Essex
A major feature of this old market town is a restored windmill that goes by the name 'Gibraltar'. A pleasant mixture of old cottages and shops complemented by the mainly 14th-century church is surveyed by a timber-framed 16th- and 17th-century hall from its hill above the River Pant.

Turn right SP 'Dunmow' and continue to Bran End. After $2\frac{1}{2}$ miles turn left on to the A130 and continue to Dunmow.

Epping Forest's many acres of varied scenery provide one of East London's most valuable leisure amenities.

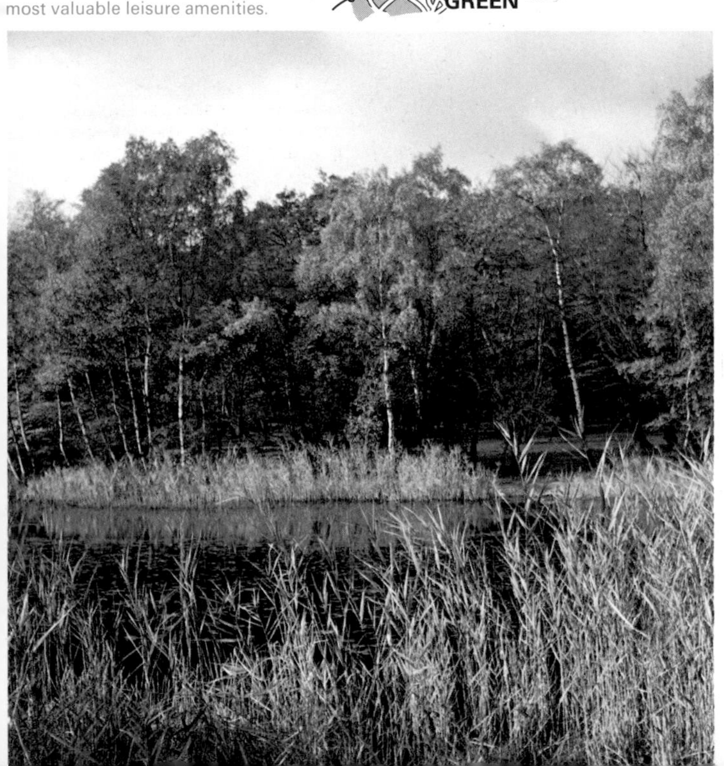

The massive timbers of Greensted Church are a unique survival.

Great Dunmow's 16th-century Clock House.

GREAT DUNMOW, Essex
The Dunmow Flitch trial is held here every 4 years to find a man and wife who have not had a domestic brawl or wished to be unmarried for 12 months and a day. A flitch of bacon is presented to the couple able to prove this enviable state of affairs. The town, a quiet enough place even without this incentive, boasts a large church and a rather small square.

Turn left again SP 'Chelmsford', then in $\frac{3}{4}$ mile turn right on to the B184 SP 'Ongar'. Continue to High Roding and Leaden Roding.

THE RODINGS, Essex
A number of attractive villages in the Roding Valley share this suffix. These include High Roding, with its thatched and gabled cottages and a 13th-century church, and Leaden Roding.

Reach the King William IV (PH) in Leaden Roding and turn right on to the A414. In 1 mile turn left on to the B184 for Fyfield. From Fyfield drive for $2\frac{1}{2}$ miles, enter a roundabout, and leave by the 2nd exit on to the A128 into Chipping Ongar.

CHIPPING ONGAR, Essex
Chipping Ongar began as a market town beneath the walls of a Norman castle. Only the mound and moat of the castle remain, but the contemporary Church of St Martin of Tours still flourishes. Explorer David Livingstone was a pupil pastor of the town's 19th-century Congregational Church.

Drive to the end of the High Street and turn right on to an unclassified road SP 'Greensted'. Pass the Two Brewers (PH) and after 1 mile pass Greensted Church on the right.

GREENSTED CHURCH, Essex
St Andrew's Church is famous as the only surviving example of a Saxon log church extant. The body of King Edmund is known to have been rested here in 1013, but the building is probably much older than that.

In a further $\frac{1}{2}$ mile turn left SP 'Stanford Rivers' and follow a narrow road, then in $1\frac{1}{4}$ miles meet crossroads and turn left again. Drive to a T-junction, turn right on to the A113 SP 'London', and in 3 miles enter a roundabout. Leave by the 2nd exit for Abridge and continue to Chigwell.

CHIGWELL, Essex
Novelist Charles Dickens used the 17th-century King's Head in Chigwell as The Maypole in his book *Barnaby Rudge*. The town's grammar school was founded in 1629 by Archbishop Harsnett, whose memorial brass can be seen inside local St Mary's Church.

After another $1\frac{3}{4}$ miles meet a T-junction and turn right, then in $\frac{3}{4}$ mile meet traffic signals and turn right again on to the A1009 SP 'Woodford Green'. Return to Woodford Green.

RESORTS AND DOWNLAND VILLAGES

High above the bright, mercurial resorts of the Sussex coast are the tranquil hamlets of the South Downs. Here change is gradual, a process to be approached with the caution born from centuries of experience.

WORTHING, W Sussex
Until the 1760s Worthing was little more than a fishing hamlet, but by the end of that century the patronage of George III's family had encouraged the smart set and the inevitable speculators to take an interest in the new town. Sadly there were no lasting major developments of any great merit, although the usual 18th-century terraces preserve something of the old gentility. Today Worthing is a popular seaside resort with a pier and an extensive pebble beach.

Leave Worthing by the A259 'Brighton' road, with occasional views of the sea to the right. Pass through South Lancing and by Shoreham Airport. Cross the River Adur and enter Shoreham-by-Sea.

Brighton's elegant pier dates from the 19th century.

SHOREHAM-BY-SEA W Sussex
Sand at low tide, good fishing in the River Adur, and a busy harbour are features of this popular seaside town. Saxon workmanship can be seen in the mainly Norman structure of St Nicholas' Church. An old chequered-flint house in the town contains the Marlipins Museum of local relics.

Continue on the A259 to Southwick.

SOUTHWICK, W Sussex
Situated on the eastern part of Shoreham Harbour, with the South Downs to the north, Southwick forms part of the Shoreham conurbation and has all but lost its own identity. Roman artefacts excavated from a villa ¼ mile north of the station can be seen in the museum at Hove.

Continue along the A259 to Portslade-by-Sea.

PORTSLADE-BY-SEA, E Sussex
The 'by Sea' part of Portslade is a fairly recent seaside development of the original village, which lies 1 mile inland and has a church with Norman origins. North of the churchyard are remains of a 12th-century flint-built manor house.

Continue along the A259 to Hove.

HOVE, E Sussex
Elegant Hove is so much a part of Brighton these days. It has a good beach, several excellent Regency terraces, a museum and art gallery and the British Engineerium with a Victorian water pumping station.

Continue into Brighton.

BRIGHTON, E Sussex
This famous resort developed as a result of the 18th-century health fad for sea bathing. Its success was assured by the patronage of George IV in 1784, and the many superb terraces preserved there today prove its continued prosperity. As with all playgrounds of the wealthy the town has a number of eccentricities. The most impressive of these is the Royal Pavilion, a magnificent Oriental-style palace built for the Prince Regent by Henry Holland in 1787. Various museums, galleries, and theatres exist in the town, and visitors are offered all the usual distractions of the British seaside holiday. An excellent aquarium can be visited near Palace Pier, and the Volk's Electric Railway – the first of its kind in the world – runs from here to the Black Rock area. Old Brighton is preserved in the winding streets of The Lanes, which contrast with the new conference centre and up-to-the-minute marina development.

Return along the seafront towards Hove, passing the King Alfred Sports Centre, and meet traffic lights. Turn right here into Hove Street and follow SP 'London'. After 1 mile cross over main A27 and in another ¾ mile at West Blatchington turn right on the A2030.

WEST BLATCHINGTON, E Sussex
An early 18th-century windmill and 19th-century St Peter's Church are all that remain of the village that originally stood in this highly-developed area.

Warehouses and sea-going vessels of all descriptions are an integral part of Portslade-by-Sea's character.

Brighton Pavilion has been remodelled several times since it was first built. Architect John Nash was largely responsible for its final appearance.

Continue to ascend the A2038. Meet crossroads and turn left on to an unclassified road SP 'Devil's Dyke'. After ½ mile keep left and ascend through open downland to Devil's Dyke.

DEVIL'S DYKE, W Sussex
Devil's Dyke is a cleft in the 711ft crest of the South Downs (see below). According to local legend the devil tried to carve a large nick to let the sea in, but failed. The spot has become popular with hang-glider enthusiasts.

THE SOUTH DOWNS
Stretching west from Beachy Head into Hampshire, the South Downs range is all that remains of a huge chalk backbone that connected England with the Continent. Some 7,000 years ago the Atlantic forced its way through to join up with the North Sea. Access for rambling and riding is available via numerous footpaths and bridleways.

Return, and after ½ mile turn left SP 'Poynings' to pass the Dyke Golf Club. After ¾ mile turn left, with views of 664ft Newtimber Hill on the right. After a further ½ mile turn sharp left and descend into Poynings.

Mosiac pavements are a feature of the Roman remains at Bignor.

POYNINGS, W Sussex
Poynings is a charming downland village with an old church that was endowed by Michael de Poynings, who died in 1369. The Rectory is of early 19th-century date.

Turn left and follow the foot of the South Downs to Fulking.

FULKING, W Sussex
Flocks of sheep graze the sides of the downland fold in which this ancient hamlet stands, and slake their thirsts at a chalk spring. A like service is offered to humankind by the pleasant Shepherd and Dog Inn.

Continue to Edburton.

EDBURTON, W Sussex
A spectacularly sheer downland escarpment towers above this tiny place, making it seem even smaller than it is. The village boasts a privately-owned craft pottery and a salmon-smoking concern. Prehistoric Castle Rings stands on Edburton Hill.

Leave Edburton with 708ft Truleigh Hill to the left and continue to the A2037. Turn left on to the A2037 for Upper Beeding.

UPPER BEEDING, W Sussex
Upper Beeding lies at the north end of a gap in the downs made by the River Adur. It has a narrow main street lined with old cottages.

Leaving Upper Beeding, turn right on to the unclassified road SP 'Steyning', and cross the River Adur into Bramber.

BRAMBER, W Sussex
Before the River Adur silted up this place was a large port. Its massive Norman castle was dismantled after the Civil War, leaving only a gateway and easily-traceable sections of wall (NT). An unusual museum is the House of Pipes, which features some 35,000 tobacco pipes from all over the world.

Continue to Steyning.

STEYNING, W Sussex
Steyning enjoys a magnificent position at the foot of the South Downs and has a late-Norman church. In Mouse Lane is a 15th-century poorhouse, and an old market house stands in the High Street. The Grammar School of 1614 can be seen in Church Street.

Leave Steyning to join the A283. On the left is Steyning Round Hill, which gives views over the Adur Valley. Continue skirting Wiston Park and Wiston.

WISTON, W Sussex
It is well worth stopping in this lovely village at the foot of downland near Chanctonbury. Unfortunately its 14th-century church was badly treated by the 19th-century restorers, but the overall atmosphere of peaceful antiquity.

Continue on the A283. In 1 mile pass an unclassified left turn leading along a wooded glade to the footpath for Chanctonbury Ring.

CHANCTONBURY RING, W Sussex
The extensive prehistoric earthworks of Chanctonbury Ring occupy a 783ft downland summit which affords views over some 30 miles of countryside.

Continue along the A283 to the edge of Washington, enter a roundabout, and leave by the 2nd exit for Storrington. Left of the road are 626ft Chantry Hill and 549ft Harrow Hill.

STORRINGTON, W Sussex
Kithurst Hill rises to 697ft above this straggling village and forms an excellent viewpoint. Celtic field patterns are preserved on its slopes, is the 28-acre Sullington Warren (NT). A large tithe barn of 1685 stands at Manor Farm.

In 1 mile pass an unclassified left turn leading to Parham House.

The nave of Steyning's parish church is a superb example of Norman architecture.

PARHAM HOUSE, W Sussex
This delightfully unpretentious Elizabethan house has a 158ft long gallery and contains fine furnishings and pictures (open).

Continue on the A283 for 1 mile farther then turn left on to an unclassified road SP 'Greatham'. In 2¼ miles cross the River Arun to Coldwaltham. Turn left on to the A29 into Watersfield, then in ½ mile turn right on to the B2138 'Petworth' road. Take the next turning left on to an unclassified road for West Burton, then turn right for Bignor.

BIGNOR, W Sussex
Several notable old houses here include the famous Old Shop, an unusual yeoman's house of the 15th century. The Roman villa sites here are one of the largest and best known in the country.

Return to West Burton then, turn left SP 'Bury' and in 1 mile turn right on to the A29 SP 'Bognor'. Ascend Bury Hill, meet a roundabout and take 1st exit into Amberley.

AMBERLEY, W Sussex
The old lime quarries now have a new lease of life as the Chalk Pits Museum, with many attractions on its industrial past.
Return to roundabout take 1st exit A284 SP 'Littlehampton'. Skirt the grounds of Arundel Park and in 2¼ miles turn left on to an unclassified road to enter Arundel.

ARUNDEL, W Sussex
Looming large over Arundel to guard a gap made in the downs by the River Arun valley is ancient and much-restored Arundel Castle, seat of the Duke of Norfolk. Behind its heavy grey walls are rooms rich in furnishings and art treasures, many of which are open to the public. A prominent town existed here before the Norman conquest, but comparatively few ancient houses remain. The only real rivals to the castle are the 14th-century Church of St Nicholas and the superb Church of Our Lady and St Philip Neri.
Continue on the A27 'Worthing' road, and in 5 miles pass an unclassified right turn to Highdown Hill.

HIGHDOWN HILL, W Sussex
Between the South Downs and the sea, about 1 mile south of the A27, is 266ft Highdown Hill (NT). This 50-acre site is of great archaeological importance for its late bronze-age, early iron-age and Saxon cemeterys, nearby is Highdown Hill Gardens.

Continue on the A27 towards Worthing. Meet a roundabout and take the 2nd exit. After ¾ mile meet another roundabout and take the 3rd exit for the return to Worthing.

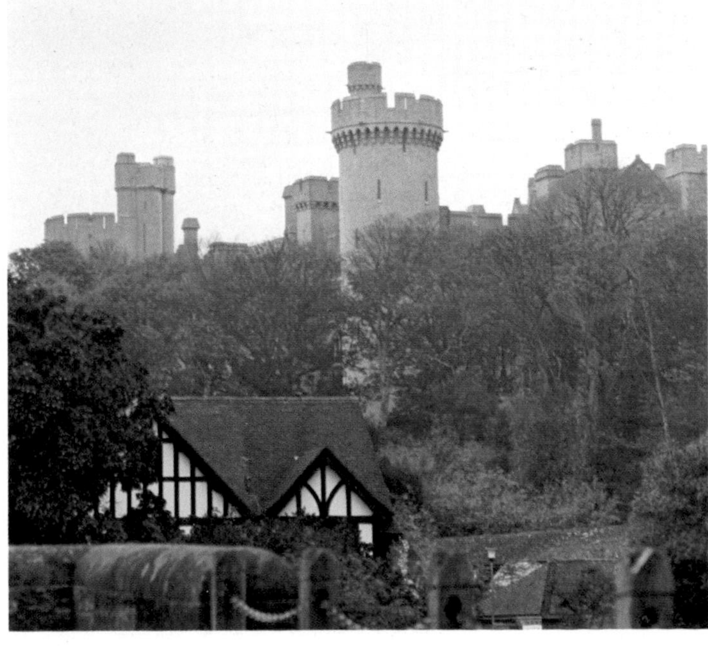

Arundel Castle, one of the most impressive Norman and medieval strongholds in the south of England, is the home of the dukes of Norfolk, hereditary Earls Marshal of England.

Key to Town Plans

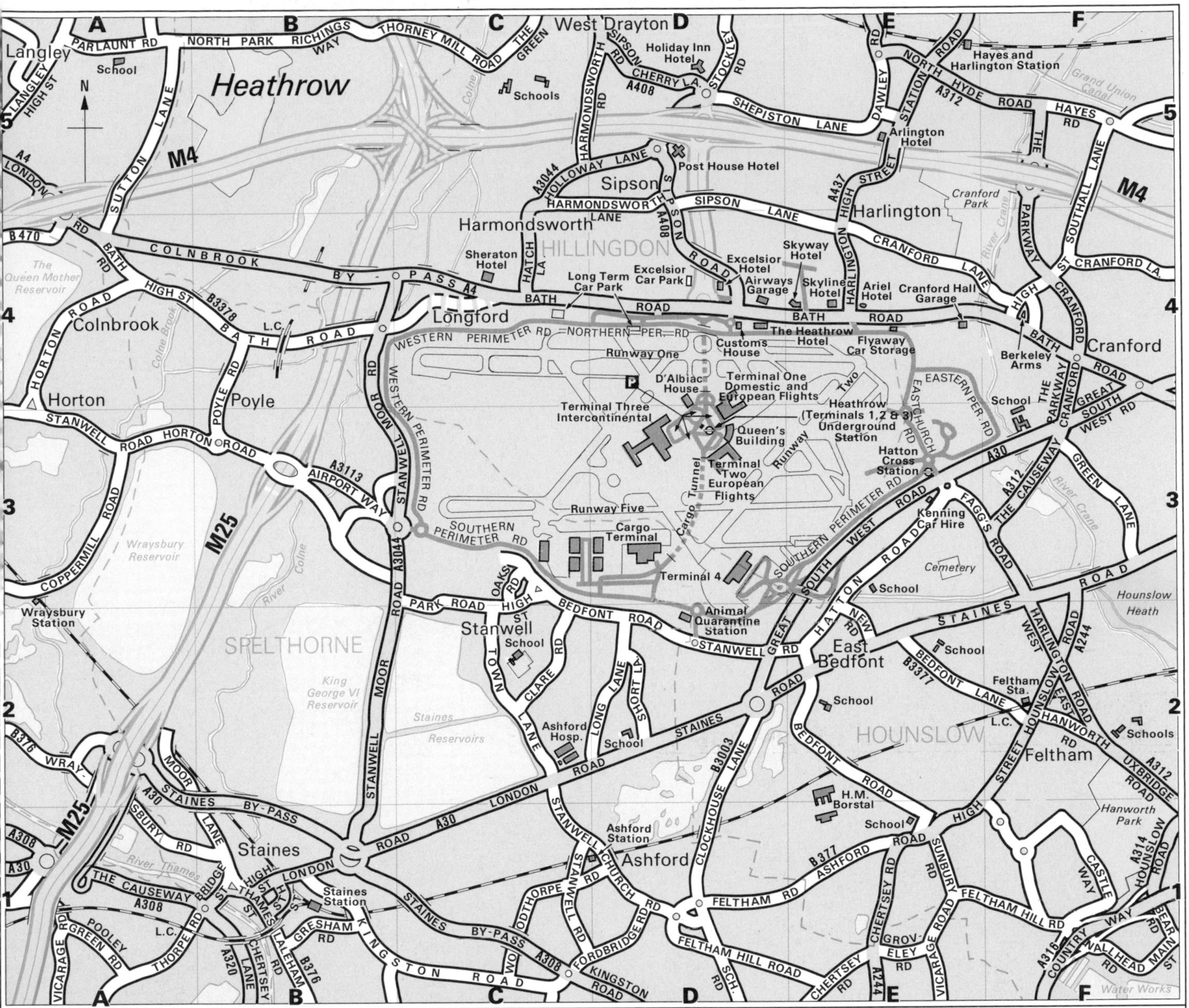

Heathrow Airport

Biggest and busiest airport in the United Kingdom, handling more international traffic than any other airport in the world, Heathrow broke its own records on 31 August 1980, when 112,880 passengers passed through. 1983 saw a total of 26,749,200 travellers, assisted by the 45,000-strong staff of the British Airports Authority and the 74 airline companies from 68 countries which operate scheduled services from the airport. Aircraft go to over 90 countries, and Heathrow's No 1 runway, 2.42 miles (3.9km) in length, is the longest used by civilian aircraft in the United Kingdom.

It all began when the site was transferred from the Air Ministry to the Ministry of Civil Aviation on 1 January 1946. On 31 May 1946, it opened as London (Heathrow) Airport, superseding the Airport of London at Croydon, established in 1928. This resulted in the operation of direct services between the United Kingdom and the United States of America. On 16 December 1955, the first three permanent buildings were opened by the Queen, and all three passenger terminals are now interlinked by pedestrian subways with moving walkways. The terminals are situated in the central area of the airport, and are also linked to the M4. A fourth terminal is under construction on the south-eastern side of the airport.

Terminal 1 is used by United Kingdom and Irish airlines for domestic and European flights, and for British Airways flights to and from certain destinations in North America. Terminal 2 is used by other European airlines except for the Irish airlines. Terminal 3 is the one used by intercontinental airlines going to Africa, America, Asia and Australia.

In 1966, the newly appointed British Airways Authority took over the responsibility for both Heathrow and the second airport at Gatwick (the two are linked by a frequent daily helicopter service). Direct rail access came in 1977 when the Underground's Piccadilly Line was extended and in the same year, Heathrow Central Station opened.

Today the Queens Building Roof Gardens and viewing gallery allow visitors to admire the aircraft and to watch the airport at work. There is a small admission charge for this.

Visitors who have come to the Queens Building Roof Gardens can also take refreshments there, at one of the many restaurants to be found throughout the airport. All three passenger terminals have licensed restaurants where full meals are served, and there are also grill bars providing hot meals. Light refreshments can also be bought.

Multi-storey car parks are sited at each of the passenger terminals for short term car parking. Heathrow also has long term car parks, situated on the northern perimeter road. A free coach carries passengers between the long term car parks and the terminals. During the night (from midnight to 6am), passengers wanting this service can contact the coach base on the special direct line telephones which are in use at the pick-up points.

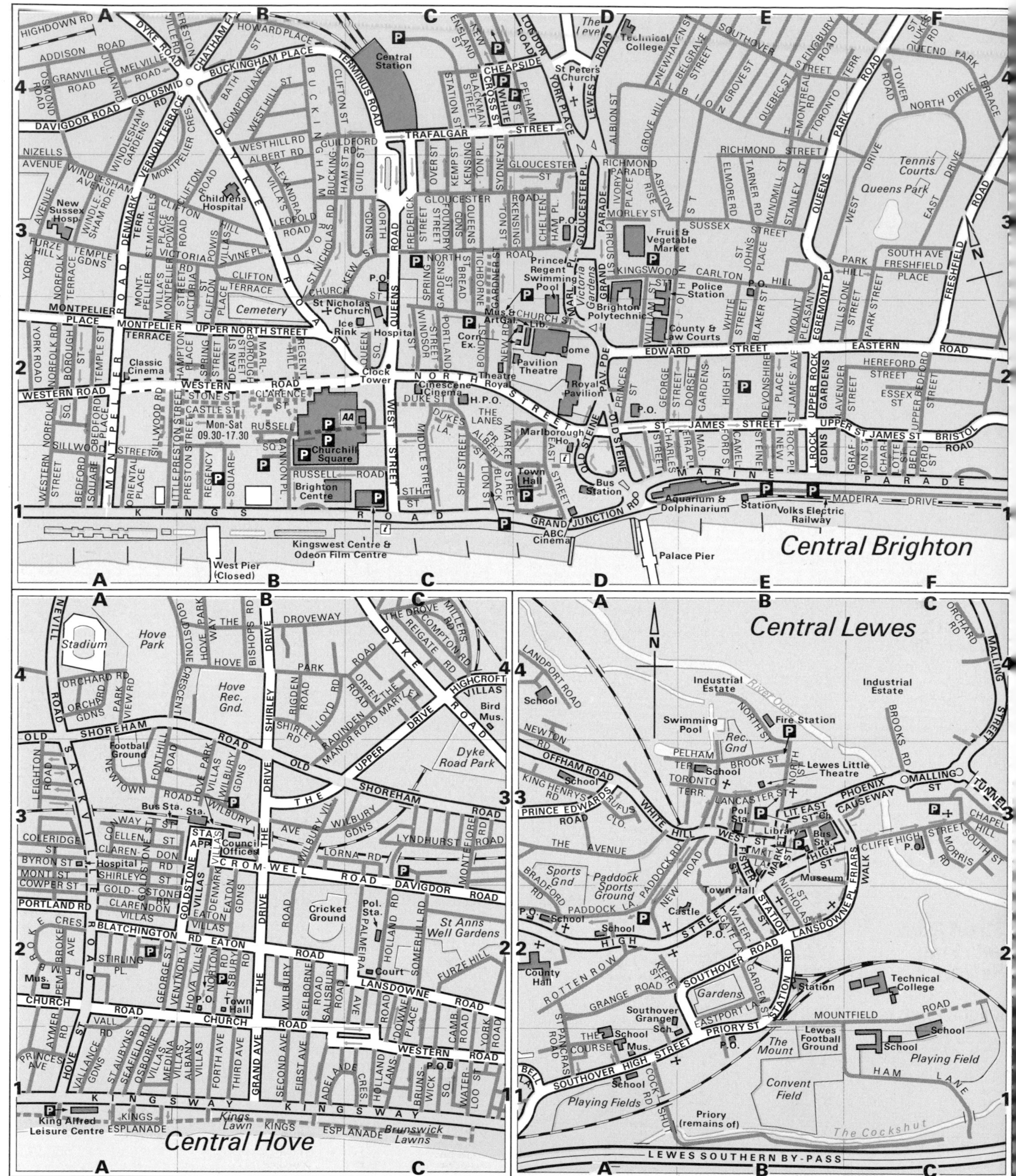

Brighton

Dr Richard Russell, from nearby Lewes, created the resort of Brighton almost singlehandedly. And he did it not by building houses or hotels, but by writing a book. His book, which praised the health-giving properties of sea-bathing and sea air, soon came to the attention of George, then Prince Regent and one day to become King George IV. He stayed at Brighthelmstone – as it was then known – in 1783 and again in 1784. In 1786 the Prince rented a villa on the Steine – a modest house that was eventually transformed into the astonishing Pavilion. By 1800 – its popularity assured by royal patronage – the resort was described in a contemporary directory as 'the most frequented and without exception one of the most fashionable towns in the kingdom'.

Perhaps the description does not quite fit today, but Brighton is a perennially popular seaside resort, as well as a shopping centre, university town and cultural venue. The Pavilion still draws most crowds, of course. Its beginnings as a villa are entirely hidden in a riot of Near Eastern architectural motifs, largely the creation of John Nash. Brighton's great days as a Regency resort *par excellence* are preserved in the sweeping crescents and elegant terraces, buildings which help to make it one of the finest townscapes in the whole of Europe.

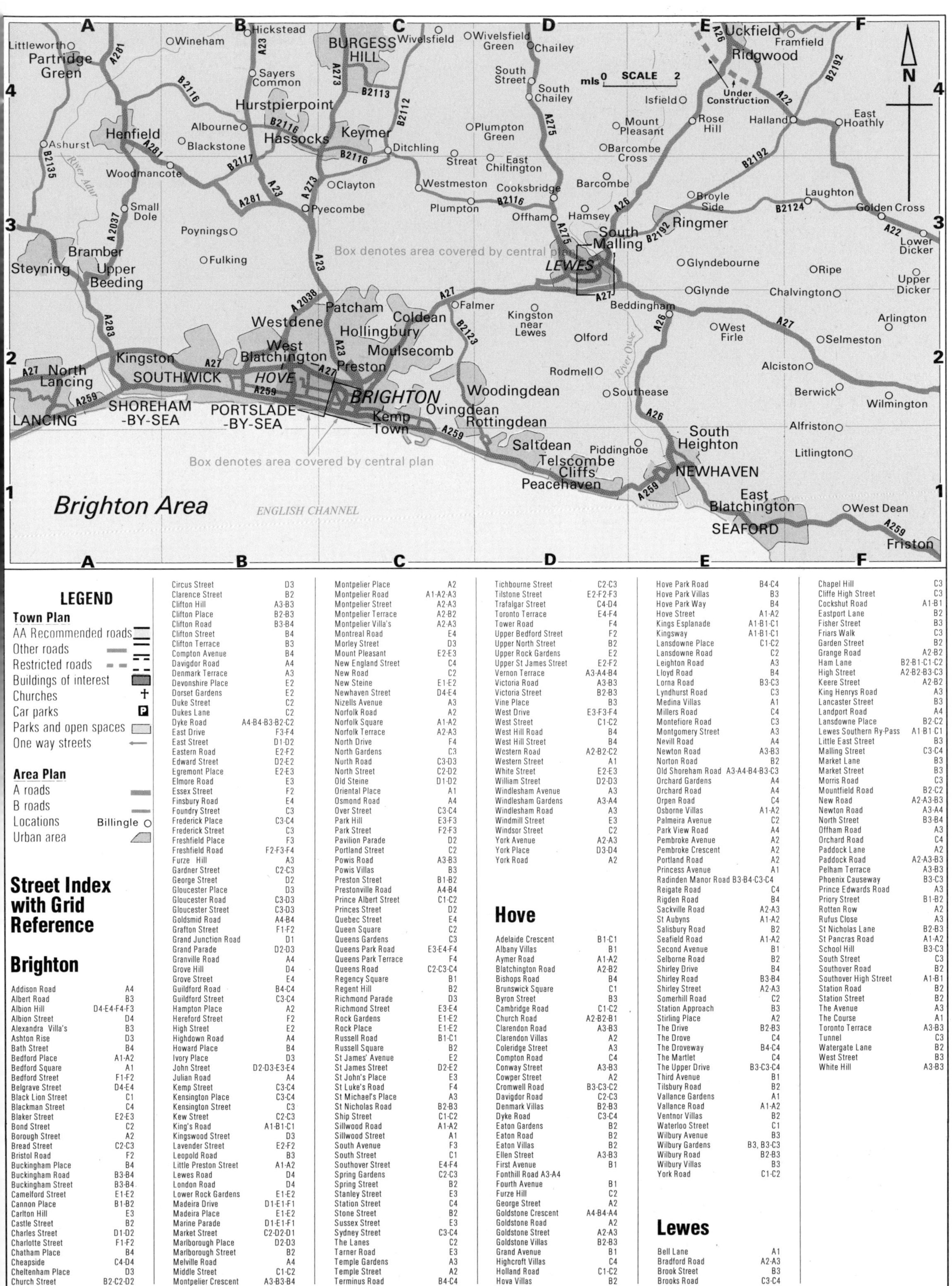

LEGEND

Town Plan

AA Recommended roads
Other roads
Restricted roads
Buildings of interest
Churches
Car parks
Parks and open spaces
One way streets

Area Plan

A roads
B roads
Locations — Billingle
Urban area

Street Index with Grid Reference

Brighton

Hove

Lewes

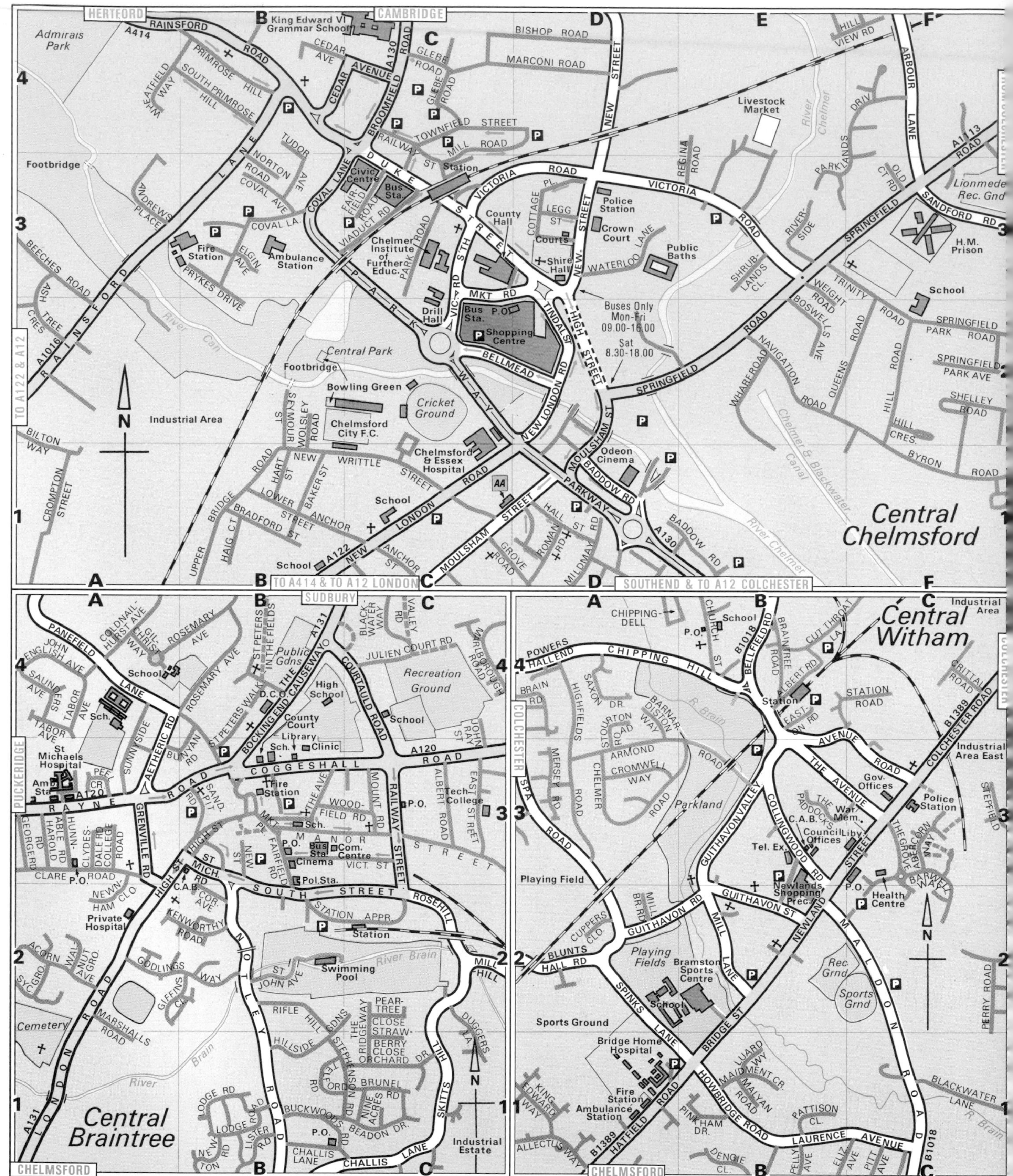

Chelmsford

Important since Roman times, this county town of Essex has undergone a good deal of expansion and development in recent years, providing it with good shopping and leisure facilities. Older buildings are concentrated in the Tindal Street area, notably the Shire Hall and the Cathedral, which dates from the 15th century. The cattle market (now on a modern site) has been going since Elizabethan days, and other places of interest include the Chelmsford and Essex Museum, which also houses the Museum of the Essex Regiment.

Braintree has been concerned with textile making since the early Middle Ages, and still keeps up the connection with the Courtaulds Group, associated with the area since the 19th century.

Maldon has retained a fascinating old quarter around All Saints Church, at the top of the High Street. A river port which has seen some industrialisation, it remains popular with holidaymakers for its position at the junction of the Blackwater and Chelmer rivers, and offers good facilities for boating along the river banks.

Witham's recent Town Development Scheme has brought expansion, incorporating housing estates, offices and factories for this ancient town on the River Brain. It has nevertheless retained some fine Georgian buildings, and several old coaching inns can be seen in the main street.

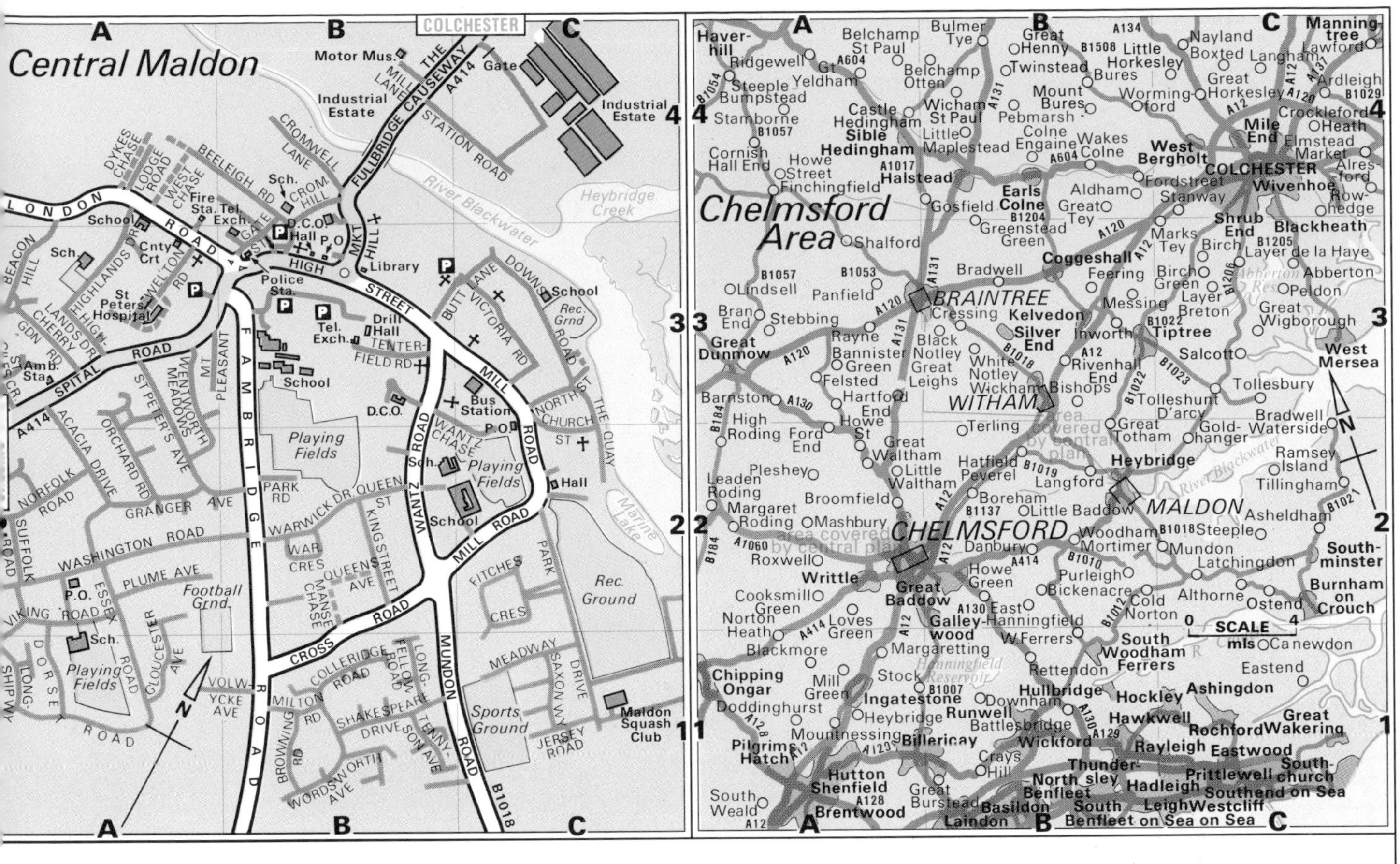

LEGEND

Town Plan

AA recommended route
Restricted roads
Other roads
Buildings of interest Theatre
Car parks
Parks and open spaces

Area Plan

A roads
B roads
Locations Notley
Urban area

Street Index with Grid Reference

Chelmsford

Anchor Street	C1
Andrews Place	A3
Arbour Lane	F4-F3
Ash Treet Crescent	A3-A2
Baddow Road	D1-E1
Baker Street	B1
Beeches Road	A3-A2
Bellmead	C2-D2
Bilton Way	A2-A1
Bishops Road	C4-D4
Boswells Avenue	E3-E2
Bradford Street	B1
Broomfield Road	C4
Byron Road	F2-F1
Cedar Avenue	B4-C4
Cottage Place	D3
Coval Avenue	B3
Coval Lane	B3-C3
Crompton Street	A1
Duke Street	C4-C3-D3
Elgin Avenue	B3
Fairfield Road	C3
Glebe Road	C4
Grove Road	C1-D1
Haig Court	B1
Hall Street	D1
Hart Street	B1
High Street	D3-D2
Hill Crescent	F2
Hill Road	F2
Hill View Road	E4-F4
Legg Street	D3
Lower Anchor Street	B1-C1
Marconi Road	C4-D4
Market Road	C3-D3
Mildmay Road	D1
Mill Road	C4-D4
Moulsham Street	C1-D1-D2
Navigation Road	E2
New London Road	B1-C1-D1-D2
New Street	D3-D4
New Writtle Street	B1-C1
Norton Road	B3
Old Court Road	F3
Parklands Drive	E3-F3-F4
Park Road	C3
Parkway	B3-C3-C2-D2-D1-E1
Primrose Hill	B4
Prykes Drive	B3-B2
Queens Road	E2-F2 F3
Railway Street	C4-C3
Rainsford Lane	A2-A3-B3-B4
Rainsford Road	A4-B4
Regina Road	E3-E4
Riverside	E3
Roman Road	D1
Sandford Road	F3
Seymour Street	B2-B1
Shelley Road	F2
Shrublands Close	E3
South Primrose Hill	A4-B4
Springfield Park Avenue	F2
Springfield Park Road	F2
Sprinfield Road	D2-E2-E3-F3-F4
Tindal Street	D3-D2
Townfield Street	C4-D4
Trinity Road	E3-F3-F2
Tudor Avenue	B4-B3
Upper Bridge Road	B1
Viaduct Road	B3-B4
Victoria Road	C3-D3-E3
Victoria Road South	C2-C3
Waterloo Lane	D3
Weight Road	E3-E2
Wharf Road	E2
Wheatfield Way	A4-B4
Wolsey Road	B1-B2

Maldon

Acacia Drive	A3-A2
Beacon Hill	A3-A4
Beeleigh Road	A4-B4
Browning Road	B1
Butt Lane	B3-C3
Cherry Garden Road	A3
Church Street	C2
Colleridge Road	B1
Cromwell Hill	B4
Cromwell Lane	B4
Cross Road	B1-B2
Dorset Road	A2-A1
Downs Road	C3
Dykes Chase	A4
Essex Road	A2-A1
Fambridge Road	B3-B2-B1
Fitches Crescent	C2
Fullbridge	B4
Gate Street	B3-B4
Gloucester Avenue	A1-A2
Granger Avenue	A2-B2
Highlands Drive	A3-A4
High Street	B3
Jersey Road	C1
King Street	B2
Lodge Road	A4
London Road	A4-A3-B3
Longfellow Road	B1
Longship Way	A1
Manse Chase	B2
Market Hill	B3-B4
Meadway	C1
Mill Lane	B4
Mill Road	B2-C2-C3-B3
Milton Road	B1
Mount Pleasant	A3
Mundon Road	B2-B1-C1
Norfolk Road	A2
North Street	C3
Orchard Road	A3-A2
Park Drive	C2-C1
Park Road	B2
Plume Avenue	A2
Queens Avenue	B2
Queen Street	B2
St Giles Crescent	A3
St Peter's Avenue	A3-B3
Saxon Way	C1
Shakespeare Drive	B1
Spital Road	A3-B3
Station Road	B4-C4
Suffolk Road	A2
The Causeway	B4-C4
The Quay	C3-C2
Tennyson Avenue	B1
Tenterfield Road	B3
Victoria Road	C3
Viking Road	A1-A2
Volwycke Avenue	A1-B1
Wantz Chase	B3-C3-C2
Wantz Road	B2-B3
Warwick Crescent	B2
Warwick Drive	B2
Washington Road	A2-B2
Wellington Road	A3
Wentworth Meadows	A3-A2
West Chase	A4
Wordsworth Avenue	B1

Witham

Abercorn Way	C3
Albert Road	B4
Allectus Way	A1
Armond Road	A3-B3
Avenue Road	B4-B3-C4-C3
Barnadiston Way	A4
Barwell Way	C3-C2
Bellfield Road	B4
Blackwater Lane	C1
Blunts Hall Road	A2
Brain Road	A4
Braintree Road	B4
Bridge Street	B1-B2
Chelmer Road	A3-B3
Chippingdell	A4-B4
Chipping Hill	A4-B4
Church Street	B4
Colchester Road	C3-C4
Collingwood Road	B3
Crittal Road	C4
Cromwell Way	A3
Cuppers Close	A2
Cut Throat Lane	B4-C4
Dengie Close	B1
Easton Road	B4
Elizabeth Avenue	B1-C1
Guithavon Road	B3-B2
Guithavon Street	B3-B2
Guithavon Valley	B3
Hatfield Road	A1-B1
Highfields Road	A4-A3
Howbridge Road	B1
King Edward Way	A1
Laurence Avenue	B1-C1
Luard Way	B1
Maidment Crescent	B1
Maldon Road	B2-C2-C1
Malyan Road	B1
Mersey Road	A3
Millbridge Road	A2
Mill Lane	B2
Newland Street	B2-B3-C3
Pattison Close	B1
Pelly Avenue	B1
Perry Road	C2
Pinkham Drive	B1
Pitt Avenue	C1
Powers Hall End	A4
Saxon Drive	A4
Spa Road	A3-A2
Spinks Lane	A2-A1-B1
Station Road	B4-C4
Stepfield	C3
Stourton Road	A3-A4
The Avenue	B3-C3
The Grove	C3
The Paddocks	B3-C3

Braintree

Acorn Avenue	A2
Albert Road	C3
Aetheric Road	A3-A4
Beadon Drive	C1
Blackwater Way	C4
Bocking End	B3-B4
Brunel Road	C1
Buckwoods Road	B1
Bunyan Road	A3-B3-B4
Challis Lane	B1-C1
Clare Road	A3
Clydesdale Road	A3
Coggeshall Road	B3-C3
Coldnailhurst Avenue	A4
College Road	A3
Coronation Avenue	B2
Courtauld Road	B4-C4-C3
Duggers Lane	C2-C1
East Street	C3
Fairfield Road	B3
George Road	A3
Giffins Close	A2-B2
Gilchrist Way	A4
Godlings Way	A2-B2
Grenville Road	A3
Harold Road	A3
High Street	A2-A3-B3
Hillside Gardens	B1-B2-C2
Hunnable Road	A3
John English Avenue	A4
John Ray Street	C4-C3
Julien Court Road	C4
Kenworthy Road	A2-B2
Lister Road	B1
Lodge Road	B1
London Road	A1-A2
Manor Street	B3-C3
Market Place	B3
Marlborough Road	C4
Marshalls Road	A2-A1
Mill Hill	C2
Mount Road	C3
Newnham Close	A2-A3
New Street	B3
Newton Road	B1
Nine Acres	C1
Wotley Road	B2-B1
Orchard Drive	C1
Panefield Lane	A4
Peartree Close	C2
Peel Crescent	A3
Railway Street	C3
Rayne Road	A3-B3
Rifle Hill	B2
Rosehill	C2
Rosemary Avenue	A4-B4
St John Avenue	B2
St Michaels Road	B3
St Peters in the Fields	B4
St Peters Walk	B3-B4
Sandpitt Road	B3
Saunders Avenue	A4
Skitts Hill	C1-C2
South Street	B3-B2-C2
Station Approach	B2-C2
Stephenson Road	B1-C1
Strawberry Close	C1
Sunnyside	A3-A4
Sycamore Grove	A2
The Avenue	B3
The Causeway	B4
The Ridgeway	C1-C2
Tabor Avenue	A4
Telford Road	B1
Valley Road	C4
Victoria Street	B3-C3
Walnut Grove	A2
Woodfield Road	B3-C3

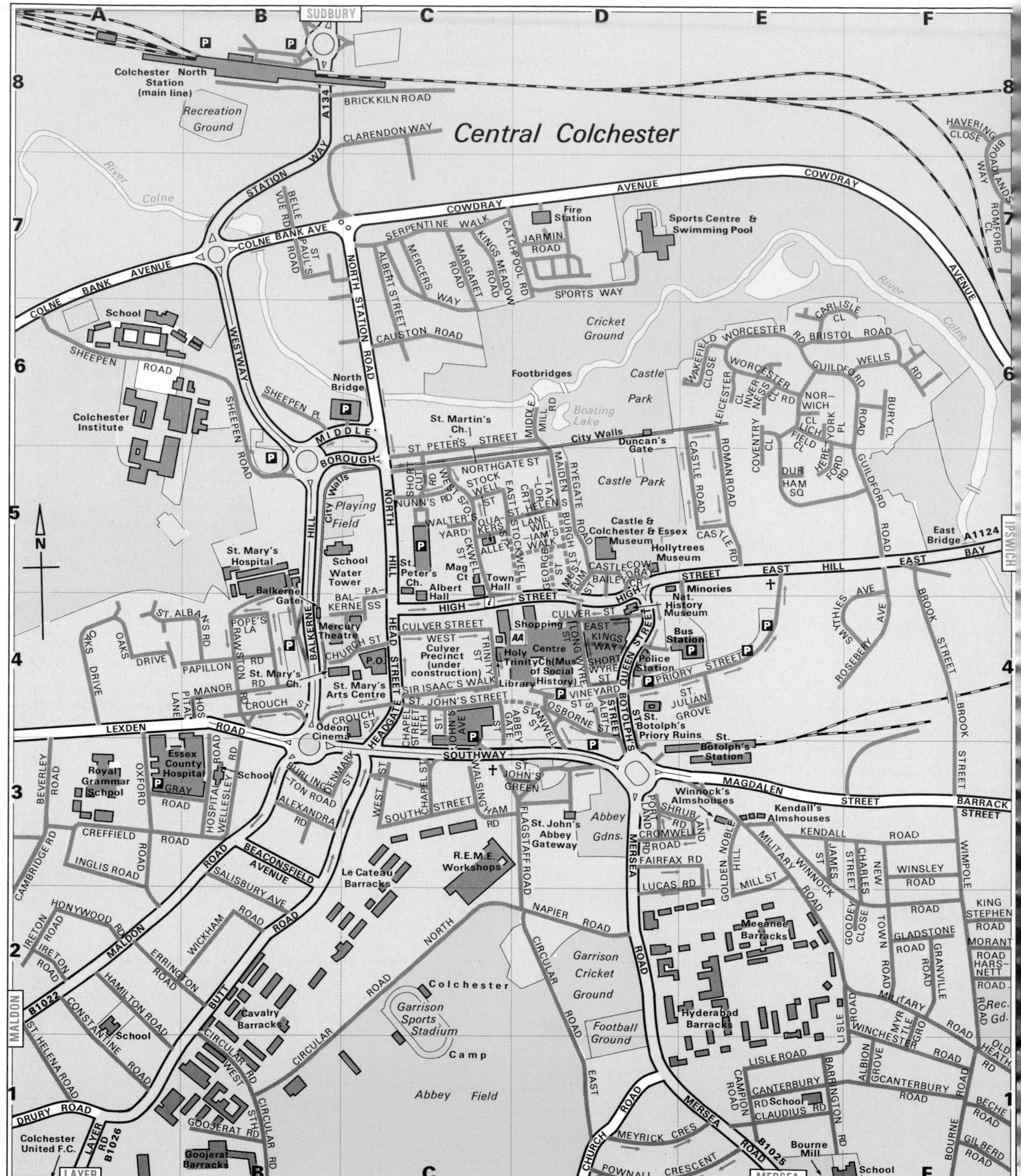

Colchester

The oldest recorded town in England, Colchester was also a Roman capital and the great walls built by the invaders stand to this day. Remains of one of their massive gateways, Balkerne Gate, have also survived. Colchester's Norman castle keep, the largest in Britain, retains an air of dark medieval menace, although it now houses nothing more sinister than the Colcester and Essex Museum where many Roman antiquities can be seen. Colchester's proximity to the continent led to the arrival of Flemish refugees during the 16th century, and they revived the cloth trade that had flourished here in the Middle Ages. Many of their attractive gabled and colour-washed houses line West Stockwell Street, known as Dutch Quarter. In contrast, much of the town centre has been turned into a modern shopping precinct.

In the High Street is Hollytrees Museum, an early 18th century house containing collections of costumes and toys, etc. Two of the town's churches have become museums in recent years; Holy Trinity is a museum of social history and All Saints houses a natural history museum.

The town hall is one of Colchester's most striking buildings; dating from the end of the 19th century, it has an ornate exterior and a 162ft tower. Colchester's other tall tower is more famous. Known as 'Jumbo', it is a vast water tower built in 1882.

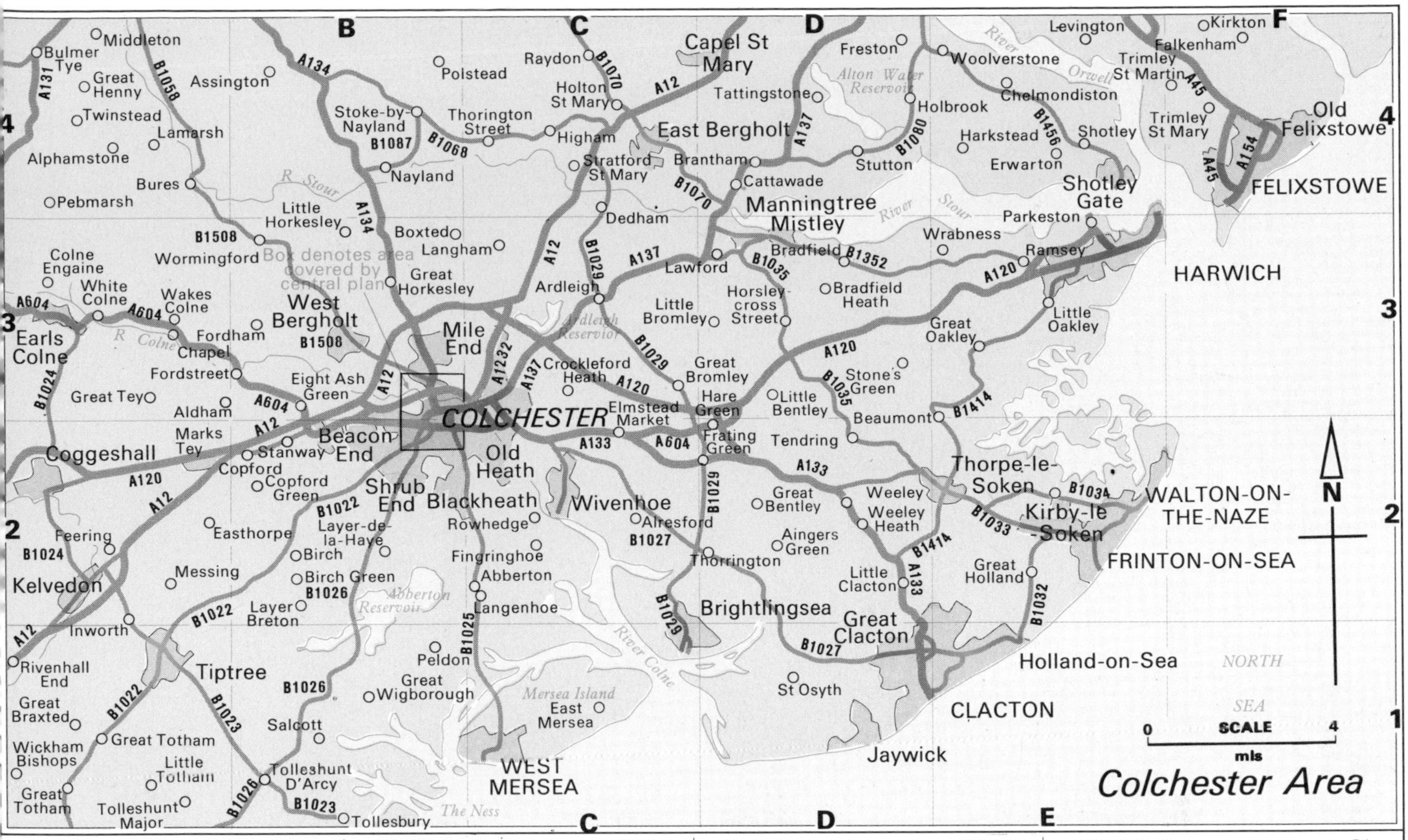

Colchester Area

LEGEND

Town Plan

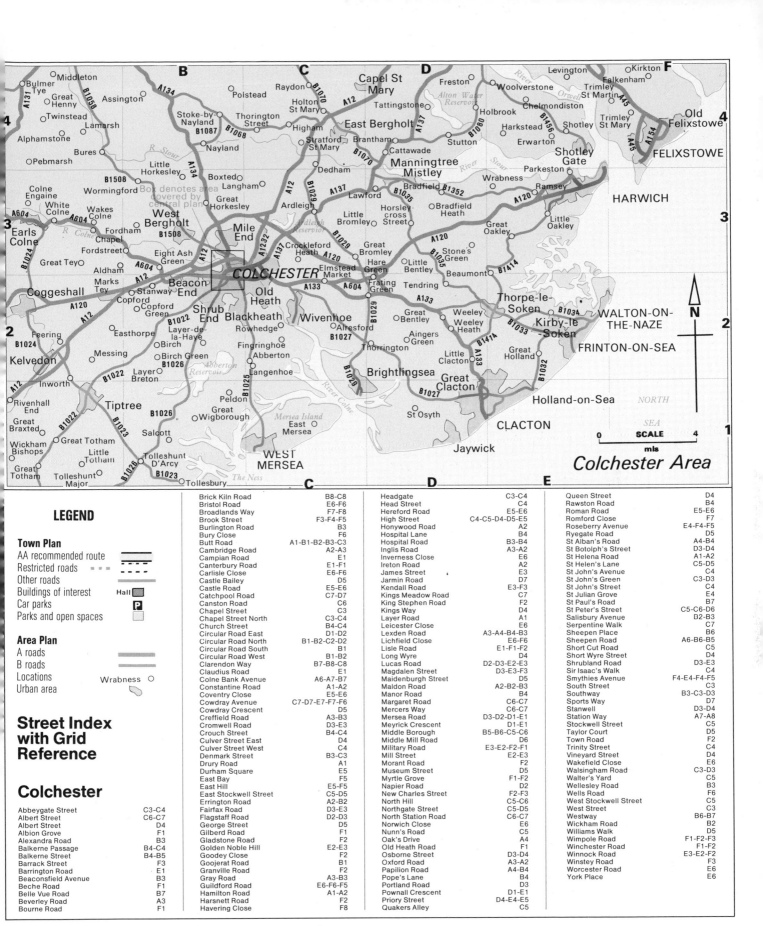

- AA recommended route
- Restricted roads
- Other roads
- Buildings of interest — Hall
- Car parks — P
- Parks and open spaces

Area Plan

- A roads
- B roads
- Locations — Wrabness
- Urban area

Street Index with Grid Reference

Colchester

Abbeygate Street	C3-C4
Albert Street	C6-C7
Albert Street	D4
Albion Grove	F1
Alexandra Road	B3
Balkerne Passage	B4-C4
Balkerne Street	B4-B5
Barrack Street	F3
Barrington Road	E1
Beaconsfield Avenue	B3
Beche Road	F1
Belle Vue Road	B7
Beverley Road	A3
Bourne Road	F1
Brick Kiln Road	B8-C8
Bristol Road	E6-F6
Broadlands Way	F7-F8
Brook Street	F3-F4-F5
Burlington Road	B3
Bury Close	F6
Butt Road	A1-B1-B2-B3-C3
Cambridge Road	A2-A3
Campian Road	E1
Canterbury Road	E1-F1
Carlisle Close	E6-F6
Castle Bailey	D5
Castle Road	E5-E6
Catchpool Road	C7-D7
Canston Road	C6
Chapel Street	C3
Chapel Street North	C3-C4
Church Street	B4-C4
Circular Road East	D1-D2
Circular Road North	B1-B2-C2-D2
Circular Road South	B1
Circular Road West	B1-B2
Clarendon Way	B7-B8-C8
Claudius Road	E1
Colne Bank Avenue	A6-A7-B7
Constantine Road	A1-A2
Coventry Close	E5-E6
Cowdray Avenue	C7-D7-E7-F7-F6
Cowdray Crescent	D5
Creffield Road	A3-B3
Cromwell Road	D3-E3
Crouch Street	B4-C4
Culver Street East	D4
Culver Street West	C4
Denmark Street	B3-C3
Drury Road	A1
Durham Square	E5
East Bay	F5
East Hill	E5-F5
East Stockwell Street	C5-D5
Errington Road	A2-B2
Fairfax Road	D3-E3
Flagstaff Road	D2-D3
George Street	D5
Gilberd Road	F1
Gladstone Road	F2
Golden Noble Hill	E2-E3
Goodey Close	F2
Goojerat Road	B1
Granville Road	F2
Gray Road	A3-B3
Guildford Road	E6-F6-F5
Hamilton Road	A1-A2
Harsnett Road	F2
Havering Close	F8
Headgate	C3-C4
Head Street	C4
Hereford Road	E5-E6
High Street	C4-C5-D4-D5-E5
Honywood Road	A2
Hospital Lane	B4
Hospital Road	B3-B4
Inglis Road	A3-A2
Inverness Close	E6
Ireton Road	A2
James Street	E3
Jarmin Road	D7
Kendall Road	E3-F3
Kings Meadow Road	C7
King Stephen Road	F2
Kings Way	D4
Layer Road	A1
Leicester Close	E6
Lexden Road	A3-A4-B4-B3
Lichfield Close	E6-F6
Lisle Road	E1-F1-F2
Long Wyre	D4
Lucas Road	D2-D3-E2-E3
Magdalen Street	D3-E3-F3
Maidenburgh Street	D5
Maldon Road	A2-B2-B3
Manor Road	B4
Margaret Road	C6-C7
Mercers Way	C6-C7
Mersea Road	D3-D2-D1-E1
Meyrick Crescent	D1-E1
Middle Borough	B5-B6-C5-C6
Middle Mill Road	D6
Military Road	E3-E2-F2-F1
Mill Street	E2-E3
Morant Road	F2
Museum Street	D5
Myrtle Grove	F1-F2
Napier Road	D2
New Charles Street	F2-F3
North Hill	C5-C6
Northgate Street	C5-D5
North Station Road	C6-C7
Norwich Close	E6
Nunn's Road	C5
Oak's Drive	A4
Old Heath Road	F1
Osborne Street	D3-D4
Oxford Road	A3-A2
Papilion Road	A4-B4
Pope's Lane	B4
Portland Road	D3
Pownall Crescent	D1-E1
Priory Street	D4-E4-E5
Quakers Alley	C5
Queen Street	D4
Rawston Road	B4
Roman Road	E5-E6
Romford Close	F7
Roseberry Avenue	E4-F4-F5
Ryegate Road	D5
St Alban's Road	A4-B4
St Botolph's Street	D3-D4
St Helena Road	A1-A2
St Helen's Lane	C5-D5
St John's Avenue	C4
St John's Green	C3-D3
St John's Street	C4
St Julian Grove	E4
St Paul's Road	B7
St Peter's Street	C5-C6-D6
Salisbury Avenue	B2-B3
Serpentine Walk	C7
Sheepen Place	B6
Sheepen Road	A6-B6-B5
Short Cut Road	C5
Short Wyre Street	D4
Shrubland Road	D3-E3
Sir Isaac's Walk	C4
Smythies Avenue	F4-E4-F4-F5
South Street	C3
Southway	B3-C3-D3
Sports Way	D7
Stanwell	D3-D4
Station Way	A7-A8
Stockwell Street	C5
Taylor Court	D5
Town Road	F2
Trinity Street	C4
Vineyard Street	D4
Wakefield Close	E6
Walsingham Road	C3-D3
Walter's Yard	C5
Wellesley Road	B3
Wells Road	F6
West Stockwell Street	C5
West Street	C3
Westway	B6-B7
Wickham Road	B2
Williams Walk	D5
Wimpole Road	F1-F2-F3
Winchester Road	F1-F2
Winnock Road	E3-E2-F2
Winstey Road	F3
Worcester Road	E6
York Place	E6

COLCHESTER
The castle keep, all that remains of Colchester's great fortress that once stretched from the High Street to the north wall of the town, was built round the masonry platform of the Roman Temple of Claudius.

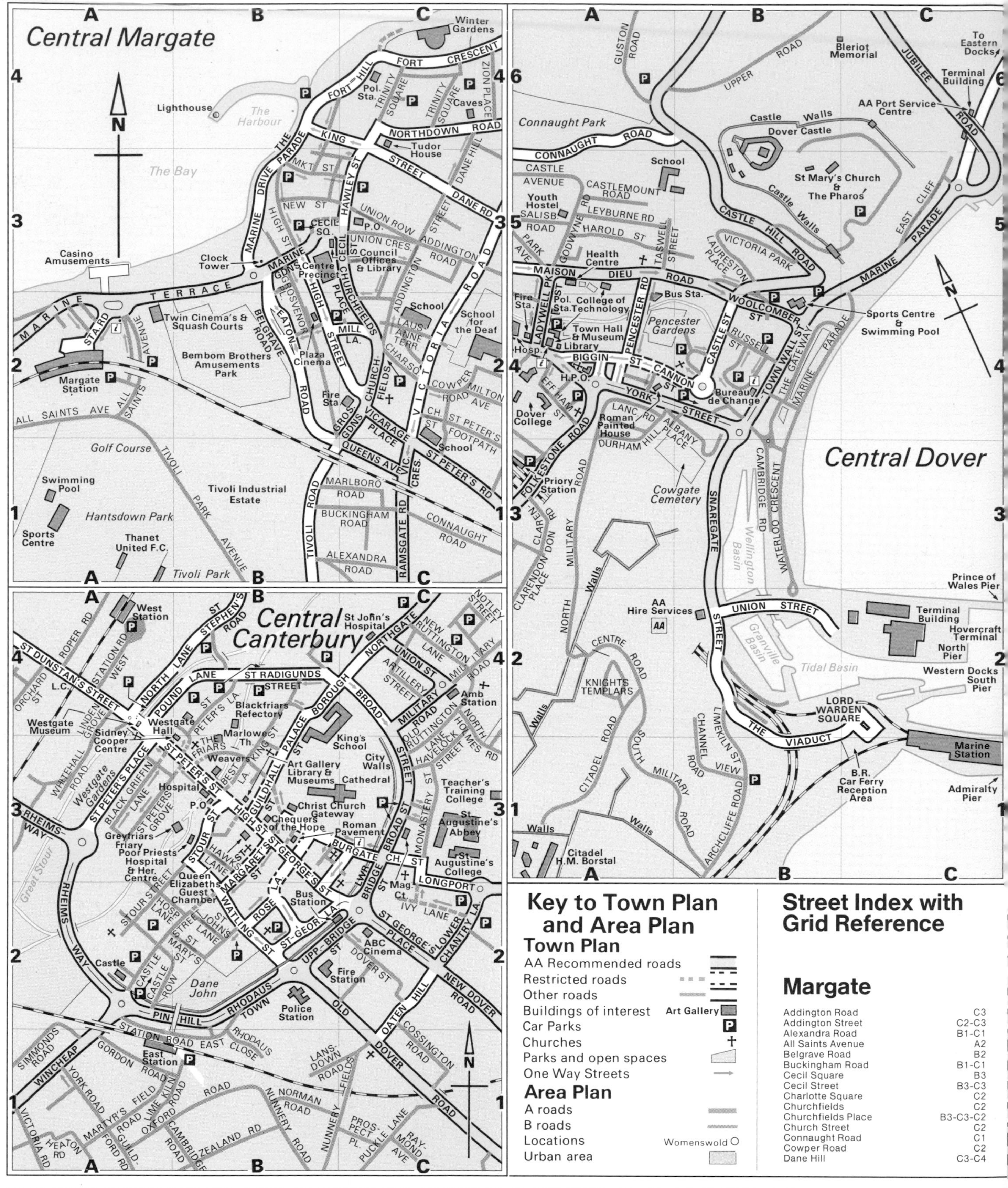

Key to Town Plan and Area Plan

Town Plan

- AA Recommended roads
- Restricted roads
- Other roads
- Buildings of interest (Art Gallery)
- Car Parks
- Churches
- Parks and open spaces
- One Way Streets

Area Plan

- A roads
- B roads
- Locations (Womenswold)
- Urban area

Street Index with Grid Reference

Margate

Addington Road	C3
Addington Street	C2-C3
Alexandra Road	B1-C1
All Saints Avenue	A2
Belgrave Road	B2
Buckingham Road	B1-C1
Cecil Square	B3
Cecil Street	B3-C3
Charlotte Square	C2
Churchfields	C2
Churchfields Place	B3-C3-C2
Church Street	C2
Connaught Road	C1
Cowper Road	C2
Dane Hill	C3-C4

Dover

Travellers tend to rush through Dover – it is one of the busiest passenger ports in England – and by so doing miss an exciting town with much of interest. Outstanding is the castle. Its huge fortifications have guarded the town since the 12th century, but within its walls are even older structures – a Saxon church and a Roman lighthouse called the Pharos. In the town itself, the town hall is housed within the walls of a 13th-century guest house called the Maison Dieu. The Roman Painted House in New Street consists of substantial remains of a Roman town house and include the best-preserved Roman wall paintings north of the Alps.

Canterbury is one of Britain's most historic towns. It is the seat of the Church in England, and has been so since St Augustine began his mission here in the 6th century. The cathedral is a priceless work of art containing many other works of art, including superb displays of medieval carving and stained glass. Ancient city walls – partly built on Roman foundations – still circle parts of the city, and a wealth of grand public buildings as well as charming private houses of many periods line the maze of lanes in the shadow of the cathedral.

Margate and ***Ramsgate*** both grew as commercial ports, but for many years they have specialised in catering for holidaymakers who like safe, sandy beaches and excellent facilities.

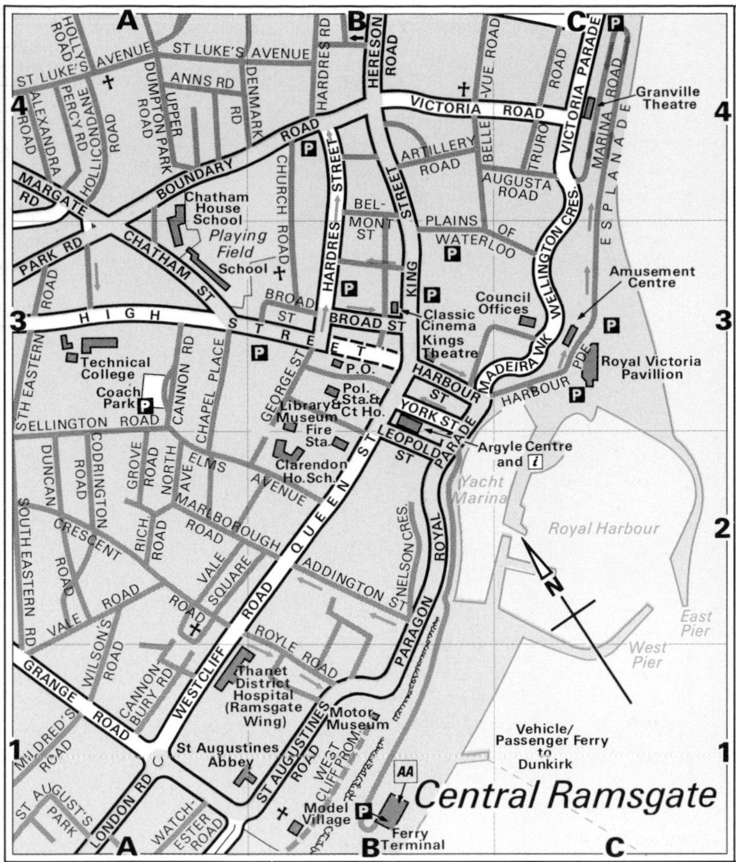

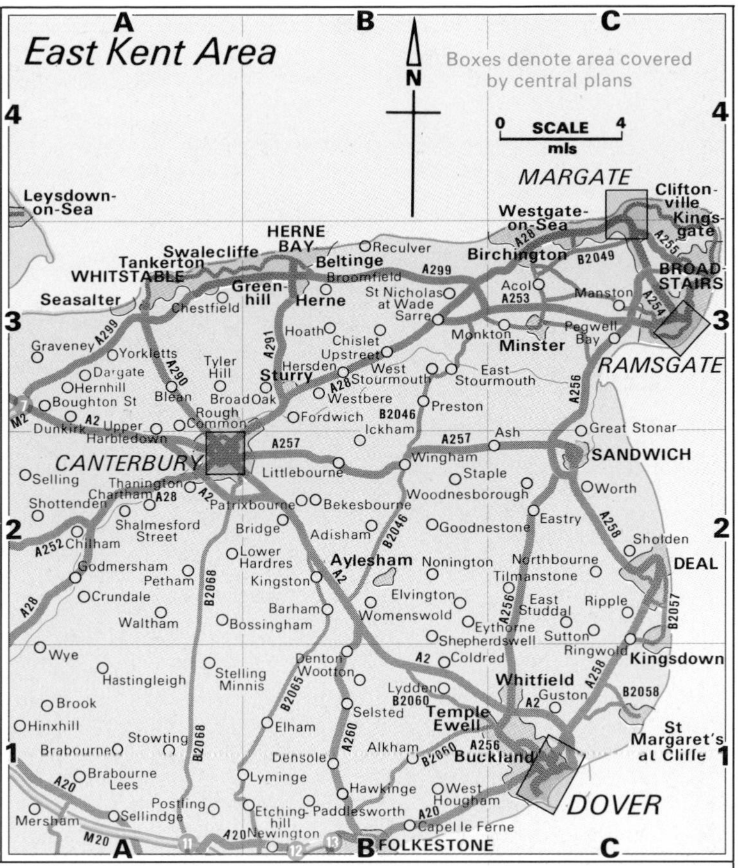

Central Ramsgate

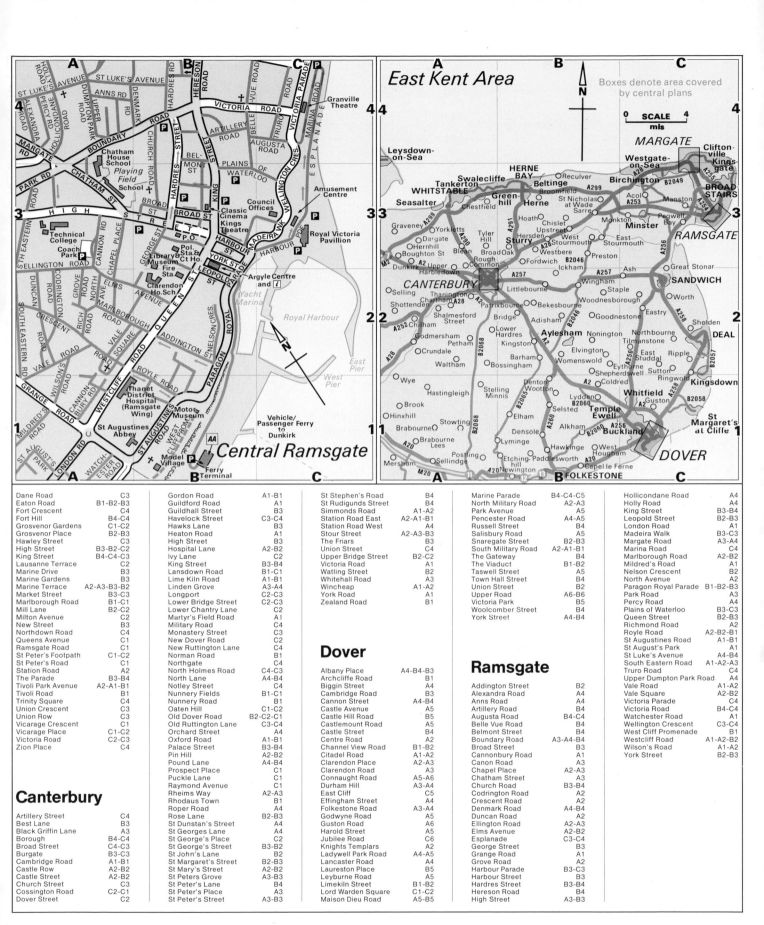

East Kent Area

Boxes denote area covered by central plans

Dane Road	C3
Eaton Road	B1-B2-B3
Fort Crescent	C4
Fort Hill	B4-C4
Grosvenor Gardens	C1-C2
Grosvenor Place	B2-B3
Hawley Street	C3
High Street	B3-B2-C2
King Street	B4-C4-C3
Lausanne Terrace	C2
Marine Drive	B3
Marine Gardens	B3
Marine Terrace	A2-A3-B3-B2
Market Street	B3-C3
Marlborough Road	B1-C1
Mill Lane	B2-C2
Milton Avenue	C2
New Street	B3
Northdown Road	C4
Queens Avenue	C1
Ramsgate Road	C1
St Peter's Footpath	C1-C2
St Peter's Road	C1
Station Road	A2
The Parade	B3-B4
Tivoli Park Avenue	A2-A1-B1
Tivoli Road	B1
Trinity Square	C4
Union Crescent	C3
Union Row	C3
Vicarage Crescent	C1
Vicarage Place	C1-C2
Victoria Road	C2-C3
Zion Place	C4

Canterbury

Artillery Street	C4
Best Lane	B3
Black Griffin Lane	A3
Borough	B4-C4
Broad Street	C4-C3
Burgate	B3-C3
Cambridge Road	A1-B1
Castle Row	A2-B2
Castle Street	A2-B2
Church Street	C3
Cossington Road	C2-C1
Dover Street	C2
Gordon Road	A1-B1
Guildford Road	A1
Guildhall Street	B3
Havelock Street	C3-C4
Hawks Lane	B3
Heaton Road	A1
High Street	B3
Hospital Lane	A2-B2
Ivy Lane	C2
King Street	B3-B4
Lansdown Road	B1-C1
Lime Kiln Road	A1-B1
Linden Grove	A3-A4
Longport	C2-C3
Lower Bridge Street	C2-C3
Lower Chantry Lane	C2
Martyr's Field Road	A1
Military Road	C4
Monastery Street	C3
New Dover Road	C2
New Ruttington Lane	C4
Norman Road	B1
Northgate	C4
North Holmes Road	C4-C3
North Lane	A4-B4
Notley Street	C4
Nunnery Fields	B1-C1
Nunnery Road	B1
Oaten Hill	C1-C2
Old Dover Road	B2-C2-C1
Old Ruttington Lane	C3-C4
Orchard Street	A4
Oxford Road	A1-B1
Palace Street	B3-B4
Pin Hill	A2-B2
Pound Lane	A4-B4
Prospect Place	C1
Puckle Lane	C1
Raymond Avenue	C1
Rheims Way	A2-A3
Rhodaus Town	B1
Roper Road	A4
Rose Lane	B2-B3
St Dunstan's Street	A4
St Georges Lane	A4
St George's Place	C2
St George's Street	B3-B2
St John's Lane	B2
St Margaret's Street	B2-B3
St Mary's Street	A2-B2
St Peters Grove	A3-B3
St Peter's Lane	B4
St Peter's Place	A3
St Peter's Street	A3-B3
St Stephen's Road	B4
St Rudigunds Street	B4
Simmonds Road	A1-A2
Station Road East	A2-A1-B1
Station Road West	A4
Stour Street	A2-A3-B3
The Friars	B3
Union Street	C4
Upper Bridge Street	B2-C2
Victoria Road	A1
Watling Street	B2
Whitehall Road	A3
Wincheap	A1-A2
York Road	A1
Zealand Road	B1

Dover

Albany Place	A4-B4-B3
Archcliffe Road	B1
Biggin Street	A4
Cambridge Road	B3
Cannon Street	A4-B4
Castle Avenue	A5
Castle Hill Road	B5
Castlemount Road	A5
Castle Street	B4
Centre Road	A2
Channel View Road	B1-B2
Citadel Road	A1-A2
Clarendon Place	A2-A3
Clarendon Road	A3
Connaught Road	A5-A6
Durham Hill	A3-A4
East Cliff	C5
Effingham Street	A4
Folkestone Road	A3-A4
Godwyne Road	A5
Guston Road	A6
Harold Street	A5
Jubilee Road	C6
Knights Templars	A2
Ladywell Park Road	A4-A5
Lancaster Road	A4
Laureston Place	B5
Leyburne Road	A5
Limekiln Street	B1-B2
Lord Warden Square	C1-C2
Maison Dieu Road	A5-B5
Marine Parade	B4-C4-C5
North Military Road	A2-A3
Park Avenue	A5
Pencester Road	A4-A5
Russell Street	B4
Salisbury Road	A5
Snaregate Street	B2-B3
South Military Road	A2-A1-B1
The Gateway	B4
The Viaduct	B1-B2
Taswell Street	A5
Town Hall Street	B4
Union Street	B2
Upper Road	A6-B6
Victoria Park	B5
Woolcomber Street	B4
York Street	A4-B4

Ramsgate

Addington Street	B2
Alexandra Road	A4
Anns Road	A4
Artillery Road	B4
Augusta Road	B4-C4
Belle Vue Road	B4
Belmont Street	B4
Boundary Road	A3-A4-B4
Broad Street	B3
Cannonbury Road	A1
Canon Road	A3
Chapel Place	A2-A3
Chatham Street	A3
Church Road	B3-B4
Codrington Road	A2
Crescent Road	A2
Denmark Road	A4-B4
Duncan Road	A2
Ellington Road	A2-A3
Elms Avenue	A2-B2
Esplanade	C3-C4
George Street	B3
Grange Road	A1
Grove Road	A2
Harbour Parade	B3-C3
Harbour Street	B3
Hardres Street	B3-B4
Hereson Road	B4
High Street	A3-B3
Hollicondane Road	A4
Holly Road	A4
King Street	B3-B4
Leopold Street	B2-B3
London Road	A1
Madeira Walk	B3-C3
Margate Road	A3-A4
Marina Road	C4
Marlborough Road	A2-B2
Mildred's Road	A1
Nelson Crescent	B2
North Avenue	A2
Paragon Royal Parade	B1-B2-B3
Park Road	A3
Percy Road	A4
Plains of Waterloo	B3-C3
Queen Street	B2-B3
Richmond Road	A2
Royle Road	A2-B2-B1
St Augustines Road	A1-B1
St August's Park	A1
St Luke's Avenue	A4-B4
South Eastern Road	A1-A2-A3
Truro Road	C4
Upper Dumpton Park Road	A4
Vale Road	A1-A2
Vale Square	A2-B2
Victoria Parade	C4
Victoria Road	B4-C4
Watchester Road	A1
Wellington Crescent	C3-C4
West Cliff Promenade	B1
Westcliff Road	A1-A2-B2
Wilson's Road	A1-A2
York Street	B2-B3

DOVER
The famous White Cliffs of Dover provide exhilarating coastal walks with views out across the Channel. Paths to the north-east lead to Walmer and to the south-east, to Folkestone.

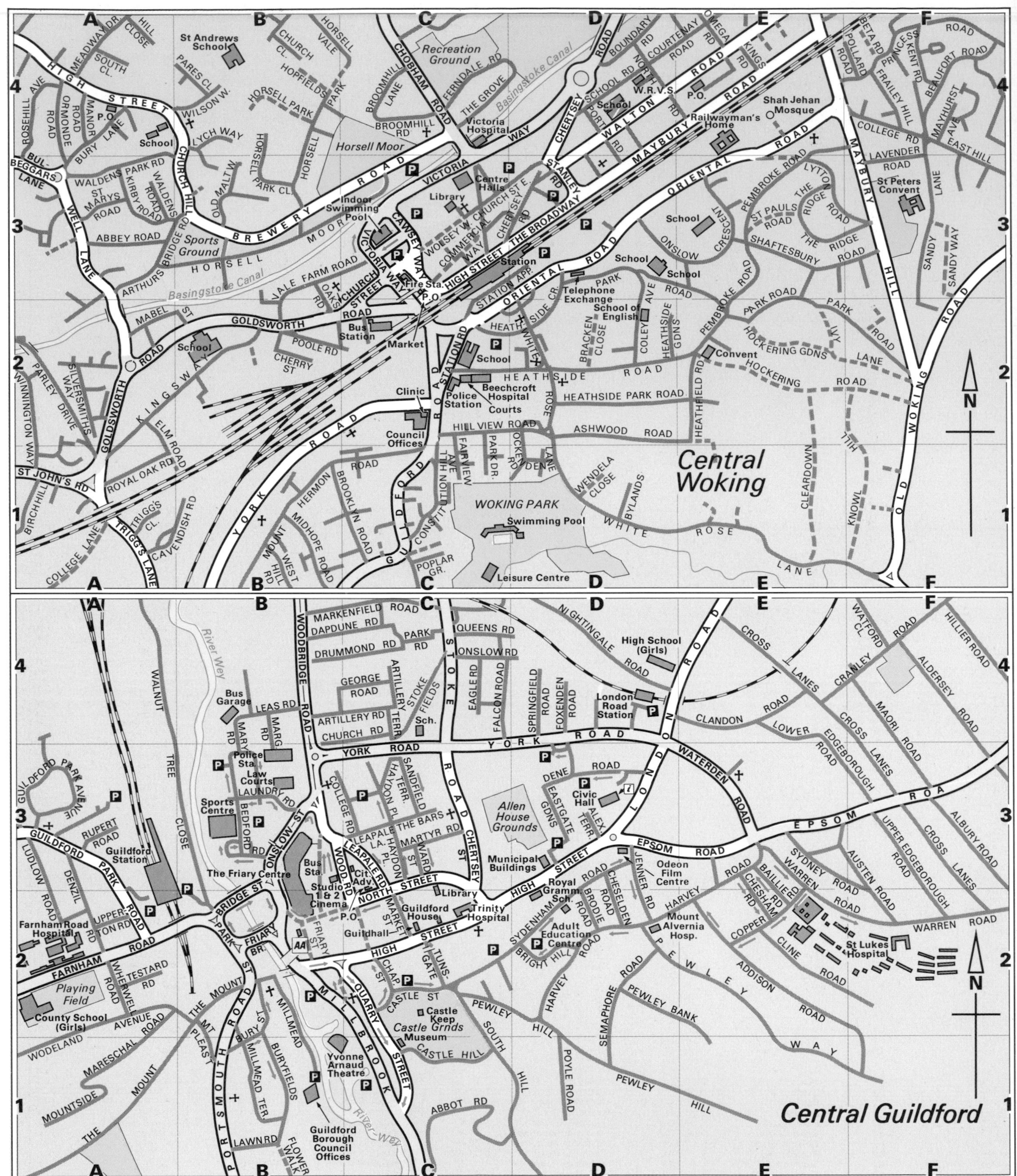

Guildford

Guildford's impressive modern redbrick Anglican cathedral, consecrated in 1961, looks down on the county town of Surrey from its hill-top setting on the outskirts. Nearby are the differently-styled modern buildings of the University of Surrey. Another example of modern architecture is the Yvonne Arnaud Theatre, which opened in 1958 on the banks of the River Wey. Despite being a busy modern shopping centre the town retains many old buildings and its steep, partly-cobbled High Street has an unchanging Georgian character. Most prominent is the Guildhall with its hexagonal bell-turret and gilded clock overhanging the pavement. All that remains of the city's castle, just off the High Street, is the 12th-century keep built by Henry II, but close by the Castle Museum has a comprehensive range of local antiquities.

Godalming An important staging post on the London to Portsmouth road in stagecoach days, this attractive North Downs town still has several old coaching inns as well as a number of other 16th-century buildings. Local artefacts can be found in the Borough Museum.

Woking A residential and commuter town on the disused Basingtoke Canal, Woking developed as a direct result of the arrival of the railway in the 1830s. Its most distinctive feature is its large Mosque, built in 1889.

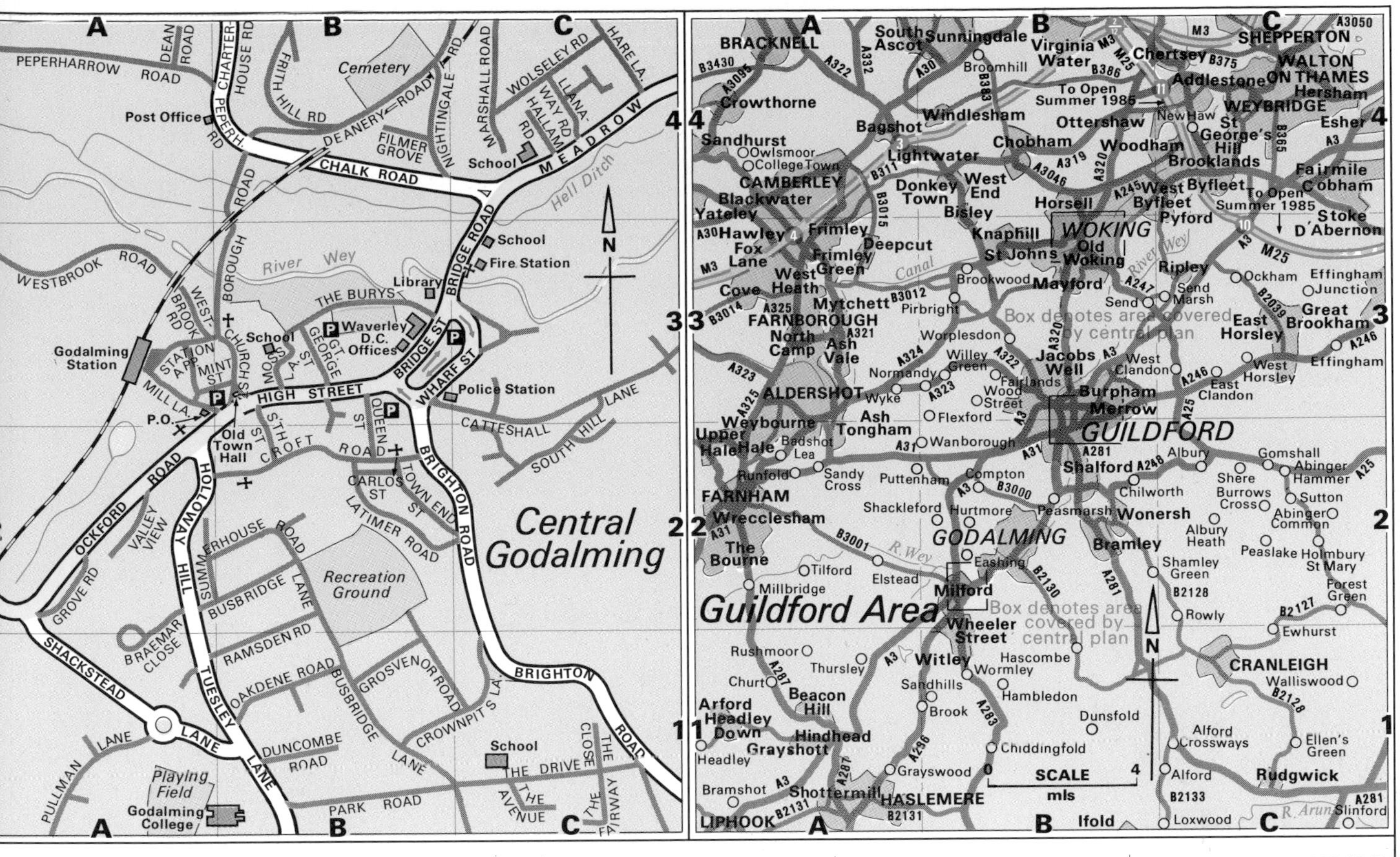

LEGEND

own Plan

A recommended route	
estricted roads	
ther roads	
uildings of interest	Station
ar parks	P
arks and open spaces	
ne way streets	

rea Plan

roads	
roads	
ocations	Fairlands
rban area	

Street Index with Grid Reference

Guildford

bbot Road	C1
ddison Road	E2-F2-F1
lbury Road	F2-F3
ldersey Road	F2-F3
lexandra Terrace	D3
rtillery Road	B4-C4
rtillery Terrace	C4
usten Road	E3-F3-F2
aillie Road	E2-E3
edford Road	B2
ridge Street	B2-B3
right Hill	D2
rodie Road	D2
uryfields	B1
ury Street	B1-B2
astle Hill	C1
astle Street	C2
hapel Street	C2
hertsey Street	C3
heselden Road	D2-D3
hesham Road	E2-E3
hurch Road	B3-B4-C4
landon Road	D4-E4
line Road	E2-F2
ollege Road	B3-C3
opper Road	E2
ranley Road	E4-F4
ross Lanes	E4-F4-F3-F2
apdune Road	B4-C4
ene Road	D3
enzil Road	A2-A3
Drummond Road	B4-C4
Eagle Road	C4
Eastgate Gardens	D3
Epsom Road	D3-E3-F3
Falcon Road	C4
Farnham Road	A2-B2
Flower Walk	B1
Foxenden Road	D4
Friary Bridge	A2-B2
Friary Street	B2
George Road	B4-C4
Guildford Park Avenue	A3
Guildford Park Road	A2-A3
Harvey Road	D2-E2-E3
Haydon Place	C3
High Street	B2-C2-D2-D3
Hillier Road	F4
Jenner Road	D2-D3
Laundry Road	B3
Lawn Road	B1
Leapale Lane	C3
Leapale Road	C3
Leas Road	B4
London Road	D3-D4-E4
Lower Edgeborough Road	E4-E3-F3
Ludlow Road	A2-A3
Maori Road	F4-F3
Mareschel Road	A1-A2
Margaret Road	B3-B4
Markenfield Road	B4-C4
Market Street	C2
Martyr Road	C3
Mary Road	B3-B4
Millbrook	B2-C2-C1
Millmead	B1-B2
Millmead Terrace	B1
Mount Pleasant	B1-B2
Mountside	A1
Nightingale Road	D4
North Street	C2-C3
Onslow Road	C4-D4
Onslow Street	B3
Park Road	C4
Park Street	B2
Pewley Bank	D2-E2-E1
Pewley Hill	C2-D2-D1-E1
Pewley Way	D2-E2-E1-F1
Portsmouth Road	B1-B2
Poyle Road	D1
Quarry Street	C2-B3-C3
Queens Road	C4-D4
Rupert Road	A3
Sandfield Terrace	C3
Semaphore Road	D1-D2
South Hill	C2-C1-D1
Springfield Road	D4
Stoke Fields	C4
Stoke Road	C3-C4
Sydenham Road	C2-D2-D3
Sydney Road	E3-F3-E2
Testard Road	A2
The Bars	C3
The Mount	A1-B1-B2
Tunsgate	C2
Upper Edgeborough Road	F2-F3
Upperton Road	A2
Walnut Treet Close	B2-B3-A3-A4
Ward Street	C3
Warren Road	E3-E2-F2
Waterden Road	D3-E3
Watford Close	F4
Wherwell Road	•A2
Woodbridge Road	B4-B3-C3-C2
Wodeland Avenue	A1-A2-B2
York Road	B3-C3-C4-D3-D4

Woking

Abbey Road	A3
Arthurs Bridge Road	A3-B4
Ashwood Road	D2-E2
Beaufort Road	F4
Beta Road	F4
Birch Hill	A1
Boundary Road	D4
Bracken Close	D2
Brewery Road	B3-C3-C4
Brooklyn	B1-C1
Broomhill Lane	C4
Broomhill Road	C4
Bulbeggars Lane	A3
Bury Lane	A3-A4
Bylands	D1
Cavendish Road	A1-B1
Cawsey Way	C3
Cherry Street	B2
Chertsey Road	C3-D3-D4
Chobham Road	C4
Church Close	B4
Church Hill	B3-B4
Church Street	C2-C3
Church Street East	C3-D3
Cleardown	E1-E2
Coley Avenue	D2-D3
College Lane	A1
College Road	F4
Commercial Way	C3
Constitution Hill	C1
Courteney Road	D4-E4
Elm Road	A2-A1
East Hill	F3-F4
Fairview Avenue	C1-C2
Ferndale Road	C4
Frailey Hill	F4
Goldsworth Road	A1-A2-B2-C2
Guildford Road	B1-C1-C2
Heathfield Road	E2
Heathside Crescent	C2-D2-D3
Heathside Gardens	D2
Heathside Park Road	C2-D2-E2
Heathside Road	C1-D1-E1
Heathside Road	E2
High Street	A3-B4
High Street	C3
Hill Close	A4
Hill View Road	C2-D2
Hockering Gardens	E2
Hockering Road	E2-F2
Hopfields	B4
Horsell Moor	A3-B3-C3
Horsell Park	B3-B4-C4
Horsell Park Close	B3-B4
Horsell Vale	B4-C4
Ivy Lane	E2-F2
Kent Road	F4
Kings Road	E4
Kings Way	A1-A2-B2
Kirby Road	A3
Knowl Hill	F1-F2
Lavender Road	F3
Lych Way	B4
Lytton Road	E3-F3
Mabel Street	A2-B2
Manor Road	A4
Maybury Hill	E4-F4-F3-F2
Maybury Road	D3-D4-E4
Mayhurst Avenue	F4
Meadway Drive	A4
Midhope Road	B1
Mount Hermon Road	B1-C1
North Road	D4-E4
Oaks Road	B2-B3
Ockenden Road	D1-D2
Old Malt Way	B3
Old Woking road	F1-F2-F3
Omega Road	E4
Onslow Crescent	D3-E3
Oriental Road	C2-C3-D2-D3-E3-E4
Ormonde Road	A3-A4
Pares Close	A4-B4
Park Drive	C1-C2
Park Road	D3-E3-E2-F2
Parley Drive	A1-A2
Pembroke Road	E2-E3-E4
Pollard Road	F4
Poole Road	B2-C2
Poplar Grove	C1
Port Road	D3-D4
Princes Road	F4
Rosehill Avenue	A4
Royal Oak Road	A1
St Johns Road	A1
St Marys Road	A3
St Pauls Road	E3
Sandy Lane	F2-F3-F4
Sandy Way	F3
School Road	D4
Shaftesbury Road	E3-F3
Silversmiths Way	A2
South Close	A4
Stanley Road	D3
Station Approach	C2-C3-D3
Station Road	C2
The Broadway	D3
The Grove	C4-D4
The Ridge	E3-F3
Trigg's Close	A1
Trigg's Lane	A1
Vale Farm Road	B2-B3-C3
Victoria Way	C2-C3-C4-D4
Waldens Park Road	A3
Waldens Road	A3
Walton Road	D3-D4-E4
Well Lane	A3
Wendella Close	D1
West Hill Road	B1
White Rose Lane	D2-D1-E1-F1
Winnington Way	A1-A2
Wilson Way	B4
Wolsey Way	C3
York Road	B1-B2-C2

Godalming

Borough Road	B3-B4
Braemar Close	A1-A2
Bridge Road	B3-C3-C4
Bridge Street	B3
Brighton Road	B3-B2-C2-C1
Busbridge Lane	A2-B2-B1
Carlos Street	B2
Catteshal Lane	B3-C3-C2-C3
Chalk Road	B4-C4
Charterhouse Road	B4
Church Street	B3
Croft Road	B2
Crownpits Lane	B1-C1
Dean Road	A4
Deanery Road	B4
Duncombe Road	B1
Filmer Grove	B4
Frith Hill Road	B4
Great George Street	B3
Grosvenor Road	B1-C1
Grove Road	A2
Hallam Road	C4
Hare Lane	C4
High Street	B3
Holloway Hill	A2
Latimer Road	B2
Llanaway Road	C4
Marshall Road	C4
Meadrow	C4
Mill Lane	A3
Mint Street	A3-B3
Moss Lane	B3
Nightingale Road	B4-C4
Oakdene Road	B1
Ockford Road	A2-A3-B2-B3
Park Road	B1
Peperharow Road	A4-B4
Pullman Lane	A1
Queen Street	B3-B2
Ramsden Road	A1-B1-B2
Shackstead Lane	A2-A1-B1
South Hill	C2-C3
South Street	B2-B3
Station Approach	A3
Summerhouse Road	A2-B2
The Avenue	C1
The Burys	B3
The Close	C1
The Drive	C1
The Fairway	C1
Town End Street	B2-C2
Tuesley Lane	A2-A1-B1
Valley View	A2
Westbrook Road	A3
Wharf Street	B3-C3
Wolseley Road	C4

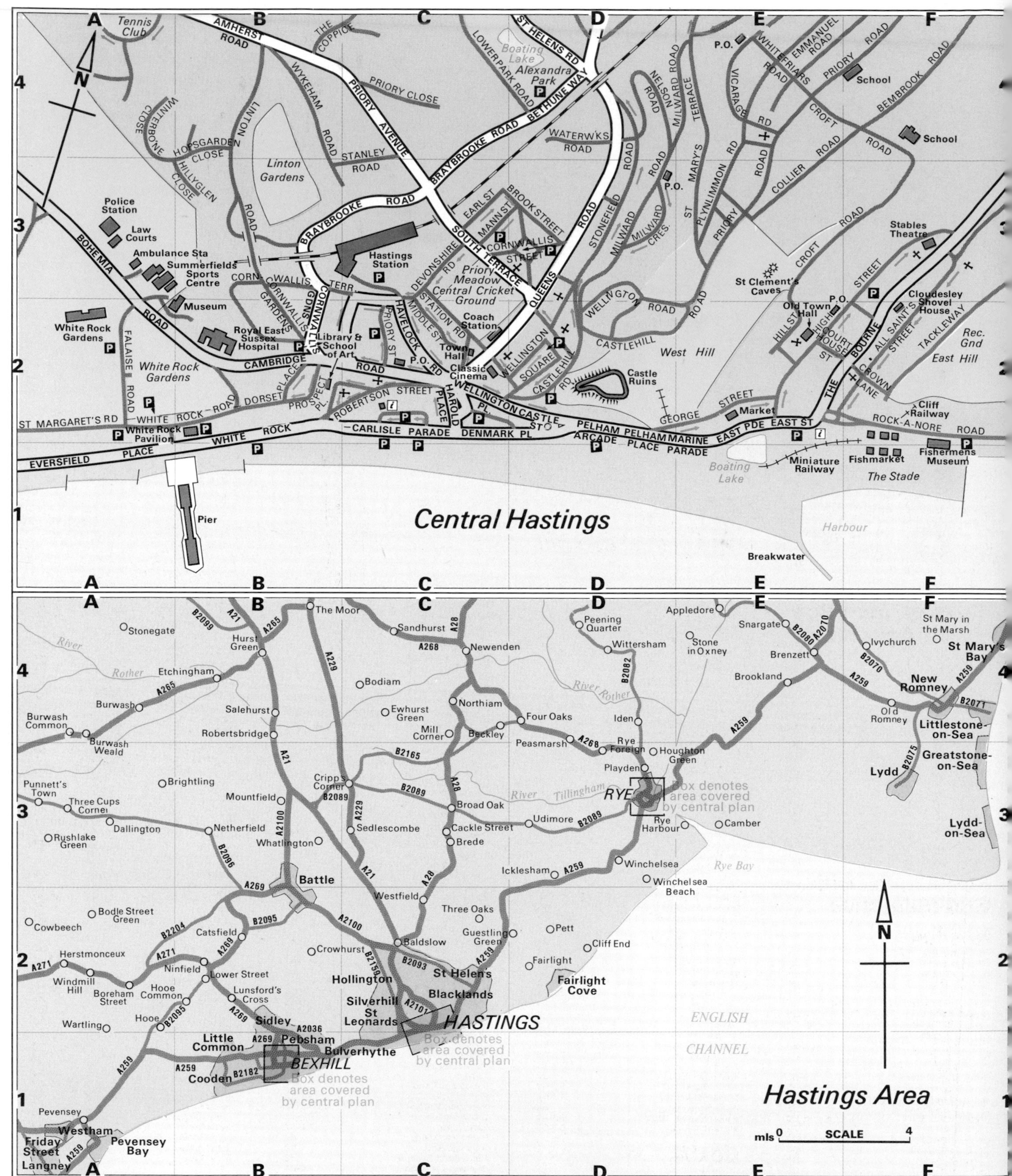

Hastings

Overlooking the beach of this popular resort are the remains of a castle established by William the Conqueror; Battle Abbey, the actual site of the great conflict of 1066, lies to the north of the town on the A2100. The Hastings Embroidery, which was commissioned in 1966 to commemorate the battle's 900th anniversary and depicts 81 memorable events in British history, can be seen at the Town Hall.

Rich in historical associations, Hastings also has a historic Old Town — a pleasant jumble of ancient buildings and narrow streets, and site of the local fish market and Fisherman's Museum. Theatres, pubs and amusement areas fill the main resort, which has all the amenities expected of a major holiday centre.

Bexhill offers the entertainment facilities of the De La Warr Pavilion, which overlooks the sands, and a good range of outdoor activities can be enjoyed in nearby Egerton Park. Manor Gardens, in the older part of the town, contains the Manor Costume Museum and the ruins of the manor house.

Rye is an atmospheric town of cobbled streets and half-timbered houses. A gang of smugglers had its headquarters at the 15th-century Mermaid Inn, and other places of interest include the Baddings Tower Museum, the Rye Town Model and the old harbour, which is now a nature reserve.

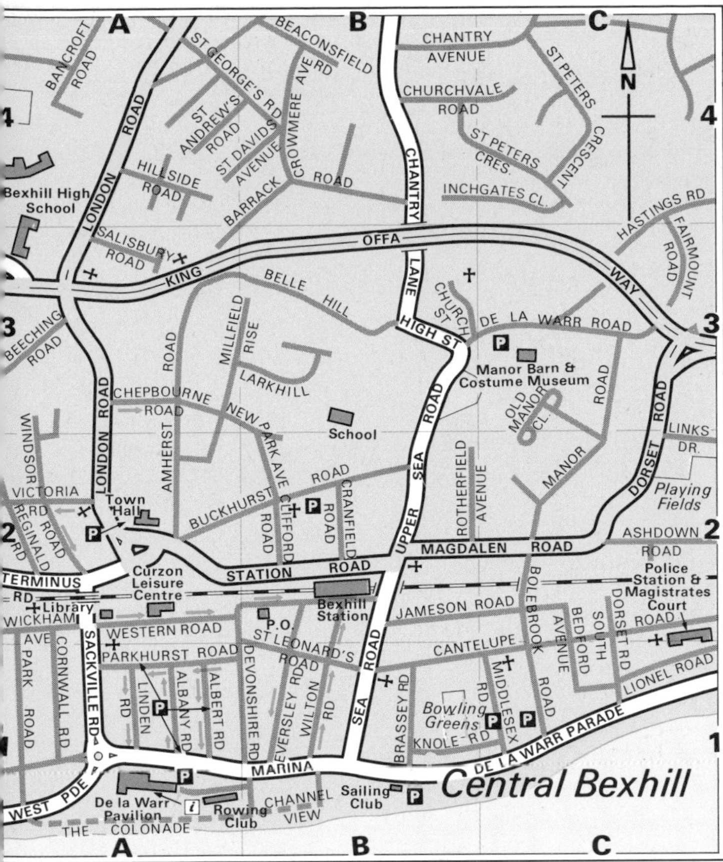

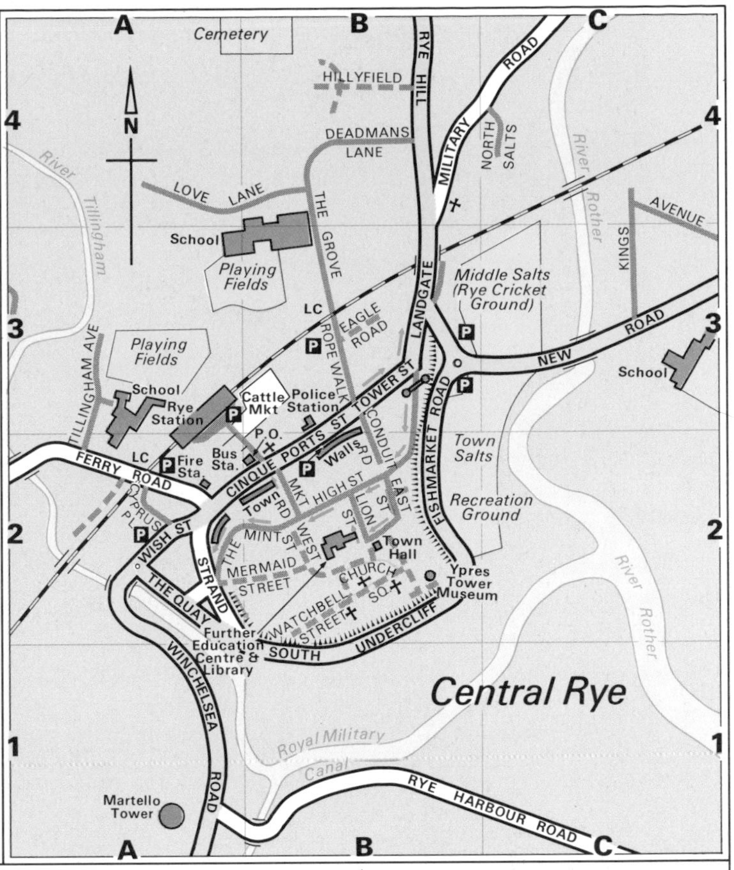

Central Bexhill

Central Rye

Key to Town Plan and Area Plan

Town Plan

- AA Recommended roads
- Restricted roads
- Other roads
- Buildings of interest — Castle
- Car Parks — P
- Churches — +
- Parks and open spaces
- One Way Streets

Area Plan

- A roads
- B roads
- Locations — Kingston
- Urban area

Street Index with Grid Reference

Hastings

Amherst Road	B4
All Saints Street	F2-F3
Bembrook Road	F4
Bethune Way	D4
Bohemia Road	A3-A2-B2
Braybrooke Road	B3-C3-C4-D4
Brook Street	C3-D3
Cambridge Road	B2-C2
Carlisle Parade	C2
Castlehill Road	D2-E2-E3
Castle Street	D2
Collier Road	E3-E4-F4
Cornwallis Gardens	B3-B2
Cornwallis Street	C3-D3
Cornwallis Terrace	B3-C3
Courthouse Street	E2
Croft Road	E4-F4-F3-E3
Crown Lane	F2
Denmark Place	C2-D2
Devonshire Road	C3
Dorset Place	B2
Earl Street	C3
East Parade	E2
East Street	E2
Emmanuel Road	E4
Eversfield Place	A1
Falaise Road	A2
George Street	D2-E2
Harold Place	C2
Havelock Road	C2
High Street	E2-F2-F3
Hill Street	E2
Hillyglen Close	B3
Hopsgarden Close	B3-B4
Linton Road	B4-B3
Lower Park Road	C4-D4
Mann Street	C3-D3
Marine Parade	D2-E2
Middle Street	C2
Milward Crescent	D3
Milward Road	D3-D4-E4
Nelson Road	D4
Pelham Arcade	D2
Pelham Place	D2
Plynlimmon Road	E3-E4
Priory Avenue	B4-C4-C3
Priory Close	C4
Priory Road	E3-E4-F4
Priory Street	C2
Prospect Place	B2
Queens Road	C2-D2-D3-D4
Robertson Street	B2-C2
Rock-a-Nore Road	F2
St Helens Road	D4
St Margaret's Road	A2
St Mary's Terrace	E3-E4
South Terrace	C3-D3
Stanley Road	B3-C3-C4
Station Road	C2-C3
Stonefield Road	D3-D4
Tackleway	F2-F3
The Coppice	B4-C4
The Bourne	E2-F2
Vicarage Road	E4
Waterworks Road	D4
Wellington Place	C2-D2
Wellington Road	D3-D2-E2
Wellington Square	D2
White Rock	B1-B2
White Rock Road	A2-B2
Whitefriars Road	E4
Winterbourne Close	A3-A4
Wykeham Road	B4-B3-C3

Bexhill

Albany Road	A1
Albert Road	A1
Amherst Road	A2-A3
Ashdown Road	C2
Bancroft Road	A4
Barrack Road	A3-B4
Beaconsfield Road	B4
Bedford Avenue	C2-C1
Beeching Road	A3
Belle Hill	B3
Bolebrook Road	C2-C1
Brassey Road	B1
Buckhurst Road	A2-B2
Cantelupe Road	B1-C1-C2
Channel View	B1
Chantry Avenue	B4-C4
Chantry Lane	B4-B3
Chelsea Close	C2
Chepbourne Road	A3
Church Street	B3
Churchvale Road	B4-C4
Clifford Road	B2
Cornwall Road	A2-A1
Cranfield Road	B2
Crowmere Avenue	B4
De la Warr Parade	B1-C1
De la Warr Road	C3
Devonshire Road	A1-B1
Dorset Road	C2-C3
Dorset Road South	C2-C1
Eversley Road	B1
Fairmount Road	C3-C4
Hastings Road	C4-C3
High Street	B3
Hillside Road	A4
Inchgates Close	B4-C4
Jameson Road	B2-C2
King Offa Way	A3-B3-C3
Knole Road	B1-C1
Larkhill	A3-B3
Linden Road	A1
Links Drive	C2
Lionel Road	C1
London Road	A4-A3-A2
Magdalen Road	B2-C2
Manor Road	C2-C3
Marina	A1-B1
Middlesex Road	C1
Millfield Rise	A3-B3
New Park Avenue	A3-B3-B2
Old Manor Close	C2-C3
Park Road	A1-A2
Parkhurst Road	A1
Reginald Road	A2
Rotherfield Avenue	B2
St Andrew's Road	A4-B4
St Davids Avenue	A4-B4
St George's Road	A4-B4
St Leonard's Road	B2-B1
St Peters Crescent	B4-C4
Sackville Road	A2-A1
Salisbury Road	A3
Sea Road	B1-B2
Station Road	A2-B2
Terminus Road	A2
The Colonade	A1
Upper Sea Road	B2-B3
Victoria Road	A2
West Parade	A1
Western Road	A2
Wickham Avenue	A2
Wilton Road	B1
Windsor Road	A3-A2

Rye

Church Square	B2
Cinque Ports Street	A2-B2-B3
Conduit Road	B3-B2
Cyprus Place	A2
Deadmans Lane	B4
Eagle Road	B3
East Street	B2
Ferry Road	A2
Fishmarket Road	B2-B3
High Street	B2
Hillyfield	B4
Kings Avenue	C3-C4
Landgate	B3
Lion Street	B2
Love Lane	A4-B4
Market Road	B2
Mermaid Street	A2-B2
Military Road	B4-C4
New Road	B3-C3
North Salts	C4
Rope Walk	B3
Rye Harbour Road	B1-C1
Rye Hill	B4
South Undercliff	B1-B2
Strand	A2
The Grove	B4-B3
The Mint	A2-B2
The Quay	A2
Tillingham Avenue	A2-A3
Tower Street	B3
Watchbell Street	B2
West Street	B2
Winchelsea Road	A1-A2
Wish Street	A2

HASTINGS
Although the harbour of this one-time Cinque Port silted up centuries ago, fishing boats are still winched up on the shingle beach, and fishermen's net-drying huts at the foot of the cliff railway are a distinctive feature.

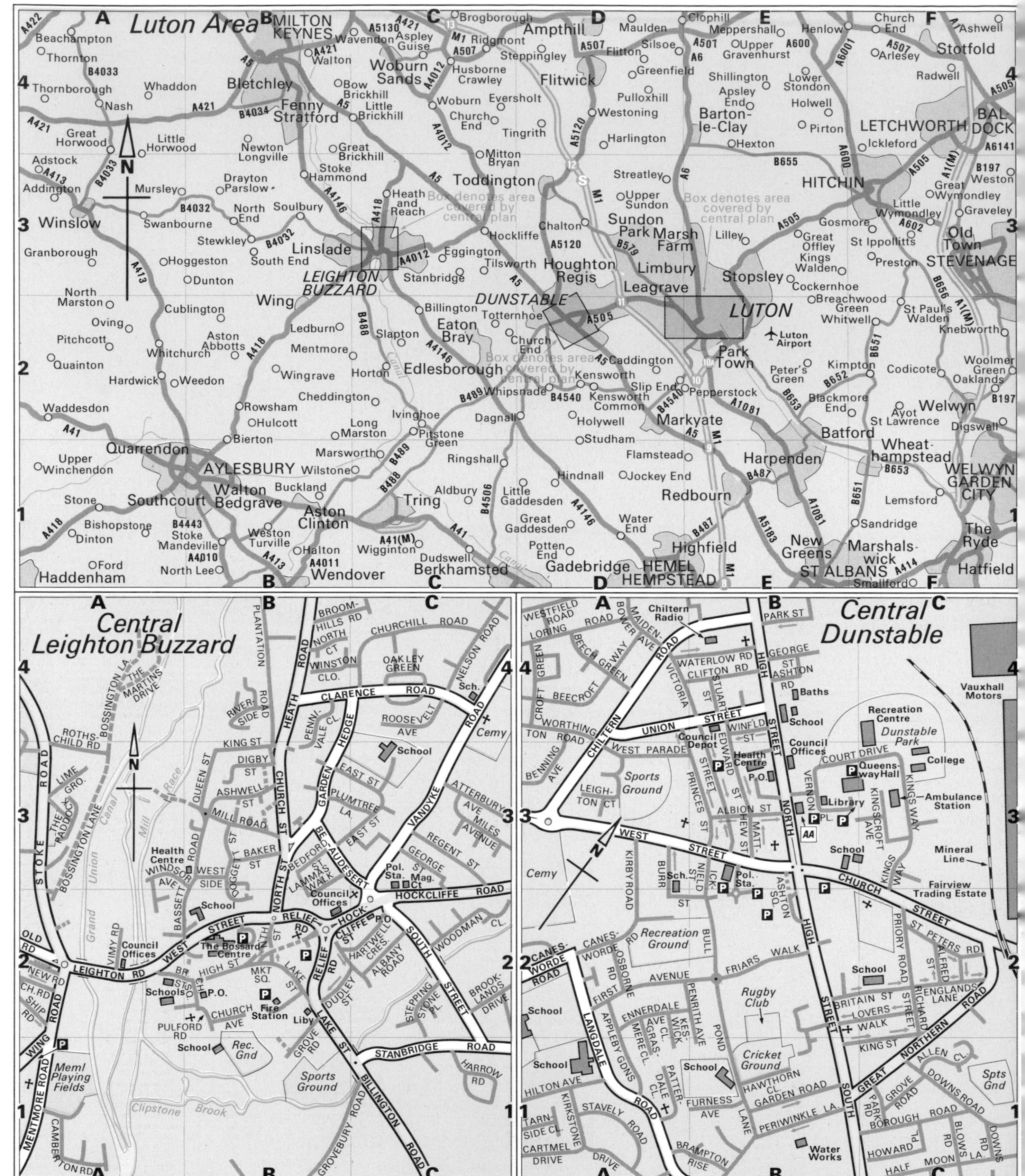

Luton

Huge numbers of people go to Luton each year; for most the stay is very brief since it is the starting-off point for holidays on the Mediterranean and all over Europe. The airport has become Luton's best-known feature, but the town prospered for a long time before the advent of aeroplanes. Straw plaiting and straw hat making were the mainstays of its fortunes from the 19th century onwards, and even today hats are still made here. In the town's museum and art gallery, at Wardown Park, are exhibits of the hat trade, and of the pillow lace trade, another of the town's traditional industries. Also in the museum are exhibits devoted to natural history and local life, including a 'Luton Life' gallery complete with reconstructed street scene. St Mary's is the parish church. It is a huge building – one of the largest churches in England – containing much of interest. It dates principally from the 13th to 15th centuries, and has a spectacular font of Purbeck marble, along with many monuments and excellent carving in stone and wood. Just to the south of the town is Luton Hoo, a palatial mansion built to the designs of Robert Adam. It contains a notable collection of pictures and tapestries and sumptuous Fabergé jewellery. The mansion is surrounded by a magnificently landscaped 1,500-acre park laid out by Capability Brown in the 18th century.

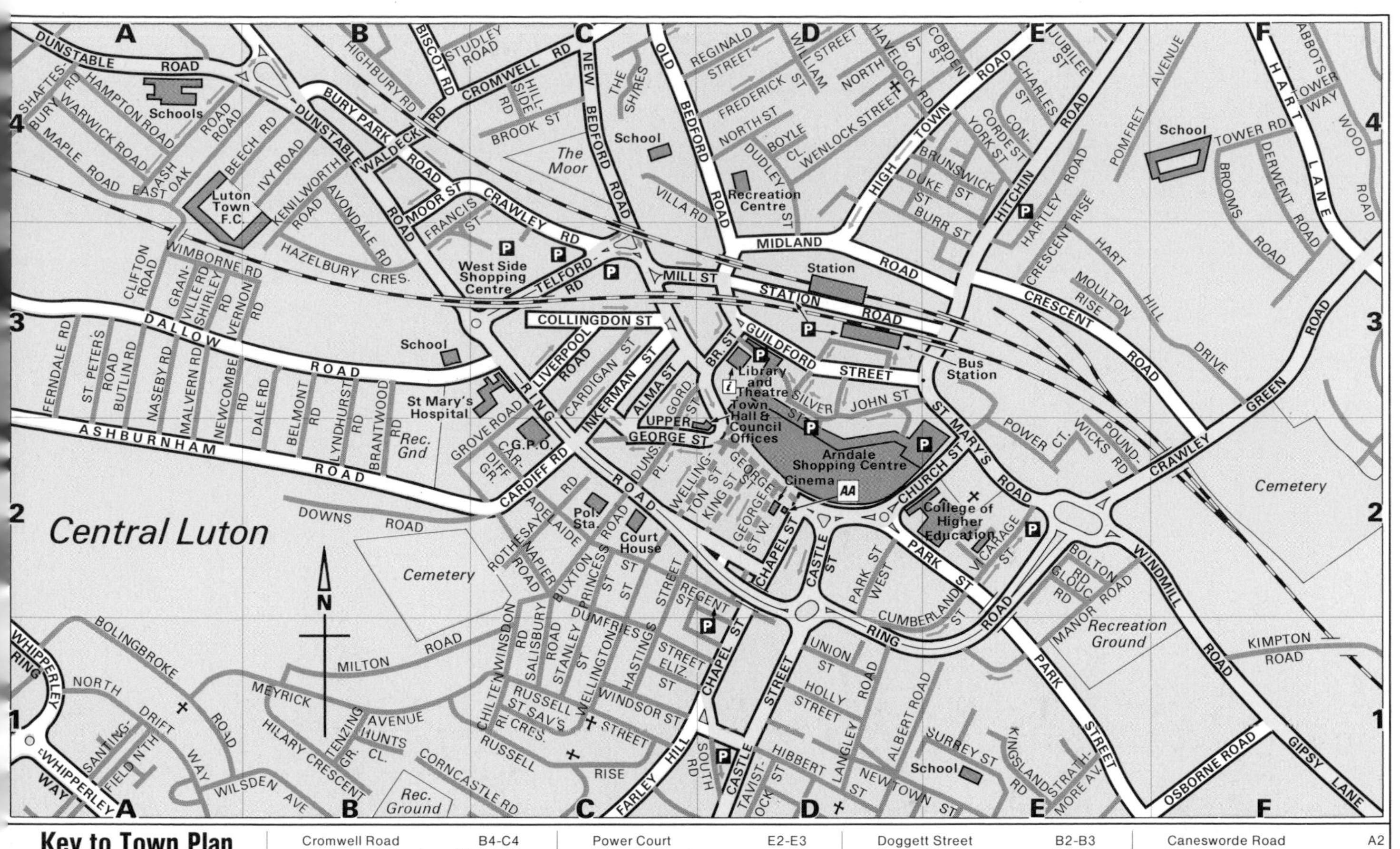

Key to Town Plan and Area Plan

Town Plan

AA Recommended roads
Other roads
Restricted roads
Buildings of interest Library
Churches
Car Parks
Parks and open spaces
AA Service Centre
One way street

Area Plan

A roads
B roads
Locations Kensworth
Urban area

Street Index

Luton

Abbots Wood Road F4
Adelaide Street C2
Albert Road D1-E1
Alma Street C2-C3
Ashburnham Road A3- 2-B2-C2
Ash Road A4
Avondale Road B4-B3
Beech Road A4-B4
Belmont Road B2-B3
Biscot Road B4
Bolingbroke Road A1
Bolton Road E2
Boyle Close D4
Brantwood Road B2-B3
Bridge Street D3
Brook Street C4
Brooms Road F3-F4
Brunswick Street D4-E4
Burr Street D4-D3-E4
Bury Park Road B4
Butlin Road A2-A3
Buxton Road C2
Cardiff Grove C2
Cardiff Road C2
Cardigan Street C3
Castle Street D1-D2
Charles Street E4
Chapel Street D1-D2
Chilton Rise C1
Church Street D2-E2
Clifton Road A3
Cobden Street E4
Collingdon Street C3
Concorde Street E4
Corncastle Road B1-C1
Crawley Green Road E2-F2-F3
Crawley Road C3-C4
Crescent Rise E3-E4
Crescent Road E3-F3-F2
Cromwell Road B4-C4
Cumberland Street D1-E1-E2
Dale Road B2-B3
Dallow Road A3-B3-C3
Derwent Road F3-F4
Downs Road B2-C2
Dudley Street D3-D4
Duke Street D4-E4
Dumfries Street C2-C1-D1
Dunstable Place C2
Dunstable Road A4-B4-B3
Elizabeth Street C1-D1
Farley Hill C1
Ferndale Road A3
Francis Street B3-B4-C4
Frederick Street D4
George Street D2
George Street West D2
Gipsy Lane F1
Gloucester Road E2
Gordon Street C2-C3-D3
Granville Road A3
Grove Road B2-C3-C3
Guildford Street D3
Hampton Road A4
Hart Hill Drive E3-F3
Hart Lane F3-F4
Hartley Road E3-E4
Hastings Street C1-C2
Havelock Road D4-E4
Hazelbury Crescent B4
Hibbert Street D1
Highbury Road B4
Hightown Road D3-D4-E4
Hilary Crescent B1
Hillside Road C4
Hitchin Road E3-E4
Holly Street D1
Hunts Close B1
Inkerman Street C2-C3
Ivy Road B4
John Street D3
Jubilee Street E4
Kenilworth Road B3-B4
Kimpton Road F1
Kingsland Road E1
King Street D2
Langley Road D1
Liverpool Road C3
Lyndhurst Road B2-B3
Malvern Road A2-A3
Manor Road E1-E2
Maple Road East A4
Meyrick Avenue A1-B1-C1
Midland Road D3-E3
Mill Street C3-D3
Milton Road B1-C1
Moor Street B3-B4-C4
Moulton Rise E3
Napier Road C2
Naseby Road A2-A3
New Bedford Road C3-C4
Newcombe Road A2-A3-B3
Newtown Street D1-E1
North Drift Way A1
North Street D4-E4
Oak Road A4-B4
Old Bedford Road C4-D4-D3
Osborne Road E1-F1
Park Street D2-E2-E1
Park Street West D2
Pomfret Avenue E4-F4
Poundwicks Road E2-E3
Power Court E2-E3
Princess Street C2
Regent Street C2-D2
Reginald Street C4-D4
Ring Road C3-C2-D2-D1-E1-E2
Rothesay Road C2
Russel Rise C1
Russell Street C1
St Mary's Road E2-E3
St Peter's Road A2-A3
St Saviors Crescent C1
Salisbury Road C1-C2
Santingfield North A1
Shaftesbury Road A4
Shirley Road A3
Silver Street D2-D3
South Road D1
Stanley Street C1-C2
Station Road D3-E3
Strathmore Avenue E1
Studley Road B4-C4
Surrey Street E1
Tavistock Street D1
Telford Road C3
Tenzing Grove B1
The Shires C4
Tower Road F4
Tower Way F4
Union Street D1
Upper George Street C2-D2
Vernon Road A3-B3
Vicarage Street E2
Villa Road C4-D4
Waldeck Road B4
Warwick Road A4
Wellington Street C1-C2-D2
Wenlock Street D4
Whipperley Ring A1
Whipperley Way A1
William Street D4
Wilsden Avenue A1-B1
Wimborne Road A3-B3
Windmill Road E2-F2-F1
Windsor Street C1
Winsdon Road C1-C2
York Street E4

Leighton Buzzard

Albany Road C2
Ashwell Street B3
Atterbury Avenue C3
Baker Street B3
Bassett Road A2-B2-B3
Beaudesert B3-C3
Bedford Street B3
Billington Road C1
Bossington Lane A2-A3-A4
Bridge Street A2-B2
Brooklands Drive C2
Broomhills Road B4-C4
Camberton Road A1
Church Avenue B2
Church Road A2
Churchill Road C4
Church Square B2
Church Street B3
Clarence Road B4-C4
Digby Street B3
Doggett Street B2-B3
Dudley Street B2-C2
East Street B3-C3
Garden Hedge B3-B4-C4
George Street C3
Grovebury Road B1-C1
Grove Road B1-B2
Harrow Road C1
Hartwell Crescent B2-C2
Heath Road B3-B4
High Street B2
Hockcliffe Road C2-C3
Hockcliffe Street B2-C2
King Street B3
Lake Street B2-B1-C1
Lammas Walk B2-B3
Leighton Road A2
Lime Grove A3
Market Square B2
Mentmore Road A1
Miles Avenue C3
Mill Road B3
Nelson Road C4
New Road A2
North Court B4
North Street B2-B3
Oakley Green C4
Old Road A2
Pennivale Close B3-B4
Plantation Road B3-B4
Plumtree Lane B3-C3
Pulford Road B2
Queen Street B3
Regent Street C3
Relief Road B2
Riverside B4
Rothschild Road A3
Roosevelt Avenue C4
Ship Road A2
South Street C1-C2
Stanbridge Road C1
Steppingstone Place C2
Stoke Road A2-A3-A4
The Martins Drive A4
The Paddock A3
Vandyke Road C2-C3-C4
Vimy Road A2
West Side B3
West Street A2-B2
Windsor Avenue A3-B3
Wing Road A1-A2
Winston Close B4-C4
Woodman Close C2

Dunstable

Albion Street B3
Alfred Street C2
Allen Close C1
Appleby Gardens A1-A2
Ashton Road B4
Ashton Square B2-B3
Beech Green A4
Beechcroft Way A4
Benning Avenue A3-A4
Blows Road C1
Borough Road C1
Brampton Rise A1-B1
Britain Street B2-C2
Bull Pond Lane B1-B2
Burr Street A3-A2-B2
Canesworde Road A2
Cartmel Drive A1
Chiltern Road A3-A4-B4
Church Street B3-C3-C2
Clifton Road A4-B4
Court Drive B3-C3
Croft Green A4
Downs Road C1
Edward Street B3-B4
Englands Lane C2
Ennerdale Avenue A2
First Avenue A2-B2
Friars Walk B2
Furness Avenue B1
Garden Road B1
George Street B4
Grasmere Close A1-A2
Great Northern Road B1-C1-C2
Grove Road C1
Half Moon Lane C1
Hawthorn Close B1
High Street North B3-B4
High Street South B3-B2-B1-C1
Hilton Avenue A1
Howard Place C1
Icknield Street B2-B3
Keswick Close A1-A2
Kingscroft Avenue C3
Kingsway C3
King Street B1-C1-C2
Kirby Road A2-A3
Kirkstone Drive A1
Langdale Road A1-A2
Leighton Court A3
Loring Road A4
Lovers Walk B2-C2
Maidenbower Avenue A4
Matthew Street B3
Osborne Road A2
Park Road C1
Park Street B4
Patterdale Close A1
Penrith Avenue A2-B2-B1
Periwinkle Lane B1
Princes Street A4-A3-B3
Priory Road C2
Richard Street C2
St Peter's Road C2
Stavely Road A1
Stuart Street B4
Tarnside Close A1
Union Street A4-B4
Vernon Place B3
Victoria Street A4-B4-B3
Waterlow Road A4-B4
Westfield Road A4
West Parade A3
West Street A3-B3
Winfield Street B4
Worthington Road A4

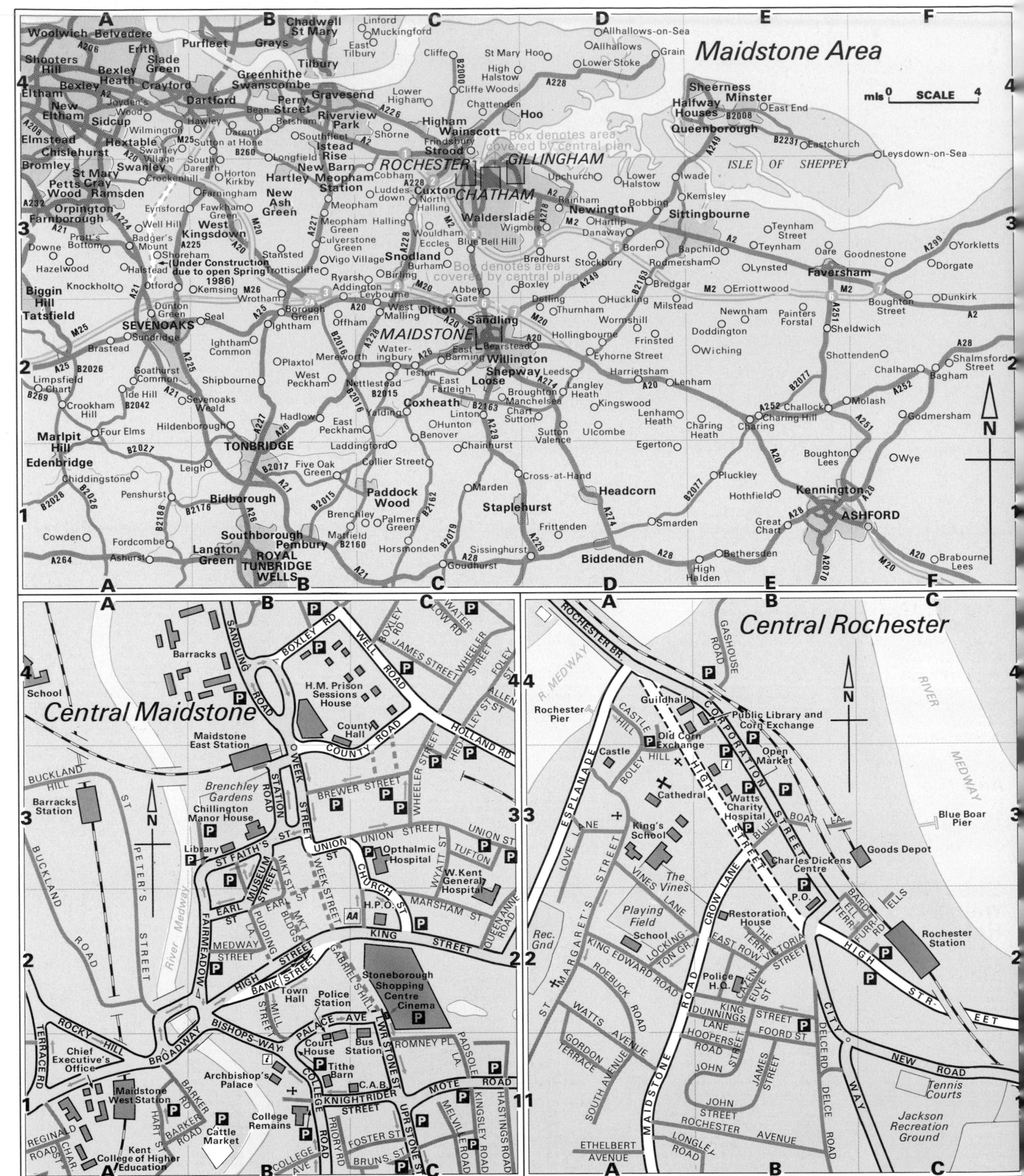

Maidstone

County town of Kent, Maidstone has long been a place of importance. The ruins of the 14th-century Archbishop's Palace overlook the River Medway, and Allington Castle dates from the 13th century. Maidstone Museum and Art Gallery explores the town's extensive history; also of interest is the Tyrwhitt-Drake Museum of Carriages, housed in the Palace stables.

Rochester Medieval walls enclose the Norman castle and cathedral of this attractive and historic town, but its quaint old shops, inns and tea shops give it a distinctly Victorian flavour. Charles Dickens spent much of his life in the area and featured Rochester in his novels: justly proud of its associations with the great man, the town boasts an award-winning Charles Dickens Centre.

Gillingham has been associated with the nearby Royal Naval Dockyard since Tudor times and it continues the tradition with the Royal Naval Barracks and the Royal School of Military Engineering, both situated in the Brompton area.

Chatham Home of the Royal Naval Dockyard since the 16th century, Chatham today is dominated by the office tower block which crowns the Pentagon Centre, a shopping and entertainments complex. Pleasant riverside gardens have been laid out on the site of the old Gun Wharf, and the Medway Heritage Centre is in Dock Road.

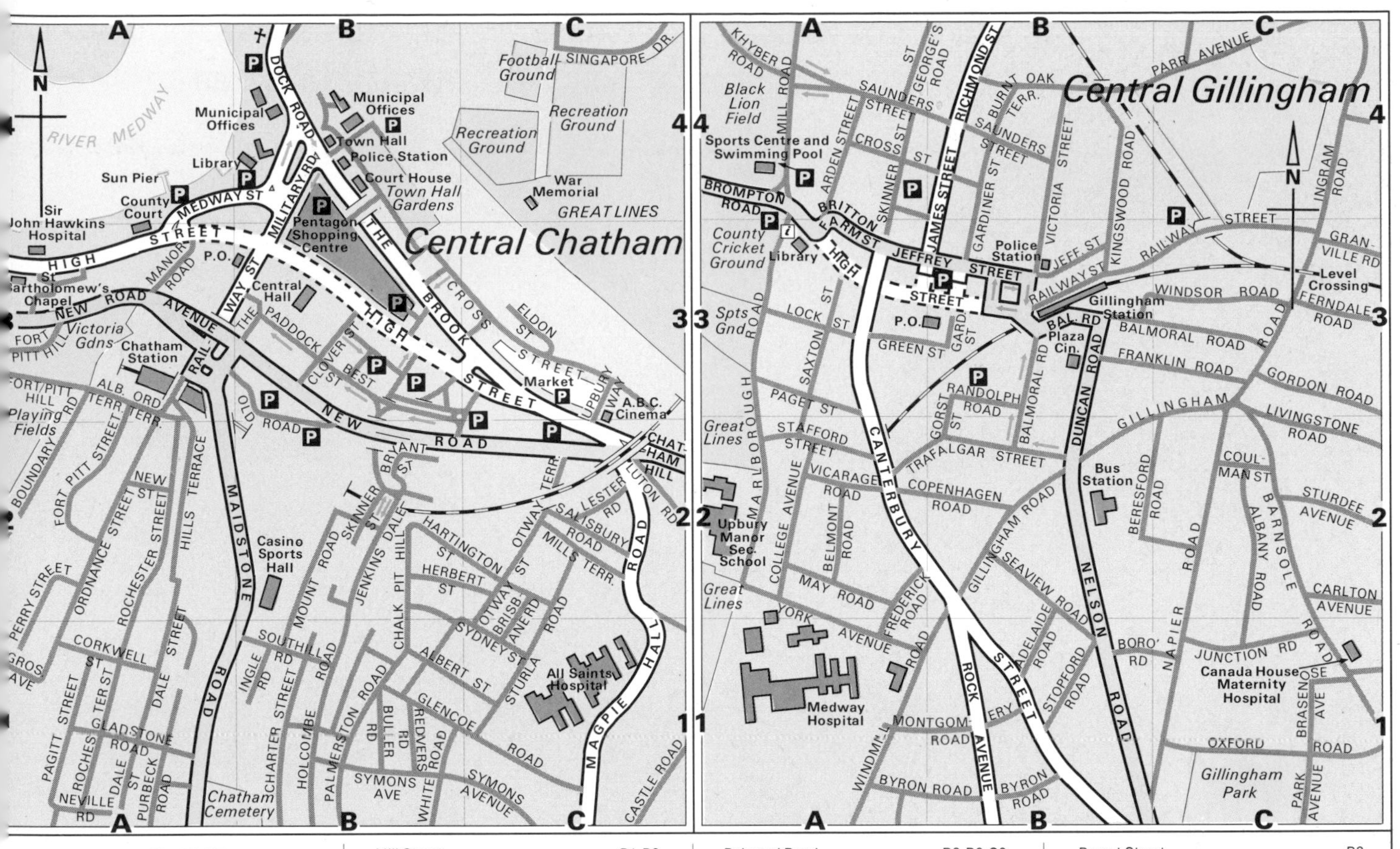

LEGEND

Town Plan

- AA Recommended roads
- Restricted roads
- Other roads
- Buildings of interest — Station
- Churches
- Parks and open spaces
- Car Parks — P
- One Way Streets

Area Plan

- A roads
- B roads
- Locations — Muckingford
- Urban area

Street Index with Grid Reference

Maidstone

Allen Street	C4
Bank Street	B2
Barker Road	A1-B1
Bishops Way	B1-B2
Boxley Road	B4-C4
Brewer Street	B3-C3
Broadway	A1-B1-B2
Brunswick Street	C1
Buckland Hill	A3
Buckland Road	A2-A3
Charles Street	A1
Church Street	C2-C3
College Avenue	B1
College Road	B1
County Road	B4-B3-C3-C4
Earl Street	B2-B3
Fairmeadow	B2-B3
Foley Street	C4
Foster Street	B1-C1
Gabriel's Hill	B2-C2
Hart Street	A1
Hastings Road	C1
Hedley Street	C3-C4
High Street	B2
Holland Road	C3-C4
James Street	C4
Kingsley Road	C1
King Street	B2-C2
Knightrider Street	B1-C1
Lower Stone Street	C1-C2
Market Buildings	B2
Market Street	B2-B3
Marsham Street	C2
Medway Street	B2
Melville Road	C1
Mill Street	B1-B2
Mote Road	C1
Museum Street	B2-B3
Padsole Lane	C1
Palace Avenue	B1-B2-C2
Priory Road	B1
Pudding Lane	B2
Queen Anne Road	C2
Reginald Road	A1
Rocky Hill	A1-A2
Romney Place	C1
St Faith's Street	B3
St Peter's Street	A2-A3
Sandling Road	B4
Station Road	B3
Terrace Road	A1-A2
Tufton Street	C3
Union Street	B3-C3
Upper Stone Street	C1
Waterlow Road	C4
Week Street	B2-B3
Well Road	B4-C4
Wheeler Street	C3-C4
Wyatt Street	C2-C3

Rochester

Bardell Terrace	B2-C2
Blue Boar Lane	B3
Boley Hill	A3
Castle Hill	A3-A4
Cazeneuve Street	B2
City Way	B2-B1-C1
Corporation Street	A4-B4-B3-B2
Crow Lane	B2-B3
Delce Road	B1-B2
Dunnings Lane	A2-B2
East Row	B2
Esplanade	A2-A3-A4
Ethelbert Avenue	A1
Foord Street	B1
Furrells Road	B2-C2
Gashouse Road	B4
Gordon Terrace	A1-A2
High Street	A4-A3-B3-B2-C2
Hoopers Road	A1-B1
James Street	B1
John Street	B2-B1-A1-B1
King Edward Road	A2
King Street	B2
Lockington Grove	A2-B2
Longley Road	A1-B1
Love Lane	A2-A3
Maidstone Road	A1-A2-B2
New Road	B1-C1
Rochester Avenue	A1-B1
Rochester Bridge	A4
Roebuck Road	A1-A2
St Margaret's Street	A1-A2-A3
South Avenue	A1
The Terrace	B2
Victoria Street	B2
Vines Lane	A3-A2-B2
Watts Avenue	A1-A2

Gillingham

Adelaide Road	B1-B2
Albany Road	C1-C2
Arden Street	A4
Balmoral Road	B2-B3-C3
Barnsole Road	C1-C2-C3
Belmont Road	A2
Beresford Road	C2-B2-C2
Borough Road	B1-C1
Brasenose Avenue	C1
Britton Farm Street	A3-A4
Brompton Road	A4
Burnt Oak Terrace	B4
Byron Road	A1-B1
Canterbury Street	A3-A2-B2-B1
Carlton Avenue	C2
College Avenue	A2
Copenhagen Road	A2-B2
Coulman Street	C2
Cross Street	A4-B4
Duncan Road	B2-B3
Ferndale Road	C3
Franklin Road	B3-C3
Frederick Road	A1-A2
Gardiner Street	B3-B4
Gillingham Road	B2-B3-C3
Gordon Road	C3
Gorst Street	B2-B3
Granville Road	C3
Green Street	A3-B3
High Street	A3-B3
Ingram Road	C3-C4
James Street	A3-B3-B4
Jeffrey Street	A3-B3
Junction Road	C1
Kingswood Road	B3-B4
Khyber Road	A4
Livingstone Road	C2-C3
Lock Street	A3
Marlborough Road	A2-A3-A4
May Road	A2
Mill Road	A4
Montgomery Road	A1-B1
Napier Road	B1-C1-C2-C3
Nelson Road	B2-B1-C1
Oxford Road	C1
Paget Street	A3
Park Avenue	C1
Parr Avenue	B4-C4
Railway Street	B3-C3
Randolph Road	B3
Richmond Street	B4
Rock Avenue	B1-B2
St George's Road	A4-B4
Saunders Street	A4-B4
Saxton Street	A2-A3
Seaview Road	B1-B2
Skinner Street	A3-A4
Stafford Street	A2
Stopford Road	B1
Sturdee Avenue	C2
Trafalgar Street	A2-B2
Vicarage Road	A2
Victoria Street	B3-B4
Windmill Road	A1-B1-B2
Windsor Road	B3-C3
York Avenue	A1-A2

Chatham

Albany Terrace	A3
Albert Street	B1-C1
Best Street	B3
Boundary Road	A2-A3
Brisbane Road	C1-C2
Bryant Street	B2
Buller Road	B1
Castle Road	C1
Chalk Pit Hill	B1-B2
Charter Street	B1
Chatham Hill	C2
Clover Street	B3
Corkwell Street	A1
Cross Street	B3-C3
Dale Street	A1-A2
Dock Road	B4
Eldon Street	C3
Fort Pitt Hill	A3
Fort Pitt Street	A2-A3
Gladstone Road	A1
Glencoe Road	B1-C1
Grosvenor Avenue	A1
Hartington Street	B2-C2
Herbert Street	B2-C2
High Street	A3-B3-C3
Hills Terrace	A2
Holcombe Road	B1-B2
Ingle Road	B1
Jenkins Dale	B2
Lester Road	C2
Luton Road	C2
Magpie Hall Road	C1-C2
Maidstone Road	A3-A2-B2-B1-A1
Manor Road	A3
Medway Street	A3-A4-B4
Military Road	B3-B4
Mills Terrace	C2
Mount Road	B1-B2
Neville Road	A1
New Road	B3-B2-C2
New Road Avenue	A3-B3
New Street	A2
Old Road	A3-B3-B2
Ordnance Street	A1-A2-A3
Ordnance Terrace	A3
Otway Street	C1-C2
Otway Terrace	C2
Pagitt Street	A1
Palmerston Road	B1
Perry Street	A1-A2
Purbeck Road	A1
Railway Street	A3-B3
Redvers Road	B1
Rochester Street	A1-A2
Salisbury Road	C2
Singapore Drive	C4
Skinner Street	B2
Southill Road	B1
Sturla Road	C1-C2
Sydney Street	B2-C2-C1
Symons Avenue	B1-C1
The Brook	B4-B3-C3
The Paddock	B3
Upbury Way	C2-C3
White Road	B1

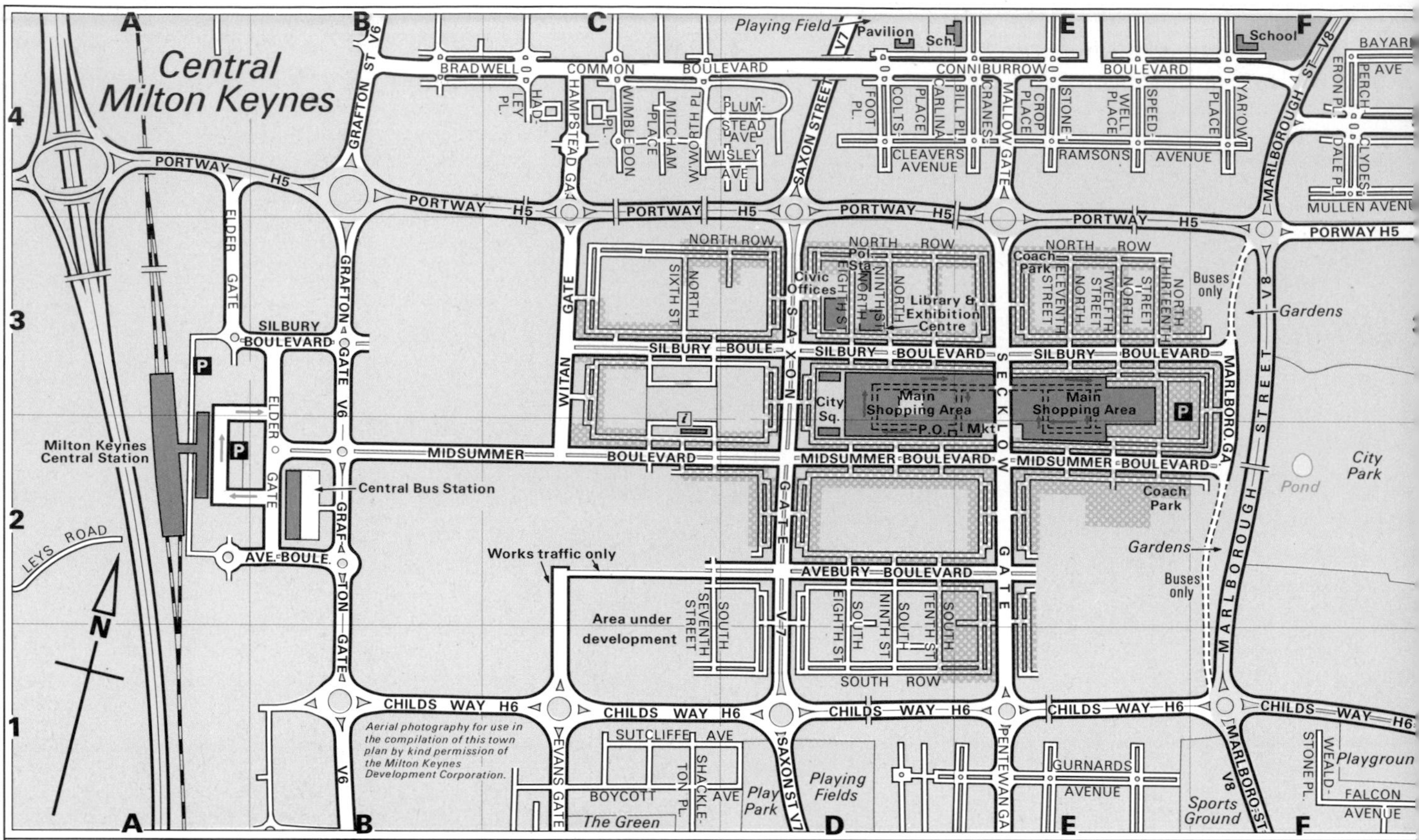

Central Milton Keynes

Aerial photography for use in the compilation of this town plan by kind permission of the Milton Keynes Development Corporation.

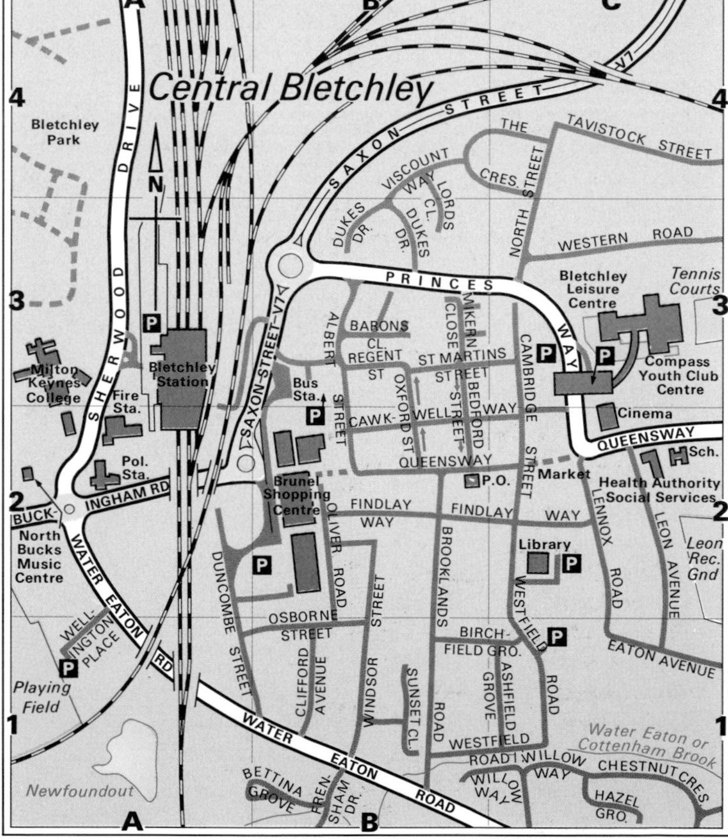

Key to Town Plan and Area Plan

Town Plan

AA Recommended roads
Other roads
Restricted roads
Buildings of interest — Library
Parks and open spaces
Car parks and car parking areas — P
One Way Streets

Area Plan

A roads
B roads
Locations — Stanford ○
Urban area

STREET INDEX- with grid reference

Milton Keynes

Avebury Boulevard	A2-B2, C2-D2-E2
Bayard Avenue	F4
Boycott Avenue	C1-D1
Bradwell Common Boulevard	B4-C4-D4
Carlina Place	D4
Childs Way	B1-C1-D1-E1-F1
Cleavers Avenue	D4-E4
Clydesdale Place	F4
Coltsfoot Place	D4
Conniburrow Boulevard	D4-E4-F4
Cranesbill Place	E4
Elder Gate	A4-A3, B3-B2
Evans Gate	C1
Falcon Avenue	F1
Grafton Gate	B1-B2-B3
Grafton Street	B4
Gurnards Avenue	E1
Hadley Place	C4
Hampstead Gate	C4
Leys Road	A2
Mallow Gate	E4
Marlborough Gate	F2-F3
Marlborough Street	F1-F2-F3-F4
Midsummer Boulevard	B2-C2-D2-E2-F2

Milton-Keynes

The most famous of Britain's New Towns, Milton Keynes was officially opened in 1973. The new city was carefully and considerately planned to integrate with the existing towns and villages and countryside, and yet provide a self-sufficient community where industry, business and housing could develop.

Milton Keynes borough covers some 22,000 acres of North Buckinghamshire, including the towns of Bletchley, Stony Stratford and Wolverton, but the hub of the region is Central Milton Keynes. Here, one of the largest and most attractive shopping areas in Britain can be found. All the shops are under cover and are reached from tall glass-walled arcades paved with marble and lined with exotic trees and shrubs.

The variety of modern housing in Milton Keynes is another of the city's exciting attractions. Purpose-built homes have been imaginatively planned to suit all ages, and the residential areas have generous areas of green open spaces.

Recreational facilities are also an integral part of the city's concept. Bletchley – one of three leisure centres – has a huge multi-purpose sports hall where international events are held, and an exotic free-form swimming pool. Here, beneath the tinted glass of the pyramidal building, real palm trees create a Mediterranean atmosphere.

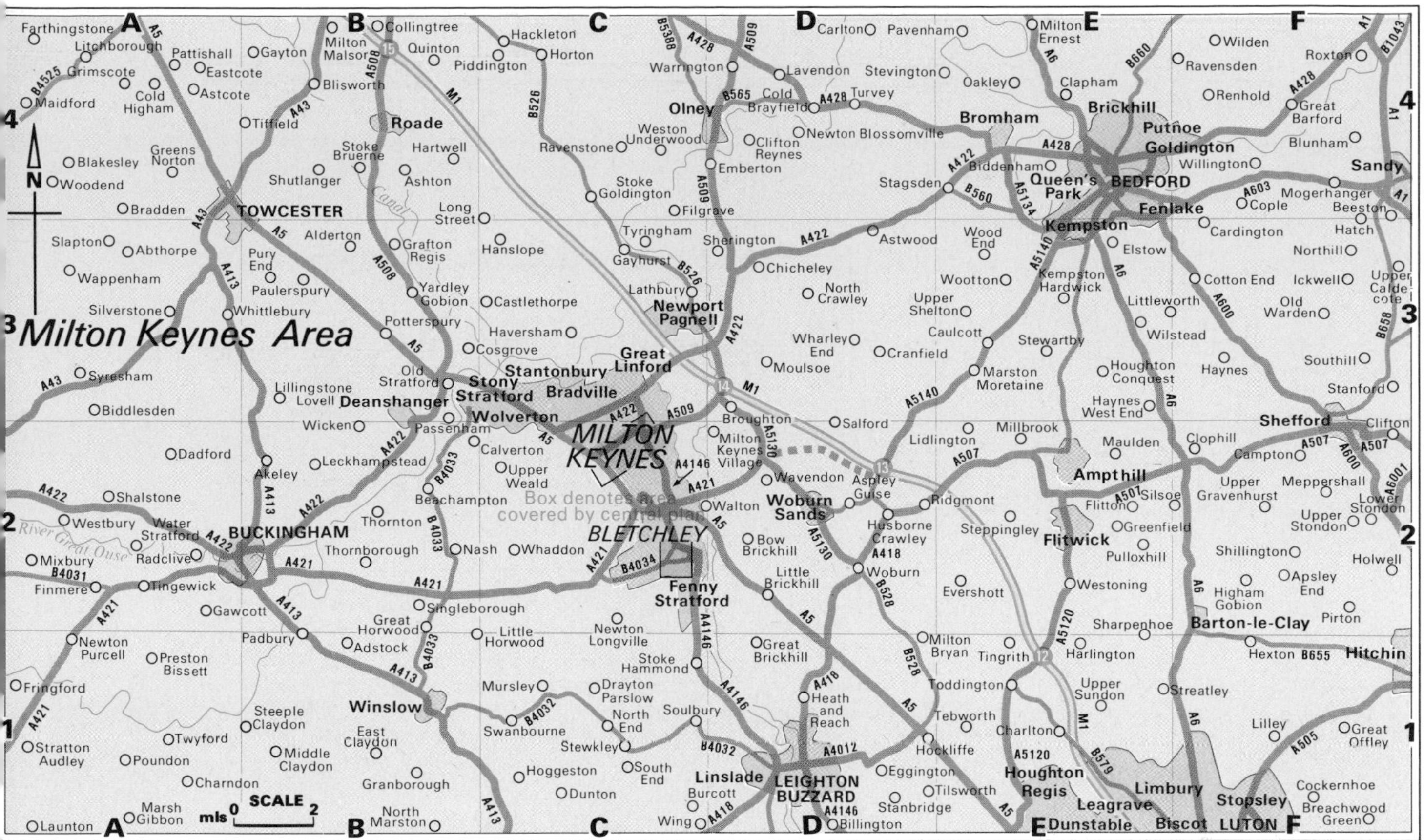

Milton Keynes Area

Mitcham Place C4
Mullen Avenue F4
North Eighth Street D3
North Eleventh Street E3
North Ninth Street D3
North Row C3-D3-E3
North Sixth Street C3
North Thirteenth Street E3
North Twelfth Steet E3
Pentewan Gate E1
Percheron Place F4
Plumstead Avenue C4-D4
Portway A4-B4-C4-D4-E4-E3-F3-F4
Ramsons Avenue E4-F4
Saxon Gate D1-D2-D3
Saxon Street D1, D4
Secklow Gate E1-E2-E3
Shackleton Place C1
Silbury Boulevard A3-B3, C3-D3-E3-F3
South Eighth Street D1-D2
South Ninth Street D1-D2
South Row D1-E1
South Seventh Street C1-C2
South Tenth Street D1-D2
Speedwell Place E4
Stonecrop Place E4
Sutcliffe Avenue C1-D1
Wandsworth Place C4
Wealdstone Place F1
Wimbledon Place C4
Wisley Avenue C4-D4
Witan Gate C2-C3
Yarrow Place F4

Bletchley

Albert Street B2-B3
Ashfield Grove C1
Barons Close B3
Bedford Street B2-B3
Bettina Grove A1-B1
Birchfield Grove B1-C1
Brooklands Road B1-B2
Buckingham Road A2
Cambridge Street C2-C3
Cawkwell Way B2-C2
Chestnut Crescent C1
Clifford Avenue B1
Dukes Drive B3
Duncombe Street A2-A1-B1
Eaton Avenue C1
Findlay Way B2-C2
Frensham Drive B1
Hazel Grove C1
Lennox Road C1-C2
Leon Avenue C1-C2
Lords Close B3-B4
Mikern Close B3
North Street C3-C4
Oliver Road B1-B2
Osborne Street A1-B1
Oxford Street B2-B3
Princes Way B3-C3
Queensway B2-C2
Regent Street B3
St Martins Street B3-C3
Saxon Street A3-A2-B2-B3-B4-C4
Sherwood Drive A2-A3-A4
Sunset Close B1
Tavistock Street C4
The Crescent B4-C4
Viscount Way B4
Water Eaton Road A2-A1-B1-C1
Wellington Place A1-A2
Western Road C3
Westfield Road B1-C1-C2
Willow Way B1-C1
Windsor Street B1-B2

MILTON KEYNES
Huge industrial estates and modern factories were built in Milton Keynes during the 1970s to provide employment for the people who moved to the New Town from London as a result of the capital's housing problems.

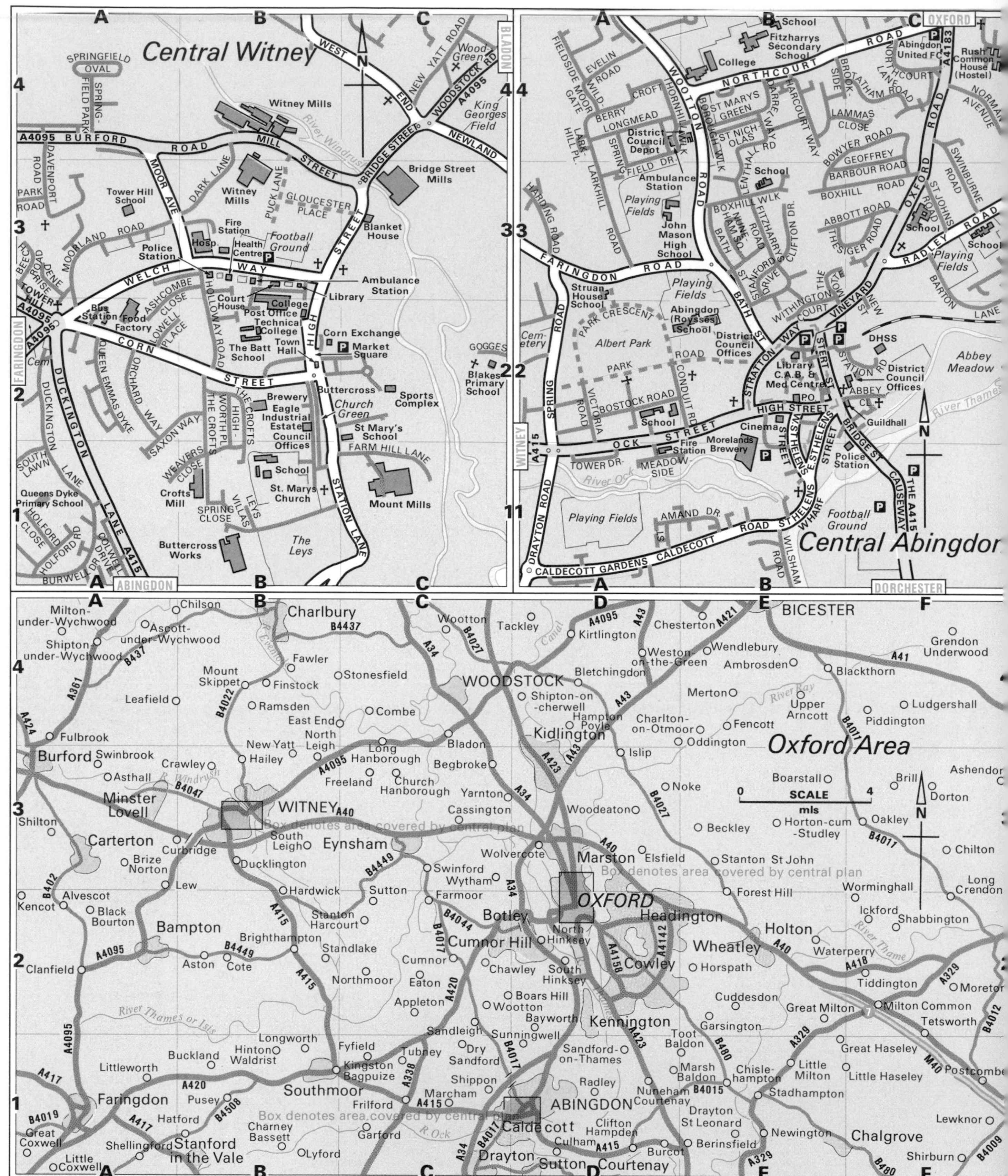

Oxford

From Carfax (at the centre of the city) round to Magdalen Bridge stretches High Street, one of England's best and most interesting thoroughfares. Shops rub shoulders with churches and colleges, alleyways lead to ancient inns and to a large covered market, and little streets lead to views of some of the finest architecture to be seen anywhere. Catte Street, beside St Mary's Church (whose lovely tower gives a panoramic view of Oxford), opens out into Radcliffe Square, dominated by the Radcliffe Camera, a great round structure built in 1749. Close by is the Bodleian Library, one of the finest collections of books and manuscripts in the world. All around are ancient college buildings. Close to Magdalen Bridge is Magdalen College, founded in 1448 and certainly not to be missed. Across the High Street are the Botanical Gardens, founded in 1621 and the oldest such foundation in England. Footpaths lead through Christ Church Meadow to Christ Church College and the cathedral. Tom Tower is the college's most notable feature; the cathedral is actually its chapel and is the smallest cathedral in England. Among much else not to be missed in Oxford is the Ashmolean Museum, whose vast collections of precious and beautiful objects from all over the world repay many hours of study; perhaps the loveliest treasure is the 9th-century Alfred Jewel.

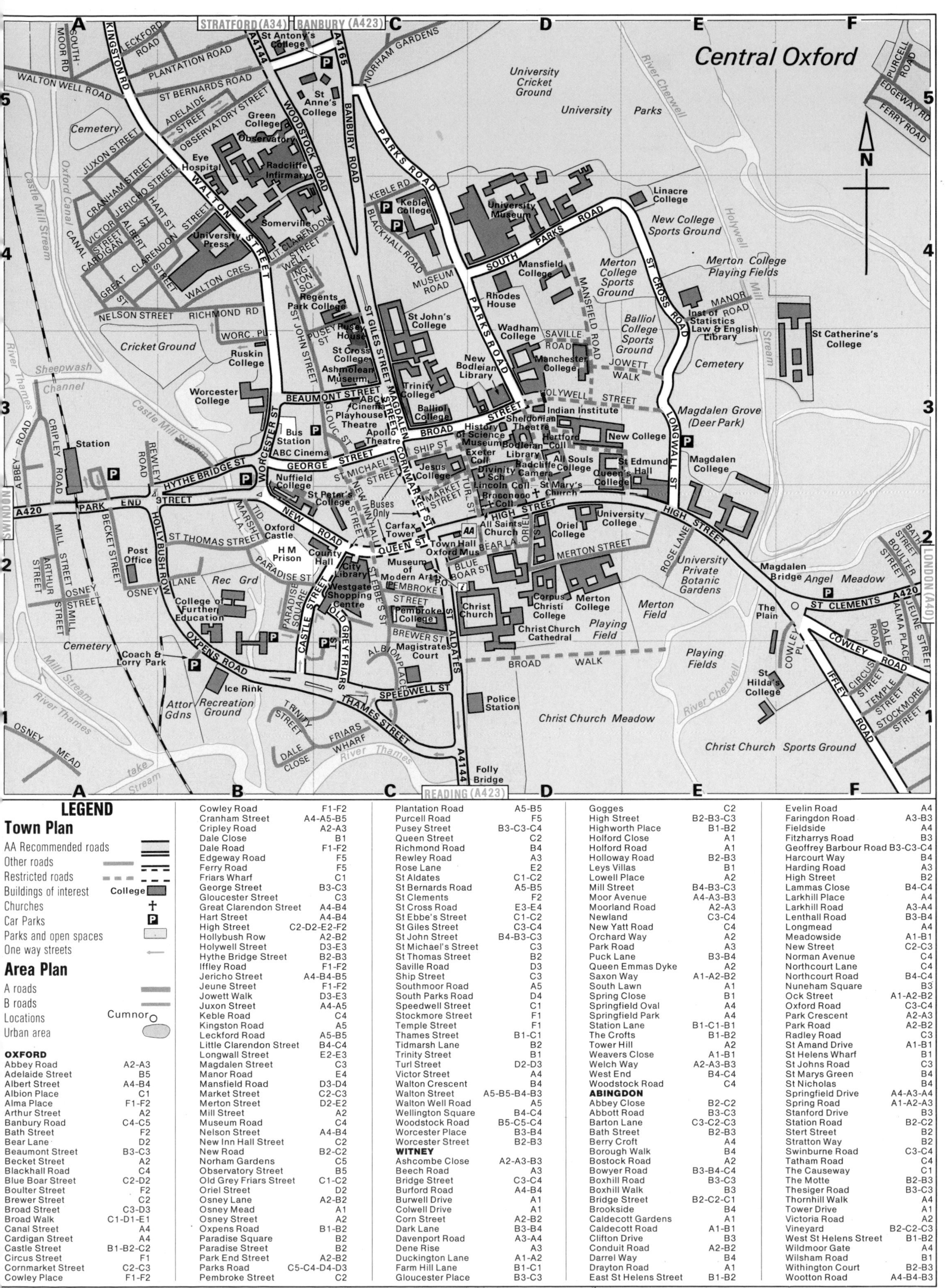

LEGEND

Town Plan

AA Recommended roads
Other roads
Restricted roads
Buildings of interest College
Churches
Car Parks
Parks and open spaces
One way streets

Area Plan

A roads
B roads
Locations Cumnor
Urban area

OXFORD

Abbey Road A2-A3
Adelaide Street B5
Albert Street A4-B4
Albion Place C1
Alma Place F1-F2
Arthur Street A2
Banbury Road C4-C5
Bath Street F2
Bear Lane D2
Beaumont Street B3-C3
Becket Street A2
Blackhall Road C4
Blue Boar Street C2-D2
Boulter Street F2
Brewer Street C2
Broad Street C3-D3
Broad Walk C1-D1-E1
Canal Street A4
Cardigan Street A4
Castle Street B1-B2-C2
Circus Street F1
Cornmarket Street C2-C3
Cowley Place F1-F2
Cowley Road F1-F2
Cranham Street A4-A5-B5
Cripley Road A2-A3
Dale Close B1
Dale Road F1-F2
Edgeway Road F5
Ferry Road F5
Friars Wharf C1
George Street B3-C3
Gloucester Street C3
Great Clarendon Street A4-B4
Hart Street A4-B4
High Street C2-D2-E2-F2
Hollybush Row A2-B2
Holywell Street D3-E3
Hythe Bridge Street B2-B3
Iffley Road F1-F2
Jericho Street A4-B4-B5
Jeune Street F1-F2
Jowett Walk D3-E3
Juxon Street A4-A5
Keble Road C4
Kingston Road A5
Leckford Road A5-B5
Little Clarendon Street B4-C4
Longwall Street E2-E3
Magdalen Street C3
Manor Road E4
Mansfield Road D3-D4
Market Street C2-C3
Merton Street D2-E2
Mill Street A2
Museum Road C4
Nelson Street A4-B4
New Inn Hall Street C2
New Road B2-C2
Norham Gardens C5
Observatory Street B5
Old Grey Friars Street C1-C2
Oriel Street D2
Osney Lane A2-B2
Osney Mead A1
Osney Street A2
Oxpens Road B1-B2
Paradise Square B2
Paradise Street B2
Park End Street A2-B2
Parks Road C5-C4-D4-D3
Pembroke Street C2
Plantation Road A5-B5
Purcell Road F5
Pusey Street B3-C3-C4
Queen Street C2
Richmond Road B4
Rewley Road A3
Rose Lane E2
St Aldates C1-C2
St Bernards Road A5-B5
St Clements F2
St Cross Road E3-E4
St Ebbe's Street C1-C2
St Giles Street C3-C4
St John Street B4-B3-C3
St Michael's Street C3
St Thomas Street B2
Saville Road D3
Ship Street C3
Southmoor Road A5
South Parks Road D4
Speedwell Street C1
Stockmore Street F1
Temple Street F1
Thames Street B1-C1
Tidmarsh Lane B2
Trinity Street B1
Turl Street D2-D3
Victor Street A4
Walton Crescent B4
Walton Street A5-B5-B4-B3
Walton Well Road A5
Wellington Square B4-C4
Woodstock Road B5-C5-C4
Worcester Place B3-B4
Worcester Street B2-B3

WITNEY

Ashcombe Close A2-A3-B3
Beech Road A3
Bridge Street C3-C4
Burford Road A4-B4
Burwell Drive A1
Colwell Drive A1
Corn Street A2-B2
Dark Lane B3-B4
Davenport Road A3-A4
Dene Rise A3
Duckington Lane A1-A2
Farm Hill Lane B1-C1
Gloucester Place B3-C3
Gogges C2
High Street B2-B3-C3
Highworth Place B1-B2
Holford Close A1
Holford Road A1
Holloway Road B2-B3
Leys Villas B1
Lowell Place A2
Mill Street B4-B3-C3
Moor Avenue A4-A3-B3
Moorland Road A2-A3
Newland C3-C4
New Yatt Road C4
Orchard Way A2
Park Road A3
Puck Lane B3-B4
Queen Emmas Dyke A2
Saxon Way A1-A2-B2
South Lawn A1
Spring Close B1
Springfield Oval A4
Springfield Park A4
Station Lane B1-C1-B1
The Crofts B1-B2
Tower Hill A2
Weavers Close A1-B1
Welch Way A2-A3-B3
West End B4-C4
Woodstock Road C4

ABINGDON

Abbey Close B2-C2
Abbott Road B3-C3
Barton Lane C3-C2-C3
Bath Street B2-B3
Berry Croft A4
Borough Walk B4
Bostock Road A2
Bowyer Road B3-B4-C4
Boxhill Road B3-C3
Boxhill Walk B3
Bridge Street B2-C2-C1
Brookside B4
Caldecott Gardens A1
Caldecott Road A1-B1
Clifton Drive B3
Conduit Road A2-B2
Darrel Way B4
Drayton Road A1
East St Helens Street B1-B2
Evelin Road A4
Faringdon Road A3-B3
Fieldside A4
Fitzharrys Road B3
Geoffrey Barbour Road B3-C3-C4
Harcourt Way B4
Harding Road A3
High Street A2
Lammas Close B4-C4
Larkhill Place A4
Larkhill Road A3-A4
Lenthall Road B3-B4
Longmead A4
Meadowside A1-B1
New Street C2-C3
Norman Avenue C4
Northcourt Lane C4
Northcourt Road B4-C4
Nuneham Square B3
Ock Street A1-A2-B2
Oxford Road C3-C4
Park Crescent A2-A3
Park Road A2-B2
Radley Road C3
St Amand Drive A1-B1
St Helens Wharf B1
St Johns Road C3
St Marys Green B4
St Nicholas B4
Springfield Drive A4-A3-A4
Spring Road A1-A2-A3
Stanford Drive B3
Station Road B2-C2
Stert Street B2
Stratton Way B2
Swinburne Road C3-C4
Tatham Road C4
The Causeway C1
The Motte B2-B3
Thesiger Road B3-C3
Thornhill Walk A4
Tower Drive A1
Victoria Road A2
Vineyard B2-C2-C3
West St Helens Street B1-B2
Wildmoor Gate A4
Wilsham Road B1
Withington Court B2-B3
Wootton Road A4-B4-B3

Portsmouth

Richard the Lionheart first recognised the strategic importance of Portsea Island and subsequently ordered the first docks, and later the town of Portsmouth, to be built. Over the centuries, succeeding monarchs improved the defences and extended the docks which now cover some 300 acres – as befits Britain's premier naval base. Of the defensive fortifications, Fort Widley and the Round Tower are the best preserved remains. Two famous ships rest in Portsmouth; *HMS Victory* and the *Mary Rose*. The former, Lord Nelson's flagship, has been fully restored and the adjacent Royal Naval museum houses numerous relics of Trafalgar. The *Mary Rose*, built by Henry VIII, lay on the sea bed off Southsea until she was spectacularly raised in 1982. She has now been put on display and there is an exhibition in Southsea Castle of artefacts that have been recovered from her. Portsmouth suffered greatly from bombing in World War II and the centre has been almost completely rebuilt. However, the old town, clustered around the harbour mouth, escaped severe damage and, now restored, forms an attractive and fashionable area of the city.

Southsea, Portsmouth's near neighbour, developed in the 19th century as an elegant seaside resort with fine houses and terraces, an esplanade and an extensive seafront common.

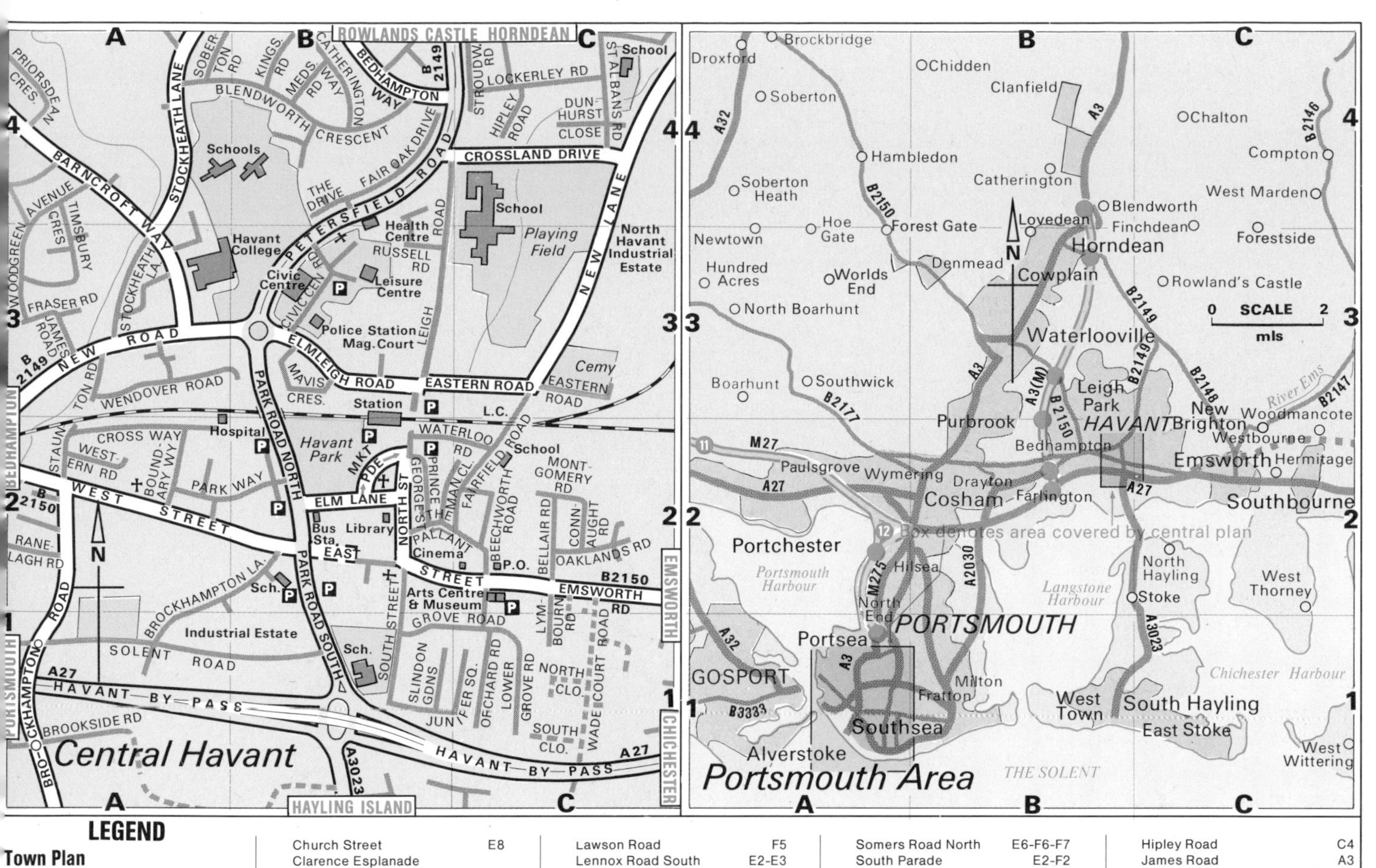

LEGEND

Town Plan
- AA recommended route
- Restricted roads
- Other roads
- Buildings of interest Station
- Car parks
- Parks and open spaces
- One way streets

Area Plan
- A roads
- B roads
- Locations ○ Lovedean
- Urban area

Street Index with Grid Reference

Portsmouth

Havant

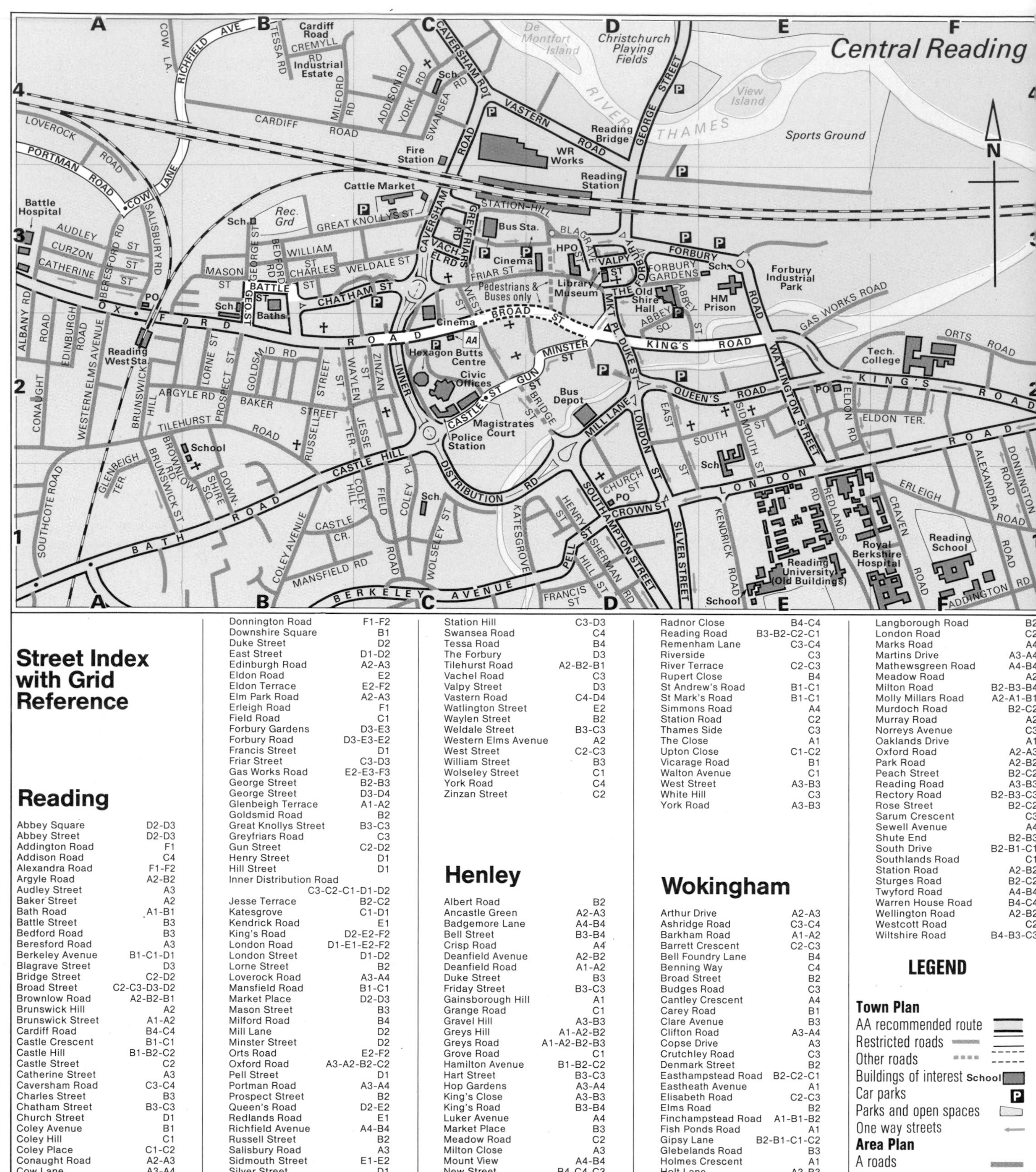

Street Index with Grid Reference

Reading

Abbey Square	D2-D3
Abbey Street	D2-D3
Addington Road	F1
Addison Road	C4
Alexandra Road	F1-F2
Argyle Road	A2-B2
Audley Street	A3
Baker Street	A2
Bath Road	A1-B1
Battle Street	B3
Bedford Road	B3
Beresford Road	A3
Berkeley Avenue	B1-C1-D1
Blagrave Street	D3
Bridge Street	C2-D2
Broad Street	C2-C3-D3-D2
Brownlow Road	A2-B2-B1
Brunswick Hill	A2
Brunswick Street	A1-A2
Cardiff Road	B4-C4
Castle Crescent	B1-C1
Castle Hill	B1-B2-C2
Castle Street	C2
Catherine Street	A3
Caversham Road	C3-C4
Charles Street	B3
Chatham Street	B3-C3
Church Street	D1
Coley Avenue	B1
Coley Hill	C1
Coley Place	C1-C2
Conaught Road	A2-A3
Cow Lane	A3-A4
Craven Road	F1-F2
Cremyll Road	B4
Crown Street	D1
Curzon Street	A3
Donnington Road	F1-F2
Downshire Square	B1
Duke Street	D2
East Street	D1-D2
Edinburgh Road	A2-A3
Eldon Road	E2
Eldon Terrace	E2-F2
Elm Park Road	A2-A3
Erleigh Road	F1
Field Road	C1
Forbury Gardens	D3-E3
Forbury Road	D3-E3-E2
Francis Street	D1
Friar Street	C3-D3
Gas Works Road	E2-E3-F3
George Street	B2-B3
George Street	D3-D4
Glenbeigh Terrace	A1-A2
Goldsmid Road	B2
Great Knollys Street	B3-C3
Greyfriars Road	C3
Gun Street	C2-D2
Henry Street	D1
Hill Street	D1
Inner Distribution Road	C3-C2-C1-D1-D2
Jesse Terrace	B2-C2
Katesgrove	C1-D1
Kendrick Road	E1
King's Road	D2-E2-F2
London Road	D1-E1-E2-F2
London Street	D1-D2
Lorne Street	B2
Loverock Road	A3-A4
Mansfield Road	B1-C1
Market Place	D2-D3
Mason Street	B3
Milford Road	B4
Mill Lane	D2
Minster Street	D2
Orts Road	E2-F2
Oxford Road	A3-A2-B2-C2
Pell Street	D1
Portman Road	A3-A4
Prospect Street	B2
Queen's Road	D2-E2
Redlands Road	E1
Richfield Avenue	A4-B4
Russell Street	B2
Salisbury Road	A3
Sidmouth Street	E1-E2
Silver Street	D1
Sherman Road	D1
Southampton Street	D1
Southcote Road	A1-A2
South Street	D2-E2
Station Hill	C3-D3
Swansea Road	C4
Tessa Road	B4
The Forbury	D3
Tilehurst Road	A2-B2-B1
Vachel Road	C3
Valpy Street	D3
Vastern Road	C4-D4
Watlington Street	E2
Waylen Street	B2
Weldale Street	B3-C3
Western Elms Avenue	A2
West Street	C2-C3
William Street	B3
Wolseley Street	C1
York Road	C4
Zinzan Street	C2

Henley

Albert Road	B2
Ancastle Green	A2-A3
Badgemore Lane	A4-B4
Bell Street	B3-B4
Crisp Road	A4
Deanfield Avenue	A2-B2
Deanfield Road	A1-A2
Duke Street	B3
Friday Street	B3-C3
Gainsborough Hill	A1
Grange Road	C1
Gravel Hill	A3-B3
Greys Hill	A1-A2-B2
Greys Road	A1-A2-B2-B3
Grove Road	C1
Hamilton Avenue	B1-B2-C2
Hart Street	B3-C3
Hop Gardens	A3-A4
King's Close	A3-B3
King's Road	B3-B4
Luker Avenue	A4
Market Place	B3
Meadow Road	C2
Milton Close	A3
Mount View	A4-B4
New Street	B4-C4-C3
Norman Avenue	B2
Queen Street	B3-B2-C2
Paradise Road	A2-A3
Park Road	C1
Radnor Close	B4-C4
Reading Road	B3-B2-C2-C1
Remenham Lane	C3-C4
Riverside	C3
River Terrace	C2-C3
Rupert Close	B4
St Andrew's Road	B1-C1
St Mark's Road	B1-C1
Simmons Road	A4
Station Road	C2
Thames Side	C3
The Close	A1
Upton Close	C1-C2
Vicarage Road	B1
Walton Avenue	C1
West Street	A3-B3
White Hill	C3
York Road	A3-B3

Wokingham

Arthur Drive	A2-A3
Ashridge Road	C3-C4
Barkham Road	A1-A2
Barrett Crescent	C2-C3
Bell Foundry Lane	B4
Benning Way	C4
Broad Street	B2
Budges Road	C3
Cantley Crescent	A4
Carey Road	B1
Clare Avenue	B3
Clifton Road	A3-A4
Copse Drive	A3
Crutchley Road	C3
Denmark Street	B2
Easthampstead Road	B2-C2-C1
Eastheath Avenue	A1
Elisabeth Road	C2-C3
Elms Road	B2
Finchampstead Road	A1-B1-B2
Fish Ponds Road	A1
Gipsy Lane	B2-B1-C1-C2
Glebelands Road	B3
Holmes Crescent	A1
Holt Lane	A3-B3
Howard Road	B2
Hughes Road	C3
Jubilee Avenue	A4-A3-B3
Keephatch Road	C3-C4
Langborough Road	B2
London Road	C2
Marks Road	A4
Martins Drive	A3-A4
Mathewsgreen Road	A4-B4
Meadow Road	A2
Milton Road	B2-B3-B4
Molly Millars Road	A2-A1-B1
Murdoch Road	B2-C2
Murray Road	A2
Norreys Avenue	C3
Oaklands Drive	A1
Oxford Road	A2-A3
Park Road	A2-B2
Peach Street	B2-C2
Reading Road	A3-B3
Rectory Road	B2-B3-C3
Rose Street	B2-C2
Sarum Crescent	C3
Sewell Avenue	A4
Shute End	B2-B3
South Drive	B2-B1-C1
Southlands Road	C1
Station Road	A2-B2
Sturges Road	B2-C2
Twyford Road	A4-B4
Warren House Road	B4-C4
Wellington Road	A2-B2
Westcott Road	C2
Wiltshire Road	B4-B3-C3

LEGEND

Town Plan
AA recommended route
Restricted roads
Other roads
Buildings of interest School
Car parks P
Parks and open spaces
One way streets
Area Plan
A roads
B roads
Locations Wilsden
Urban area

Reading

Shopping and light industry first spring to mind when thinking of Reading, but the town actually has a long and important history. Its rise to significance began in 1121 when Henry I founded an abbey here which became the third most important in England. However, after the Dissolution of the Monasteries, only a few ruins were left. Reading also used to be one of the major centres of the medieval cloth trade, but, already declining in the early 17th century, this source of income was reduced still further as a result of Civil War disturbances.

A fascinating collection of all types of farm implements and domestic equipment can be found in the extremely comprehensive Museum of English Rural Life, situated in the University Campus at Whiteknights Park. The town's own museum has major displays about nearby Silchester – the powerful Roman town of *Calleva*.

Henley-on-Thames, famous for its annual rowing regatta, is a lovely old town, well-provided with old coaching inns, Georgian façades and numerous listed buildings.

Wokingham has been a market town for centuries and over the years has been known for its silk industry and its bell-foundry. Half-timbered gabled houses can be seen in the town centre, although modern development surrounds it.

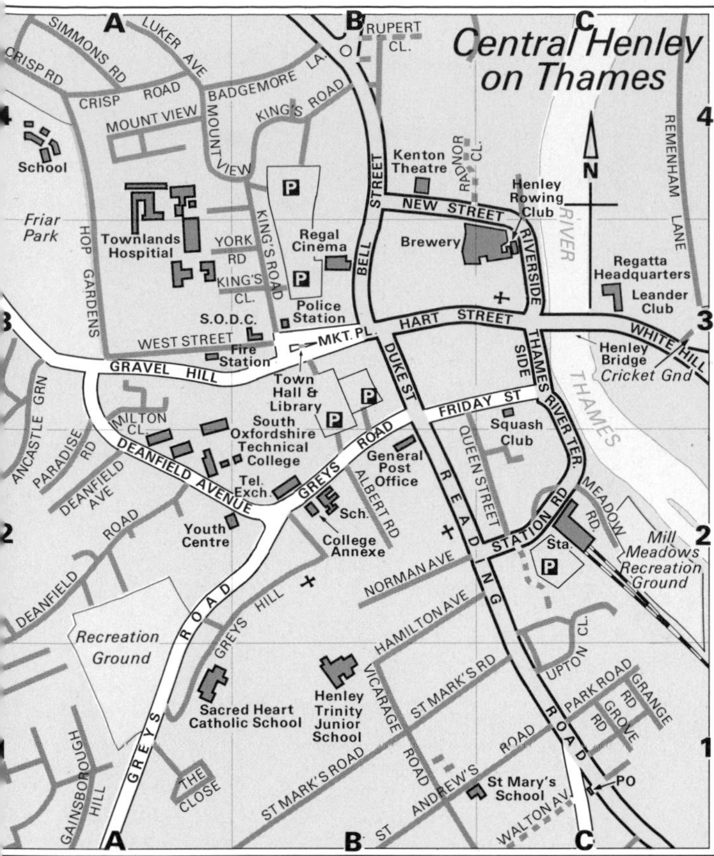

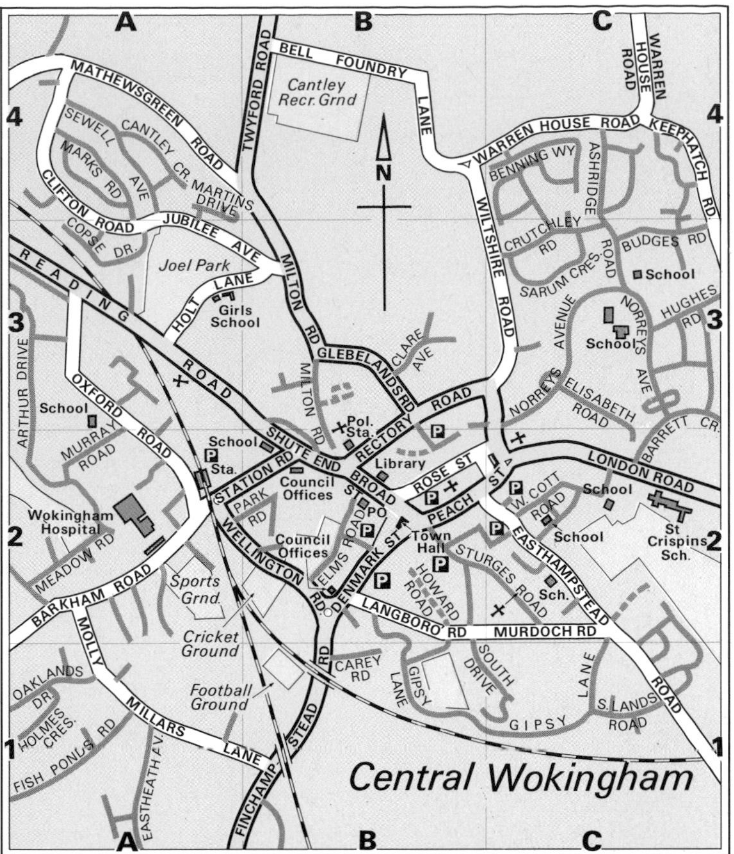

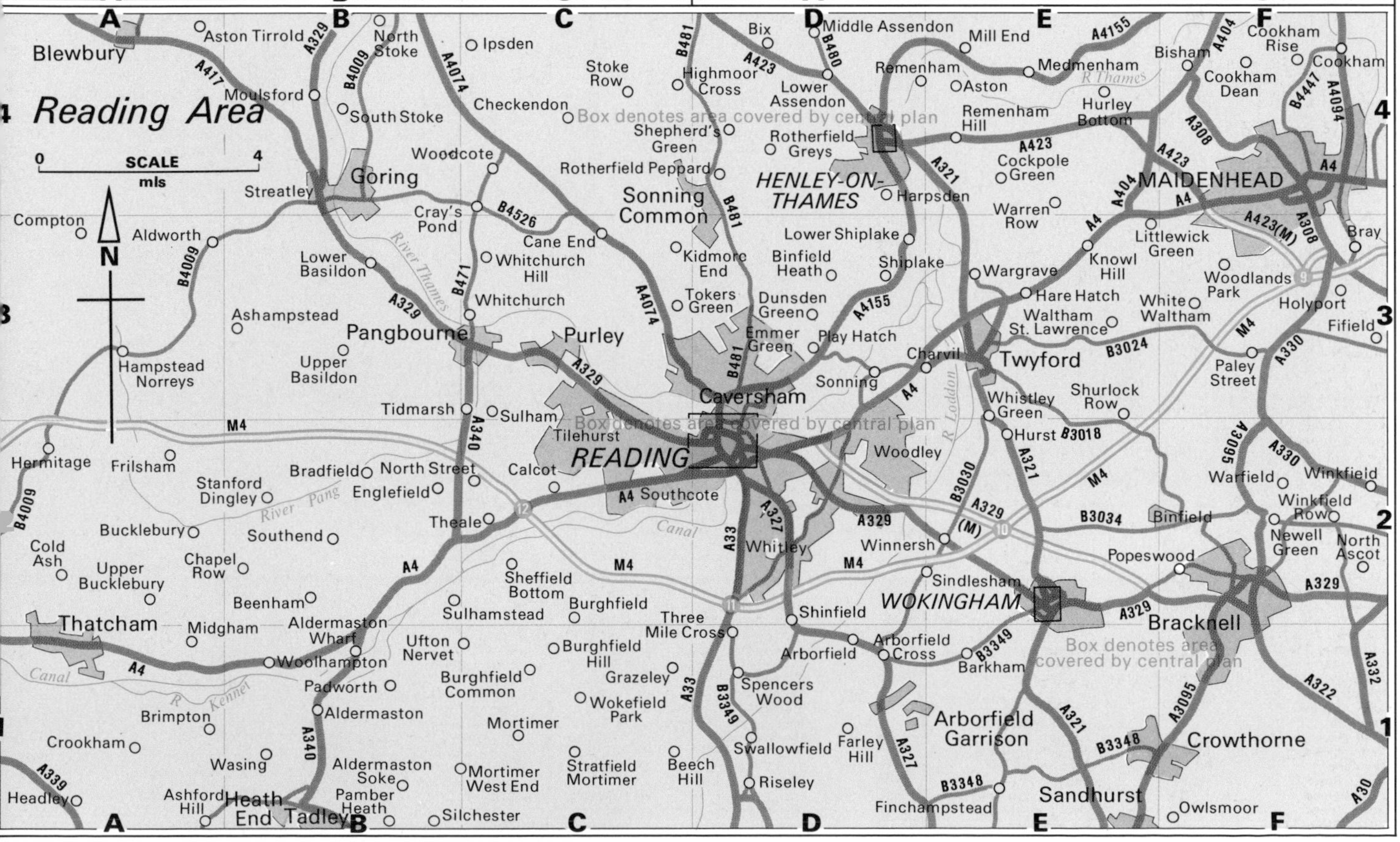

Central Henley on Thames

Central Wokingham

Reading Area

READING
Whiteknights, which consists of 300 acres of landscaped parkland, provides Reading's modern university with an incomparable campus setting and includes a conservation area and a biological reserve for research purposes.

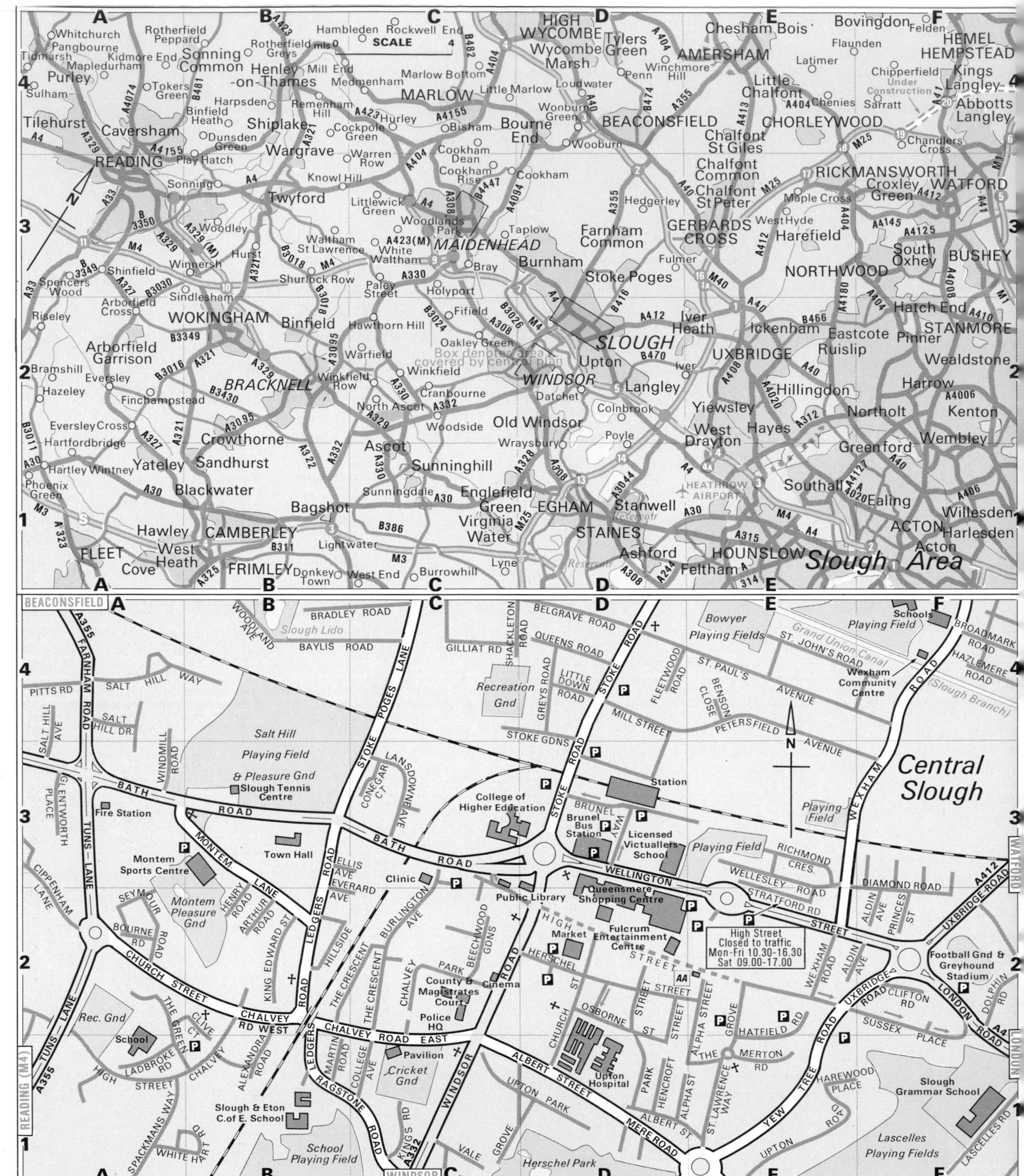

Slough

The town is something of a non-starter as far as architectural beauty or historical interest is concerned. However, it is a good shopping centre and has plenty of sports and leisure facilities.

Windsor The distinctive outline of the castle's towers and battlements above the Thames completely dominates the town. First built by the Normans to guard the approaches to London, it has been altered and added to at different times by various kings, but Henry III and Edward III contributed most to its present haphazard shape. The State Apartments are magnificent, as is St George's Chapel, with its superb fan-vaulted ceiling. Queen Mary's Dolls' House is an exquisite model house of the 1920s, complete down to the last detail. The town itself, squeezed between the castle walls and the river, has several attractive streets graced with fine buildings. One 17th-century colonnaded building by Sir Christopher Wren contains a small museum of local interest, and a recent new attraction is the Madame Tussaud's Royalty and Railways Exhibition.

Maidenhead used to be an important stage-post on the London to Bath road and is now a prosperous Thameside residential town. Oldfield House, near the ancient bridge designed by Brunel, contains the Henry Reitlinger Bequest Museum, specialising in glass and ceramics.

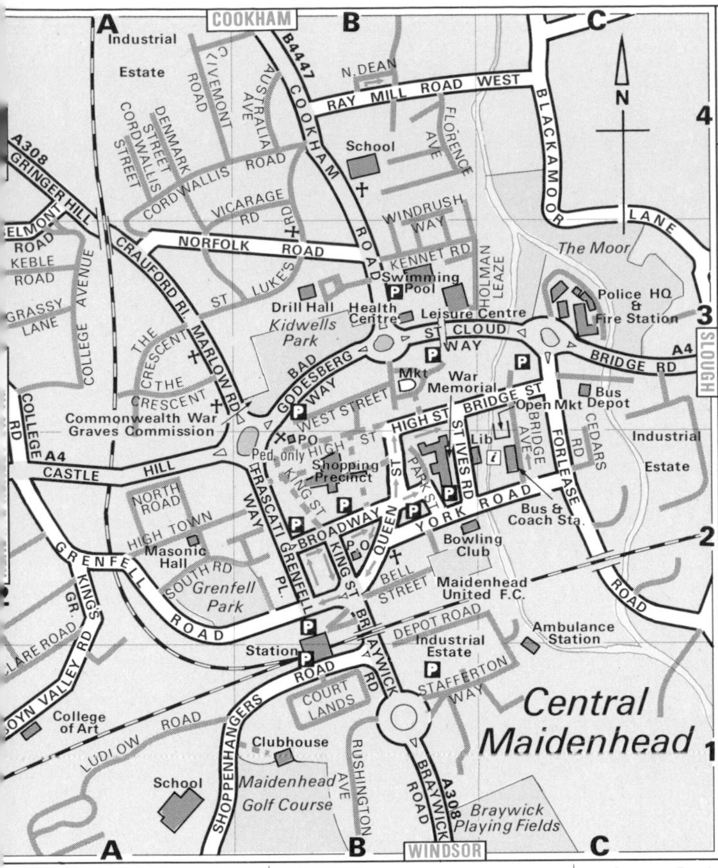

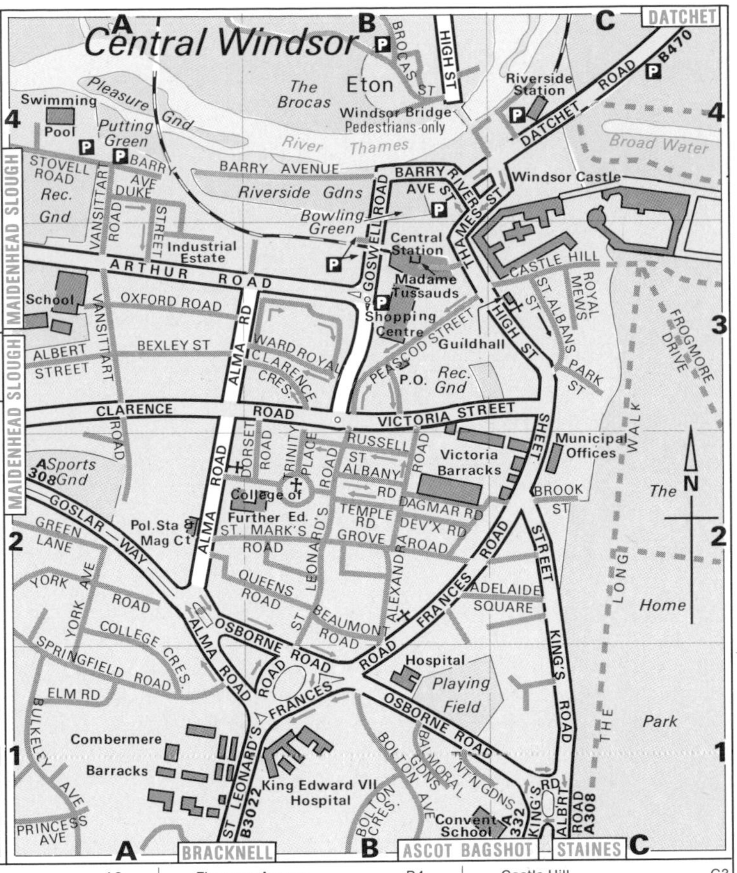

Central Maidenhead

Central Windsor

LEGEND

Town Plan
- AA recommended route
- Restricted roads
- Other roads
- Buildings of interest — Station
- Car parks
- Parks and open spaces
- One way streets

Area Plan
- A roads
- B roads
- Locations — Hightown
- Urban area

Street Index with Grid Reference

SLOUGH
Salt Hill Park in the centre of Slough features a bowling green, tennis courts and a children's play area, as well as pleasant walks through landscaped gardens. This is one of several recreational areas scattered throughout the town.

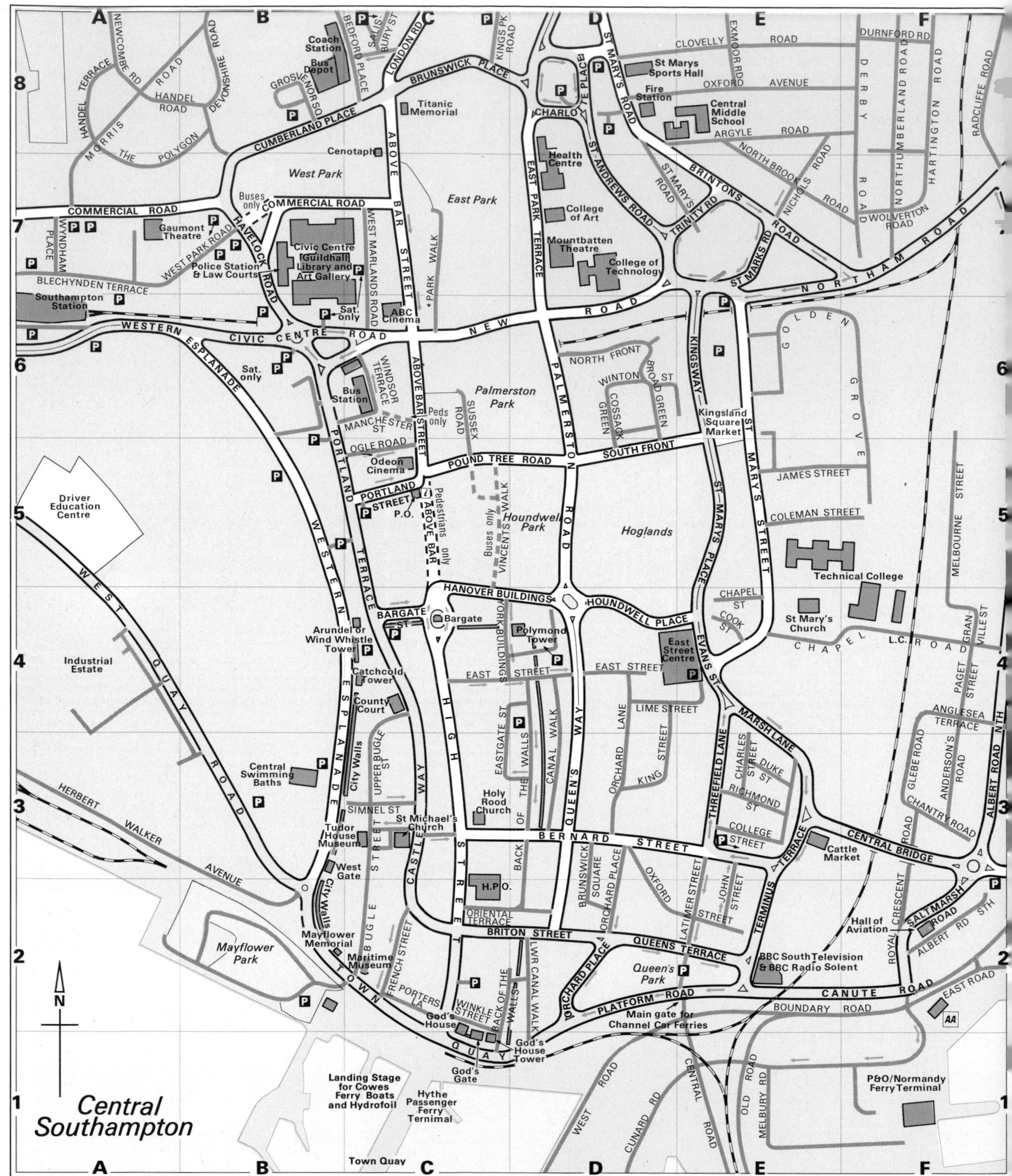

Southampton

In the days of the great ocean-going liners, Southampton was Britain's premier passenger port. Today container traffic is more important, but cruise liners still berth there. A unique double tide caused by the Solent waters, and protection from the open sea by the Isle of Wight, has meant that Southampton has always been a superb and important port. Like many great cities it was devastated by bombing raids during World War II. However, enough survives to make the city a fascinating place to explore. Outstanding are the town walls, which stand to their original height in some places, especially along Western Esplanade. The main landward entrance to the walled town was the Bargate – a superb medieval gateway with a Guildhall (now a museum) on its upper floor. The best place to appreciate old Southampton is in and around St Michael's Square. Here is St Michael's Church, oldest in the city and founded in 1070. Opposite is Tudor House Museum, a lovely gabled building housing much of interest. Down Bugle Street are old houses, with the town walls, pierced by the 13th-century West Gate, away to the right. At the corner of Bugle Street is the Wool House Maritime Museum, contained in a 14th-century warehouse. On the quayside is God's House Tower, part of the town's defences and now an archaeological museum.

Central Eastleigh

Southampton Area

Key to Town Plan and Area Plan

Town Plan

A.A. Recommended roads
Other roads
Restricted roads
Buildings of interest — Cinema
A A Service Centre — AA
Car Parks — P
Parks and open spaces
One way streets

Area Plan

A roads
B roads
Locations — Ower O
Urban Area

SOUTHAMPTON

Above Bar	C5
Above Bar Street	C5-C6-C7-C8
Albert Road North	F3-F4
Albert Road South	F2
Anderson's Road	F3-F4
Anglesea Terrace	F4
Argyle Road	E8-F8
Back of the Walls	C1-C2-D2-D3-D4
Bargate Street	C4
Bedford Place	B8-C8
Bernard Street	C3-D3-E3
Blechynden Terrace	A7
Boundary Road	E2-F2
Briton Street	C2-D2
Britons Road	D8-E8-E7
Broad Green	D6
Brunswick Place	C8-D8
Brunswick Square	D2-D3
Bugle Street	C2-C3
Canal Walk	D3-D4
Canute Road	E2-F2
Castle Way	C2-C3-C4
Central Bridge	E3-F3
Central Road	E1-E2
Chantry Road	F3
Chapel Road	E4-F4
Chapel Street	E4
Charles Street	E3
Charlotte Place	D8
Civic Centre Road	B6-C6
Clovelly Road	D8-E8-F8
Coleman Street	E5-F5
College Street	E3
Commercial Road	A7-B7-C7
Cook Street	E4
Cossack Green	D5-D6
Cumberland Place	B7-B8-C8
Cunard Road	D1-E1
Derby Road	F7-F8
Devonshire Road	B8
Duke Street	E3
Durnford Road	F8
East Road	F2
East Street	C4-D4
East Park Terrace	D6-D7-D8
Eastgate Street	D3-C3-C4-D4
Evans Street	E4
Exmoor Road	E8
French Street	C2
Glebe Road	F3-F4
Golden Grove	E6-F6-F5
Granville Street	F4
Grosvenor Square	B8
Handel Road	A8-B8
Handel Terrace	A8
Hanover Buildings	C5-C4-D4
Hartington Road	F7-F8
Havelock Road	B6-B7
Herbert Walker Avenue	A3-B3-B2
High Street	C1-C2-C3-C4
Houndwell Place	D4-E4
James Street	E5-F5
John Street	E2-E3
Kingsway	E6-E7
King Street	D3-D4
Kings Park Road	C8
Latimer Street	E2-E3
Lime Street	D4-E4
London Road	C8
Lower Canal Walk	D1-D2
Manchester Street	B6-C6
Marsh Lane	E3-E4
Melbourne Street	F4-F5-F6
Melbury Road	E1
Morris Road	A7-A8-B8
New Road	E6-D6-D7
Newcombe Road	A8
Nichols Road	E7-E8
North Brook Road	E8-E7-F7
North Front	D6
Northam Road	E6-E7-F7
Northumberland Road	F7-F8
Ogle Road	C5
Old Road	E1-E2
Orchard Lane	D3-D4
Orchard Place	D2-D3
Oriental Terrace	C2-D2
Oxford Avenue	D8-E8-F8
Oxford Street	D3-D2-E2
Paget Street	F4
Palmerston Road	D5-D6
Park Walk	C6-C7
Platform Road	D2-E2
Porters Lane	C2
Portland Street	C5
Portland Terrace	B6-B5-C5-C4
Pound Tree Road	C5-D5
Queens Terrace	D2-E2
Queen's Way	D2-D3-D4
Radcliffe Road	F7-F8
Richmond Street	E3
Royal Crescent Road	F2-F3
St Andrews Road	D7-D8
St Marks Road	E7
St Mary's Place	E4-E5
St Mary's Road	D8-D7-E7
St Mary's Street	E4-E5-E6
Salisbury Street	C8
Saltmarsh Road	F2-F3
Simnel Street	C3
South Front	D5-E5-E6-D6
Sussex Road	C5-C6
The Polygon	A8-A7-B7-B8
Terminus Terrace	E2-E3
Threefield Lane	E3-E4
Town Quay	B2-C2-C1-D1
Trinity Road	D7-E7
Upper Bugle Street	C3-C4
Vincents Walk	C5
West Marlands Road	C6-C7
West Road	D1-D2-E2
West Park Road	A7-B7
West Quay Road	A5-A4-B4-B3
Western Esplanade	B2-B3-B4-B5-B6-A6
Windsor Terrace	C6
Winkle Street	C1-C2
Winton Street	D6-E6
Wolverton Road	F7
Wyndham Place	A7
York Buildings	C4-D4

EASTLEIGH

Abbots Road	A1
Archers Road	C3
Blenheim Road	B2-C2
Brookwood Avenue	B3
Burns Road	A1
Campbell Road	C1
Cedar Road	A1
Chadwick Road	A2-B2
Chamberlayne Road	B1-B2-B3
Chandlers Ford By-pass	A4
Cherbourg Road	A1-B1-C1
Chestnut Avenue	A1-B1-C1
Coniston Road	B2
Cranbury Road	C1-C2-C3
Darwin Road	C4
Cranbury Road	C1-C2-C3
Darwin Road	C4
Derby Road	A2-A1-B1-C1
Desborough Road	B1-C1-C2
Dew Lane	A3-B3
Elizabeth Way	C4
Factory Road	B2-C2
George Street	C3
Goldsmith Road	B1
Goodwood Road	A4
Grantham Road	B1-B2-C2-C1
High Street	C1-C2
Kelvin Road	A2-B2
Kipling Road	A3-B3
Lawn Road	C4
Leigh Road	A3-B3-C3-C2
Locksley Road	A1
Magpie Lane	A1-A2
Mansbridge Road	B1
Market Street	C1-C2-C3
Monks Way	A1-B1
Mount View	C3-C4
Newtown Road	C3
Nightingale Avenue	C3
Nutbeem Road	B1-B2-B3
O'Connell Road	A2
Owen Road	A2
Parnham Drive	A4-B4
Passfield Avenue	A1-A2-A3
Romsey Road	B3-C3
Ruskin Road	C4
Stanstead Road	A4
Stoneham Lane	A1
St John's Road	C4
St Lawrence Road	C4
Scott Road	A2
Selborne Drive	B4
Shakespeare Road	B4-C4
Shelley Road	B1
Southampton Road	C1-C2
The Crescent	C3
The Quadrangle	C4
Tennyson Road	A1-A2-B2
Toynbee Road	B3
Twyford Road	C3-C4
Whyteways	B4
Wilmer Road	B2
Woodside Avenue	A3-A4
Woodside Road	A4

SOUTHAMPTON
Although liners still use Southampton's docks which handled all the great ocean-going passenger ships before the age of air travel replaced sea travel, the port is chiefly used by commercial traffic today.

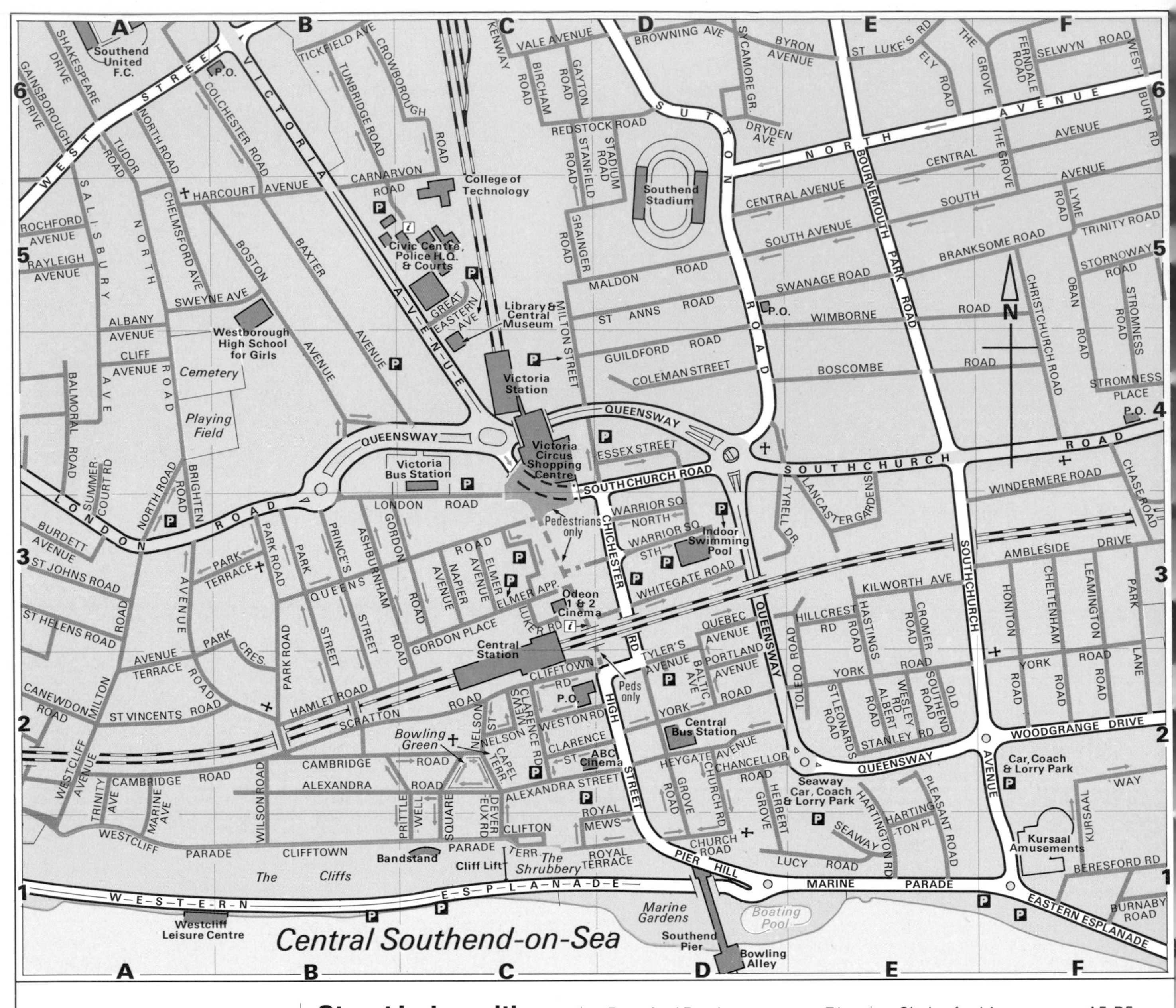

Key to Town Plan and Area Plan

Town Plan

A A Recommended roads
Other roads
Restricted roads
Buildings of interest Pavilion
Car Parks P
Parks and open spaces
Churches +
One Way Streets

Area Plan

A roads
B roads
Locations Parkston ○
Urban area

Street Index with Grid Reference

Southend-on-Sea

Southend

The longest pleasure pier in the world and brilliant illuminations along the seafront in autumn are just two of the attractions of this thriving, immensely popular seaside resort, which offers the visitor every facet of the traditional holiday. Dance halls, theatres, amusement arcades and funfairs fill the Marine Parade area, with Peter Pan's Playground next to the pier and the Kursall Amusement Park at the eastern end of the seafront both attracting crowds of visitors. The Pier itself offers entertainments (not least a wax museum housed in the replica of Sir Francis Drake's *Golden Hind* which lies alongside) and its $1\frac{1}{4}$ mile length is usually liberally dotted with fishermen. The most popular beaches are at Westcliffe and Thorpe Bay, while Leigh-on-Sea, linked to Southend by a lengthy promenade, makes a peaceful contrast to the main seafront area.

Places of interest include the village of Prittlewell, on the northern edge of town, with its 12th-century Priory and 13th-century church, 13th- to 14th-century Southchurch Hall (a timber-framed manor house with period furniture and beautiful grounds) and the Central Museum, which traces the history of south-east Essex back to the Romans. Good shopping and sports facilities, pleasant parks, professional cricket and football, and greyhound racing are other features of the town.

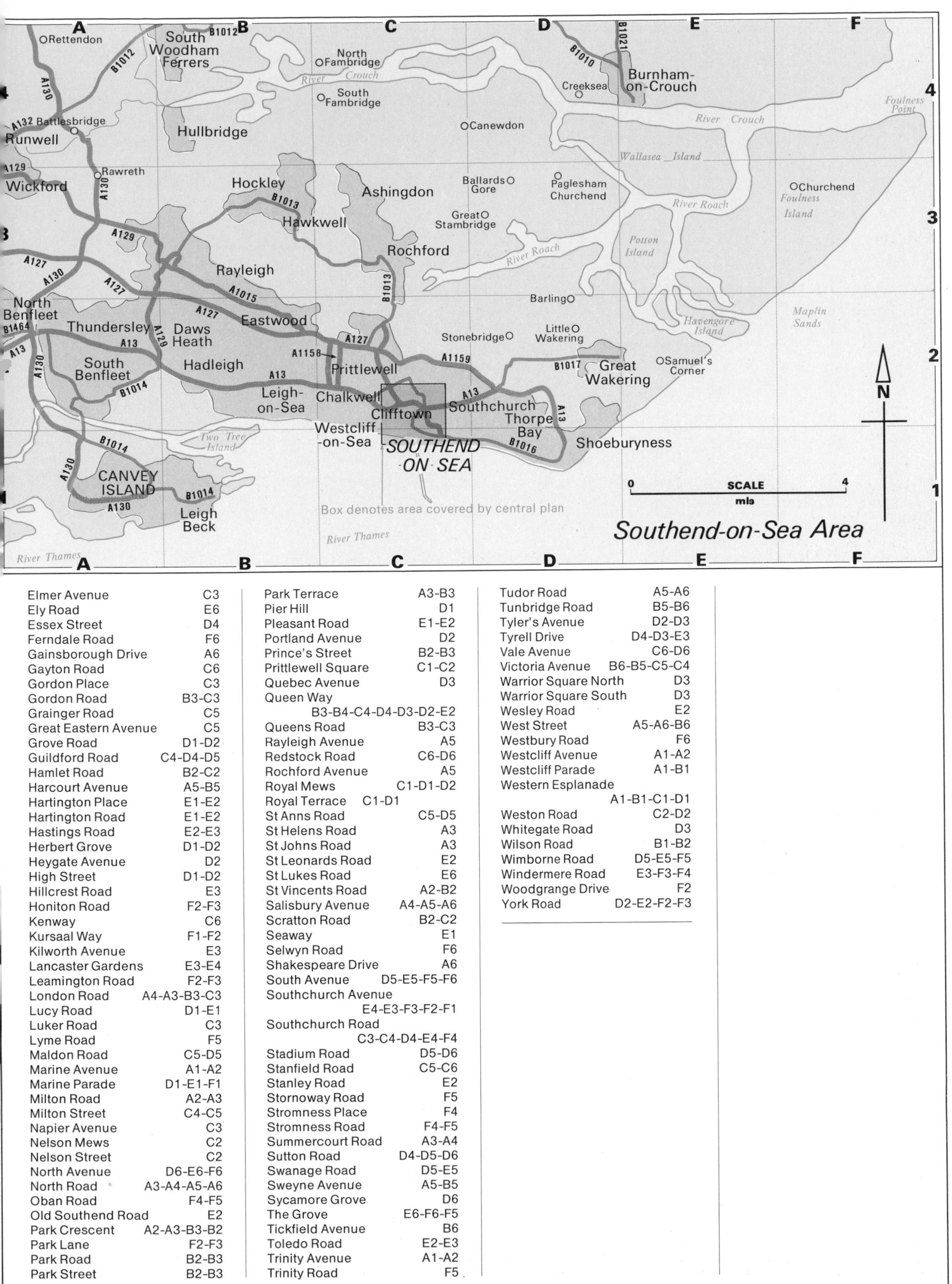

A
B
C
D
E
F
1
2
3
4
Rettendon
South Woodham Ferrers
B1012
B1012
A130
North Fambridge
River Crouch
South Fambridge
B1010
B1021
Creeksea
Burnham-on-Crouch
Foulness Point
A132 Battlesbridge
Runwell
Hullbridge
Canewdon
River Crouch
Wallasea Island
A129
Rawreth
Wickford
A130
Hockley
B1013
Ashingdon
Ballards Gore
Paglesham Churchend
Churchend
Foulness Island
River Roach
Hawkwell
Great Stambridge
A129
Rochford
Potton Island
River Roach
A127
A130
A127
Rayleigh
B1013
A1015
North Benfleet
A127
Eastwood
Barling
Maplin Sands
B1464
Thundersley
A129
Daws Heath
A13
A127
Stonebridge
Little Wakering
Havengore Island
A13
A130
South Benfleet
Hadleigh
A1158
Prittlewell
A1159
B1017
Great Wakering
Samuel's Corner
N
B1014
A13
Leigh-on-Sea
Chalkwell
A13
Southchurch
Thorpe Bay
A13
Clifftown
Westcliff-on-Sea
Two Tree Island
SOUTHEND-ON-SEA
B1016
Shoeburyness
B1014
A130
CANVEY ISLAND
B1014
A130
Leigh Beck
0 SCALE 4
mls
Box denotes area covered by central plan
River Thames
River Thames
Southend-on-Sea Area

Legend to Atlas

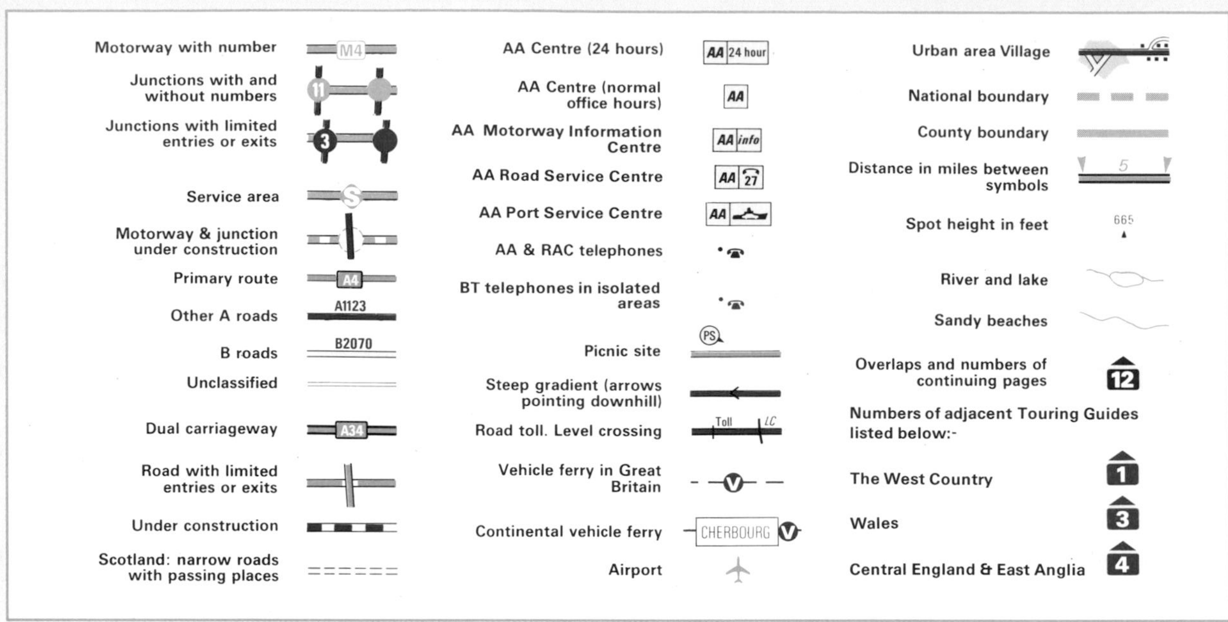

Abbey or Cathedral
Ruined Abbey or Cathedral
Castle
House and Garden
House
Garden
Industrial Interest
Museum or Collection
Prehistoric Monument
Famous Battle Site
Preserved Railway or Steam Centre
Windmill
Sea Angling

Coastal- Launching Site
Surfing
Climbing School
County Cricket Ground
Gliding Centre
Artificial Ski Slope
Golf Course
Horse Racing
Show Jumping/Equestrian Centre
Motor Racing Circuit
Cave
Country Park
Dolphinarium or Aquarium

Nature Trail
Wildlife Park (mammals)
Wildlife Park (birds)
Zoo
Forest Drive
Lighthouse
Tourist Information Centre
Tourist Information Centre (summer only)
Long Distance Footpath
AA Viewpoint
Other Place of Interest
Boxed symbols indicate tourist attractions in towns

The National Grid

The National Grid provides a system of reference common to maps of all scales. The grid covers Britain with an imaginary network of 100 kilometre squares. Each square is identified by two letters, *eg* TR. Every 100 kilometre square is then subdivided into 10 kilometre squares which appear as a network of blue lines on the map pages. These blue lines are numbered left to right 0-9 and bottom to top 0-9. These 10 kilometre squares can be further divided into tenths to give a place reference to the nearest kilometre.

Key to Road Maps

Thurso
Wick
Stornoway
Outer Hebrides
Ullapool
Shetland Islands
Banff
Portree
Inverness
Peterhead
Aberdeen
Fort William
Orkney Islands
Pitlochry
Oban
Perth
Dundee
Edinburgh
Largs
Glasgow
Berwick
Peebles
Campbeltown
Ayr
Dumfries
Newcastle upon Tyne
Stranraer
Workington
Middlesbrough
Kendal
Isle of Man
Scarborough
Douglas
Lancaster
York
Blackpool
Leeds
Hull
Grimsby
Liverpool
Manchester
Sheffield
Caernarfon
Chester
Lincoln
Stoke
Nottingham
King's Lynn
Shrewsbury
Norwich
Leicester
Great Yarmouth
Peterborough
Aberystwyth
Birmingham
Coventry
Northampton
24/25
26/27
Cambridge
Worcester
Fishguard
Carmarthen
Hereford
Felixstowe
Gloucester
16/17
18/19
Oxford
20/21
22/23
Chelmsford
Pembroke
Swansea
LONDON
Cardiff
Bristol
Reading
12/13
8/9
10/11
Maidstone
14/15
Guildford
Dover
Barnstaple
Salisbury
Folkestone
Taunton
Southampton
4/5
6/7
Brighton
Newhaven
2/3
Exeter
Weymouth
Bournemouth
Truro
Plymouth
Scilly Isles

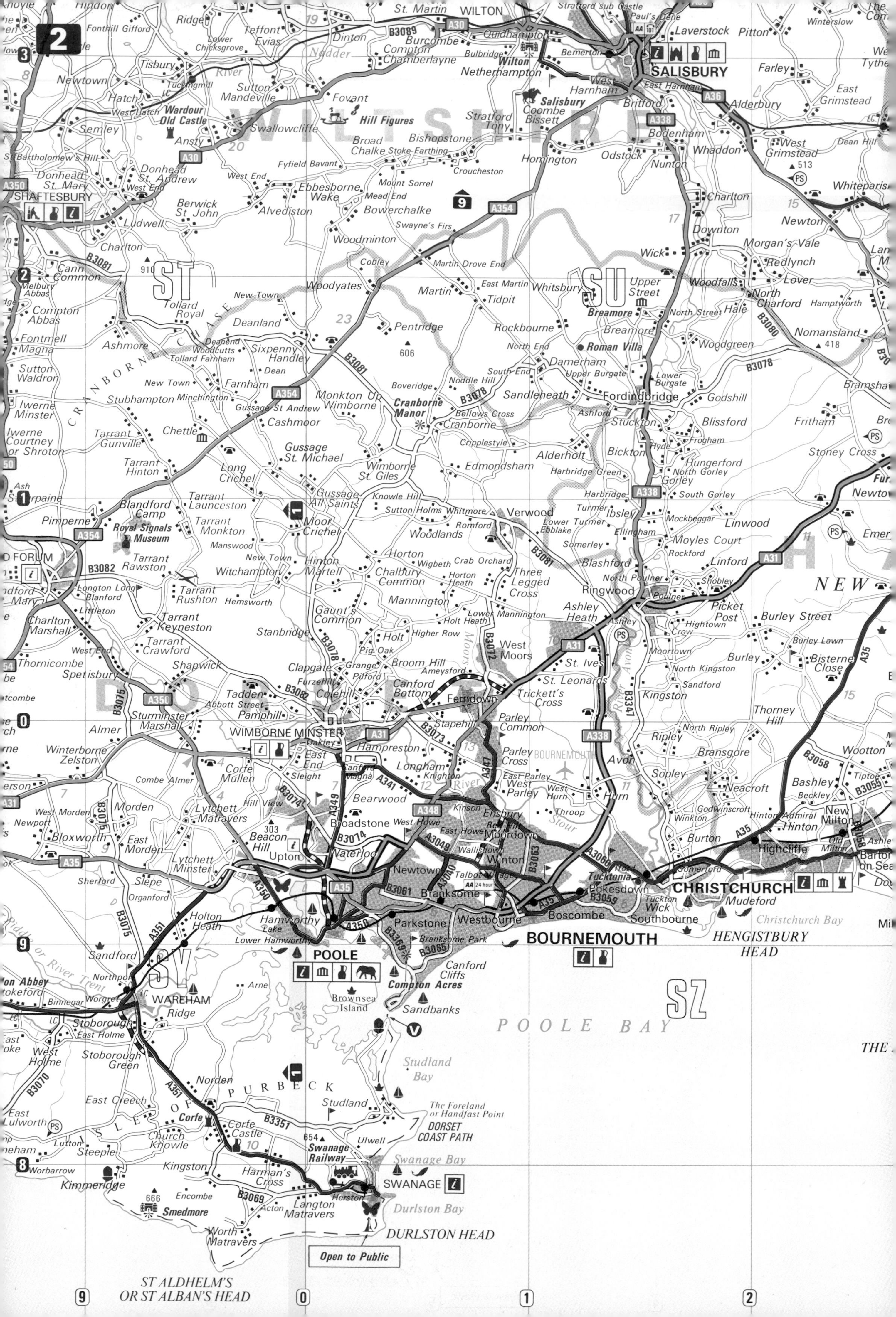
2
WILTSHIRE
DORSET
NEW FOREST
ST
SU
SY
SZ
SALISBURY
WILTON
St. Martin
Stratford sub Castle
Laverstock
Pitton
Winterslow
Fonthill Gifford
Ridge
Teffont Evias
Lower Chicksgrove
Dinton
Burcombe
Compton Chamberlayne
Quidhampton
Bemerton
Bulbridge
Wilton
Netherhampton
West Harnham
East Harnham
Farley
East Grimstead
Tisbury
Newtown
Tuckingmill
Hatch
Sutton Mandeville
Fovant
Hill Figures
Wardour Old Castle
West Hatch
Semley
Ansty
Swallowcliffe
Salisbury
Coombe Bissett
Stratford Tony
Britford
Alderbury
Bishopstone
Broad Chalke
Stoke Farthing
Bodenham
Whaddon
West Grimstead
Dean Hill
St Bartholomew's Hill
Donhead St. Andrew
Donhead St. Mary
Fyfield Bavant
Croucheston
Homington
Odstock
Nunton
West End
Ebbesborne Wake
Mount Sorrel
Mead End
SHAFTESBURY
Berwick St John
Alvediston
Bowerchalke
Charlton
Whiteparish
Ludwell
Swayne's Firs
Newton
Downton
Woodminton
Charlton
Wick
Morgan's Vale
Redlynch
Cann Common
Cobley
Martin Drove End
Melbury Abbas
Woodyates
Martin
East Martin
Tidpit
Whitsbury
Upper Street
Woodfalls
Lover
North Charford
Hale
Hamptworth
Compton Abbas
Tollard Royal
New Town
Deanland
Pentridge
Breamore
North Street
Breamore
Rockbourne
Nomansland
Woodgreen
Fontmell Magna
Ashmore
Deanend
Woodcutts
Tollard Farnham
Sixpenny Handley
Dean
North End
Roman Villa
Damerham
Upper Burgate
Lower Burgate
South End
Noddle Hill
Sutton Waldron
CRANBORNE CHASE
New Town
Farnham
Boveridge
Sandleheath
Fordingbridge
Godshill
Bramshaw
Iwerne Minster
Stubhampton
Minchington
Gussage St Andrew
Monkton Up Wimborne
Cranborne Manor
Bellows Cross
Cranborne
Ashford
Stuckton
Blissford
Fritham
Iwerne Courtney or Shroton
Tarrant Gunville
Chettle
Cashmoor
Cripplestyle
Frogham
Hyde
Stoney Cross
Tarrant Hinton
Long Crichel
Gussage St. Michael
Wimborne St. Giles
Edmondsham
Alderholt
Bickton
Hungerford
North Gorley
Gorley
Harbridge Green
Harbridge
South Gorley
Ash
Stourpaine
Tarrant Launceston
Gussage All Saints
Knowle Hill
Sutton Holms
Whitmore
Verwood
Turmer
Lower Turmer
Ebblake
Ibsley
Mockbeggar
Linwood
Newtown
Pimperne
Blandford Camp
Royal Signals Museum
Tarrant Monkton
Moor Crichel
Romford
Woodlands
Ellingham
Moyles Court
Rockford
Emery Down
Manswood
Horton
Wigbeth
Crab Orchard
Somerley
Blashford
Linford
FORUM
Tarrant Rawston
New Town
Witchampton
Hinton Martell
Chalbury Common
Horton Heath
Three Legged Cross
North Poulner
Shobley
Poulner
Ringwood
Picket Post
Burley Street
Longton
Long Blandford
Tarrant Rushton
Hemsworth
Littleton
Charlton Marshall
Tarrant Keyneston
Gaunt's Common
Mannington
Lower Mannington
Holt Heath
Ashley Heath
Ashley
Hightown
Crow
Burley Lawn
Stanbridge
Holt
Higher Row
West Moors
Moortown
Burley
Bisterne Close
Tarrant Crawford
Pig Oak
Broom Hill
St. Ives
North Kingston
West End
Thornicombe
Spetisbury
Shapwick
Clapgate
Grange
Pilford
Ameysford
St. Leonards
Sandford
Furzehill
Canford Bottom
Trickett's Cross
Kingston
Tadden
Abbott Street
Colehill
Ferndown
Pamphill
Sturminster Marshall
Stapehill
Parley Common
Thorney Hill
Almer
WIMBORNE MINSTER
Oakley
Hampreston
North Ripley
Ripley
Wootton
Winterborne Zelston
East End
Parley Cross
BOURNEMOUTH
Bransgore
Corfe Mullen
Sleight
Canford Magna
Longham
Knighton
Avon
Combe Almer
East Parley
West Parley
Sopley
Tiptoe
Bashley
Neacroft
Beckley
West Hurn
Hurn
Throop
Godwinscroft
Winkton
Hinton Admiral
Hinton
New Milton
Bearwood
Kinson
Ensbury
West Morden
Morden
Lytchett Matravers
Hill View
Broadstone
West Howe
Redhill
Moordown
Newport
Bloxworth
East Morden
Beacon Hill
East Howe
Burton
Old Milton
Ashley
Barton on Sea
Upton
Waterloo
Wallisdown
Winton
Iford
Highcliffe
Tuckton
Lytchett Minster
Newtown
Talbot Village
Tucktonia
Sherford
Slepe
Pokesdown
CHRISTCHURCH
Branksome
Somerford
Organford
Tuckton
Wick
Mudeford
Hamworthy
Parkstone
Westbourne
Boscombe
Southbourne
Christchurch Bay
Holton Heath
Lake
Lower Hamworthy
Branksome Park
HENGISTBURY HEAD
POOLE
Canford Cliffs
Sandford
Compton Acres
Northport
Bindon Abbey
Wool
Stokeford
Arne
Brownsea Island
WAREHAM
Binnegar
Worgret
Ridge
Sandbanks
POOLE BAY
Stoborough
East Holme
THE
East Stoke
West Holme
Stoborough Green
Studland Bay
Norden
PURBECK
ISLE OF PURBECK
East Creech
Studland
The Foreland or Handfast Point
DORSET COAST PATH
East Lulworth
Corfe
Corfe Castle
Church Knowle
Lutton
Steeple
Ulwell
Swanage Railway
654
Swanage Bay
Tyneham
Worbarrow
Kingston
Harman's Cross
SWANAGE
Kimmeridge
666
Encombe
Smedmore
Herston
Acton
Langton Matravers
Durlston Bay
Worth Matravers
DURLSTON HEAD
Open to Public
ST ALDHELM'S OR ST ALBAN'S HEAD
River Nadder
River Stour
River Avon
River Piddle or River Trent
Moors River
A30
A36
A338
A354
A350
A31
A35
A348
A341
A349
A347
A3049
A3040
A3063
A3060
A3065
A3066
A351
B3089
B3081
B3078
B3080
B3082
B3078
B3073
B3072
B3074
B3075
B3061
B3059
B3058
B3055
B3369
B3070
B3351
B3069
B3347
B3014
910
606
513
418
303
9
0
1
2
8

3
WINCHESTER
Houghton
Ashley
Sparsholt
Headbourne Worthy
Easton
Avington
Ovington
New Alresford
Gilbert Street
Ropley
Bishop's Sutton
Ropley Dean
Horsebridge
King's Somborne
Dean
Tichborne
1644
West Tisted
East Tytherley
Brook
Cheriton
North End
Bramdean
Hinton Marsh
Filmore Hill
Bailey Green
Privett
Lower Brook
Mottisfont
Mottisfont Abbey
Spearywell
Standon
Oliver's Battery
Pitt
Chilcomb
Hinton Ampner
West Meon Woodlands
Michelmersh
Compton
Beauworth
Shorley
Brockwood Park
West Meon Hut
Froxfield Green
Braishfield
Hillier Aboretum
Hursley
Morestead
Kilmeston
Dunbridge
Kent's Oak
Timsbury
Shawford
Twyford
Lane End
West Meon
East End
Lower Bordean
Ampfield
Knapp Hill
Awbridge
Colden Common
Owslebury
Warnford
Langrish
Ripplington
Ratley
Otterbourne
Abbotswood
Ratlake
Hiltingbury
Brambridge
Highbridge
Marwell Zoo
Exton
East Meon
Coombe Cross
ROMSEY
Whitenap
Hensting
Upham
Corhampton
Coombe
East Wellow
North Baddesley
Fryern Hill
Chandler's Ford
Allbrook
Fisher's Pond
Crowdhill
Lower Upham
Ashton
Dean
Meonstoke
West Wellow
Broadlands
Chilworth
Bishopstoke
Durley Street
Droxford
Brockbridge
Ashfield
Toot Hill
Fair Oak
Chidden
Lee
EASTLEIGH
Horton Heath
Palace
Bishop's Waltham
Clanfield
Upton
Rownhams
Durley
Hoe
Soberton
Wigley
Ower
Bassett
SOUTHAMPTON AIRPORT
Waltham Chase
Swanmore
Vineyard & Winepress
Hambledon
Stonyford
Nursling
Swaythling
Long Common
Hillpound
Calmore
Hillstreet
Testwood
Moorgreen
West End
Boorley Green
Shirrell Heath
Catherington
Copythorne
Totton
Shirley
AA 24 hour
Portswood
Bitterne
Shedfield
Soberton Heath
Cadnam
Millbrook
Wildern
Curdridge
Kingsmead
Anthill Common
Hordean
Northam
Thornhill
Botley
Newtown
Hundred Acres
Hoe Gate
Worlds End
Lovedean
Bartley
Netley Marsh
Eling
Foxhills
Colbury
SOUTHAMPTON
Hedge End
Wickham
Sholing
Curbridge
Denmead
Anmore
Woodlands
Ashurst
Pooksgreen
Marchwood
Woolston
Toll
Burridge
North Boarhunt
Furzeley Corner
Soake
Bursledon
Lower Swanwick
Swanwick
Purbrook
New Forest Butterfly Farm
Dibden
Netley
Sarisbury
Park Gate
Funtley
Boarhunt
Southwick
Purbrook Park
Stakes
Lyndhurst
Beaulieu River
Hythe
Locks Heath
Titchfield Abbey
Wallington
Wymering
Portsdown Hill
Bedhampton
Langdown
Hamble
Titchfield Common
Catisfield
FOREST
Dibden Purlieu
FAREHAM
Drayton
Butsash
Fleetend
Cosham
Beaulieu Heath
Warsash
Titchfield
Portchester
Hardley
Little Posbrook
Balmerlawn
Holbury
Fawley
Stubbington
Bridgemary
Portsmouth Harbour
Hilsea
Peel Common
North End
Beaulieu
Ashlett
Ower
Hill Head
Elson
Hardway
Hill Top
Otterwood
Blackfield
Hatchet Gate
East Boldre
Langley
Calshot
Rowner
Portsea
PORTSEA ISLAND
Setley
GOSPORT
Fratton
Lee-on-the-Solent
Battramsley
Bucklers Hard
Exbury
Alverstoke
Southsea
Eastney
Stansore Point
Pilley Bailey
Lower Exbury
Boldre
Norleywood
Pilley
Lepe
Stokes Bay
Spinners
Needs Ore Point
Gilkicker Point
Portmore
East End
South Baddesley
COWES
Norris Castle
PORTSMOUTH
Buckland
Pennington
Walhampton
LYMINGTON
Thorns Beach
East Cowes
Osborne
Woodside
Gurnard
Rew Street
Hillis Corner
Barton Manor
Whippingham
Lymore
Lower Pennington
Fishbourne
RYDE
Puckpool Point
Nettlestone Point
Mark's Corner
Northwood
Porchfield
Parkhurst
Wootton Bridge
Wootton
Quarr Abbey
Binstead
Seaview
Keyhaven
Hamstead
Cranmore
Newtown
Shalfleet
Whitehouse
Wootton Common
Havenstreet
Nettlestone
Hurst Sconce Point
Yarmouth
Bouldnor
St Helens
Norton
Gunville
Carisbrooke
Isle of Wight Steam Railway
Bembridge Point
Norton Green
Ningwood
Roman Villa
Staplers
Robin Hill
Bembridge
Totland
Thorley Street
Newbridge
NEWPORT
East Ashey
Brading
FORELAND
Freshwater
Wellow
Bowcombe
Shide
Downend
Nunwell
Steyne Cross
Alum Bay
Afton
Calbourne
Blackwater
Alverstone
Yarbridge
Freshwater Bay
Watermill
Shalcombe
Arreton Manor
Arreton
Haseley Manor
Roman Villa
Morton
Bembridge Down
Easton
Rowborough
Gatcombe
Merstone
Newchurch
Queen's Bower
Culver Cliff
Yaverland
Freshwater Bay
Brook
Cheverton
Mortown
Winford
Chillerton
Yafford Water Mill
Limerstone
Rookley
Branstone
SANDOWN
Mottistone
Shorwell
Lake
Apse Heath
Sandown Bay
Godshill
Sandford
Whiteley Bank
SHANKLIN
Brighstone
Chilton Chine
Thorncross
Yafford
Kingston
Shanklin Chine
Brighstone Bay
Roud
Wroxall
Luccombe Village
Chale Green
Little Atherfield
Luccombe Chine
Atherfield Point
Pyle
Southford
Appuldurcombe
DUNNOSE
Whitwell
Nettlecombe
Bierley
VENTNOR
Chale
Blackgang Chine
Blackgang
Niton
St. Lawrence
The Undercliff
ST CATHERINE'S POINT
Open to Public
THE SOLENT
ISLE OF WIGHT
4
5
6

4
Winslade
Tunworth
South Warnborough
Crondall
Upper Hale
Farnham
Tongham
Seale
Puttenham
Compton
Littleton
Loseley
Farleigh Wallop
Ellisfield
Weston Corbett
Weston Patrick
Herriard
Long Sutton
Well
Runfold
The Sands
Shackleford
Farncombe
Upper Common
Lower Common
Bagmore
Nash's Green
Southrope
Lower Froyle
Bentley
Wrecclesham
Waverley Abbey
Elstead
Peper Harow
Hurtmore
Eashing
Godalming
Axford
Shalden Green
Golden Pot
Upper Froyle
Isington
Bucks Horn Oak
Birdworld
Rowledge
Old Kiln
Shortfield Common
Tilford
Milford
Busbridge
Lasham
Shalden
Cuckoo's Corner
Blacknest
Spreakley
Millbridge
Bradley
Holybourne
Binsted
Frensham
Tuesley
Lower Wield
Neatham
Batt's Corner
Rushmoor
Wheelerstreet
Hydestile
Alton
Anstey
Wilsdon
Wyck
Wheatley
The Straits
Frithend
Thursley
Pitch Place
Witley
Culmer
Hydons Ball
Hambledon
Bentworth
Halt End
Thedden Grange
Upper Wield
Wivelrod
The Butts
Beech
East Worldham
B3004
Sleaford
Green Cross
Cross Place
Wormley
Churt
Beacon Hill
Bowlhead Green
Brook
Sandhills
Combe Common
Loxhill
Medstead
Chawton
Jane Austen House
West Worldham
Hartley Mauditt
Kingsley
Bordon
Arford
Headley Down
Hearn
Hindhead
Chiddingfold
Hattingley
South Town
Lower Farringdon
Shortheath
Oakhanger
Lindford
Headley
Grayshott
Gibbet Hill
894
West End
Soldridge
Four Marks
Upper Farringdon
Standford
Sydenhurst
Highstreet Green
North Street
Hawthorn
Gilbert White Museum
Selborne
Whitehill
Bramshott
Grayswood
Mid Hants Railway
Kitwood
Blackmoor
Shottermill
Critchmere
Haslemere
Ramsnest Common
Gilbert Street
Newton Valence
Conford
Liphook
Hammer
Camelsdale
Anstiebury
Haste Hill
The Buildings
Bishop's Sutton
Ropley
Ropley Dean
Charlwood
East Tisted
Longmoor Camp
Griggs Green
Bohunt Manor
Gospel Green
Fisherstreet
Monkwood
Colemore
Empshott
Greatham
Linchmere
Kingsley Green
West Tisted
Hawkley
Liss Forest
Langley
Hollycombe Steam Museum
Plaistow
Bramdean
Filmore Hill
Bailey Green
Burgates
Oakshott
Milland
Northchapel
Hillgrove
Lurgashall
Hinton Ampner
West Meon Woodlands
Privett
High Cross
Liss
East Liss
Steep Marsh
Fernhurst
Woodmansgreen
Dial Green
Milland Marsh
Rake
Brockwood Park
West Meon Hut
Froxfield Green
Stoner Hill
Hill Brow
Redford
Henley
Lickfold
Balls Cross
Steep
Borden
West Meon
East End
Lower Bordean
Stroud
Bell Hill
Sheet
Tarwick Common
Rogate
Tote Hill
Bexleyhill
Warnford
Langrish
Ripplington
Eastshaw
Iping
Lodsworth
Keyfox
Chithurst
Woolbeding
Petersfield
Upperton
Petworth
East Meon
Habin
Trotton
Easebourne
Halfway Bridge
River
Exton
Coombe Cross
Ramsdean
Weston
Causeway
Nursted
West Harting
Nyewood
Stedham
Tillington
Minsted
Midhurst
Butser Hill
889
Coombe
South Mill
Buriton
Elsted
Lower Elsted
West Lavington
South Ambersham
Selham
Meonstoke
Cocking Causeway
Coultershaw Bridge
Little Bognor
South Harting
East Harting
Treyford
Heyshott Green
Fittleworth
Brockbridge
Chidden
Didling
Heyshott
Upper Norwood
Lower Fittleworth
Uppark
Bepton
Duncton
Lower Horncroft
Soberton
Clanfield
Chalton
North Marden
Cocking
Graffham
Vineyard & Winepress
Hambledon
Catherington
Chilgrove
East Lavington
Duncton Hill
Barlavington
Soberton Heath
Compton
East Marden
Sutton
Bignor
Blendworth
Anthill Common
West Marden
Up Marden
Singleton
Upwaltham
West Burton
Horndean
Finchdean
Lovedean
Forestside
West Dean
Charlton
East Dean
Hoe Gate
Worlds End
Deanlane End
Rowland's Castle
Stoughton
Open Air Museum
South Downs Way
North Boarhunt
Denmead
Anmore
Soake
Cowplain
Madehurst
Furzeley Corner
Waterlooville
Lordington
Walderton
Eartham
Purbrook
Havant
Aldsworth
Woodend
West Stoke
Lavant
Goodwood
Slindon
Southwick
Stakes
Westbourne
Funtington
Halnaker
Portsdown Hill
Purbrook Park
New Brighton
West Ashling
Goodwood Aerodrome
Strettington
Westerton
Boxgrove
Crockerhill
Fontwell
Arundel
Wymering
Bedhampton
Woodmancote
East Ashling
Westhampnett
Tangmere
Norton
Fontwell Park
Binstead
Drayton
Hermitage
Breach
Hambrook
Roman Palace
Boxgrove Priory
Aldingbourne
Nyton
Walberton
Portchester
Cosham
Emsworth
Southbourne
Chichester
Westergate
Eastergate
Langstone
Prinsted
Broadbridge
Oving
Woodgate
Barnham
Portsmouth Harbour
Hilsea
Northney
Thorney Island
Walton
Fishbourne
Colworth
Yapton
North End
Langstone Harbour
North Hayling
Chidham
Bosham
Apuldram
Dell Quay
North Mundham
Merston
Shripney
Hardway
Portsea Island
Tye
Stoke
West Thorney
Bosham Hoe
Donnington
Elbridge
North Bersted
Flansham
Climping
Portsea
Fleet
Hayling Island
West Itchenor
Crouchers
Hunston
Runcton
South Mundham
Ancton
Fratton
Chichester Harbour
Shipton Green
Sidlesham Common
Fisher
Bersted
South Bersted
Elmer
Southsea
Eastney
West Town
South Hayling
Eastoke
Birdham
Street End
Rose Green
Middleton-on-Sea
Felpham
Sandy Beach Estate
Somerley
Nyetimber
Aldwick
Bognor Regis
Bay Estate
Portsmouth
Hayling Bay
West Wittering
Highleigh
Sidlesham
Almodington
Earnley
Pagham Beach Estate
Pagham
Bracklesham
East Wittering
Norton
Church Norton
East Beach
Ryde
Puckpool Point
Nettlestone Point
Seaview
Selsey
SU
SZ
To Jersey and Guernsey
Le Havre
St Malo Cherbourg Caen Le Havre
Selsey Bill
7
8
9

5
Shere
Gomshall
A25
Westcott
Brockham
12
Dovers Green
Earlswood
South Nutfield
Ridge Green
Godstone Station
Crowhurst Lane End
Albury
Burrows Cross
Abinger Hammer
Wotton
Bushbury
Strood Green
Dawesgreen
North Holmwood
Leigh
Salfords
South Godstone
Blindley Heath
Crouch House Green
Blackheath
Brook
Albury Heath
Sutton
Abinger Common
Sidlowbridge
Old Mill
Watermill Museum
Farley Green
Peaslake
South Holmwood
Holmwood Corner
Nalderswood
Outwood
Lingfield Common
Waterside
Abinger Bottom
Coldharbour
Felday
Norwood Hill
Horne
Lingfield
Plaistow Street
Shamley Green
Holmbury St. Mary
Holmwood Station
Beare Green
Parkgate
Hookwood
Weatherhill
Smallfield
Leith Hill Tower
Povey Cross
Horley
Newchapel
Lingfield
Dormans Land
Forest Green
Newdigate
Gatwick Airport London
Burstow
Mormon Temple
Felcourt
Rowly
Thorn's Flush
Ewhurst
Capel
Charlwood
Gatwick Garden
Fernhill
Black Corner
Shipley Bridge
Felbridge
Baldwins Hill
Dormans Park
Ockley
Russ Hill
Lowfield Heath
Copthorne
Cranleigh
Ewhurst Green
Clark's Green
Old Bonnetts
Tinsley Green
North End
Hammerwood
East Grinstead
Walliswood
Ifieldwood
Three Bridges
Crawley Down
Oakwoodhill
Rusper
Ifield
Pound Hill
Sunnyside
Ashurst Wood
Baynard's Park
Kingsfold
Lambs Green
Worth
Turner's Hill
Standen
Saint Hill
Laker's Green
Alfold Crossways
Ellen's Green
Crawley
Tilgate
War Museum
Faygate
Selsfield Common
Cox Green
Rowhook
Warnham
Worth Abbey
Forest Row
Rudgwick
Colgate
Pease Pottage
Priests House
Sharpthorne
Tisman's Common
Cricketers Inn
Loxwood
Bucks Green
Broadbridge Heath
Roffey
St Leonards Forest
Tilgate Forest Row
Balcombe Lane
West Hoathly
Wakehurst Place
Tyes Cross
Park Street
Slinfold
Horsham
Doomsday Green
Handcross
Balcombe
Highbrook
Tanyard
The Haven
Ashfold Crossways
Nymans
Staplefield
Ardingly
Horsted Keynes
Birchgrove
Five Oaks
Itchingfield
Buckman Corner
Manning's Heath
Ardingly Reservoir
Chelwood Common
Newpound Common
Southwater Street
Slaugham
Barns Green
Monk's Gate
Lower Beeding
Bluebell Railway
Danehill
New Bridge
Nuthurst
Whitemans Green
Brook Street
Borde Hill
Furner's Green
Billingshurst
Southwater
Leonardslee
Slough Green
Warninglid
Lindfield
Wisborough Green
Brooks Green
Copsale
Crabtree
Cuckfield
Haywards Heath
Sheffield Green
Parbrook
Coneyhurst Common
Dragons Green
Maplehurst
Ansty
Adversane
Coolham
Green Street
Bolney
Bolney Common
Scayne's Hill
Fletching
Fletching Common
Shipley
Legh Manor
North Heath
Broadford Bridge
Belloc's Mill
Cowfold
Crosspost
North Common
Gay Street
Whitehall
West Grinstead
Kent Street
Twineham Green
Wivelsfield Station
Wivelsfield
Newick Rough
Chailey
Broomer's Corner
Butcher's Row
Wineham
Hickstead
Goddards Green
Broomershill
Woods Hill
Littleworth
Shermanbury
Wivelsfield Green
Pulborough
Nutbourne
West Chiltington
Dial Post
Partridge Green
Twineham
Burgess Hill
Marehill
Sayers Common
South Common
South Street
Town Littleworth
Nutbourne Common
Thakeham
Bines Green
High Cross
Albourne Green
Hurstpierpoint
Plumpton Green
Wiggonholt
West Chiltington Common
Spear Hill
Ashurst
Henfield
West End
Blackstone
South Chailey
Greatham
Ashington
Albourne
Ditchling
Plumpton
Northpark Wood
Cootham
Storrington
Nep Town
Oreham Common
Woodmancote
Newtimber Place
Hassocks
Keymer
Streat
East Chiltington
Parham Park
Hole Street
Horsebridge Common
Bunction
Clayton
Westmeston
Cooksbridge
Rackham
Sullington
Rock
Newtimber Place
Pyecombe
Ditchling Beacon
Plumpton
Amberley
The Chantry
Washington
Small Dole
Kithurst Hill
Wiston
Edburton
Poynings
Mount Harry
Offham
Hamsey
Steyning
Bramber
Saddlescombe
Fulking
South Malling
North Stoke
South Stoke
549
Harrow Hill
North End
Upper Beeding
Stanmer
Lewes
Falmer
Burpham
Wepham
Findon
Botolphs
Patcham
Coldean
Hollingbury
Kingston near Lewes
Iford
Wildfowl Trust
Warningcamp
The Vale
Coombes
Shoreham-by-Sea
West Blatchington
Hangleton
Moulsecoomb
Mile Oak
Portslade
Preston
Bevendean
Rodmell
Patching
Hammerpot
Clapham
High Salvington
Upper Cokeham
Shoreham Airport
Kingston by Sea
Southwick
Brighton
Woodingdean
Cross Bush
Salvington
Durrington
Old Shoreham
Southease
Poling Corner
Poling
Highdown
Sompting
Lancing
Portslade-by-Sea
Hove
Brighton Race Hill
Ovingdean
Telscombe
Deans
Angmering
Hangleton
Broadwater
Kemp Town
Saltdean
Piddinghoe
Rustington
East Preston
Kingston
Ferring
West Worthing
Worthing
Goring-by-Sea
Rottingdean
Telscombe Cliffs
Peacehaven
Littlehampton
Kingston Gorse
Newhaven
TQ
TV
1
2
3
4

6
Oxted
Tandridge
Hurst Green
Chartwell
Crockham Hill
Toy's Hill
Emmetts
Long Barn
Sevenoaks Weald
Shipbourne
Hildenborough
Hadlow
Golden Green
East Peckham
Nettlestead Green
Yalding
Godstone Station
South Godstone
Marlpit Hill
Four Elms
Chiddingstone Causeway
Hall Place
Penshurst Station
Leigh
TONBRIDGE
Laddingford
Blindley Heath
Old Mill
Crowhurst
Edenbridge
Hever
Chiddingstone
Penshurst Place
Tudeley
Five Oak Green
Paddock Wood
Lingfield
Marsh Green
Penshurst
Bidborough
SOUTHBOROUGH
Matfield
Brenchley
Newchapel
Dormans Land
Cowden Station
Cowden
Markbeech
Fordcombe
Speldhurst
Pembury
Felbridge
Felcourt
Hammerwood
EAST GRINSTEAD
Ashurst
Langton Green
ROYAL TUNBRIDGE WELLS
Horsmonden
Crawley Down
Sunnyside
Ashurstwood
Groombridge
Frant
Lamberhurst
Owl House
Standen
Saint Hill
Hartfield
Eridge Green
Bayham Abbey
Scotney Castle
Forest Row
Coleman's Hatch
Withyham
Eridge Station
Bells Yew Green
Kilndown
Priests House
Sharpthorne
West Hoathly
Boarshead
Wadhurst
Cousley Wood
Wych Cross
ASHDOWN FOREST
Crowborough
Mark Cross
Three Leg Cross
Highbrook
Tanyard
Chelwood Gate
Tidebrook
Ticehurst
Horsted Keynes
Nutley
Duddleswell
Jarvis Brook
Rotherfield
Stonegate
Bluebell Railway
Danehill
Fairwarp
Mayfield
Etchingham
Lindfield
High Hurstwood
River Rother
Witherenden Hill
Robertsbridge Aeronautical Museum
HAYWARDS HEATH
Maresfield
Five Ashes
Burwash
Burwash Common
Fletching
Uckfield
Buxted
Hadlow Down
Batemans
Heathfield
Robertsbridge
Newick
Broadoak
Cade Street
Wivelsfield
Wivelsfield Green
Chailey
Beeches Farm
Ridgewood
Framfield
Blackboys
Cross in Hand
Little London
Punnett's Town
Brightling
Mountfield
Waldron
Dallington
Netherfield
South Street
Isfield
Little Horsted
Horam
Rushlake Green
Plumpton Green
Halland
Vines Cross
Penhurst
Ditchling
Plumpton
Barcombe Cross
Bentley Wildfowl
East Hoathly
Foul Mile
Shortgate
Chiddingly
Cowbeech
Bodle Street Green
Westmeston
Cooksbridge
Whitesmith
Herstmonceux
Ringmer
Laughton
Golden Cross
Hellingly
Windmill Hill
Ninfield
MOUNT HARRY
Offham
Hamsey
South Malling
Glyndebourne
Ripe
Horsebridge
Magham Down
Royal Observatory
Boreham Street
LEWES
CLIFFE HILL
Glynde Place
Glynde
Chalvington
Upper Dicker
Michelham Priory
Hailsham
Wartling
Hooe
Falmer
Kingston near Lewes
Beddingham
West Firle
Firle Place
Selmeston
Arlington
Moulsecoomb
Rodmell
SOUTH DOWNS WAY
FIRLE BEACON
Alciston
Little Common
Bevendean
Woodingdean
Southease
Tarring Neville
Berwick
Drusilla
Wilmington
Polegate
Pevensey
Norman's Bay
Brighton
Ovingdean
Telscombe
Alfriston Clergy House
South Heighton
Folkington
Stone Cross
Westham
Pevensey Bay
Saltdean
Piddinghoe
Denton
Alfriston
Litlington
Willingdon
Langney
Rottingdean
Telscombe Cliffs
Peacehaven
Norton
Bishopstone
Jevington
Hampden Park
Langney Point
NEWHAVEN
East Blatchington
Westdean
WILLINGDON HILL
SEAFORD
Exceat
East Dean
Friston
EASTBOURNE
Birling Gap
BEACHY HEAD
DIEPPE
TV
A21
A22
A26
A27
A259
A264
A267
A272
A275

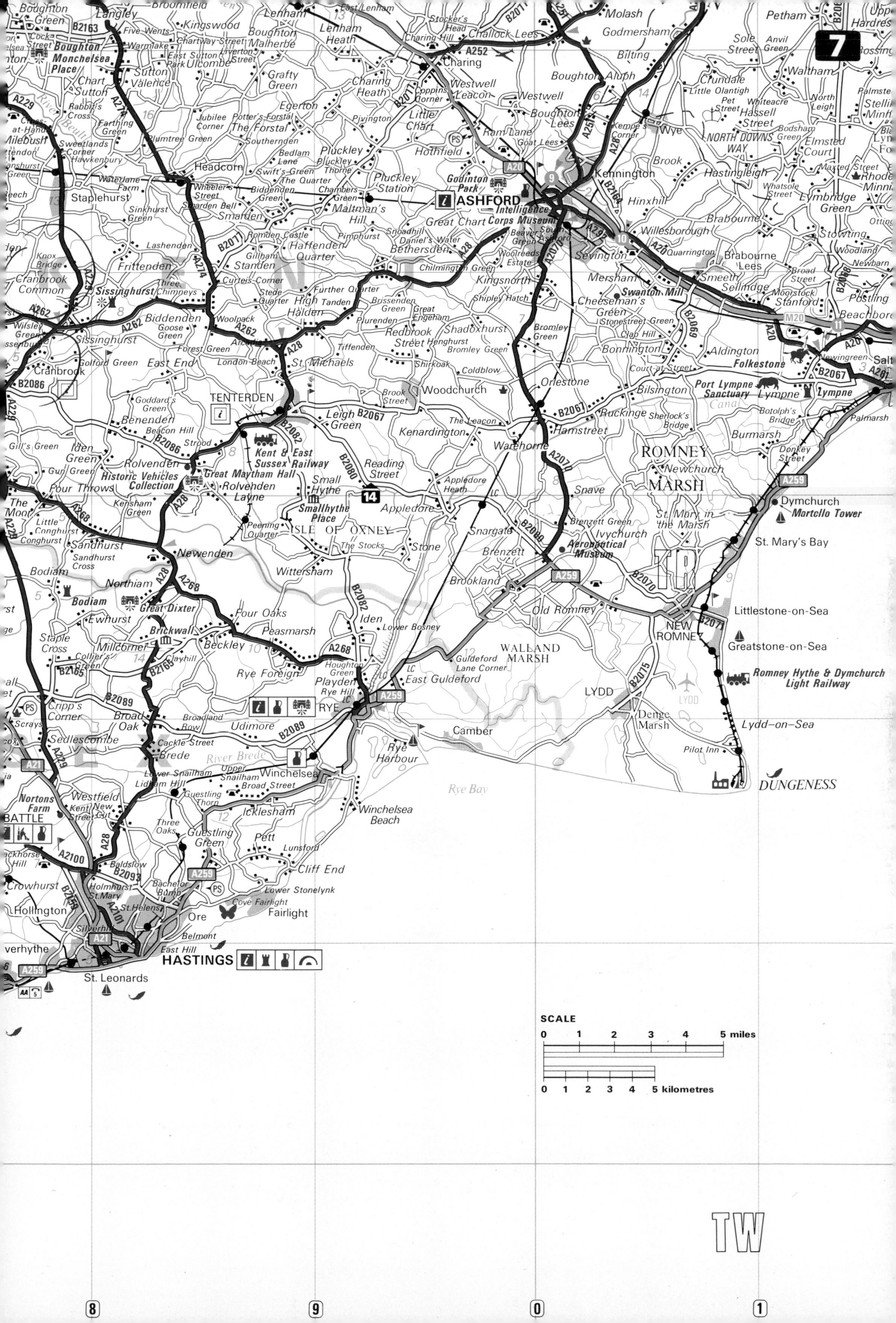
7
Boughton Green
Langley
Broomfield
Lenham
East Lenham
Stocker's Head
Molash
Petham
Upper Hardres
Boughton Monchelsea Place
Five Wents
Kingswood
Boughton Malherbe
Lenham Heath
Charing Hill
Challock Lees
Godmersham
Sole Street
Anvil Green
Bossingham
Warmlake
Chartway Street
Liverton Street
East Sutton
Ulcombe
Charing
Westwell Leacon
Bilting
Crundale
Waltham
Sutton Valence
Chart Sutton
Grafty Green
Charing Heath
Coppins Corner
Westwell
Boughton Aluph
Little Olantigh
Palmstead
Rabbit's Cross
Farthing Green
Jubilee Corner
Potter's Forstal
The Forstal
Egerton
Pivington
Little Chart
Boughton Lees
Pet Street
Whiteacre
Hassell Street
North Leigh
Stelling Minnis
Milebush
Sweetlands Corner
Hawkenbury
Plumtree Green
Southernden
Bedlam Lane
Pluckley
Hothfield
Ram Lane
Goat Lees
Kempe's Corner
Wye
Bodsham Green
Elmsted Court
NORTH DOWNS WAY
Headcorn
Swift's Green
Pluckley Thorne
The Quarter
Brook
Hastingleigh
Maxted Street
Rhodes Minnis
Waterlane Farm
Wheeler's Street
Biddenden Green
Chambers Green
Pluckley Station
Godinton Park
Kennington
Whatsole Street
Staplehurst
Smarden Bell
ASHFORD
Intelligence Corps Museum
Great Chart
Hinxhill
Lymbridge Green
Sinkhurst Green
Smarden
Maltman's Hill
Brabourne
Romden Castle
Pimphurst
Snoadhill
Daniel's Water
Beaver Green
South Ashford
Willesborough
Stowting
Lashenden
Gillham
Haffenden Quarter
Bethersden
Woolreeds Estate
Sevington
Quarrington
Brabourne Lees
Woodland
Knox Bridge
Frittenden
Standen
Chilmington Green
Kingsnorth
Mersham
Smeeth
Sellindge
Broad Street
Newbarn
Cranbrook Common
Sissinghurst
Three Chimneys
Curteis Corner
Stede Quarter
High Halden
Further Quarter
Tanden
Brissenden Green
Great Engeham
Shipley Hatch
Swanton Mill
Cheeseman's Green
Moorstock
Stanford
Postling
Biddenden
Goose Green
Woolpack
Plurenden
Shadoxhurst
Stonestreet Green
Clap Hill
Beachborough
Wilsley Green
Sissinghurst
Forest Green
Arcadia
Tiffenden
Redbrook Street
Henghurst
Bromley Green
Bonnington
Aldington
Newingreen
Saltwood
Golford Green
East End
London Beach
St. Michaels
Shirkoak
Coldblow
Folkestone
Cranbrook
TENTERDEN
Woodchurch
Orlestone
Court-at-Street
Port Lympne Sanctuary
Lympne
Goddard's Green
Brook Street
Bilsington
Canal
Benenden
Beacon Hill
Leigh Green
The Leacon
Kenardington
Ruckinge
Sherlock's Bridge
Botolph's Bridge
Palmarsh
Iden Green
Strood
Hamstreet
Warehorne
Burmarsh
Gill's Green
Rolvenden
Kent & East Sussex Railway
Reading Street
ROMNEY MARSH
Newchurch
Donkey Street
Gun Green
Historic Vehicles Collection
Great Maytham Hall
Appledore Heath
Four Throws
Rolvenden Layne
Small Hythe
Snave
Dymchurch
Martello Tower
The Moor
Kensham Green
Smallhythe Place
Appledore
Little Conghurst
Peening Quarter
ISLE OF OXNEY
Snargate
Brenzett Green
St. Mary in the Marsh
Conghurst
Sandhurst
Stone
The Stocks
Ivychurch
St. Mary's Bay
Newenden
Brenzett
Aeronautical Museum
Sandhurst Cross
Wittersham
Bodiam
Northiam
Brookland
Old Romney
Littlestone-on-Sea
Great Dixter
Four Oaks
Ewhurst
Iden
Lower Bosney
NEW ROMNEY
Staple Cross
Peasmarsh
Brickwall
Beckley
WALLAND MARSH
Greatstone-on-Sea
Millcorner
Collier's Green
Clayhill
Guldeford Lane Corner
Houghton Green
Rye Foreign
Playden
Rye Hill
East Guldeford
Romney Hythe & Dymchurch Light Railway
Cripp's Corner
LYDD
Broad Oak
RYE
Denge Marsh
Scrays
Broadland Row
Udimore
Camber
Lydd-on-Sea
Sedlescombe
Cackle Street
Brede
River Brede
Rye Harbour
Pilot Inn
Lower Snailham
Upper Snailham
Winchelsea
DUNGENESS
Norton's Farm
Lidham Hill
Westfield
Broad Street
Rye Bay
Guestling Thorn
Kent Street
New Cut
BATTLE
Icklesham
Winchelsea Beach
Three Oaks
Guestling Green
Pett
Lunsford
Baldslow
Cliff End
Crowhurst
Holmhurst St. Mary
Bachelor Bump
Lower Stonelynk
St. Helens
Cove Fairlight
Hollington
Ore
Fairlight
Silverhill
Belmont
East Hill
Bulverhythe
HASTINGS
St. Leonards
A20
A28
A21
A229
A252
A259
A262
A268
A274
A2070
A2100
M20
B2067
B2070
B2075
B2077
B2080
B2082
B2086
B2089
B2093
B2165
SCALE
0 1 2 3 4 5 miles
0 1 2 3 4 5 kilometres
TQ
TR
TW
8
9
0
1

38
8
Westerleigh
Wapley
Turville
Drew
Leigh Delamere
Stanton St. Quintin
Upper Seagry
Bradenstoke
Stoke Gifford
Henfield
Ram Hill
Codrington
B4465
Tormarton
M4
Burton
Sevington
Sutton Benger
Christian Malford
MANGOTSFIELD
Hinton
Nettleton
Castle Combe
Kington St. Michael
A429
Kington Langley
Foxham
16
Pucklechurch
Shortwood
Dyrham Park
Dyrham
West Kington
Castle Combe
Yatton Keynell
Allington
Langley Burrell
Soundwell
B4465
West Littleton
North Wraxall
Ford
B4039
Spirthill
Siston
Upper Wraxall
West Yatton
A420
Hardenhuish
East Tytherton
BRISTOL
A420
Warmley
Webb's Heath
Bridgeyate
Doynton
The Shoe
Giddeahall
Sheldon Manor
West Tytherton
KINGSWOOD
A420
Marshfield
Slaughterford
CHIPPENHAM
Pennsylvania
Lucknam
Biddestone
Hanham
Wick
Cold Ashton
Colerne
Thickwood
Cross Keys
A46
Upper Pickwick
Corsham Court
Studley
Brislington
A4175
Oldland
Upton Cheyney
Langridge
St Catherine
Colerne
Pickwick
A4
Derry Hill
Bowood
A4
Ditteridge
Corsham
Notton
A432
North Stoke
Swainswick
Alcombe
Northend
Box
Lacock
Mile Elm
A37
Queen Charlton
KEYNSHAM
780
Kelston
Lansdown
Charlcombe
Batheaston
Ashley
Wadswick
Neston
B3353
Gastard
Lacock Abbey
Sandy Lane
Bath
A4
Bowden Hill
Stockley
Chewton Keynsham
Saltford
A4
BATH
A363
Bathford
Monkton Farleigh
B3109
A365
Purlpit
Whitley
Beanacre
Chittoe
Compton Dando
B3116
Corston
Weston
Bathampton
Atworth
Shaw
Westbrook
Bromham
Norton Malreward
Burnett
A39
South Wraxall
Norrington Common
Sandridge
Blackmore Forest
Woollard
Stanton Prior
Newton St. Loe
Twerton
Claverton
A3102
St. Edith's Marsh
Stanton Drew
Pensford
Whiteway
Farleigh Wick
Bradford Leigh
Broughton Gifford
MELKSHAM
Hunstrete
Wilmington
Monkton Combe
Conkwell
Chalfield
Redstocks
A368
Englishcombe
Priston Mill
A3062
Woolley Green
Holt
The Courts
Seend Cleeve
Sells Green
Chelwood
Marksbury
Priston
Inglesbatch
A367
B3108
Turleigh
B3107
A350
A361
A37
680
Midford
BRADFORD ON AVON
Staverton
Semington
Seend
Clutton Hill
Farmborough
South Stoke
Limpley Stoke
Winsley
Freshford
Little Marsh
Horseshoes
Poulshot
Clutton
B3115
Timsbury
Tunley
Dunkerton
Combe Hay
Twinhoe
Hinton Priory
Westwood
Hilperton
Great Hinton
Meadgate
Carlingcott
Wellow
Farleigh
Westwood
Bulkington
Temple Cloud
High Littleton
Peasedown St. John
Hinton Charterhouse
Trowle Common
A361
Ashton Common
Keevil
Hinton Blewett
Hallatrow
Camerton
A366
Wingfield
TROWBRIDGE
Steeple Ashton
Marston
Worton
B3355
Stony Littleton
B3110
Farleigh Hungerford
Southwick
Farrington Gurney
Paulton
A362
Shoscombe
A36
Woodmarsh
Rood Ashton
West Ashton
A39
MIDSOMER NORTON
Clandown
RADSTOCK
A366
Norton St. Philip
Tellisford
Tropical Bird Gardens
East Coulston
Great Cheverell
Writhlington
Faulkland
B3110
North Bradley
Yarnbrook
Dunge
Ston Easton
Westfield
Norton Hill
Clapton
B3355
Woolverton
Rode
Heywood
Erlestoke
Little Cheverell
Downside Abbey
Kilmersdon
Hemington
Hawkeridge
Chilcompton
Hardington
Laverton
Brokerswood
Edington
B3114
A37
B3139
Charlton
Babington
Lullington
Rudge
B3098
Bratton
Bratton Camp
878
Stratton-on-the-Fosse
A362
Buckland Dinham
Beckington
Standerwick
Hill Figure
WESTBURY
Chalford
Holcombe
Newbury
Dilton Marsh
Highbury
Upper Vobster
Mells
Oldford
Gurney Slade
A367
Berkley
Westbury Leigh
Nettlebridge
Great Elm
Clink
Chalcot
Coleford
Vobster
A3098
A350
Ashwick
Soho
Little Green
Whatley
FROME
Upton Scudamore
Oakhill Manor
Oakhill
Leigh upon Mendip
Lower Whatley
Chapmanslade
A36
Stoke St. Michael
East End
Chantry
Little Keyford
Corsley
WARMINSTER
682
Thrupe
Nunney
Lye's Green
Corsley Heath
Cold Harbour
Downside
Downhead
Holwell
Lane End
A362
Waterlip
Darshill
SHEPTON MALLET
Dean
Leighton
Nunney Catch
Tytherington
Boreham
Norton Bavant
A361
Cloford
East Woodlands
Bishopstrow
B390
Charlton
Doulting
Cranmore
Trudoxhill
West Woodlands
Longleat
Crockerton
Sutton Veny
Heytesbury
East Somerset Railway
Weston Town
A359
River Frome
Horningsham
Shear Cross
Knook
East Compton
Chesterblade
Witham Friary
Newbury
Longbridge Deverill
B3095
Upton Lovell
Wanstrow
B3092
A36
Royal Bath & West Showground
Higher Alham
Tytherington
Codford St. Peter
Prestleigh
Gare Hill
Pottle Street
Brixton Deverill
Corton
Codford St. Mary
Westcombe
Upton Noble
Hill Deverill
Boyton
Fisherton de la Mere
Evercreech
Stoney Stratton
Batcombe
Maiden Bradley
Sherington
Milton Clevedon
Monkton Deverill
Stockton
Pye Hill
B3081
945
Ditcheat
A371
Brewham
Norton Ferris
Kingston Deverill
A37
Lamyatt
South Brewham
Kilmington
A350
Kilmington Street
Pertwood
Stourhead
Wyke Champflower
Hardway
Chicklade
A303
Stourton
B3092
B3095
Berwick St. Leonard
Fonthill Bishop
Bruton
Cole
Redlynch
Gasper
13
Mere
A303
B3089
Teffont Magna
Sutton
Pitcombe
Ansford
Castle Cary
Stoney Stoke
Shepton Montague
Barrow
Penselwood
Coombe Street
Zeals
Wolverton
B3092
West Knoyle
Hindon
B3089
Chilmark
Alford
B3152
B3081
Chaltoh Musgrove
B3081
Bleak Street
Queen Oak
Bourton
Barrow Street
The Green
Fonthill Gifford
Ridge
Teffont Evias
Lovington
Galhampton
Bratton Seymour
East Knoyle
Lower Chicksgrove
Holloway
Wincanton
Leigh Common
West Bourton
B3092
Tisbury
North Cadbury
Yarlington
Wincanton
Stoke Trister
Silton
B3095
Newtown
A359
A371
Bayford
Hale
Milton on Stour
Sedgehill
Tuckingmill
Sutton Mandeville
Woolston
A303
Cucklington
North End
Hatch
West Hatch
Wardour Old Castle
Holton
Maperton
B3081
Gillingham
Semley
Swallowcliffe
South Cadbury
Compton Pauncefoot
Blackford
Lattiford
North Cheriton
Quarr
Wyke
Ham Common
Elm Hill
Ansty
Eccliffe
Motcombe
A30
Fyfield
South Cheriton
B3145
Buckhorn Weston
Langham
St Bartholomew's Hill
20
Sutton Montis
Charlton Horethorne
Rodgrove
Horsington
Sandley
Bugley
B3092
DORSET
Donhead St. Mary
Donhead St. Andrew
West End
Kington Magna
West Stour
Knap Corner
A350
Sherborne Causeway
Berwick St. John
Corton Denham
A357
Abbas Combe
A30
SHAFTESBURY
Stowell
Higher Nyland
East Stour
Enmore Green
Ludwell
Alvediston
Rimpton
7
Templecombe
8
Stour
Cann
9

9
Tockenham
The Barton
Broadtown Lane
Chiseldon
Overtown
Badbury
Brightwalton
Church End
Thornhill
Broad Town
Bushton
Wroughton
Draycot Foliat
17
Lambourn
Preston
Uffcott
PS
Barbury Castle
Upper Upham
Baydon
Chaddleworth
Clyffe Pypard
Broad Hinton
A4361
A345
Woodsend
B4192
B4001
Eastbury
East Garston
A338
Leckhampstead Thicket
Clevancy
Aldbourne
Woodlands St Mary
Great Shefford
East Shefford
Winterbourne Bassett
Highway
Ogbourne St. George
Southend
892
Preston
B4000
Welford
Berwick Bassett
12
Ogbourne St. Andrew
Whittonditch
Weston
Compton Bassett
Rockley
Ramsbury
Crooked Soley
Straight Soley
10
14
Winterbourne Monkton
Ogbourne Maizey
New Town
B4192
Knighton
Chilton Foliat
Hungerford Newton
Wickham Green
Easton
Wickham
Cherhill
Yatesbury
Little London
River Kennet
Avebury
Mildenhall
3
Clapton
Elcot
Halfway
A4
Avebury
Fyfield
Axford
Stitchcombe
Hungerford
12
Hill Figure
West Kennet
A4
MARLBOROUGH
Froxfield
Beckhampton
PS
10
A4
Avington
Manton
Marsh Benham
A361
West Overton
East Kennett
Lockeridge
Hill Figure
Cadley
Chisbury
Little Bedwyn
Kintbury
Layland's Green
8
Clench Common
Savernake Forest
Durley
Kintbury Cross Ways
Bourton
964
Hill Figure
Great Bedwyn
Bagshot
Inkpen
Hell Corner
Hamstead Marshall
TAN HILL
Huish
A345
A346
Newtown
Upper Green
North End
Allington
Stanton St. Bernard
950
Wootton Rivers
Crofton Beam Engines
Shalbourne
Ham
West Woodhay
Horton
West Stowell
Oare
Stibb Green
Crofton
WALBURY HILL
Heath End
Coate
Alton Priors
New Mill
Westcourt
Burbage
Eastcourt
Rivar
974
All Cannings
Honeystreet
Pewsey
Wilton
A338
Combe
East Woodhay
Wilcot
Fyfield
B3087
Marten
Buttermere
Etchilhampton
Woodborough
Milton Lilbourne
Easton Royal
West Grafton
East Grafton
Beechingstoke
Broad Street
Oxenwood
Southcott
Wexcombe
Linkenholt
Faccombe
Patney
Gores
North Newnton
Manningford Bruce
A338
Wedhampton
Marden
Hill Figure
Tidcombe
Littledown
Fosbury
Netherton
Wilsford
Manningford Bohune
Vernham Street
Ashmansworth
Chirton
Charlton
Aughton
Brunton
Urchfont
Vernham Dean
Rushall
Upavon
A342
Collingbourne Kingston
Upper Chute
Upton
Lower Everleigh
Sunton
Cadley
17
Everleigh
Collingbourne Ducis
Lower Chute
Ibthorpe
Woodcott
Chute Cadley
West Chisenbury
East Chisenbury
East Everleigh
Tangley
Hurstbourne Tarrant
Wadwick
Compton
Littlecott
Ludgershall
Chute Lodge
Wildhern
Stoke
Enford
Longstreet
Coombe
735
Hatherden
A342
10
Swampton
Upper Enham
Fifield
Fittleton
A338
Appleshaw
Duck Street
Little London
Tilshead
Netheravon
North Tidworth
Clanville
Enham-Alamein
Smannell
Haxton
SU
Penton Grafton
Penton Mewsey
Finkley
Westdown Camp
Figheldean
South Tidworth
Kimpton
Fyfield
East Anton
Picket Piece
Tinker's Hill
Charlton
B3400
A345
Shipton Bellinger
5
Thruxton
Orcheston
Brigmerston
Ablington
Milston
Thruxton
Weyhill
Andover Down
Elston
B3086
Larkhill
9
ANDOVER
Maddington
Durrington
East Cholderton
Monxton
Anna Valley
Shrewton
Woodhenge
Bulford Barracks
A303
Quarley
Amport
Upper Clatford
A303
Forton
B390
A360
Stonehenge
Bulford
Countess
5
Bury Hill
Cottage End
Harewood Forest
B3083
Abbotts Ann
B3048
Winterbourne Stoke
West Amesbury
Amesbury
Cholderton
B3084
Grateley
Goodworth Clatford
A3057
Wherwell
Newton Stacey
A303
Normanton
A343
Westover
Wilsford
Newton Toney
Palestine
Berwick St. James
River Avon
Allington
Fullerton
Chilbolton
B3420
Steeple Langford
Lake
8
R. Bourne
Over Street
Upper Woodford
Great Durnford
Boscombe
Over Wallop
Middle Wallop
Longstock
Leckford
Stapleford
A338
A30
Middle Woodford
High Post
Idmiston
PS
Porton
18
Nether Wallop
Stoford
Netton
12
Lopcombe Corner
A343
B3084
Crawley
Salterton
Winterbourne Gunner
Little Langford
Great Wishford
Lower Woodford
Winterbourne Dauntsey
A30
Stockbridge
A272
River Wylye
A345
Middle Winterslow
Broughton
South Newton
Little Durnford
Hurdcott
A36
Winterbourne Earls
West Winterslow
Barford St. Martin
Old Sarum
Castle Hill
A30
Little Somborne
Up Somborne
WILTON
Stratford sub Castle
The Common
Winterslow
Houghton
A30
Paul's Dene
Laverstock
Pitton
Sparsholt
B3089
Quidhampton
Burcombe
Bulbridge
Bemerton
West Tytherley
Horsebridge
King's Somborne
Ashley
Compton Chamberlayne
Wilton
SALISBURY
PS
Netherhampton
West Harnham
East Harnham
Farley
B3084
Brook
Harnham
A3057
East Tytherley
584
WINCHE
Salisbury
A36
East Grimstead
11
Figures
Coombe Bissett
Britford
Alderbury
West Dean
Lockerley
Spearywell
Mottisfont Abbey
Mottisfont
Stratford Tony
Michelmersh
Standon
A338
Bishopstone
Bodenham
Dean Hill
East Dean
Dunbridge
Stoke Farthing
Whaddon
West Grimstead
Homington
Odstock
Braishfield
Nunton
513
Carter's Clay
Kent's Oak
Croucheston
Hillier Arboretum
Hursley
Mount Sorrel
PS
Whiteparish
Timsbury
End
Charlton
15
A27
Newtown
B3084
Ampfield
2
A354
Ratley
Awbridge
Ratlake
Swayne's Firs
17
16
Abbotswood
Downton
Newton
River
1
2
3
ROMSEY
4
Wick
Morgan's Vale
Landford Manor
Sherfield English
B303

10
Letcombe Bassett
Chilton
Blewbury
Tirrold
North Stoke
Ipsden
Wellplace Bird Farm
Highmoor
OXFORDSHIRE
Moulsford
South Stoke
Stoke Row
Checkendon
Shepherd's Green
West Ilsley
18
THE RIDGEWAY PATH
871
Upper Lambourn
Fawley
Farnborough
East Ilsley
Streatley
Woodcote
Exlade Street
Rotherfield Peppard
Goring
Greenmoor Hill
Cray's Pond
Sonning Common
South Fawley
Catmore
Compton
Cold Harbour
Cane End
Lambourn
Brightwalton
Lilley
Stanmore
Aldworth
Basildon
Whitchurch Hill
Brightwalton Green
Brightwalton Holt
Four Points
Child Beale Wildlife Trust
Whitchurch
Chazey Heath
Mapledurham
Chaddleworth
Mell Green
Beedon
Beedon Hill
World's End
Ashampstead
Ashampstead Green
East Garston
Eastbury
Woodlands St Mary
Leckhampstead Thicket
Peasemore
Upper Basildon
Basildon
Toll
Great Shefford
East Shefford
Leckhampstead
Bothampstead
Hampstead Norreys
Pangbourne
Westwood Row
Purley
Watermill
Downend
Sulham
Yattendon
Tidmarsh
Chieveley
Horsemoor
Little Hungerford
Burnt Hill
Little Heath
Tilehurst
Weston
Welford
Frilsham
Bradfield
North Street
Calcot
Wickham Green
Westbrook
Hermitage
Straight Soley
Crooked Soley
Hungerford Newton
Winterbourne
Curridge
Wellhouse
Stanford Dingley
Englefield
Calcot Row
READING
Chilton Foliat
Wickham
Easton
Boxford
Ownham
Bucklebury
The Slade
South End
Theale
Hunt's Green
Clapton
Wickham Heath
Cold Ash
Upper Bucklebury
Sheffield Bottom
Hungerford
Elcot
Halfway
Bagnor
Stockcross
Donnington
Chapel Row
Beenham
Sulhamstead
Sulhamstead Bannister
Burghfield
Avington
1644
Speen
Shaw
Thatcham
Midgham
Woolhampton
Ufton Nervet
Burghfield Hill
Three Mile Cross
Kintbury
Layland's Green
Enborne
NEWBURY
Aldermaston Wharf
Burghfield Common
Grazeley
Bagshot
1643
Skinners Green
Sandleford Close
Newbury Greenham
R Kennet
Aldermaston
Padworth
Padworth Common
Aldermaston Court
Wokefield Park
Hamstead Marshall
Inkpen
Upper Green
Hell Corner
Red Hill
Enborne Row
Goldfinch Bottom
Brimpton
Crookham
Wasing
Mortimer
Beech Hill
North End
Trapshill
Ball Hill
Newtown
Aldermaston Soke
Mortimer West End
Stratfield Mortimer
Ham
West Woodhay
Broad Laying
Bishop's Green
Headley
Heath End
B3051
Calleva
Stratfield Saye
Rivar
Heath End
Woolton Hill
Sandham Memorial Chapel
Brock's Green
Plastow Green
Ashford Hill
New Town
Silchester
West End Green
Stratfield Saye
Combe
East Woodhay
East End
Pound Street
Burghclere
Tadley
Pamber Heath
Fair Oak Green
Stratfield Turgis
Buttermere
Highclere
Baughurst
Wolverton Common
Pamber Green
Little London
Oxenwood
Whitway
Browninghill Green
Bramley Green
Spanish Green
Linkenholt
Faccombe
Highclere Street
Old Burghclere
Ecchinswell
Towns End
Pamber End
Bramley
Littledown
West Heath
Fosbury
Netherton
Sydmonton
Kingsclere
Wolverton
Charter Alley
Sherfield on Loddon
Hartley Wespall
Vernham Street
Ashmansworth
Crux Easton
Ramsdell
The Vyne
Church End
Vernham Dean
Monk Sherborne
Sherborne St. John
Rotherwick
Upton
Hannington
Ibworth
Chineham
Ibthorpe
Woodcott
Litchfield
North Oakley
Upper Wootton
Lower Chute
Dunley
Basing
Old Basing
Chute Cadley
Binley
Wadwick
Egbury
Wootton St. Lawrence
Winklebury
Tangley
Hurstbourne Tarrant
Stoke
Quidhampton
Newfound
BASINGSTOKE
Hatch
Chute Lodge
Clarken Green
Hatherden
Wildhern
St. Mary Bourne
Cole Henley
Deane
Oakley
East Oakley
Mapledurwell
Dunhill Street
Upper Enham
Little London
Southington
Ashe
Kempshott
Clanville
Enham-Alamein
Smannell
Freefolk
Overton
Pardown
Upton
Penton Mewsey
Picket Piece
Laverstoke
Steventon
Cliddesden
Winslade
Tunworth
Penton Grafton
East Anton
Tinker's Hill
Tufton
Whitchurch
Broadmere
Weston Corbett
Weyhill
Charlton
Farleigh Wallop
Ellisfield
Herriard
Andover Down
Hurstbourne Priors
North Waltham
Nash's Green
Sarson
ANDOVER
East Aston
Dummer
Monxton
Anna Valley
Longparish
Upper Common
Lower Common
Bagmore
Southrope
Upper Clatford
Forton
Middleton
Army Camp
Nutley
Shalden Green
Abbotts Ann
Bury Hill
Cottage End
Harewood Forest
Popham
Axford
Lasham
Goodworth Clatford
Bransbury
Woodmancott
Preston Candover
Micheldever Station
Upper Bullington
Lower Bullington
Newton Stacey
Westover
Wherwell
West Stratton
MICHELDEVER FOREST
Chilton Candover
Bradley
Fullerton
Barton Stacey
East Stratton
Lower Wield
Chilbolton
Wonston
Northbrook
Bentworth
Halt End
Thedden Grange
Middle Wallop
Longstock
Leckford
Sutton Scotney
Stoke Charity
Micheldever
Brown Candover
Upper Wield
Wivelrod
Northington
Totford
Nether Wallop
Swarraton
Medstead
South Wonston
Hattingley
South Town
Stockbridge
Crawley
Abbotstone
Old Alresford
Bighton
West End
Soldridge
Four Marks
Broughton
Kings Worthy
Littleton
Itchen Abbas
North Street
Gundleton
Little Somborne
Abbots Worthy
Martyr Worthy
Itchen Stoke
Mid Hants Railway
Hawthorn
Houghton
Up Somborne
New Alresford
Kitwood
Gilbert Street
Sparsholt
Headbourne Worthy
Easton
Avington
Ovington
Ropley
Charlwood
Ashley
Bishop's Sutton
Ropley Dean
Horsebridge
King's Somborne
Dean
Weeke
Monkwood
B3404
Tichborne
West Tisted
1644
Brook
WINCHESTER
Cheriton
North End
Lower Brook
Stanmore
Bramdean
Filmore Hill
Bailey Green
Mottisfont
Hinton Marsh
Chilcomb
Privett
Standon
Oliver's

11
Lower Assendon
Mill End
Medmenham
Bisham Abbey
Remenham
Remenham Hill
Hurley
HENLEY ON THAMES
Cockpole Green
MAIDENHEAD
Cookham
Cookham Dean
Cookham Rise
Cliveden
Taplow
Burnham Beeches
Farnham Common
Farnham Royal
Stoke Poges
Fulmer
Iver Heath
Denham
Ickenham
Uxbridge
HILLINGDON
Harpsden
Littlewick Green
Warren Row
Wargrave
Knowl Hill
Shire Horse Centre
Woodlands Park
Burnham
Bray
Dorney
Boveney
Windsor
Eton Wick
SLOUGH
Langley
Iver
Richings Park
West Drayton
Yiewsley
Cowley
Hayes
Shiplake
Dunsden Green
Play Hatch
Sonning
Hare Hatch
Waltham St. Lawrence
Twyford
White Waltham
Holyport
ETON
Datchet
WINDSOR
Colnbrook
Poyle
Sipson
Harmondsworth
Heston
Longford
HEATHROW AIRPORT LONDON
Hatton
Fifield
Touchenend
Oakley Green
Eton College
Shurlock Row
Paley Street
Hawthorn Hill
Windsor Safari Park
Old Windsor
Wraysbury
Horton
Stanwell Moor
Stanwell
East Bedfont
Feltham
Whistley Green
Woodley
Hurst
Winkfield
Warfield
Cranbourne
The Village
Englefield Green
Hythe End
Dinton Pastures Country Park
Earley
Winnersh
Binfield
Newell Green
Winkfield Row
Woodside
Savill
EGHAM
STAINES
Ashford
Sindlesham
Burleigh
Ascot
Thorpe
Thorpe Park
Laleham
Littleton
SUNBURY
Shinfield
Arborfield
Arborfield Cross
WOKINGHAM
BRACKNELL
Easthampstead
South Ascot
Sunninghill
Sunningdale
Virginia Water
Lyne
Shepperton
R.E.M.E. Museum
Barkham
Arborfield Garrison
Farley Hill
CHERTSEY
WALTON ON-THAMES
Addlestone
WEYBRIDGE
Crowthorne
SURREY HILL
Windlesham
Bagshot
Burrowhill
Ottershaw
Finchampstead
Owlsmoor
Sandhurst
College Town
Lightwater
Chobham
Woodham
Eversley
Yateley
Eversley Cross
Blackbushe
BLACKBUSHE AIRPORT
Frogmore
Blackwater
Bagshot Heath
West End
Byfleet
Cobham
CAMBERLEY
FRIMLEY
Hawley
Deepcut
Knaphill
Horsell
WOKING
Pyrford
Wisley
Stoke D'Abernon
Hazeley
Mattingley
Hartfordbridge
Hartley Wintney
Fox Lane
Cove
Bisley
Brookwood
Mayford
Ripley
Ockham
Phoenix Green
FLEET
FARNBOROUGH
Mytchett
Pirbright
Send
West Horsley
East Horsley
Winchfield
Dogmersfield
Henley Park
Worplesdon
Jacobs Well
West Clandon
Church Crookham
Crookham Village
ALDERSHOT
Normandy
Wood Street
Stoughton
Burpham
Clandon Park
East Clandon
Odiham
Ash
Flexford
Onslow Village
GUILDFORD
Shere
Gomshall
Crondall
Ewshot
Upper Hale
Tongham
Wanborough
Seale
Puttenham
Compton
Loseley
Chilworth
Albury
FARNHAM
Runfold
The Sands
Shackleford
Farncombe
Shalford
Wonersh
Blackheath
Peaslake
Sutton
Bentley
Waverley Abbey
Elstead
Peper Harow
Godalming
Bramley
Holmbury St. Mary
Rowledge
Birdworld
Tilford
Millbridge
Milford
Busbridge
Shamley Green
Thorncombe Street
Forest Green
Blacknest
Frensham
Rushmoor
Wheelerstreet
Witley
Hydestile
Winkworth Arboretum
Hascombe
Ewhurst
Cranleigh
Thursley
Hambledon
Kingsley
West Worldham
Bordon
Churt
Hindhead
Grayshott
Chiddingfold
Dunsfold
Alfold Crossways
Ellen's Green
Headley
Oakhanger
Selborne
Alfold
Rudgwick
Bramshott
Shottermill
HASLEMERE
Camelsdale
Grayswood
Liphook
Longmoor Camp
Fisherstreet
Ifold
Loxwood
Bucks Green
Greatham
Linchmere
Kingsley Green
Plaistow
Langley
Hollycombe Steam Museum
Northchapel
Roundstreet Common
Five Oaks
Liss
Milland
Fernhurst
Lurgashall
Newpound Common
WEST SUSSEX
NORTH DOWNS WAY

12
BERKHAMSTED
Whelpley Hill
Bourne End
Felden
Bovingdon
Lye Green
Botley
Chipperfield
Flaunden
Kings Langley
Abbots Langley
Bucks Hill
Bedmond
Pimlico
Potters Crouch
Chiswellgreen
De Haviland Mosquito Aircraft Museum
Primrosehill
Bricket Wood
Colney Heath
London Colney
Colney Street
Shenleybury
Shenley
Radlett
South Mimms
Welham Green
Brookmans Park
Northaw
Cuffley
POTTERS BAR
Crews Hill Station
Epping Green
West End
Newgate Street
Appleby Street
Goff's Oak
Latimer
Sarratt
Chenies
Little Chalfont
Chorleywood West
CHORLEYWOOD
AMERSHAM
Coleshill
Chandler's Cross
WATFORD
Croxley Green
Garston
Aldenham
Round Bush
Letchmore Heath
Green Street
Ridge
Bentley Heath
Ganwick Corner
Hadley Wood
Monken Hadley
Botany Bay
Forty Hill
ENFIELD
Borehamwood
BUSHEY
Oxhey
Elstree
Arkley
BARNET
Totteridge
Cockfosters
East Barnet
New Barnet
Winchmore Hill
Southgate
Chalfont St. Giles
Chalfont Common
Jordans
Heronsgate
RICKMANSWORTH
Maple Cross
Batchworth Heath
West Hyde
Harefield
Horn Hill
Bushey Heath
Merry Hill
Hatch End
South Oxhey
Eastbury
Northwood
Stanmore
Edgware
Highwood Hill
Mill Hill
Friern Barnet
Wood Green
Edmonton
Tottenham
Chalfont St. Peter
Gerrards Cross
Hedgerley Green
Hedgerley
Denham Green
Newyears Green
Pinner
Pinner Green
HARROW
Wealdstone
RAF Museum
Kingsbury
Kenton
Hendon
Church End
Finchley
HARINGEY
Hornsey
Golders Green
Highgate
Eastcote
Ruislip
Harrow on the Hill
Neasden
Hampstead
Stoke Newington
Burnham Beeches
Fulmer
Denham
Ickenham
Northolt Park
Wembley
Willesden
CAMDEN
ISLINGTON
Stoke Poges
Iver Heath
New Denham
North Hillingdon
Northolt
BRENT
Harlesden
Shoreditch
Stoke Green
Wexham
Uxbridge
HILLINGDON
Greenford
Perivale
Paddington
Finsbury
CITY OF LONDON
St. Marylebone
Love Green
Iver
Cowley
Hayes End
Hayes
Yeading
Southall
EALING
Acton
CITY OF WESTMINSTER
SLOUGH
Shreding Green
Yiewsley
Richings Park
West Drayton
Norwood Green
Brentford
HAMMERSMITH
Bermondsey
SOUTHWARK
Upton
Langley
Sipson
Harmondsworth
Heston
Cranford
Osterley Park
Kew
Chiswick
KENSINGTON AND CHELSEA
Datchet
ETON
WINDSOR
Colnbrook
Poyle
Longford
HEATHROW AIRPORT LONDON
Hatton
Isleworth
HOUNSLOW
Mortlake
Barnes
Fulham
Battersea
LAMBETH
Clapham
Brixton
Horton
Stanwell
Stanwell Moor
West Bedfont
East Bedfont
Twickenham
RICHMOND UPON THAMES
Putney
WANDSWORTH
Roehampton
Dulwich
Old Windsor
Wraysbury
The Village
Feltham
Ham
Upper Tooting
Streatham
Englefield Green
Hythe End
EGHAM
Ashford
Hanworth
Felthamhill
Hampton
Teddington
Wimbledon
Tooting
West Norwood
Savill Garden
Valley Gardens
Thorpe Lea
STAINES
Kempton Park
SUNBURY
KINGSTON UPON THAMES
MERTON
Norbury
Thornton Heath
Sunningdale
Thorpe Park
Thorpe
Laleham
Littleton
East Molesey
Hampton Court Palace
Morden
Mitcham
Virginia Water
Knowlehill
Lyne
Shepperton
Lower Halliford
Thames Ditton
Surbiton
Malden
Broomhall
Addlestone
CHERTSEY
WALTON-ON-THAMES
Sandown
ESHER
Long Ditton
Tolworth
Worcester Park
The Wrythe
Whitgift Hospital
Beddington
Carshalton
CROYDON
Albury Bottom
WEYBRIDGE
Oatlands Park
West End
Hersham
Hook
Chessington
Cheam
SUTTON
Wallington
South Croydon
Burrowhill
Ottershaw
New Haw
Claygate
Purley
Brimshot
Woodham
Brox
St George's Hill
Whiteley Village
Horton
EWELL
Belmont
Sanderstead
Chobham
Anthonys
Castle Green
West Byfleet
Byfleet
Fairmile
Cobham
Oxshott Heath
Oxshott
Malden Rushett
EPSOM
Little Woodcote
Woodmansterne
Coulsdon
Kenley
Whyteleafe
Horsell
Mayburry
Pyrford
Wisley
Stoke D'Abernon
Epsom Downs Station
BANSTEAD
Old Coulsdon
Newark Priory
WOKING
St Johns
Ripley
Ockham
Downside
May's Green
Martyr's Green
Ashtead
Epsom
Burgh Heath
Chipstead
Mayford
Old Woking
Send Marsh
Effingham Common
LEATHERHEAD
Fetcham
Tadworth
Kingswood
Hooley
Chaldon
CATERHAM
Cartbridge
Burntcommon
West Horsley
East Horsley
Little Bookham
Great Bookham
Headley
Walton on the Hill
Send
Sendgrove
Sutton Green
Jacobs Well
Pitch Place
West Clandon
Hatchlands
Clandon Park
Effingham
Polesden Lacey
Mickleham
Box Hill
Lower Kingswood
Merstham
South Merstham
Godstone
Wood Street
Stoughton
Burpham
Merrow
East Clandon
Westhumble
Denbies
Buckland
Bedhill
Brewer Street
Holmethorpe
Nutfield
Bletchingley
Onslow Village
GUILDFORD
Shere
Gomshall
NORTH DOWNS WAY
DORKING
Betchworth
Brockham
REIGATE
Earlswood
South Nutfield
HERTFORDSHIRE
SURREY
ELSTREE AERODROME
EAVESDEN AERODROME
M25
M1
M4
M3
M10
A1(M)

13
CHELMSFORD
Nazeing
Epping Green
Thornwood Common
North Weald Basset
Fyfield
Willingale
Writtle
Great Baddow
Galleywood
CHESHUNT
TL
Waltham Abbey
Upshire
EPPING
Coopersale Common
Chipping Ongar
Blackmore
Margaretting
West Hanningfield
Theydon Bois
Fiddlers Hamlet
Stanford Rivers
Stondon Massey
Fryerning
Ingatestone
Stock
21
High Beach
Loughton
Abridge
Stapleford Tawney
Navestock
Kelvedon Hatch
Doddinghurst
Mountnessing
South Hanningfield
Epping Forest Museum
Buckhurst Hill
Chigwell
Lambourne End
Stapleford Abbotts
Navestock Side
Pilgrims Hatch
Hutton
Shenfield
BILLERICAY
22
Runwell
Wickford
BRENTWOOD
Ingrave
Little Burstead
Woodford Green
Grange Hill
Hainault
Havering-atte-Bower
Harrold Hill
Herongate
Great Burstead
Nevendon
Woodford Bridge
Collier Row
Gidea Park
Harold Wood
Great Warley
Little Warley
Dunton Wayletts
North Benfleet
BASILDON
REDBRIDGE
Romford
Squirrel's Heath
Hornchurch
HAVERING
Cranham
Laindon
Pitsea
Vange
Wanstead
Seven Kings
Ilford
Becontree
BARKING
Rush Green
Upminster
West Horndon
Bulphan
Bowers Gifford
One Tree Hill
Forest Gate
West Ham
Eastbury Manor
East Ham
Dagenham
Elm Park
South Hornchurch
North Ockendon
Horndon on the Hill
Fobbing
Corringham
Dutch Cottage
NEWHAM
Creekmouth
Beckton
Rainham
South Ockendon
Baker Street
Orsett
Stanford le Hope
Coryton
Canning Town
River Thames
Thamesmead
Wennington
North Stifford
Mucking
Thames Haven
Aveley
Little Thurrock
Chadwell St. Mary
Linford
Woolwich
Abbey Wood
Belvedere
Purfleet
West Thurrock
GRAYS
West Tilbury
Halstow Marshes
Charlton
Lesnes Abbey
Erith
East Tilbury
Kidbrooke
East Wickham
Welling
Slade Green
TILBURY
Cliffe
Cooling
LEWISHAM
Eltham
BEXLEY
Crayford
Greenhithe
Stone
NORTHFLEET
GRAVESEND
Church Street
DARTFORD
SWANSCOMBE
Hither Green
Eltham Palace
New Eltham
Catford
Mottingham
Sidcup
Wilmington
Bean
Singlewell or Ifield
Chalk
Lower Higham
Cliffe Woods
Grove Park
Chislehurst
North Cray
Hawley
Darenth
Betsham
Southfleet
Shorne
Higham
Wainscott
Upnor
Bromley
Hextable
Sutton at Hone
Longfield
Thong
Frindsbury
Widmore
St. Pauls Cray
Swanley
South Darenth
Strood
Shortlands
Bickley
Petts Wood
St. Mary Cray
Horton Kirby
Hartley
Cobham
ROCHESTER
Bromley Common
Orpington
Crockenhill
Farningham
Fawkham Green
Meopham Station
Cuxton
West Wickham
Hayes
BROMLEY
Eynsford
New Ash Green
Meopham
Luddesdown
CHATHAM
Keston
Farnborough
Chelsfield
Roman Villa
Lullingstone
Brands Hatch
Halling
Green Street Green
Well Hill
West Kingsdown
Ash
Culverstone Green
Wouldham
New Addington
Badgers Mount
Stansted
NORTH DOWNS WAY
Snodland
Burham
Blue Bell Hill
Leaves Green
Downe
Pratt's Bottom
Shoreham
Fairseat
Vigo
Trottiscliffe
Birling
Cudham
Knockholt Pound
Halstead
Ryarsh
Priory
Eccles
Aylesford
Biggin Hill
Otford
Heaverham
Wrotham
New Hythe
Kemsing
Borough Green
Addington
Leybourne
Tatsfield
Chevening
Dunton Green
Seal
Ightham
West Malling
Offham
Ditton
Sandling
Allington
Chipstead
Riverhead
Wrotham Heath
Platt
St Leonards Tower
British Legion Village
East Malling
Brasted
Sundridge
SEVENOAKS
Knole
Great Comp
Claygate Cross
Old Soar
Mereworth
Wateringbury
Barming Heath
MAIDSTONE
Westerham
Brasted Chart
Quebec
Squerryes Court
Underriver
Plaxtol
Detillens
Limpsfield
Oxted
Ide Hill
Emmetts
Whitley Row
Black Charles
Shipbourne
Dunk's Green
West Peckham
Nettlestead
Nettlestead Green
West Farleigh
East Farleigh
Loose
Long Barn
Chartwell
Crockham Hill
Toy's Hill
Hurst Green
Sevenoaks Weald
Oakhurst
Hadlow
East Peckham
Hale Street
Yalding
Coxheath
Hunton
Hildenborough
Four Elms
Marlpit Hill
Linton
4
5
6
7

14
Chadwell St. Mary
Linford
Muckingford
East Tilbury
Low Street
TILBURY
Halstow Marshes
Allhallows-on-Sea
Allhallows
St. Mary's Hoo
Cuckold's Green
Stoke
ISLE OF GRAIN
Grain
Wallend
A228
B2001
Cliffe
Cooling
High Halstow
Church Street
Cooling Street
Fenn Street
Sharnal Street
North Street
GRAVESEND
Milton
Denton
Lower Higham
Chalk
Shorne
Cliffe Woods
Lee Green
Wainscott
Higham
Broad Street
Chattenden
Hoo
Lower Upnor
Upnor
Frindsbury
Strood
Thong
Henhurst
Shorne Ridgeway
A2
A226
ROCHESTER
Cobham
Owletts
Henley Street
Cuxton
Borstal
Luddesdown
Foxendown
Meopham
Meopham Green
North Halling
Halling
Priestwood Green
Harvel
Upper Halling
Holborough
Snodland
NORTH DOWNS WAY
Birling
Ryarsh
Addington
Leybourne
Offham
West Malling
East Malling
St Leonards Tower
Herne Pound
East Malling Heath
Wateringbury
Burham
Wouldham
Eccles
Aylesford
New Hythe
Larkfield
Ditton
Priory
British Legion Village
Allington
Sandling
Barming Heath
East Barming
Teston
Tovil
MAIDSTONE
Brompton
Grange
GILLINGHAM
CHATHAM
Luton
Wayfield
Capstone
Hempstead
Walderslade
Lidsing
Blue Bell Hill
Darland
Wigmore
Rainham
Moor Street
Farthing Corner
Hartlip
Bayford
Ham Green
Wetham Green
Upchurch
East Rainham
Otterham Quay
Lower Halstow
Iwade
Breach
Bobbing
Key Street
Newington
Howt Green
Kemsley
Milton Regis
SITTINGBOURNE
Sailing Barge Museum
Bapchild
Tonge Corner
Blacketts
Conyer
Teynham Street
Teynham
Luddenham Court
Uplees
The Swale
SHEERNESS
Marine Town
Mile Town
Halfway Houses
West Minster
Minster
Queenborough
Rushenden
Chetney
Eastchurch
Warden
Mud Row
Warden Point
ISLE OF SHEPPEY
ELMLEY ISLAND
ISLE OF HARTY
A249
A250
B2008
B2231
Bredhurst
Dunn Street
Stockbury
Hill Green
Oad Street
Borden
Tunstall
Rodmersham
Rodmersham Green
Highsted
Rawling Street
Newbury
Lewson Street
Lynsted
Deerton Street
FAVERSHAM
Oare
Davington Hill
Preston
Ospringe
Westfield Sole
Pollyfield
Lower Cox Street
South Green
Bredgar
Boxley
Hucking
Swanton Street
Bicknor
Baxon
Milsted
Dungate
Erriottwood
Hansletts Forstal
Painter's Forstal
Whitehill
Detling
Thurnham
Broad Street
Wormshill
Doddington
Frinsted
Newnham
Ringlestone
Seed
Tong
Eastling
Throwley
Wichling
Bearsted
Eyhorne Manor
Hollingbourne
Grove Green
Otham
Eyhorne Street
West Street
Tong Green
Leaveland
Badlesmere
Woodside Green
Harrietsham
Stalisfield Green
Caring
Leeds
Shepway
Otham Hole
Broomfield
Leeds Castle
Warren Street
East Lenham
Lenham
Lenham Heath
Stocker's Head
Charing Hill
Challock Lees
Kingswood
Langley
Five Wents
Chartway Street
Boughton Malherbe
Warmlake
East Sutton Park
Ulcombe
Liverton Street
Charing
Westwell Leacon
Westwell
Boughton Aluph
Boughton Lees
Grafty Green
Charing Heath
Egerton
Coppins Corner
Little Chart
Ram Lane
Goat Lees
Loose
East Farleigh
West Farleigh
Yalding
Coxheath
Hunton
Boughton Monchelsea
Cock Street
Boughton Monchelsea Place
Linton
Chart Sutton
Sutton Valence
Rabbit's Cross
Farthing Green
Jubilee Corner
Potter's Forstal
The Forstal
Southernden
Pivington
Hothfield
Plumtree Green
Headcorn
Bedlam Lane
Pluckley
Pluckley Thorne
Swift's Green
The Quarter
Chambers Green
Pluckley Station
Godinton Park
ASHFORD
Intelligence Corps Museum
Nettlestead
Nettlestead Green
Hale Street
Bush
East Peckham
Barnes Street
Beltring
Laddingford
Benover
Chainhurst
Stile Bridge
Mockbeggar
Collier Street
Underling Green
Cross-at-Hand
Milebush
Little Pattenden
Great Pattenden
Claygate
Fowlhall
Rhoden Green
Gain Hill
Queen Street
Paddock Wood
Badsell
Mile Oak
Matfield
Pearsons Green
Marden
Marden Beech
Marden Thorn
Wanshurst Green
Sweetlands Corner
Hawkenbury
Waterlane Farm
Staplehurst
Wheeler's Street
Biddenden Green
Smarden Bell
Smarden
Sinkhurst Green
Maltman's Hill
Great Chart
Pimphurst
Snoadhill
Daniel's Water
Bethersden
South Ashford
Beaver Green
Woolreeds Estate
Sevington
Castle Hill
The Corner
Brenchley
Burr's Hill
Winchet Hill
Curtisden Green
Knox Bridge
Lashenden
Romden Castle
Haffenden Quarter
Gillbam
Standen
Chilmington Green
Kingsnorth
Petteridge
Kipping's Cross
Horsmonden
Gravelhurst
Cranbrook Common
Frittenden
Curteis Corner
Stede Quarter
Further Quarter
High Halden
Tanden
Brissenden Green
Great Engeham
Shipley Hatch
Broad Ford
Goudhurst
Flishinghurst
Sissinghurst
Three Chimneys
Biddenden
Woolpack
Plurenden
Redbrook Street
Shadoxhurst
Henghurst
Bromley Green
Spelmonden
Iden Green
Wilsley Green
Glassenbury
Goose Green
Forest Green
Arcadia
Tiffenden
Owl House
Lamberhurst
Smugley
Cranbrook
Golford Green
East End
London Beach
St. Michaels
Shirkoak
Coldblow
Orlestone
Scotney Castle
Risedown
Hook Green
Lamberhurst Down
Bewlbridge
Kilndown
Hartley
Pinetum
Bedgebury Forest
Goddard's Green
Benenden
Beacon Hill
TENTERDEN
Leigh Green
Brook Street
Woodchurch
Kenardington
The Leacon
Hamstreet
Warehorne
Cousley Wood
Pell Green
Stonecrouch
Wadhurst
Whiligh
Three Leg Cross
Bewl Bridge Reservoir
Flimwell
Primrose Hill
High Street
Gill's Green
Iden Green
Strood
Kent & East Sussex Railway
Reading Street
Dale Hill
Union Street
Hawkhurst
Gun Green
Rolvenden
Historic Vehicles Collection
Great Maytham Hall
Rolvenden Layne
Small Hythe
Appledore Heath
Snave
Wallcrouch
Ticehurst
The Moor
Pour Throws
Kensham Green
Smallhythe Place
Appledore
Brenzett Green
Ivychurch
Bardown
The Horns
Stonegate
Little Conghurst
Conghurst
Peening Quarter
ISLE OF OXNEY
Snargate
Aeronautical Museum
Cooper's Corner
Burgh Hill
Hurst Green
Sandhurst
Sandhurst Cross
Newenden
Wittersham
The Stocks
Stone
Brenzett
Etchingham
Bodiam
Northiam
Brookland
A259
Southover
Holton Hill
Robertsbridge Aeronautical Museum
Salehurst
Bodiam
Great Dixter
Four Oaks
Old Romney
Copper's Green Hill
Burwash
Batemans
Northbridge Street
Ewhurst
Staple Cross
Brickwall
Peasmarsh
Iden
Lower Bosney
Robertsbridge
Millcorner
Collier's Green
Clayhill
Beckley
Rye Foreign
Houghton Green
WALLAND MARSH
Gudeford Lane Corner
East Guldeford
Burwash Weald
Vinehall
KENT
EAST SUSSEX
NORTH DOWNS

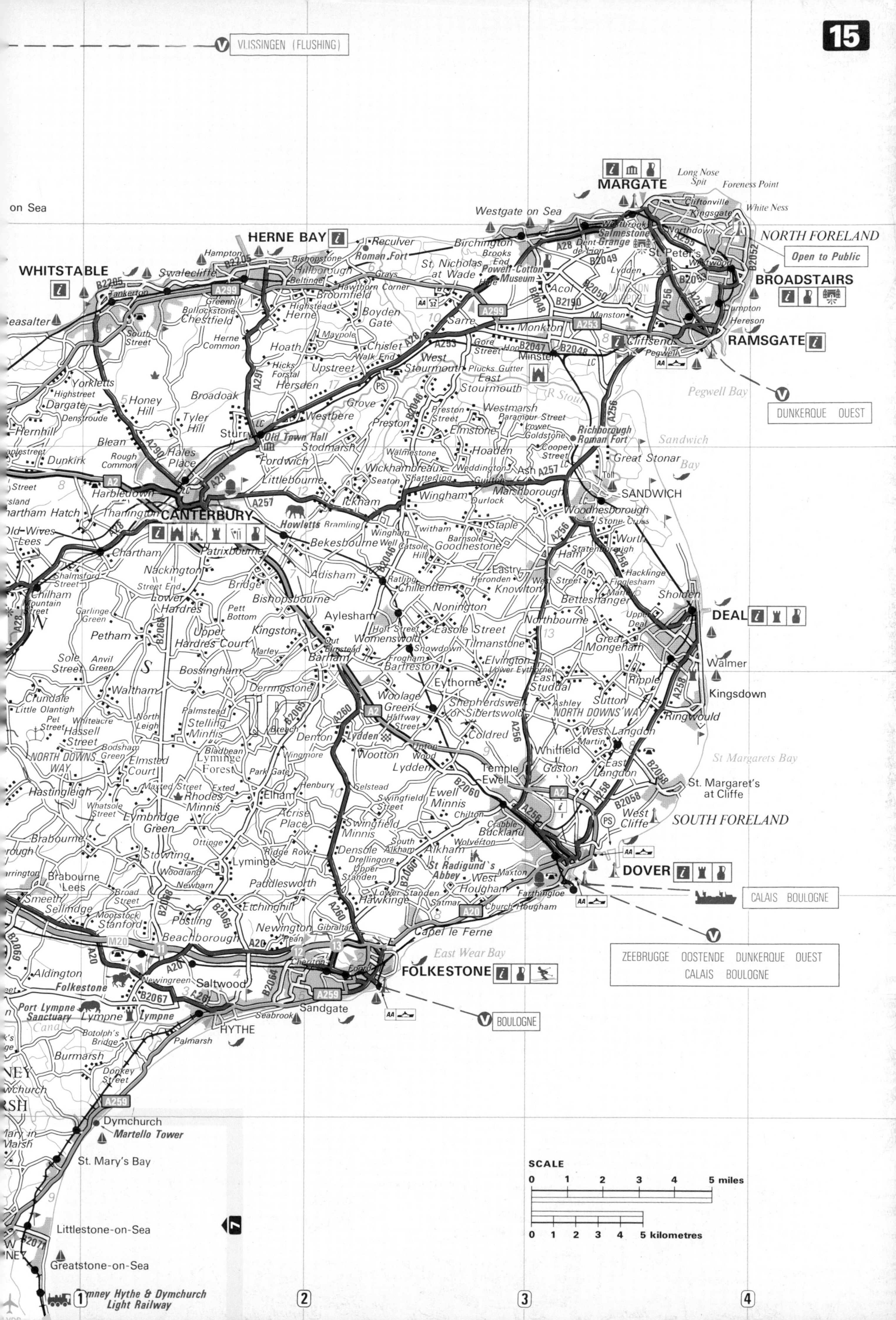
VLISSINGEN (FLUSHING)
MARGATE
Long Nose Spit
Foreness Point
Cliftonville
Kingsgate
White Ness
NORTH FORELAND
Open to Public
BROADSTAIRS
RAMSGATE
Pegwell Bay
DUNKERQUE OUEST
Westgate on Sea
Birchington
HERNE BAY
Reculver
Roman Fort
WHITSTABLE
Swalecliffe
Tankerton
Seasalter
Herne
Hoath
Chislet
Sarre
Monkton
Minster
Manston
Acol
St. Nicholas at Wade
Powell-Cotton Museum
Cliffsend
Pegwell
Sturry
Old Town Hall
Fordwich
CANTERBURY
Harbledown
Thanington
Chartham
Blean
Dunkirk
Littlebourne
Howletts
Bekesbourne
Patrixbourne
Wingham
Ickham
Sandwich
SANDWICH
Great Stonar
Richborough Roman Fort
Woodnesborough
Eastry
Ash
Staple
Adisham
Aylesham
Nonington
Barham
Bishopsbourne
Bridge
Kingston
Petham
Chilham
Waltham
Elham
Denton
Lydden
Temple Ewell
Whitfield
Coldred
Shepherdswell or Sibertswold
Eythorne
Northbourne
DEAL
Walmer
Kingsdown
Ringwould
Sholden
Betteshanger
St Margarets Bay
St. Margaret's at Cliffe
SOUTH FORELAND
West Cliffe
DOVER
CALAIS BOULOGNE
ZEEBRUGGE OOSTENDE DUNKERQUE OUEST
CALAIS BOULOGNE
Capel le Ferne
East Wear Bay
FOLKESTONE
Sandgate
Seabrook
BOULOGNE
Hawkinge
Alkham
Swingfield Minnis
Lyminge
Paddlesworth
Etchinghill
Newington
Postling
Stanford
Sellindge
Brabourne
Stowting
Hastingleigh
Saltwood
HYTHE
Palmarsh
Lympne
Port Lympne Sanctuary
Aldington
Burmarsh
Dymchurch
Martello Tower
St. Mary's Bay
Littlestone-on-Sea
Greatstone-on-Sea
Romney Hythe & Dymchurch Light Railway
A2
A20
A28
A256
A258
A259
A260
A299
M20
SCALE
0 1 2 3 4 5 miles
0 1 2 3 4 5 kilometres
1
2
3
4

16
Lower Buckenhill
Sollers Hope
Bounds
Much Marcle
Donnington
Bromsberrow Heath
Portway
M50
Pendock
White End
Long Green
Hardwick Green
Eldersfield
TEWKESBURY
A38
Walton Cardiff
Ashchurch
Pamington
Ballingham
Falcon
Lyne Down
Stocking
Dymock
Greenway
Broome Green
Ryton
Redmarley D'Abitot
Playley Green
Lowbands
Lime Street
Forthampton
Linkend
Chaceley
Odda's Chapel
Fiddington
How Caple
Yatton
Fawley Chapel
Kempley
Kempley Green
Fishpool
Hole-in-the-Wall
Poolhill
Hethelpit Cross
Pillows Green
Corse Lawn
Town Street
Deerhurst
Apperley
Tredington
Stoke Orchard
A417
A449
B4024
B4208
B4211
B4213
Hill of Eaton
Upton Crews
Upton Bishop
Four Oaks
Botloe's Green
Brand Green
Staunton
Oridge Green
Snigs End
Tirley
Deerhurst Walton
Brampton Abbotts
Shaw Common
Oxenhall
Upleadon
The Haw
Coombe Hill
Hardwicke
Elmstone Hardwicke
Gorsley
B4221
B4215
Hasfield
The Stream
Lower Apperley
Leigh
Pitt's Elm
Bridstow
ROSS-ON-WYE
Rudhall
Linton
Gorsley Common
Kilcot
B4227
Newent
Blackwellsend Green
Hartpury
Corse
Tithe Barn
Ashleworth
Boddington
Barrow
Uckington
Swindon
Little Gorsley
Anthony's Green
Bishop's Norton
Prior's Norton
A40
Aston Crews
Bromsash
Ryeford
B4222
Aston Ingham
Clifford's Mesne
Kent's Green
Highleadon
Norton
Staverton
Golden Valley
Ashfield
Tudorville
B4228
Weston under Penyard
Crews Hill
Woolridge
Down Hatherley
Staverton Bridge
Sandhurst
Coughton
Lea
Glasshouse
Taynton
Tibberton
Rudford
Maisemore
Twigworth
GLOUCESTER CHELTENHAM
Goodrich
Howle Hill
Pontshill
Boxbush
Glasshouse Hill
Bright's Hill
Highnam Green
Woodgreen
Highnam
Over
Longford
Churchdown
Up Hatherley
Walford
Hope Mansell
East Dean
Dursley Cross
Little London
Huntley
Bulley
Badgeworth
Leckhampton
Kerne Bridge
Kiln Green
Mitcheldean
Crooked End
A4136
Longhope
Abenhall
Birdwood
Nottswood Hill
Oakle Street
Churcham
Linton
Barnwood
Hucclecote
Shurdington
Ruardean
B4227
Drybrook
Blaisdon
Upper Ley
Calcott's Green
Minsterworth
GLOUCESTER
A48
Brockworth
The Butts
Bentham
Ullenwood
Ruardean Woodside
Ruardean Hill
Nailbridge
Flaxley
Northwood Green
Elmore Back
Hempsted
A4173
Roman Villa
Little Witcombe
English Bicknor
Brierley
Cinderford
Westbury Court
Farleys End
Elmore
Tuffley
Robinswood Hill
Upton St. Leonards
Great Witcombe
Birdlip
Stockwell
Upper Lydbrook
Broadmoor
Bilson Green
Elton
Chaxhill
Stantway
Waterend
Quedgeley
Bondend
Prinknash
Cranham
Dean Hall
A4151
Littledean
Westbury-on-Severn
Hardwicke
Whaddon
Edge End
B4226
Broadoak
Newnham
Boxbush
Longney
Four Mile Elm
Brookthorpe
Prinknash Bird Park
Brimpsfield
Five Acres
FOREST OF DEAN
Ruspidge
Rodley
Epney
Paradise
Sheepscombe
Mile End
Cannop
Ruddle
Upper Soudley
Milton End
Farestield
Whiteway
Caudle Green
Broadwell
B4221
Arlingham
Upper Framilode
Moreton Valence
Edge
Painswick
Syde
Milkwall
Ancient Iron Mines
B4234
Lower Soudley
207
Saul
M5
Harescombe
Wishanger
Miserden
Winstone
Duntisbourne
B4431
Parkend
Aylford
Northington
Awre
Standish
Pitchcombe
Slad
B4070
The Camp
Throughman
Ellwood
Brain's Green
Whitminster
Stroud Green
881
Sudgrove
Yorkley
Blakeney Hill
Blakeney
Frampton on Severn
B4071
Randwick
Whiteshill
Duntisbourne Abbots
Bream's Meend
Nibley
Claypits
Westend
Nastend
Alkerton
B4419
Stonehouse
Ebley
A46
STROUD
Bisley
Edgeworth
Duntisbourne
Dean Forest Railway Society
Whitecroft
Bream
Oldcroft
Etloe
A48
Purton
River Severn
Middle Street
Eastington
Nashend
Eastcombe
Bournes Green
Daglingworth
Briavels
Lydney
Allaston
Wildfowl Trust
Shepherd's Patch
Dudbridge
King's Stanley
Selsley
Bussage
Chalford
Far Oakridge
Sapperton
Primrose Hill
Sharpness
Newerne
Purton
Slimbridge
Moorend
Cambridge
Frocester
Leonard Stanley
B4066
Thrupp
Brimscombe
Oakridge
Hewelsfield
Aylburton Common
Tutnalls
Brookend
Halmore
Gossington
Coaley
Woodchester
Frampton Mansell
Aylburton
Newtown
St Chloe
Burleigh
Hyde
Alvington
Wanswell
Lower Cam
Far Green
Amberley
Minchinhampton
Breadstone
Ashmead Green
Nympsfield
Windsoredge
Crackstone
Berkeley
Hook Street
B4066
The Quarry
Berkeley Road
Cam
Uley Bury
NAILSWORTH
Box
Ball's Green
Cherington
Tarlton
Berkeley Heath
Crawley
Downend
B4014
Ham
Stinchcombe
Uley
B4058
Horsley
Rodmarton
Nag's Head
Bevington
Newport
Lower Wick
Dursley
Owlpen
Avening
Barton End
Woodmancote
812
Nupdown
Hystfield
Woodford
Nibley Green
Millend
A4135
Tiltups End
Culkerton
Upper Hill
Hill
B4059
North Nibley
Pitt Court
Kingscote
Chavenage
Tetbury Upton
Ashley
Shepperdine
Stone
Lower Stone
B4060
Bournstream
Newington Bagpath
Chelworth
Oldbury Naite
Rockhampton
Damery
Tortworth
Wotton-under-Edge
Lasborough
Beverston
Tetbury
Crudwell
Falfield
B4058
Kingswood
Boxwell
Pullens Green
Oldbury-on-Severn
Lower Morton
Whitfield
B4509
Wortley
Long Newnton
Murcott
Cowhill
Littleton-on-Severn
Morton
Milbury Heath
Bibstone
Charfield
Leighterton
B4014
Hankerton
Townwell
Talbot's End
Alderley
Tresham
Westonbirt Aboretum
A433
Doughton
Kington
Thornbury
Cromhall
Cromhall Common
B4061
Hillesley
Lower Kilcott
Westonbirt
Shipton Moyne
Brokenborough
Elberton
Filands
Charlton
A38
Gravesend
Oldbury on the Hill
Upper Kilcott
Starveall
Willesley
MALMESBURY
B4461
Olveston
Old Down
Alveston
West End
Wickwar
Hawkesbury Upton
Knockdown
Didmarton
Easton Grey
Milbourne
Green Hill
Tytherington
Itchington
Bagstone
Hawkesbury
Sherston
Foxley
Lea
Awkley
M4
Rudgeway
Rangeworthy
Dunkirk
Sopworth
B4042
Tockington
Woodhouse Down
Earthcott Green
Horton Court
657
B4040
Foxley Green
Almondsbury
M5
Latteridge
B4059
Engine Common
Horton
Petty France
Luckington
Corston
A429
Little Somerford
Gaunt's Earthcott
Iron Acton
Little Sodbury End
Little Badminton
A46
Badminton
Norton
Over
B4055
Frampton Cotterell
Chipping Sodbury
Little Sodbury
Great Badminton
Alderton
Rodbourne
Patchway
Watley's End
Nibley
Yate
Old Sodbury
Hullavington
New Town
Startley
Catbrain
B4057
Great Stoke
Coalpit Heath
A432
Dodington
Lower Stanton St. Quintin
Lower Seagry
Seagry Heath
Winterbourne
Ram Hill
Rudford
Wapley
B4040
Acton Turville
Littleton Drew
Grittleton
Stanton St. Quintin
Upper Seagry
Filton
Stoke Gifford
Westerleigh
Kendleshire
Doddington
Leigh Delamere
Sutton Benger
A4174
Hambrook
Mogreen
Codrington
B4465
Tormarton
Burton
B4039
Sevington
Horfield
Frenchay
M32
MANGOTSFIELD
Nettleton
Upper Draycot
Foxham
Lockleaze
Blackhorse
Hinton
M4
Castle Combe
Kington St. Michael
Kington Langley
Redland
B4056
B4058
A432
Downend
Pucklechurch
West Kington
Castle Combe
Yatton Keynell
Soundwell
B4465
Dyrham Park
Dyrham
West Littleton
North Wraxall
Ford
West Yatton
Allington
B4279
Langley
GLOUCESTER
SO
ST
AVON
WILTS

17
Seven Wells
Batsford Arboretum
Bourton-on-the-Hill
Dorn
Batsford
Great Wolford
Wolford
Long Compton
Norton
Alderton
Toddington
Stanway
Snowshill
4
New Town
A438
B4078
A44
Moreton-in-Marsh
Barton-on-the-Heath
24
A34
Great Rollright
Swerford
Didbrook
Taddington
Stumps Cross
Cutsdean
1001
Sezincote
A424
A429
Longborough
Greet
Hailes
Gretton
Hailes Abbey
Ford
Farmcote
Evenlode
Little Compton
Little Rollright
Rollright Stones
A361
Winchcombe
B4077
Condicote
Donnington
Temple Guiting
Cotswolds Farm Park
Chastleton
Salford
Over Norton
Dunthrop
Little Tew
Broadwell
Adlestrop
Heythrop
Sudeley Castle & Gardens
Kineton
Upper Swell
Stow-on-the-Wold
A436
Cornwell
B4450
CHIPPING NORTON
Old Chalford
Church Enstone
B4022
Belas Knap
Chalk Hill
Lower Swell
Barton
Oddington
Daylesford
Charlton Abbots
Guiting Power
B4068
Maugersbury
Churchill
Lidstone
B4030
Naunton
Upper Slaughter
Kingham
Enstone
A34
HAM
Hawling
Brockhampton
Wick Rissington
Icomb
B4026
Chadlington
Fulwell
Sarsden
Dean
Taston
Aylworth
Lower Slaughter
Bledington
Foscot
Kiddington
Sevenhampton
Bourton-on-the-Water
Gawcombe
Westcote
Nether Westcote
Lyneham
Greenend
Spelsbury
Ditchley
Ditchley Park
Whittington
A436
Notgrove
Model Village
Syreford
Hampden
A40
Idbury
Chilson
Charlbury
Andoversford
Salperton
Cold Aston
Shipton Oliffe
Shipton
Little Rissington
A424
Fifield
Ascott-under-Wychwood
B4437
Compton Abdale
Hazleton
Turkdean
Clapton-on-the-Hill
Milton-under-Wychwood
Shipton-under-Wychwood
Fawler
Finstock
18
A429
Great Rissington
Farmington
Langley
Leafield
Hampnett
Northfield Barn
B4437
Ramsden
Withington
Cassey Compton
SP
Great Barrington
Taynton
A361
South Lawn
B4022
Roman Villa
East End
Yanworth
Oxpens
Northleach
A40
Sherborne
Westhall Hill
Fulbrook
Fordwells
Whiteoak Green
New Yatt
Roman Villa
Windrush
Swinbrook
Delly End
Asthall Leigh
Hailey
Eastington
Little Barrington
Upton
Widford
A435
Chedworth
Burford
Asthall
Minster Lovell
Crawley
A4095
A433
Fossebridge
Coln St. Dennis
B4047
Minster Lovell Hall
WITNEY
Rendcomb
Aldsworth
Signet
B4020
A40
Charterville Allotments
Newland
Calcot
Westwell
Coln Rogers
Kilkenny
Holwell
A361
Calmsden
Winson
16
Bradwell Grove
Curbridge
High Cogges
North Cerney
Cotswold Wild Life Park
Shilton
Ablington
Brize Norton
Ducklington
R Leach
A4095
Arlington
A433
Bibury
Carterton
Bagendon
Barnsley House Garden
Eastleach Turville
BRIZE NORTON
OXFORDSHIRE
A415
Cokethorpe
Hardwick
Eastleach Martin
Kencot
Alvescot
Lew
Coln St. Aldwyns
Yelford
A435
A429
Wiggold
Hatherop
Filkins
Black Bourton
Brighthampton
A417
Baunton
Barnsley
Broughton Poggs
Aston
Quenington
Fyfield
Broadwell
B4449
A433
Ampney Crucis
Sunhill
B4020
Bampton
Cote
Ampney St. Mary
Southrop
Weald
Standlake
Fairford Park
Langford
NCESTER
Betty's Grave
Little Faringdon
Little Clanfield
Clanfield
Shifford
A417
Ampney St. Peter
Poulton
Fairford
Newbridge
R Thames
A429
Chesterton
Milton End
Grafton
Chimney
Preston
A417
Harnhill
Radcot
Carswell Marsh
Duxford
Longworth
Siddington
A419
Poulton Priory
Meysey Hampton
Horcott
Welford
Lechlade
Kelmscot
Thrup
Hinton Waldrist
Driffield
Driffield Cross Roads
Inglesham
Eaton Hastings
Buckland
Southmoor
Ewen
South Cerney
Marston Meysey
Dunfield
Kempsford
A361
Down Ampney
A417
Buscot
Littleworth
Pusey
Kingston Bagpuize
Shorncote
Down Ampney
River Thames
Upper Inglesham
Buscot Park
A420
Pusey
Upperup
North End
Cerney Wick
Latton
Faringdon
Charney Bassett
Hatford
Castle Eaton
Hannington Wick
A417
B4508
Kent End
Ashton Keynes
Somerford Keynes
SU
Coleshill
Shellingford
Cricklade
Great Coxwell Barn
River Ock
Stanford in the Vale
Chelworth Upper Green
B4041
Calcutt
Westrop
B4019
Little Coxwell
Great Coxwell
Minety Lower Moor
Hannington
Hampton
Eastrop
Highworth
Goosey
Fernham
Chelworth Lower Green
Leigh
Brook
B4040
Minety
Purton Stoke
A419
Broad Blunsdon
Blunsdon Hill
Stanton Fitzwarren
B4508
Watchfield
Baulking
Denchworth
Grove
B4019
B4000
Longcot
A417
A361
Sevenhampton
Blunsdon St. Andrew
B4534
A4311
Braydon
Red Lodge
Purton
Haydon Wick
Kingsdown
Upper Stratton
South Marston
Shrivenham
Uffington
West Challow
East Challow
Queen Street
Woolstone
Kingston Lisle
Sparsholt
Dogridge
Green Hill
Lydiard Green
Common Platt
B4006
Stratton St. Margaret
A420
Bourton
Compton Beauchamp
Childrey
The Common
Lydiard Millicent
Gorse Hill
Nine Elms
Greatfield
514
Wayland's Smithy
Hill Figure
Letcombe Regis
Callow Hill
B4041
Hook
Lydiard Park
B4006
Walcot
Ashbury
Uffington Castle
Letcombe Bassett
B4042
Toothill
SWINDON
Horpit
Bishopstone
Idstone
Lambourn Downs
A338
A3102
AA 24 hour
Coate
A419
Dauntsey Green
Wootton Bassett
16
Grittenham
Nore Marsh
A4361
A4259
Hinton Parva
Wanborough
Ashdown
B4001
Fawley
A3102
B4005
Wroughton
North Wroughton
M4
15
Liddington
THE RIDGEWAY PATH
B4000
Upper Lambourn
Tockenham Wick
Lyneham
Elcombe
B4005
Wroughton
Tockenham
B4041
Broadtown Lane
Thornhill
Overtown
Chiseldon
Badbury
South Fawley
10
LYNEHAM
Church End
Wroughton
Broad Town
Draycot Foliat
B4192
Lambourn
Lambourn
9
Preston
Bushton
A4361
Uffcott
Barbury Castle
9
Upper Upham
Baydon
East Garston
Goatacre
Clyffe Pypard
Broad Hinton
A3
2
1
Woodsend
13
12
Eastbury
3
B4000
Woodlands
Clevancy
Aldbourne
Great

18
NORTHAMPTONSHIRE
OXFORDSHIRE
BERKSHIRE
Brailes
Sibford Gower
Swalcliffe
Broughton
Newington
Tadmarton
Stourton
Sibford Ferris
Bodicote
Twyford Gardens
Adderbury
Bloxham
Milton
Upper Astrop
Astrop
Newbottle
King's Sutton
Charlton
Walton Grounds
Rowler
Farthinghoe
Steane
BRACKLEY
Whitfield
Turweston
Dadford
Akeley
Stowe House
Shalstone
Chackmore
Hinton-in-the-Hedges
R. Great Ouse
Evenley
Westbury
Water Stratford
Radclive
Finmere
Mixbury
Whichford
Ascott
Hook Norton
Milcombe
Barford St John
Barford St. Michael
R. Swere
Wigginton
South Newington
Clifton
Aynho
Croughton
Little Tingewick
Tingewick
Mount Gawcott
Great Rollright
Swerford
Hempton
Deddington
Souldern
Cottisford
Newton Purcell
Barton Hartshorn
Hillesden
Preston Bissett
Nether Worton
Potato Town
Great Tew
Little Tew
Dunthorp
Over Worton
North Aston
Duns Tew
Hardwick
Baynard's Green
Hethe
Chetwode
Fritwell
Fewcott
Stoke Lyne
Fringford
Godington
Cowley
Twyford
Heythrop
Sandford St. Martin
Ledwell
Middle Barton
Somerton
Middle Aston
Steeple Aston
Ardley
Upper Heyford
Bucknell
Bainton
Stratton Audley
Poundon
CHIPPING NORTON
Old Chalford
Church Enstone
Gagingwell
Westcott Barton
Steeple Barton
Lower Heyford
Caversfield
BICESTER
Woodfield
Charndon
Calvert
Lidstone
Enstone
R. Glyme
Caulcott
Rousham
Middleton Stoney
Northbrook
Highfield
Town's End
Launton
Marsh Gibbon
Edgcott
Chadlington
Dean
Taston
Over Kiddington
Kiddington
Ditchley
Glympton
Tackley
R. Dorn
Chesterton
Greenend
Spelsbury
Ditchley Park
Grendon Underwood
R. Ray
Chilson
Charlbury
Wootton
Kirtlington
Wendlebury
Blackthorn
Ascott-under-Wychwood
Fawler
WOODSTOCK
Old Woodstock
Bletchingdon
Weston-on-the-Green
Ambrosden
Ludgershall
Finstock
Stonesfield
Shipton-on-Cherwell
Merton
Arncott
Piddington
Leafield
Blenheim Palace
Thrupp
Hampton Poyle
Charlton-on-Otmoor
Fencott
Murcott
Wotton Underwood
Ramsden
Combe
Long Hanborough
Bladon
R. Cherwell
Boarstall Duck Decoy & Nature Reserve
Boarstall
Dorton
Whiteoak Green
Roman Villa
East End
OXFORD AIRPORT
Islip
Oddington
Brill
Upper Pollicott
Lower Pollicott
Field Assarts
New Yatt
Delly End
Begbroke
Kidlington
Noke
Studley
Asthall Leigh
Hailey
North Leigh
Church Hanborough
Water Eaton
Beckley
Little London
Oakley
Chilton
Crawley
Minster Lovell
Freeland
Cassington
Yarnton
Woodeaton
Studley Priory Hotel
Woodperry
Stanton St. John
Easington
WITNEY
Barnard Gate
Minster Lovell Hall
Eynsham
Sunnymead
Elsfield
Church End
Curbridge
South Leigh
Toll
Wytham
Wolvercote
Summertown
Binsey
Worminghall
Peppershill
Ickford
Lower End
Forest Hill
Brize Norton
High Cogges
Swinford
Farmoor
Marston
New Marston
Barton
Holton
Waterperry
Shabbington
Ducklington
Sutton
Farmoor Reservoir
Stanton Harcourt
AA 24 hour
Headington
Hardwick
Cokethorpe
Botley
Dean Court
North Hinksey
Osney
Horspath
Wheatley
Draycot
Waterstock
Albury
Rycote Chapel
Tiddington
Lew
Yelford
West End
Brighthampton
OXFORD
Cumnor
Eaton
Cutts End
Iffley
Cowley
Cuddesdon
Milton Common
Moreton
Aston
Northmoor
Bessels Leigh
Wootton
Boars Hill
Kennington
Littlemore
Blenheim
Denton
Great Milton
Great Haseley
Tetsworth
Bampton
Weald
Cote
Standlake
Rock End
Appleton
Sandleigh
Sandford-on-Thames
Garsington
Southend
Latchford
Little Haseley
Shifford
Newbridge
R. Thames or Isis
Chimney
Sunningwell
Toot Baldon
Little Milton
Adwell
Carswell Marsh
Duxford
Longworth
Dry Sandford
Cothill
Radley
Marsh Baldon
Chislehampton
Stoke Talmage
Hinton Waldrist
Eyfield
Shippon
Nuneham Courtenay
Stadhampton
Wheatfield
South Weston
Buckland
Southmoor
Tubney
1643
Easington
Lewknor
ABINGDON
Golden Balls
Berinsfield
Chalgrove
Pusey
Kingston Bagpuize
Frilford
Fyfield Wick
Nuneham
Clifton Hampden
Newington
Pyrton
Garford
Marcham
Caldecott
Burcot
Drayton St. Leonard
Cuxham
Hatford
Charney Bassett
Sutton Wick
Culham
Appleford
Dorchester
Berrick Prior
Berrick Salome
Brightwell Baldwin
Watlington
River Ock
Drayton
Warborough
Stanford in the Vale
Lyford
East Hanney
Sutton Courtenay
Long Wittenham
Little Wittenham
Overy
Pendon
Shillingford
Britwell Salome
Shellingford
Goosey
West Hanney
Steventon
Milton
Milton Manor
Railway Museum
Wittenham Clumps
Benson
Ewelme
Greenfield
Baulking
Denchworth
Priory Cottages
Milton Hill
Didcot
Preston Crowmarsh
Grove
Ardington Wick
West Hendred
Brightwell
Mackney
WALLINGFORD
Cookley Green
Uffington
West Challow
East Challow
Ardington
Harwell
North Moreton
Park Corner
Kingston Lisle
Sparsholt
Charlton
West Lockinge
East Hendred
West Hagbourne
East Hagbourne
South Moreton
Winterbrook
Crowmarsh Gifford
Nettlebed
WANTAGE
Childrey
Letcombe Regis
Upton
Aston Upthorpe
Cholsey
West End
Aston Tirrold
Nuffield
Hailey
Hill Figure
West Ginge
East Ginge
Chilton
Blewbury
North Stoke
Ipsden
Wellplace Bird Farm
Highmoor
Letcombe Bassett
Stoke Row
Lambourn Downs
West Ilsley
THE RIDGEWAY PATH
871
Moulsford
South Stoke
Checkendon
Shepherd's Green
Rotherfield Peppard
Upper Lambourn
Fawley
Farnborough
East Ilsley
Streatley
Woodcote
Exlade Street
Greenmoor Hill
Cray's
Sonning
SU
A34
A361
A43
A422
A423
A41
A413
A421
A4095
A4260
A44
A40
A420
A415
A4144
A4158
A4142
A418
A329
A4074
A4130
A4183
A338
A417
A4185
A34
B4031
B4030
B4022
B4026
B4027
B4437
B4044
B4449
B4017
B480
B4015
B4009
B4016
B4493
B4494
B4001
B4508
B4011
B4047
B4526
B4471
B481

19
MILTON KEYNES
Passenham
Calverton
Leckhampstead
Upper Weald
Loughton
Shenley Church End
Beachampton
Shenley Brook End
Thornton
Thornborough
Nash
Whaddon
BLETCHLEY
Fenny Stratford
Wavendon
Walton
Simpson
Bow Brickhill
Woburn Sands
Aspley Guise
Little Brickhill
Brogborough
Lidlington
Millbrook
Houghton
AMPTHILL
Ridgmont
Husborne Crawley
Higher Berry End
Eversholt
Woburn
Woburn Abbey
Steppingley
Flitwick
Westoning
Maulden
Clophill
Silsoe
Wrest Park
Flitton
Greenfield
Pulloxhill
Higham Gobion
Barton in the Clay
Harlington
Tingrith
Milton Bryan
Potsgrove
Battlesden
Toddington
Sharpenhoe
Upper Sundon
Streatley
Great Horwood
Singleborough
Little Horwood
Newton Longville
Great Brickhill
Adstock
Winslow
Mursley
Drayton Parslow
Stoke Hammond
Heath and Reach
Addington
Soulbury
Swanbourne
North End
Stewkley
Hockliffe
Tebworth
LEIGHTON BUZZARD
LINSLADE
Wingfield
Chalton
Lower Sundon
Sundon Park
Lilley
Stopsley
East Claydon
Hoggeston
Granborough
Dunton
Wing
Ascott
Eggington
Tilsworth
Stanbridge
Houghton Regis
Leagrave
North Marston
Cublington
Billington
Totternhoe
DUNSTABLE
Oving
Quainton
Whitchurch
Ledburn
Slapton
Eaton Bray
Mentmore
Pitchcott
Aston Abbotts
Quainton Railway Society
Hardwick
Wingrave
Crafton
Horton
Edlesborough
Dunstable Downs
Whipsnade
Kensworth
Caddington
Kensworth Common
Waddesdon
Weedon
Rowsham
Cheddington
Ivinghoe
Ivinghoe Aston
Long Marston
Dagnall
Markyate
HARPENDEN
Waddesdon Manor
AYLESBURY
Bierton
Hulcott
Pitstone
Studham
Upper Winchendon
Burcott
Astrope
Puttenham
Marsworth
Ringshall
Little Gaddesden
Flamstead
Lower Winchendon
Lower Hartwell
Hartwell
Stone
Aston Clinton
Wilstone
Buckland
New Mill
TRING
Aldbury
Ashridge Management College
Great Gaddesden
Redbourn
Upton
Weston Turville
Stoke Mandeville
Westlington
Halton
Hastoe
Wigginton
Nettleden
Water End
Cuddington
Bishopstone
Ford
Wendover
THE RIDGEWAY PATH
Northchurch
Dudswell
Berkhamsted
Piccotts End
Potten End
Haddenham
Kimble Wick
North Lee
Nash Lee
Aston Sandford
Kimble
St. Leonards
Cholesbury
HEMEL HEMPSTEAD
Owlswick
THE THREE HUNDREDS OF AYLESBURY
BERKHAMSTED
Kingsey
Meadle
Ellesborough
Buckland Common
Kingsash
Lee Gate
Bellingdon
Ashley Green
Bourne End
Boxmoor
Two Waters
Longwick
Askett
Dunsmore
The Lee
Lee Clump
Chartridge
Whelpley Hill
Felden
Bedmond
Towersey
The Ford
Pitch Green
Princes Risborough
Hampden
Ballinger Common
Bovingdon
Henton
Bledlow
Parkfield
Great Missenden
CHESHAM
Lye Green
Ley Hill
Chipperfield
Kings Langley
Abbots Langley
Saunderton
South Heath
Botley
Hampden Row
Hyde Heath
Chinnor
Loosley Row
Flaunden
Bucks Hill
Oakley
Crowell
Lacey Green
Prestwood
Little Kingshill
Latimer
Sarratt
Kingston Blount
Speen
Great Kingshill
Chesham Bois
Little Chalfont
Chenies
WATFORD
Bledlow Ridge
Upper North Dean
Heath End
Little Missenden
Radnage
Hughenden Valley
Holmer Green
AMERSHAM
CHORLEYWOOD
Chandler's Cross
The City
Stokenchurch
Bradenham
Naphill
Hughenden Manor
Penn Street
Coleshill
Croxley Green
Beacon's Bottom
West Wycombe
Hazlemere
Winchmore Hill
Chalfont St. Giles
Heronsgate
Ibstone Common
Downley
Tylers Green
RICKMANSWORTH
West Wycombe Park
HIGH WYCOMBE
Cadmore End
Penn
Seer Green
Chalfont Common
Maple Cross
South Oxhey
Ibstone
Wycombe Marsh
Horn Hill
West Hyde
Turville
Bolter End
Fingest
Lane End
Booker
Bekonscot Model Village
Loudwater
Jordans
Harefield
Eastbury
Summer Heath
Skirmett
Flackwell Heath
BEACONSFIELD
Chalfont St. Peter
Northwood
Stonor Park
Frieth
Chisbridge Cross
Little Marlow
Marlow Bottom
Wooburn Moor
Wooburn Green
Gerrards Cross
Denham Green
Stonor
Parmoor
Rockwell End
Eastcote
Lower Woodend
Bovingdon Green
Wooburn
Hedsor
Hedgerley
Hedgerley Green
Pheasant's Hill
Fawley
Hambleden
MARLOW
Bourne End
Cores End
Burnham Beeches
Littleworth Common
Denham
Ruislip
Mill End
Lower Assendon
Medmenham
Bisham
Bisham Abbey
Cookham
Cookham Dean
Cookham Rise
Dropmore
Cliveden
Farnham Common
Fulmer
Ickenham
Northolt
Remenham
Aston
Remenham Hill
Hurley
Park Corner
East Burnham
Farnham Royal
Stoke Poges
Iver Heath
Iver
New Denham
North Hillingdon
Uxbridge
HILLINGDON
HENLEY ON THAMES
Cockpole Green
MAIDENHEAD
Burchett's Green
Littlewick
Taplow
Lent
Burnham
Stoke Green
Wexham
Love Green
Shreding
Cowley
Harpsden
LUTON AIRPORT
Luton Hoo
East Hyde
Verulamium Theatre
Gorhambury
Primrosehill
M1
M25
M40
A5
A6
A41
A413
A418
A4010
A404
A355
A40
A412
A4146
A421

20
MILTON KEYNES
Wavendon
Woburn Sands
Brogborough
Lidlington
Millbrook
Houghton
Clophill
Shefford
Henlow
Campton
AMPTHILL
Maulden
Upper Gravenhurst
Meppershall
Ridgmont
Husborne Crawley
Steppingley
Flitton
Wrest Park
Silsoe
Arlesey
BLETCHLEY
Bow Brickhill
Aspley Guise
Flitwick
Greenfield
Shillington
Upper Stondon
Fenny Stratford
Little Brickhill
Woburn
Eversholt
Westoning
Pulloxhill
Higham Gobion
Apsley End
Holwell
Ickleford
Woburn Abbey
Tingrith
Milton Bryan
Harlington
Barton in the Clay
Hexton
Pirton
Great Brickhill
Newton Longville
Potsgrove
Battlesden
Sharpenhoe
HITCHIN
Stoke Hammond
Heath and Reach
Toddington
Upper Sundon
Streatley
Drayton Parslow
Soulbury
Hockliffe
Tebworth
Lower Sundon
Great Offley
Gosmore
LEIGHTON BUZZARD
LINSLADE
Stewkley
Wingfield
Chalton
Sundon Park
Lilley
Preston
Eggington
Tilsworth
Stopsley
Cockernhoe Green
Dunton
Wing
Stanbridge
Houghton Regis
Leagrave
King's Walden
St. Paul's Walden
Ascott
Cublington
Billington
Totternhoe
LUTON
Breachwood Green
Ledburn
Slapton
Eaton Bray
DUNSTABLE
Church End
LUTON AIRPORT
Astor Abbotts
Mentmore
Northall
Edlesborough
Caddington
Whitwell
Wingrave
Crafton
Horton
Dunstable Downs
Kensworth
Slip End
Luton Hoo
Kimpton
Codicote
Rowsham
Cheddington
Whipsnade
Kensworth Common
East Hyde
Ivinghoe Aston
Long Marston
Ivinghoe
HARPENDEN
Bierton
Hulcott
Pitstone
Dagnall
Markyate
Ayot St. Lawrence
Shaw's Corner
Studham
Puttenham
Marsworth
Ringshall
Little Gaddesden
Flamstead
Aston Clinton
Buckland
New Mill
Ashridge Management College
Redbourn
Wheathampstead
Weston Turville
TRING
Aldbury
Great Gaddesden
Hatching Green
Water End
Piccotts End
Sandridge
Halton
Hastoe
Wigginton
Potten End
ST. ALBANS
Wendover
THE RIDGEWAY PATH
Northchurch
Berkhamsted
Verulamium Theatre
Nash Lee
St. Leonards
Cholesbury
HEMEL HEMPSTEAD
Gorhambury
THE THREE HUNDREDS OF AYLESBURY
BERKHAMSTED
Ellesborough
Buckland Common
Ashley Green
Bourne End
Dunsmore
Lee Gate
Bellingdon
Colney Heath
Bedmond
Chiswellgreen
De Havilland Mosquito Aircraft Museum
London Colney
Hampden
Lee Clump
Chartridge
Whelpley Hill
Felden
Princes Risborough
Ballinger Common
Bovingdon
Great Missenden
CHESHAM
Lye Green
Primrosehill
Colney Street
Shenleybury
Chipperfield
Kings Langley
Abbots Langley
Bricket Wood
South Heath
Botley
Hampden Row
Shenley
Prestwood
Little Kingshill
Hyde Heath
Bucks Hill
Flaunden
Radlett
Speen
Latimer
Sarratt
Great Kingshill
Chesham Bois
Little Chalfont
Chenies
WATFORD
Aldenham
Little Missenden
Chandler's Cross
Letchmore Heath
Hughenden Valley
Holmer Green
AMERSHAM
Naphill
CHORLEYWOOD
Croxley Green
BUSHEY
Borehamwood
Hughenden Manor
Penn Street
Coleshill
Hazlemere
Winchmore Hill
Chalfont St. Giles
Heronsgate
Oxhey
Elstree
Downley
Tylers Green
Bushey Heath
RICKMANSWORTH
South Oxhey
H WYCOMBE
Penn
Wycombe Marsh
Bekonscot Model Village
Seer Green
Chalfont Common
Maple Cross
West Hyde
Horn Hill
Hatch End
Stanmore
Edgware
Loudwater
Jordans
Eastbury
Harefield
Northwood
Pinner
Flackwell Heath
BEACONSFIELD
Chalfont St. Peter
Wealdstone
Kingsbury
Little Marlow
Wooburn Green
Denham Green
HARROW
Kenton
Eastcote
Gerrards Cross
Wooburn
Hedgerley
Hedsor
MARLOW
Bourne End
Burnham Beeches
Ruislip
Harrow on the Hill
Cookham
Denham
Dropmore
Northolt Park
Wembley
BRENT
Cliveden
Cookham Rise
Fulmer
Ickenham
Bisham Abbey
Farnham Common
Iver Heath
Northolt
Hurley
Stoke Poges
New Denham
Uxbridge
Farnham Royal
Taplow
Greenford
HILLINGDON
Perivale
MAIDENHEAD
EALING
Burnham
Cowley
Yeading
Littlewick
Hayes
Southall
SP
SU

21
Barley
Chrishall
Audley End
Radwinter
Newnham
Therfield
Reed
Smith's End
Shaftenhoe End
Little Chishill
Bridge Green
Wendens Ambo
Sewards End
Wimbish
Kelshall
Bygrave
Nuthampstead
Langley
Arkesden
Audley End Station
Debden
Wimbish Green
Baldock
Wallington
Sandon
Barkway
Buckland
Anstey
Clavering
Newport
Wicken Bonhunt
Howlett End
Mill End
Rushden
Chipping
Meesden
Brent Pelham
Rickling
Quendon
Widdington
Mole Hall
Debden Cross
Thaxted
Clothall
Weston
Throcking
Buntingford
Wyddial
Great Hormead
Berden
Cottered
Hare Street
Stocking Pelham
Ugley
Henham
Bardfield
Cromer
Aspenden
Furneux Pelham
East End
Ugley Green
Broxted
Lindsell
Walkern
Westmill
Patmore Heath
Farnham Green
Manuden
Elsenham
Great Easton
STEVENAGE
Aston End
Wood End
Nasty
Braughing
Albury
Farnham
Stansted Mountfitchet
Molehill Green
Benington
Puckeridge
Little Hadham
Birchanger
Little Easton
Aston
Standon
Hadham Ford
STANSTED AIRPORT
Takeley
Great Dunmow
Knebworth
Watton-at-Stone
Dane End
Collier's End
Bury Green
BISHOP'S STORTFORD
Sacombe
Thorley
Great Hallingbury
Datchworth
Much Hadham
High Cross
Hadham Cross
Little Hallingbury
Great Canfield
Woolmer Green
Stapleford
Tonwell
Wadesmill
Baker's End
Spellbrook
High Roding
Burnham Green
Bramfield
Perry Green
SAWBRIDGEWORTH
Hatfield Heath
Aythorpe Roding
Hatfield Broad Oak
Tewin
WARE
Widford
Wareside
White Roding
High Easter
HERTFORD
Waterford
Hunsdon
Leaden Roding
WELWYN GARDEN CITY
Great Amwell
High Wych
Sheering
Stanstead Abbotts
Eastwick
Matching
Margaret Roding
Hertingfordbury
Little Amwell
Matching Tye
Matching Green
Abbess Roding
HARLOW
Letty Green
Hertford Heath
Hailey
Potter Street
THE RODINGS
HODDESDON
Essendon
Bayford
Hacketts
Broxbourne
Roydon
Foster Street
High Laver
Little Laver
Beauchamp Roding
Great Parndon
Magdalen Laver
Little Berkhamsted
Broadley Common
Hastingwood
Willingale
Epping Green
Nazeing
Moreton
Fyfield
West End
Wormley
Lower Nazeing
Thornwood Common
Bobbingworth
Norton Heath
Newgate Street
Appleby Street
Bumble's Green
North Weald Bassett
High Ongar
Epping Upland
Coopersale Common
Greensted
Chipping Ongar
Nine Ashes
Goff's Oak
Cuffley
Northaw
CHESHUNT
Upshire
EPPING
Toot Hill
Blackmore
POTTERS BAR
Crews Hill Station
Waltham Abbey
Waltham Cross
Fiddlers Hamlet
Stanford Rivers
Mill Green
Stondon Massey
Fryerning
Theydon Bois
Little End
Kelvedon Hatch
Botany Bay
Forty Hill
Enfield Lock
Stapleford Tawney
Doddinghurst
Enfield Wash
High Beach
Navestock
Mountnessing
ENFIELD
Forty Hall
Cockfosters
Ponders End
Loughton
Abridge
Stapleford Abbotts
Navestock Side
Pilgrims Hatch
Winchmore Hill
East Barnet
Epping Forest Museum
Lambourne End
Bournebridge
South Weald
Shenfield
Southgate
Chingford
Buckhurst Hill
Chigwell
Chigwell Row
Noak Hill
BRENTWOOD
Friern Barnet
Edmonton
Grange Hill
Hainault
Havering-atte-Bower
Harrold Hill
Brook Street
Ingrave
Wood Green
Tottenham
Woodford Green
Collier Row
Herongate
Finchley
WALTHAM FOREST
Woodford Bridge
Gidea Park
Harold Wood
Great Warley
Little Warley
HARINGEY
Barkingside
REDBRIDGE
Romford
Squirrel's Heath
HAVERING
Cranham
Golders Green
Hornsey
Walthamstow
Wanstead
Seven Kings
Hornchurch
West Horndon
Highgate
Stoke Newington
Leyton
Becontree
Rush Green
Hampstead
ISLINGTON
HACKNEY
Ilford
BARKING
Upminster
Bulphan
CAMDEN
Forest Gate
Elm Park
North Ockendon
Bethnal Green
West Ham
Eastbury Manor
Dagenham
South Hornchurch
Finsbury
Shoreditch
CITY OF LONDON
TOWER HAMLETS
NEWHAM
East Ham
Creekmouth
St. Marylebone
Poplar
Beckton
Rainham
South Ockendon
Baker Street
CITY OF WESTMINSTER
River Thames
Thamesmead
Wennington
A10
A505
A507
A120
A414
A1184
M11
M25
A12
A127
A13
A406
B1038
B1368
B1004

Radwinter
Hempstead
Chapelend Way
Stambourne
Grass Green
Gestingthorpe
Great Henny
Little Cornard
Assington
Wimbish
Cole End
Tye Green
Great Sampford
Spain's End
Robinhood End
Toppesfield
Pool Street
Audley End
Colne Valley
Castle Hedingham
Wickham St. Paul
Twinstead
Workhouse Green
Cornish Hall End
Le Hurst
Gainsford End
Delvin End
Highstreet Green
Great Maplestead
Lucking Street
Little Maplestead
Alphamstone
Lamarsh
Bures Green
Bures
Upper Green
Wimbish Green
Elder Street
Debden
Howlett End
Little Sampford
Howe Street
Spain's Hall
Morris Green
Sible Hedingham
Pebmarsh
Cross End
Mount Bures
Debden Green
Debden Cross
Mole Hall
Boyton End
Hawkspur Green
Guildhall and Museum
Finchingfield
Daw Street
Forry's Green
Southey Green
Wethersfield
Whiteash Green
Doe's Corner
Wakes Colne Green
Wormingford
Thaxted
Little Bardfield
Bardfield End Green
Cutler's Green
Hamperden End
Bridge End
Great Bardfield
Waltham's Cross
Blackmore End
Colne Engaine
Countess Cross
HALSTEAD
Bardfield Cottage
Monk Street
Sibley's Green
Holder's Green
Oxen End
Shalford
Church End
Beazley End
Gosfield
White Colne
Wakes Colne
Chappel & Wakes Colne Station
Henham
Lindsell
Bardfield Saling
Shalford Green
Greenstead Green
Earls Colne
Rose Green
Chappel
Fordham
Duton Hill
Broxted
Gallow Green
Tilty
Duck End
Jasper's Green
High Garrett
Burton's Green
Swan Street
Fordstreet
Crow's Green
Great Easton
Brick End
Bran End
Great Saling
Folly Green
Tumbler's Green
Great Tey
Molehill Green
Butcher's Pasture
Panfield
Bocking Churchstreet
Dowsland Green
Markshall
Aldham
Stebbing Park
Stebbing
Stisted
Little Easton
Great Dunmow
Church End
Stebbing Green
Blake End
Rayne
Bocking
Pattiswick
Bradwell
Coggeshall
Tilkey
Broad Green
Little Tey
Marks Tey
Takeley
Canfield End
BRAINTREE
Stockstreet
Paycocke's
Surrex
Skye Green
Copford Green
Pott's Green
Bannister Green
Little Dunmow
Molehill Green
White Court
Beddall's End
Perry Green
Blackwater
Langley Green
Heckfordbridge
Hope End Green
Bacon End
Puttock's End
Row Green
Willows Green
Black Notley
Tye Green
Cressing
Hawbush Green
Coggeshall Hamlet
Feering
Easthorpe
Great Canfield
Barnston
North End
Felsted
The Green
Silver End
Gore Pit
Kelvedon
Hardy's Green
Messing
Birch Green
Philpot End
Bishop's Green
Wellstye Green
Causeway End
Cock Green
Young's End
White Notley
ESSEX
Taverners Green
Broad Green
Street
Hatfield Broad Oak
High Roding
Rodingbury
Hounslow Green
Hartford End
Littley Green
Great Leighs
Rank's Green
Faulkbourne
Inworth
Haynes Green
Smythe's Green
Little Leighs
Fairstead
Rivenhall End
Layer Marney Tower
Layer Marney
Aythorpe Roding
Ford End
Fuller Street
Chipping Hill
Tiptree Heath
Tiptree
High Easter
Roundbush Green
Stagden Cross
Howe Street
Powershall End
WITHAM
Little Braxted
Great Braxted
Tolleshunt Knights
White Roding
Leaden Roding
Pleshey
Chatham Green
Terling
Oxley Green
Clatterford End
Great Waltham
Little Waltham
Russell Green
Wickham Bishops
Great Totham
Margaret Roding
Good Easter
Broad's Green
Chignall Smealy
Abbess Roding
Fambridge End
Chalk End
Mashbury
Hatfield Peverel
Little Totham
Woodend
Pepper's Green
THE RODINGS
Broomfield
Great Totham
Tolleshunt Major
Beauchamp Roding
Boyton Cross
Roxwell
Chignall St. James
Boreham
Nounsley
Langford
Ulting Wick
Norwood End
Birds Green
Shellow Bowells
Little Baddow
Beeleigh Abbey
Heybridge
Goldhanger
Miller's Green
Willingale
Cooksmill Green
Great Oxney Green
Springfield
CHELMSFORD
Woodham Walter
Heybridge Basin
River Blackwater
OSEA IS
The Stone
Fyfield
Writtle
Elm Green
Danbury
MALDON
NORTHEY IS
Norton Mandeville
Norton Heath
Widford
Great Baddow
Sandon
Gay Bowers
Woodham Mortimer
High Ongar
Shelley
Hylands
Galleywood
Howe Green
Butt's Green
Hazeleigh
Rudley Green
Mundon Hill
Chipping Ongar
King Street
Nine Ashes
Loves Green
Bicknacre
Cock Clarks
Lower Mayland
Paslow Wood Common
Blackmore
Handley Green
Galleywood
Margaretting
Purleigh
Roundbush
Mayland
Mill Green
Margaretting Tye
West Hanningfield
East Hanningfield
Farther Howegreen
Latchingdon & Snoreham
Stondon Massey
Fryerning
Ingatestone
Stock
Chapel Row
Stow Maries
Woodham Ferrers
Cold Norton
Althorne
Wyatt's Green
Doddinghurst
Hanningfield Reservoir
South Hanningfield
Rettendon
Heybridge
Fox Hatch
Mountnessing
South Hanningfield
Ramsden Heath
Tye
Coalhill
Rettendon Place
South Woodham Ferrers
North Fambridge
Fambridge Station
Ostend
Bentley
Pilgrims Hatch
Downham
South Fambridge
Havering's Grove
BILLERICAY
Runwell
Canewdon
Hutton
Shenfield
Ramsden Bellhouse
Hullbridge
South Weald
Crouch
BRENTWOOD
South Green
Battlesbridge
Rawreth
Hockley
Paglesham
Brook Street
Ingrave
Little Burstead
Crays Hill
Wickford
Shotgate
Hockley Hall
Mill Hill
Ashingdon
Ballards Gore
Herongate
Great Burstead
Nevendon
Hawkwell
Great Stambridge
Rochford
Dunton Wayletts
RAYLEIGH
Stroud Green
Great Warley
Little Warley
North Benfleet
Barling
BASILDON
Thundersley
SOUTHEND AIRPORT
Aircraft
R Roach
Stonebridge
Burtons
HAVERING
Cranham
East Horndon
Dunton Hall
Laindon
Pitsea
Daws Heath
Eastwood
Jordons
West Horndon
Landon Hills
Lee Chapel
Vange
Bowers Gifford
SOUTH BENFLEET
Hadleigh
Prittlewell
Bournes Green
Great Wakering
Upminster
Bulphan
Garlesters
Westley Heights
Hope's Green
Hadleigh
Leigh-on-Sea
Westcliff-on-Sea
Southchurch
North Shoebury
Great Malgraves
One Tree Hill
Thorpe Bay
North Ockendon
Fobbing
Dutch Cottage
Winter Gardens
SOUTHEND-ON-SEA
Horndon on the Hill
Corringham
Balstonia
CANVEY ISLAND
Northwick
South Ockendon
Baker Street
Orsett
Stanford le Hope
Coryton
Leigh Beck
Thames Haven
Mucking
Pump Street
Surfleet
Little

Whitestreet Green
Shelley
Polstead
Raydon
Great Wenham
Wenham
Lower Raydon
Holton St. Mary
Capel St. Mary
Bentley
Freston
Woolverstone
Tattingstone White Horse
Pinmill
River Orwell
Levington
Falkenham
Lower Falkenham
Trimley Heath
Felixstoweferry
Thorpe Common
Chelmondiston
Trimley Lower Street
Trimley
Mill Street
Thorington Street
Higham
Four Sisters
East Bergholt
Tattingstone
Alton Water
Holbrook
Harkstead
Shotley Street
Walton
Old Felixstowe
Nayland
Stratford St. Mary
Flatford Mill & Lock
East End
Upper Street
Brantham
Stutton
Lower Holbrook
Shop Corner
Erwarton
Shotley Gate
Walton Lower Street
R. Stour
Dedham
Cattawade
Holbrook Bay
FELIXSTOWE
Boxted
Langham
Boxted Cross
River Stour
Wrabness
Parkeston
Bath Side
HARWICH
Manningtree
New Mistley
Castle
Mistley
Mistley Towers
Harwich Harbour
ZEEBRUGGE
Great Horkesley
Langham Moor
Langham Wick
Ardleigh Heath
Lawford
Ardleigh
Foxash Estate
Little Bromley
Bradfield
Bradfield Heath
Ramsey
Upper Dovercourt
Dovercourt
KRISTIANSAND Summer Only
Little Oakley
Horsleycross Street
Horsley Cross
Burnt Heath
Wix Green
Wix
ESBJERG GOTEBORG
HAMBURG HOEK VAN HOLLAND
HIRTSHALLS OSLO
COLCHESTER
Parson's Heath
Goose Green
Stones Green
Great Oakley
Cabbage Row
TM
Mile End
Great Bromley
Tendring Heath
Tendring Green
Crockleford Heath
Greenstead
Little Bentley
Beaumont
Elmstead Market
Hare Green
Tendring
Goose Green
Frating Green
Thorpe Green
The Naze
Old Heath
Wivenhoe Cross
Elmstead Heath
Frating
Great Bentley
Weeley
Thorpe-le-Soken
Kirby le Soken
Naze Park
Rowhedge
Maypole Green
WIVENHOE
Upper Kirby
Walton Ashes
WALTON ON THE NAZE
Blackheath
Alresford
Weeley Heath
Kirby Cross
Malting Green
Fingringhoe
High Park Corner
Tenpenny Heath
Aingers Green
South Green
Thorrington
Row Heath
Cook's Green
Great Holland
Abberton
Langenhoe
South Heath
Samson's Corner
Little Clacton
FRINTON-ON-SEA
St Osyth Heath
Great Clacton
BRIGHTLINGSEA
Hurst Green
St Osyth Priory
St. Osyth
Holland-on-Sea
Rush Green
MERSEA ISLAND
East Mersea
Point Clear
St Osyth Marsh
CLACTON-ON-SEA
Seawick Sands
Jaywick
WEST MERSEA
Colne Point
Bradwell Waterside
Sales Point
Bradwell-on-Sea
Tillingham
Dengie
Old Montsale
Deal Hall
Holliwell Point
East Wick
Foulness Point
Courtsend
Churchend
FOULNESS ISLAND
TR
SCALE
0 1 2 3 4 5 miles
0 1 2 3 4 5 kilometres
A12
A120
A133
A131
A134
A45
B1068
B1029
B1035
B1352
B1414
B1456
B1080
B1027
B1028
B1025
B1026
B1032
B1033
B1034
B1021
0
1
2
3
4

24
NUNEATON
Attleborough
Stockingford
Chilvers Coton
Arbury Hall
BEDWORTH
Bulkington
Flamville
Sharnford
Frolesworth
Astley
Leire
Ashby Magna
Shearsby
Saddington
Gumley
Smeeton Westerby
Dunton Bassett
Peatling Parva
Bruntingthorpe
Mowsley
Laughton
LEICESTERSHIRE
Claybrooke Magna
Ashby Parva
Gilmorton
Walton
Lubenham
Theddingworth
Wibtoft
Wolvey
Ullesthorpe
Kimcote
Cloudesley Bush
Willey
Bitteswell
Lutterworth
Misterton
Husbands Bosworth
Withybrook
Monks Kirby
Brockhurst
Walcote
North Kilworth
Sibbertoft
Shilton
Barnacle
Ansty
Cotesbach
South Kilworth
Sulby Reservoir
Welford
Naseby
COVENTRY
Foleshill
Walsgrave on Sowe
Stretton under Fosse
Pailton
Churchover
Swinford
Stanford Hall
Stanford on Avon
Shawell
Catthorpe
Clay Coton
Cold Ashby
Thornby
Stoke
Binley
Brinklow
Easenhall
Harborough Magna
Newton
Lilbourne
Earlsdon
Stivichall
Willenhall
Brandon
Bretford
Church Lawford
Newbold on Avon
Clifton upon Dunsmore
Yelvertoft
Winwick
Guilsborough Grange
Guilsborough
Lunt Roman Fort
Baginton
Coventry Airport
Ryton-on-Dunsmore
Wolston
Long Lawford
New Bilton
Hillmorton
Crick
West Haddon
Coton Manor
Stoneleigh
Kenilworth
National Agricultural Centre
Stretton-on-Dunsmore
RUGBY
Cawston
Bilton
Dunchurch
Kilsby
Bubbenhall
Princethorpe
Wappenbury
Bourton on Dunsmore
Thurlaston
Barby
Ravensthorpe
East Haddon
Weston under Wetherley
Frankton
Draycote
Marton
Birdingbury
Kites Hardwick
Woolscott
Willoughby
Ashby St Ledgers
Watford
Cubbington
Eathorpe
Hunningham
Leamington Hastings
Grandborough
Braunston
Welton
Long Buckby
ROYAL LEAMINGTON SPA
Offchurch
Radford Semele
Long Itchington
Broadwell
Sawbridge
Wolfhampcote
Whilton
Great Brington
Althorp
Nethercote
Cuttle
Stockton
Tomlow
Lower Shuckburgh
Flecknoe
Norton
Little Brington
Whitnash
Bascote
Bascote Heath
Napton
Staverton
DAVENTRY
Nobottle
Ufton
Southam
Upper Shuckburgh
Dodford
Harpole
Bishop's Tachbrook
Napton on the Hill
Catesby
Newnham
Badby
Flore
Upper Heyford
Harbury
Ladbroke
Marston Doles
Priors Marston
Hellidon
Upper Weedon
Weedon
Stowehill
Nether Heyford
Ashorne
Chesterton Green
Cross Green
Everdon
Church Stowe
Bugbrooke
Moreton Morrell
Bishop's Itchington
Priors Hardwick
Charwelton
Fawsley
Upper Stowe
Rothersthorpe
Lighthorne
Farthingstone
Preston Capes
Little Preston
Church Charwelton
Pattishall
Gaydon
Knightcote
Wormleighton
Upper Boddington
Hinton
Litchborough
Eastcote
Astcote
Chadshunt
Wharf
Byfield
Grimscote
Cold Higham
Maidford
Northend
Kineton
Magpie Hill
Lower Boddington
Woodford Halse
Fenny Compton
Aston le Walls
West Farndon
Canons Ashby
Adstone
Foxley
Blakesley
Duncote
Combrook
Little Kineton
Avon Dassett
Claydon
Eydon
Quinbury End
Caldecote
Butlers Marston
Appletree
Moreton Pinkney
Woodend
Greens Norton
Arlescote
Farnborough
Farnborough Hall
Chipping Warden
Woodend Green
Plumpton
Bradden
Radway
Warmington
Hay's Bridge
Edgcote
R Cherwell
Culworth
Weedon Lois
Towcester
Pillerton Hersey
Cropredy
Wardington
Weston
Slapton
Foscote
Ratley
Mollington
Abthorpe
Oxhill
Shotteswell
Upper Wardington
Thorpe Mandeville
Sulgrave Manor
Milthorpe
Wappenham
Lower Tysoe
Upton
Hornton
Great Bourton
Williamscot
Sulgrave
Whatcote
Middle Tysoe
Horley
Chacombe
Little Bourton
Stuchbury
Helmdon
Silverstone
Upper Tysoe
Alkerton
Hanwell
Middleton Cheney
Marston St Lawrence
Falcut
Shenington
Balscote
Wroxton
Greatworth
Crowfield
Syresham
Olney
Silverstone
Brackley Hatch
Winderton
Epwell
Drayton
Lower Middleton Cheney
Thenford
Radstone
High Cross
Biddlesden
Lillingstone Dayrell
BANBURY
Great Purston
Halse
Pimlico
Lower Brailes
Shutford
North Newington
Farthinghoe
Steane
Whitfield
Sibford Gower
Broughton
Swalcliffe
BRACKLEY
Dadford
Akeley
Sutton-under-Brailes
OXFORDSHIRE
Bodicote
Twyford Gardens
Upper Astrop
Newbottle
Turweston
Stowe House
Stourton
Tadmarton
Sibford Ferris
Astrop
Hinton-in-the-Hedges
R Great Ouse
Shalstone
Chackmore
Bloxham
Adderbury
Milton
King's Sutton
Charlton
Rowler
Evenley
Westbury
Water Stratford
Whichford
Ascott
Hook Norton
Milcombe
Walton Grounds
Barford St John
Barford
Mixbury
Finmere
Radclive
SP
M1
M6
M45
A5
A45
A46
A423
A425
A426
A427
A428
A429
A361
A41
A422
A43
A444
A445
A452
A50
B4112
B4113
B4114
B4109
B4029
B4455
B4027
B4428
B4429
B4453
B4452
B4451
B4086
B4035
B4036
B4037
B4038
B4525
B4031
B5414
B5385
B577
B578
B581

25
Thorpe Langton
Weston by Welland
Rockingham
Rockingham Castle
Cottingham
Deenethorpe
Southwick
Tansor
Warmington
Sutton Bassett
Ashley
Middleton
Weldon
East Carlton
Upper Benefield
Glapthorn
Cotterstock
OUNDLE
Ashton
A427
A43
A6116
A6003
CORBY
Lower Benefield
A605
Lutton
Dingley
Wilbarston
Little Bowden
Brampton Ash
Stoke Albany
Little Oakley
ROCKINGHAM FOREST
Polebrook
MARKET HARBOROUGH
A6
B669
Pipewell
A6014
Stanion
Lyreden New Bield
Stoke Doyle
Barnwell St. Andrew
Hemington
Brigstock
Pilton
Lilford Park
Great Oxendon
Braybrooke
DESBOROUGH
Great Oakley
Geddington
A6116
Wadenhoe
Barnwell All Saints
Luddington in the Brook
Thurning
A508
Triangular Lodge
Newton
Eleanor Cross
Achurch
Wigsthorpe
Rushton
Sudborough
Arthingworth
Weekley
Grafton Underwood
Aldwincle
Thorpe Waterville
Winwick
Thorpe Underwood
ROTHWELL
Lowick
Clopton
Orton
Warkton
Slipton
Twywell
Islip
Titchmarsh
Harrington
B576
KETTERING
Cranford St. Andrew
B662
Loddington
Thorpe Malsor
Thrapston
Old Weston
Maidwell
Barton Seagrave
A604
Woodford
B660
Great Cransley
Little Cransley
Cranford St. John
R Nene
Denford
Molesworth
Brington
Draughton
Broughton
BURTON LATIMER
Great Addington
Ringstead
Keyston
Leighton Bromswold
Bythorn
Lamport
Lamport Hall
Pytchley
Bottom End
Isham
A510
Finedon
Little Addington
B663
Church End
Catworth
Brook End
Old
Orlingbury
RAUNDS
Little Catworth
Scaldwell
Walgrave
B574
Great Harrowden
Stanwick
Pitsford Reservoir
Hannington
Little Harrowden
A509
Hargrave
Covington
Stow Longa
A605
B571
Tilbrook
IRTHLINGBOROUGH
Chelveston
Holcot
Hardwick
WELLINGBOROUGH
HIGHAM FERRERS
Caldecott
Shelton
Lower Dean
Grafham Water
Pitsford
A45
Upper Dean
Kimbolton
Newtown
Stonely
Sywell
Mears Ashby
River Til
Chapel Brampton
RUSHDEN
Yielden
Moulton
Wilby
Knuston
B569
Swineshead
Wood End
Overstone
B51
Little Irchester
London End
Little Wymington
Newton Bromswold
Melchbourne
Chadwell End
Pertenhall
Boughton
Irchester
Green End
Overstone Solarium
Wymington
Great Staughton
Kingsthorpe
Boothville
A4500
New Barton
B573
Great Doddington
Farndish
Riseley
Brook End
Ecton
Knotting
Keysoe
West End
Little Staughton
Queen's Park
Weston Favell
Earls Barton
Great Billing
Wollaston
Podington
Knotting Green
Top End
Hardwick End
Hatch End
NORTHAMPTON
Little Billing
Abington
Strixton
Souldrop
Lower End
Whiston
Hinwick
Keysoe Row
Cogenhoe
Grendon
Bourne End
Bolnhurst
Delapre Abbey
Little Houghton
Brafield-on-the-Green
Castle Ashby
Santa Pod
Sharnbrook
Church End
Cross End
Eleanor Cross
A428
Great Houghton
Coffle End
Bletsoe
Colmworth
Far Cotton
Castle Ashby
Easton Maudit
Bozeat
Odell
Felmersham
Thurleigh
Chapel End
Channel's End
Hardingstone
Denton
Little Odell
Radwell
Scald End
Duck's Cross
Wootton
Harrold
Yardley Hastings
Chellington
Milton Ernest
The Grange
Wilden
B526
Hackleton
Collingtree
Carlton
Pavenham
Stafford Bridge
Oakley
Ravensden
East End
Milton Malsor
Quinton
Horton
Lavendon
Sevicks End
Piddington
Warrington
B5388
West End
Quinton Green
Cold Brayfield
Clapham
Renhold
Courteenhall
B565
Stevington
R Great Ouse
Blisworth
Roade
Olney
Turvey
Village Green
Salph End
Great Barford
Bromham
Waterways Museum
Hartwell
Eakley Lanes
Weston Underwood
Goldington
Clifton Reynes
Newton Blossomville
A6
A428
Willington
Water End
Ravenstone
Ashton
Emberton
Stagsden Bird Gardens
Stagsden
A422
Biddenham
Queen's Park
BEDFORD
A603
Cople
Petsoe End
B560
A5134
B531
Long Street
Stoke Goldington
Filgrave
Stocking Green
Hardmead
KEMPSTON
Cardington
Tyringham
Astwood
Moot Hall
Harrowden
Grafton Regis
Hungate End
Hanslope
Tathall End
Gayhurst
Sherington
Wood End
Keeley Green
Elstow
A421
Chicheley
Chicheley Hall
Bourne End
Wootton
A600
Cotton End
Yardley Gobion
Castlethorpe
Lathbury
North Crawley
Kempston Hardwick
Herring's Green
Moor End
Little Linford
Brook End
Upper Shelton
Wilshamstead
Old Warden
Haversham
NEWPORT PAGNELL
Gossard's Green
Wootton Broadmead
Stewartby
Potterspury
Cosgrove
Lower Shelton
Puxley
New Bradwell
Great Linford
Wharley End
East End
Chapel End
Silver End
A5
Old Wolverton
Cranfield
Caulcott
Old Stratford
Stony Stratford
Wolverton
Moulsoe
Marston Moretaine
How End
Houghton Conquest
Haynes
Deanshanger
Willen
Broughton
Millbrook Station
Haynes West End
Little Woolstone
Bradwell
A422
Escheat
A421
Houghton
Passenham
Calverton
A509
Salford
Holcot
Lidlington
Millbrook
Clophill
Beadlow
MILTON KEYNES
Brogborough
Hall End
Leckhampstead
Upper Weald
Shenley Church End
Loughton
Wavendon
Lower End
Woburn Sands
Boughton End
Ridgmont
AMPTHILL
Maulden
Upper Gravenhurst
Beachampton
Walton
Simpson
Bow Brickhill
Dene End
Flitton
Wardhedges
Wrest Park
Thornton
Shenley Brook End
A5130
Aspley Guise
Husborne Crawley
A507
A5120
Silsoe
Thornborough
Whaddon
Nash
BLETCHLEY
Birchmoor Green
Higher Berry End
Steppingley
Church End
Greenfield
Lower Gravenhurst
Hanscombe End
Flitwick
Pulloxhill
Higham

26
Tansor
Warmington
Morborne
Norman Cross
North End
Whittlesey Mere
Pondersbridge
Ramsey Mereside
Copalder Corner
Benwick
Primrose Hill
Folksworth
Caldecote
Holme
Stilton
Ramsey St. Mary's
Middle Moor
Ashton
Chapel End
Lutton
Denton
Glatton
Polebrook
Barnwell St. Andrew
Hemington
Conington
Sawtry
Ramsey Forty Foot
West moor
Slade Field
RAMSEY
Bury
Ramsey Heights
Lilford Park
Barnwell All Saints
Luddington in the Brook
Thurning
Great Gidding
Chapel End
Green End
Little Gidding
Wigsthorpe
Church End
Upwood
Great Raveley
Tick Fen
Wistow Fen
Turf Fen
Mill End
Horseley Fen
Thorpe Waterville
Winwick
Steeple Gidding
Wood Walton
Wistow
Warboys
Little End
Chapel Head
Clopton
Titchmarsh
Coppingford
Hamerton
Upton
Wennington
Abbots Ripton
Little Raveley
Mill End
Fenton
Pidley Fen
Pidley
Broughton
Church End
Chatteris Fen
Old Weston
Molesworth
Brington
Buckworth
Alconbury Weston
Alconbury
Little Stukeley
Kings Ripton
Oldhurst
Somersham
Colne
Wood End
Earith
Keyston
Bythorn
Leighton Bromswold
Barham
Woolley
Great Stukeley
Sapley
Woodhurst
Bluntisham
Church End
Catworth
Brook End
Spaldwick
HUNTINGDON
Huntingdon
Stanton Butts
St. Peter's Hill
Hartford
ST. IVES
Houghton
Green End
Needingworth
Little Catworth
Easton
Ellington
Wyton
Hemingford Abbots
Covington
Tilbrook
Stow Longa
Ellington Thorpe
Brampton
Church End
Holywell
Over
GODMANCHESTER
Hemingford Grey
West End
Shelton
Grafham
Grafham Water
Newtown
Fen Drayton
Church End
Lower Dean
Upper Dean
Kimbolton
Stonely
East Perry
Buckden
Buckden Palace
Fenstanton
Swavesey
Middle Watch
Rampton
Swineshead
Wood End
West Perry
Offord Cluny
Offord Darcy
Littleworth End
Hilton
Conington
Boxworth End
Melchbourne
Chadwell End
Green End
Pertenhall
Staughton Green
Dillington
Staughton Highway
Stirtloe
Diddington
Boughton
Papworth St. Agnes
Elsworth
Boxworth
Oakington
Riseley
Brook End
Great Staughton
Green End
Southoe
Duck End
Great Paxton
Graveley
Kisby's Hut
Papworth Village
Lolworth
Bar Hill
Keysoe
West End
Little Staughton
Hail Weston
Little Paxton
Toseland
Yelling
Papworth Everard
Knapwell
High Street
Dry Drayton
Girton
Top End
Hardwick End
Hatch End
Keysoe Row
Duloe
ST. NEOTS
Eaton Ford
Green End
Bourne End
Bolnhurst
Bushmead
Staploe
Upper Staploe
Eaton Socon
Weald
Croxton
Eltisley
Caxton Gibbet
Highfields
Madingley
Church End
Bletsoe
Church End
Cross End
Eynesbury
Caxton End
Caxton
Bourn
Coton
Thurleigh
Chapel End
Channel's End
Colmworth
Hardwick
Scald End
Wyboston
Little Barford
Abbotsley
Great Gransden
Caxton End
Caldecote
Comberton
Green End
Milton Ernest
The Grange
Wood End
Wilden
Duck's Cross
Chawston
Bourn
Toft
Barton
Church End
Colesden
East End
Roxton
Waresley
Little Gransden
Longstowe
Kingston
Claypit Hill
Ravensden
Sevicks End
Langford End
Great Eversden
Haslingfield
Clapham
Renhold
Green End
Tempsford
Gamlingay Cinques
B1046
Little Eversden
Salph End
Goldington
Great Barford
Everton
Gamlingay
Hatley St. George
Harlton
Harston
Water End
Willington
Blunham
Gamlingay Great Heath
Wimpole Hall
Arrington
Orwell
Cockayne Hatley
East Hatley
BEDFORD
Mogerhanger
SANDY
Croydon
New Wimpole
Barrington
Queen's Park
Cople
St. Johns
Cardington
Hatch
Potton
Wrestlingworth
Wendy
Shepreth
Foxton
Thorncote Green
Beeston
The Lodge
Stratford
Tadlow
Shingay
Whaddon
Frog End
Moot Hall
Elstow
Harrowden
Northill
Sutton
Bassingbourn
Meldreth
BEDFORDSHIRE
Upper Caldecote
Eyeworth
R. Cam or Rhee
Kempston Hardwick
Cotton End
Herring's Green
Ickwell Green
Swiss Garden
Abington Pigotts
Kneesworth
Chiswick End
Fowlmere
Wilshamstead
Old Warden
Shuttleworth Collection
New Town
Dunton
Guilden Morden
North End
North Brook End
South End
Bassingbourn
Melbourn
Stewartby
Chapel End
Broom
BIGGLESWADE
Litlington
Silver End
Southill
Steeple Morden
ROYSTON
Houghton Conquest
Haynes
Ireland
Stanford
Langford
Edworth
Ashwell End
Haynes West End
Houghton
Shefford
Clifton
Henlow
Hinxworth
Ashwell
The Thrift
Barley
Millbrook
Clophill
Beadlow
Hall End
Campton
Astwick
Caldecote
Newnham
Odsey
Therfield
Maulden
Upper Gravenhurst
Church End
Smith's End
Reed
Flitton
Wardhedges
Wrest Park
Meppershall
Henlow Camp
Brook End
Arlesey
Stotfold
Slip End
Kelshall
Bygrave
Radwell
Reed End
Chapel Green
Barkway
Nuthampstead
Greenfield
Silsoe
Lower Gravenhurst
Upper Stondon
Upton End
Shillington
Hanscombe End
Higham
Pulloxhill
Norton
Wallington
Roe Green
Sandon
Green End
Buckland
BALDOCK
A1
A14
A45
A604
A141
A1123
A1096
A1303
A603
A428
A6
A421
A600
A6001
A507
A505
A10
A605
A427
A142
B660
B662
B663
B1090
B1043
B1040
B1089
B1086
B1050
B1096
B1093
B1098
B1046
B1042
B658
B661
B1428
B1041
B1039
B1368
B531
B530
A5120
R. Nene (Old Course)
River Til
R. Kym
AA 24 hour

Boot's Bridge
Manea
The Biggins
Purls Bridge
Welches Dam
Oxlode
Pymore
Downham
Black Bank
Apes Hall
Mare Fen
Littleport
Littleport Bridge
Burnt Fen
Brandon Creek
Brandon Bank
Feltwell Anchor
Feltwell
Hockwold cum Wilton
Hockwold Fens
Weeting
Grimes Graves
Santon Downham
Brandon
Town Street
Lakenheath Halt
Little Ouse River
New Bedford River or Hundred Foot Drain
Vardy Hill
Chettisham
West Fen
Coveney
Witcham
ELY
Queen Adelaide
Prickwillow
Mile End
Shippea Hill Halt
Wangford Fen
Lakenheath
Warren Lodge
Thetford Warren
Undley
Little Erlswell
Kennyhill
Holmsey Green
Elveden
Eriswell
Wentworth
Witchford
Middle Fen
Stuntney
Great Fen
Mildenhall Fen
Beck Row
River Lark
Little Thetford
Broad Hill
Thistley Green
Holywell Row
Mildenhall
West Row
Wilburton
Stretham
Barway
Soham Cotes
Isleham
Worlington
Barton Mills
Icklingham
Aldreth
Green End
Elford Closes
Soham Mere
Soham
Green Hills
Fordham
Freckenham
Tuddenham
Smithey Fen
Upware
Wicken
New River
Redlodge Warren
Lackford
West Stow
Brockley
Ingham
Culford
Chittering
Chippenham
Herringswell
Cavenham
Flempton
Hengrave
Green End
Cottenham
Denny Abbey
River Bank
Adventurers' Fen
North Street
Landwade
Kennett
Tuddenham Corner
Fornham All Saints
Waterbeach
Reach
Burwell
Snailwell
Kennett End
Kentford
Risby
Landbeach
Waterbeach
Swaffham Prior
Exning
Needham Street
Gazeley
Lower Green
Higham
Westley
Clayhithe
Commercial End
Newmarket Heath
Moulton
Upper Green
Barrow
Burthorpe Green
Little Saxham
Milton
Horningsea
Anglesey Abbey
Lode
Swaffham Bulbeck
NEWMARKET
Newmarket
Ashley
Dalham
Denham End
Great Saxham
Horringer
Stow cum Quy
Bottisham
Cheveley
Denham
Ickworth
Fen Ditton
Saxon Street
Broad Green
Dunstall Green
Hargrave Lady's Green
Chevington
Frog End
Teversham
Little Wilbraham
Stetchworth
Woodditton
Upend
Ousden
Hargrave Green
Tan Office Green
Church End
Dullingham
Ditton Green
Kirtling
Lidgate
Stonecross Green
Great Wilbraham
Six Mile Bottom
Baxter's Green
Depden Green
Chedburgh
CAMBRIDGE
Cherry Hinton
Fulbourn
Holme End
Burrough End
Westley Waterless
Burrough Green
Kirtling Green
Boyden End
Thorns
Ashfield Green
Rede
Gulling Green
Trumpington
Sharp's Corner
Great Bradley
Attleton Green
Wickhambrook
Brockley Green
Wandlebury Ring
Gog Magog Hills
Willingham Green
Brinkley
Lambfair Green
Pound Green
Wickham Street
Clopton Green
Great Shelford
Weston Colville
Cowlinge
Denston
Hawkedon
Cross Green
Stapleford
West Wratting
Carlton
Little Bradley
Cock & End
Farley Green
Stradishall
Stansfield
Somerton
Hartest
R Granta
Carlton Green
Little Thurlow
Assington Green
Thurston End
Boxted
Fenstead End
Little Shelford
Babraham
Weston Green
Balsham
Thurlow
Sowley Green
Upper Street
Fishers
Little Abington
Temple End
Sawston
Pampisford
West Wickham
Great Wratting
Hundon
Babel Green
Barnardiston
Poslingford
Hildersham
Great Abington
Linton
Horseheath
Streetly End
Withersfield
Mount Pleasant
Chilton Street
Glemsford
Nether Hall
Vineyards
The Spike
Hanchet End
Little Wratting
Brockley Green
Cavendish
Duxford
Zoological Gardens
Cardinal's Green
Bartlow
Mill Green
HAVERHILL
Burton End
Kedington
Clare
Pentlow Street
Foxearth
Melford
Duxford Airfield
Hinxton
Nosterfield End
Hazel Stub
Boyton End
Pentlow
Hickford Hill
Stump Cross
Hadstock
Shudy Camps
Castle Camps
Sturmer
Wixoe
Stoke by Clare
Belchamp St. Paul
Borley
Borley Green
Ickleton
Great Chesterford
Steventon End
Wiggens Green
New England
Baythorne End
Ovington
Ashdon
Camps End
Pale Green
Birdbrook
Ashen
Little Chesterford
Little Walden
Church End
Olmstead Green
Helions Bumpstead
Belchamp Otten
Belchamp Walter
Elmdon
Strethall
Littlebury
Water End
Steeple Bumpstead
Moyns Park
Ridgewell
Tilbury Green
Knowl Green
Puttock End
Belchamp Hall
Smith's Green
SAFFRON WALDEN
Radwinter End
Great Yeldham
Little Yeldham
Bulmer Tye
Littlebury Green
Chrishall
Audley End
Millfield
Radwinter
Hempstead
Chapelend Way
Dyer's End
Stambourne
Grass Green
Gestingthorpe
Audley End
Bridge Green
Wendens Ambo
Sewards End
Spain's End
Robinhood End
Toppesfield
Pool Street
Audley End
Wickham St. Paul
Colne Valley
Wimbish
Cole End
Tye Green
Great Sampford
Cornish Hall End
Le Hurst
Castle Hedingham
Audley End Station
Gainsford End
Delvin Green
Langley
River Pant
Little London
Great Maplestead
Arkesden
Bird Green
Elder Street
Debden
Upper Green
Wimbish Green
Delvin End
Highstreet Green
Lucking Street
Howe Street
Sible Hedingham
Little Maplestead
Stickling Green
Hill Green
Newport
Howlett End
Little Sampford
Spain's Hall
Morris Green
Doe's

INDEX

As well as the page number of each place name the index also includes an appropriate atlas page number together with a four figure map reference (see National Grid explanation on page 108).

In a very few instances place names appear without a map reference. This is because either they are not shown on the atlas or they lie just outside the mapping area of the guide. However, each tour does include a detailed map which highlights the location of all places mentioned on the route.